Ruling a Quarter of Mankind: Chiang and Mao

Paul H. Tai

Ruling a Quarter of Mankind: Chiang and Mao

Copyright © 2016 by Paul H. Tai

All rights reserved.

No part of this book may be reproduced without the written permission of the author.

ISBN: 978-1530844494

Library of Congress Control Number: 2016905787

Printed in America
Available from Amazon. Com, CreateSpace. Com, and other retail outlet stores.

In memory of my father,

Lieutenant General Tai Minchuan

CONTENTS

*President Franklin D. Roosevelt's
     Remarks on China, 1943*   viii
PREFACE   ix
NOTATIONS ON THE TEXT   xv

PART ONE: UNCANNY SIMILARITIES

Chapter One: They Could Have Been Sworn Brothers   2
    From birth to death   2
    The Southerners   3
    Naughty kids, studious adults   4
    Wives of abiding loyalty   6
    The petered out political posterity   7
    Still other coincidences   8

Chapter Two: The Same Path to Power   13
    The starting point   13
    The Soviet Factor   16
    History-mandated goals   18
    Resorting to arms   23
    Reading books   27
    Rising above others   30

PART TWO: WIELDING THE TWO BARRELS

Chapter Three: The Barrel of the Gun   41
    Use the gun to change destiny   41
    Chiang's barrel of the gun   42
    Mao's barrel of the gun   46
    How did Mao win   51

Chapter Four: The Barrel of the Pen, I: Inspiring Trust   64
    Instrument and style   64
    Chiang: Moralizing leadership   65
    Mao: Empowering poems   70

Contents

Chapter Five: The Barrel of the Pen, II: Orthodoxy and Guidance   79
    Establishing orthodoxy   79
    Chiang: To the right of Sun's ideology   80
    Mao: To the left of Marxism   83
    Guidance through sloganeering   87
    A more powerful communicator   96

PART THREE: THE ART OF THE POSSIBLE

Chapter Six: Chiang, Appeal to Emotions   101
    All in the family   101
    Honoring the dead   108
    Celebrating the living   113

Chapter Seven: Chiang, What Is Meant by Cunning   117
    Loyalty for purchase   117
    Action of removal   122
    Divide and rule   127
    Dictatorship in the guise of democracy   131
    The art of withdrawal   135

Chapter Eight: Mao, The Spy Warfare   147
    A man devoid of emotions   147
    The massive underground network   150
    Dagger in the heart   164

Chapter Nine: Mao, The Campaigns of Struggle   170
    Conflict resolution in the political universe   170
    A list of the campaigns   172
    Taming the masses   172
    Forging the cadres as a submissive workforce   176
    Never let the intellectuals kill people with their pens   178
    Removing the second most powerfuls   183
    The only revolution of its kind   191
    Reaching the limit of the art of the possible   194

PART FOUR: TOWARD A PROSPEROUS AND STRONG NATION

Chapter Ten: Handling Foreign Friends and Foes, I   204
    Chiang and Mao: Shared traits   205

Contents

    Chiang: Multi-power diplomacy, 1931-1945   207
    Chiang: Single-power dependency, 1945-1975   225

Chapter Eleven: Handling Foreign Friends and Foes, II   253
    Mao: One, two, three grand strategy   253
    Mao: Sino-American détente and strategic triangle   273
    Chiang and Mao: Build up China as a big power   280

Chapter Twelve: Seeking National Wealth   290
    Concepts of economic growth   290
    Approaches to policymaking   293
    Record of performance   304
    Appraisal of differences   308
    Path to prosperity   311

Chapter Thirteen: Conclusion, from Enemies to Comrades   322
    Quality of leadership   322
    Achievements and failures   331
    Comrades for an emerging superpower   345

APPENDIX: CHIANG KAI-SHEK'S CONFESSION AND REDEMPTION   357

INDEX   362

President Franklin D. Roosevelt's Remarks on China, 1943

China ... has given remarkable proof of her vitality and has made an astounding progress. But this progress should be accelerated so that she should become a great power. Indeed, I believe she will become the greatest power in the world.

****

I said to him [Winston Churchill], Chiang may die just as you or me, and still there will be a China. Split she may into North and South, and still it will be China. Split into Communist and Kuomintang, China will still be China. China, I said...is bound to become the strong power in the Far East.

(Full citations appear in Chapter Ten)

PREFACE

In modern world history, no national leaders governed so many people for so long as Chiang Kai-shek and Mao Zedong did in China. Coming to power in 1928, Chiang remained the leader on the Chinese mainland until 1949, when he retreated to Taiwan and served there as president until his death in 1975. Mao rose to power in 1949 and tightly controlled the mainland until he died in 1976. Together the two men ruled for nearly a half of a century a people that accounted for a quarter of mankind.[1]

Following the establishment of the Chinese Republic in 1912, a succession of warlords dominated the government in Beijing before Chiang and Mao's times, but each of them exercised authority for a short time and over only part of China. Chiang and Mao were truly the first-generation national leaders effectively governing the continental and island parts of the country. They were, in fact, co-rulers of China from the late 1920s to the mid1970s.[2] Over the decades, they fought each other in bitter wars but also shared common goals, among which was to build a "prosperous and strong nation." By the time they departed from the scene, they had not reached this goal but had set the foundation for China to become an emerging superpower in the 21st century.

This book addresses a number of specific questions about the two Chinese leaders: What kind of men were they? With what means did they rise to power? How did they insure millions upon millions of their countrymen submit to their authority? How did they contend with foreign powers while seeking their assistance to make China a strong power in the world? What measures did they adopt in their endeavor to make China rich? Given the controversies their policies have aroused, how are their legacies to be assessed? In an attempt to answer these questions, this book delves into the similarities and differences between the two men. Such an exercise will hopefully lead to a full understanding and a judicious appraisal of their political leadership.

A study of the governing experiences of Chiang and Mao portends matters of great significance. It allows us to assess their enduring impact on not only China but also the world's major powers, particularly the United States, Russia, and Japan. It helps us identify the antecedent political requisites of the phenomenal economic transformation of China today. And it enables us to differentiate the two

Preface

leaders' unique ruling skills from the political craftsmanship common to all national leaders.

This book is not a biographical study of Chiang and Mao but provides only essential background information on their life and politics. This is seen in "Part One, Uncanny Similarities" (Chapters One and Two), which is a shorthanded way of introducing the subject personalities, on which many works have been published. This Part also serves as a foreground of their striving to create a "prosperous and strong nation" that is extensively examined in Part Four.

Part Two and Part Three provide the substance of the book: Chiang and Mao's rulership skills. These parts are so designed as to allow a focused, yet in-depth treatment of a subject of considerable magnitude. Part Two deals with how Chiang and Mao used the same two sets of primary instruments of governance—what Mao graphically called "the barrel of the gun" and "the barrel of the pen." They also used a variety of supplementary instruments of governance, which I group as the art of the possible—a subject to be examined in detail in Part Three.

Late in the research, I came to a rather stunning discovery. I realized that if Chiang and Mao started out as comrades and became subsequently entrenched enemies, they ended up as comrades again—if viewed posthumously. In their long tenure of service, Chiang and Mao had built up China as a Big Power through wars, diplomacy, and territorial consolidation. In addition, Chiang developed economic policies that were embraced by Mao's successors to make China a wealthy nation. Together they created the preconditions of an emerging superpower in the 21st century.

The research for this book involved extensive consultation of a variety of materials relevant to the two Chinese leaders. They include academic works; official collections from mainland China and Taiwan; archival documents from the Second Historical Archives of China in Nanjing, China and the Hoover Institution of Stanford University; memoirs by individuals and other types of publication reminiscent of the activities and policies of Chiang and Mao; periodical literature; and proceedings of several conferences held in the first decade of the 21st century—specifically, on the Republican China sponsored respectively by the Chinese Academy of Social Sciences in Beijing and Fudan University in Shanghai and on the Chinese-Japanese war organized by Harvard University.

Two special sources of information deserve attention. One is the extensive conversations I had with Dr. Li Zhisui (author of *The Private Life of Chairman Mao*, which I translated from Chinese to English).

Preface

Serving as Mao's personal physician for twenty-two years, Li lived in the Zhongnanhai compound near the residence of Mao, who not only constantly sent for him for medical services but also frequently summoned him at night for talks. Their talks concerned mainly Mao's ruminations on historical matters, personal activities, and politics. To facilitate my work of translation, Li revealed many of these talks to me. They helped me gain insight into Mao's inner world—his unguarded thoughts and feelings about events, policies, and personalities.

The second source is the Chiang Kai-shek diaries. Covering nearly every day from 1917 to 1972, the diaries were deposited with the Hoover Institution, which released them in segments from 2006 to 2009.[3] In these years and also in 2010, I made five annual trips to the Hoover Institution, reading and copying down those diary entries pertinent to my research. Chiang's diaries were intensely personal and astonishingly frank. Judging against his other voluminous writings, one can vouch that everything he wrote down in his diaries was truthful, as he saw it, though he did not record every significant event that had happened. More importantly, the diaries were extraordinarily rich in content. They included, in addition to matters of his personal life, his views on domestic and foreign policies, his conduct of military affairs, and his relations with Chinese and foreign leaders. Of particular interest are many previously unrevealed background developments leading to his policy decisions, which, I am convinced, would necessitate a reassessment or reinterpretation of what the public has perceived as his positions on Chinese politics.

A Chinese version of this book was published in July 2015, with the following information: Hung-chao Tai, *Qiang Gan, Bi Gan He Quanshu: Chiang Kai-shek yu Mao Zedong Zhi Guo Zhi Dao* [*Gun, Pen and Power Play: How Chiang Kai-shek and Mao Zedong Ruled China*], Taipei, Taiwan: Shibao Chu Ban She, 2015. The Chinese version is based on a previously completed manuscript in English.

It is to be emphasized that the bibliographic notes in this Chinese version of the book are more comprehensive than those in the English version and that the cited Chinese references are listed in the Chinese language rather than transliterated ones. When these bibliographic notes are cited in the present book, they will be identified as Tai, *CMRC* [Chiang and Mao Ruled China] followed with page number(s).

To close these introductory remarks, I would like to identify a number of unique textual developments of this book:

Preface

- A refutation of the general perception that Chiang and Mao had diametrically opposite policies and orientations through a careful scrutiny of the similarities in their personal dispositions, instruments of governance, and goals.
- A delineation of the dialectical pattern of their political relations: from comrades to enemies and from enemies to comrades.
- A narration of Chiang's extraordinary effort at cementing emotional and social bond with his countrymen.
- An inquiry into Chiang's highly successful diplomatic strategies in regard to Japan, the Soviet Union, Great Britain, and the United States during the Second World War.
- A thorough investigation of Mao's devastatingly effective spy warfare against the Nationalist army in the Chinese civil war.
- An examination of how Mao dominated the masses, the cadres, the intellectuals, and his recalcitrant comrades through a masterful application of the theory of contradiction.
- A reasoned and fair assessment of the two leaders' accomplishments and failures.

These textual developments, I believe, open a new path for a comparative study of Chiang and Mao's politics, for these developments are either completely untouched or not systematically treated by extant published works on Chiang and Mao in the English language.

In making comparison of the two leaders, it should be noted, analysis on Chiang generally precedes that on Mao. This is so because Chiang came to power twenty-one years earlier.

While engaged in this study, I had extensive consultation with colleagues and other people interested in the subject. I want to take this opportunity to acknowledge a great intellectual debt to them: Thomas J. Bellows (University of Texas, San Antonio), Li Chang (Academia Sinica), Su-ya Chang (Academia Sinica), Nai-ruenn Chen (formerly with the U.S. Department of Commerce and Cornell University), T. J. Cheng (College of William and Mary), Hsi-sheng Chi (Hong Kong University of Science and Technology), June Teufel Dreyer (University of Miami), Edward Friedman (University of Wisconsin), Thomas B. Gold (University of California, Berkeley) Emily M. Hill (Queen's University, Canada), Choyun Hsu (University of Pittsburgh), Yilin Jin (Chinese Academy of Social Sciences, Beijing), Stanton Jue (formerly with the U.S. Department of State), Tai-chun Kuo (Hoover, Stanford), Sherman Lai (Oxford University), Hsiao-ting Lin (Hoover, Stanford), Charles

Preface

Lindsey (Hoover, Stanford), Roderick MacFarquhar (Harvard University), Jerry McBeath (University of Alaska), Ramon H. Myers (Hoover, Stanford), Andrew J. Nathan (Columbia University), Shelley Rigger (Davidson College), Theresa Shen (Wayne County College, Michigan), Shirley Soong (Hoover, Stanford), Richard Sousa (Hoover, Stanford), Robert Sutter (George Washington University), Julia C. Tai (University of Michigan, Dearborn), Jay Taylor (Harvard University), Steve Tsang (University of Nottingham), James Tsao (Houston Baptist University), Hans Van de Ven (Cambridge University), Jingping Wu (Fudan University, Shanghai), Sing-yung Wu (University of California, Irvine), Tianshi Yang (Chinese Academy of Social Sciences, Beijing), and Richard Yin (George Washington University).

All of them have read one or more chapters of the manuscript—in its finished or pre-revision version. Many of them made a more thorough review of the materials than I could expect and offered heuristic suggestions that still run through my mind at this writing; others engaged in frequent dialogues with me over some parts of the content of the project. Though variance of opinions between the reviewers and the author over minor matters remains, I am heartened by the fact that the reviewers are virtually unanimous on the acceptability of the quality of the project and of the narrative style in which it is presented.

Finally, I would like to pay tribute to the Hoover Institution of Stanford University for its rich and varied collections on China and its superb service to researches; to the Second Historical Archives of China in Nanjing for making available to me its microfilm collection on the Republican China prior to 1949; to the Library System of the University of California at San Diego for its prompt acquisition of voluminous books and documents from the People's Republic of China; and to the Chinese Academy of Social Sciences in Beijing and Fudan University in Shanghai for their endeavor to foster an atmosphere of free academic inquiry, in which my major research findings were first presented.

PHT
Carlsbad, CA, USA

Preface

NOTES

[1] For information on world population, see "Historical Estimate of World Population," Http://WWW.census.gov/ipc/www/worldhis.html. Compiled from eight studies by the United Nations and the U.S. government, and several academicians, this document estimated that the world population ranged from 2,400 million to 2,556 million in 1950. If 1953 is taken as the base year for calculation of Chinese population, since it is roughly at the middle point of the Chiang and Mao's period of rule in China, from 1928 to 1976, the Chinese population of that year stood at 601,938,000, according to a census conducted in China. Thus, the Chinese population then accounted for approximately one quarter of the world population.

[2] It should be pointed out that during Chiang Kai-shek's rule of mainland China, the Chinese Communists ruled separately territories under their control. These territories were of substantial size—as large as England in the 1940s. See p. 40, note 4, below. It should be further pointed out that while the Chiang-ruled Taiwan was incomparably smaller than the Mao-ruled Chinese mainland, the island is larger than many nations in size, including Belgium, Albania, Haiti, and Israel.

[3] In 2004 Elizabeth Chiang (widow of Chiang Kai-shek's grandson, Hsiao-yung), acting as a representative of the Chiang family, deposited the original set of Chiang Kai-shek's diaries with the Hoover Institution of Stanford University for 50 years. Chiang Kai-shek wrote them in longhand with a brush pen, in classic language, mostly without punctuation. The diaries covered the years from 1917 to 1972, with the exception of 1924, which was lost.

NOTATIONS ON THE TEXT

Chinese words are transliterated according to the Pinyin system, excepting certain Anglicized terms that have been in popular use for some time, such as, for example, Hong Kong and Manchuria.

- Wade-Giles-based personal names that have gained wide currency or that are preferred by the individuals concerned (for example, Sun Yat-sen, Chiang Kai-shek, Soong May-ling) are used as they are. However, "Chiang Kai-shek" in Chinese language works is transliterated as "Jiang Jieshi," because an overwhelming majority of these works were written by authors from the Chinese mainland, who prefer to use the pinyin system.

Chinese personal names are identified by family names first, excepting in cases where the concerned individuals prefer otherwise.

With reference to bibliographical citations,

- Names of Chinese authors of publications in Chinese language are cited with the last name first.
- Names of Chinese authors of publications in Western languages are cited with the first name first.
- Books published in Chinese language will be listed in Romanized titles, italicized. The translated titles, in English, will be italicized also, which will be used in later citations.
- Internet-sourced information has been verified for authenticity against other credible sources.
- Chiang Kai-shek Diaries will be cited as CKSD, follow by the date of entry such as, 9/18/31—referring to September 18, 1931. Reference to the diaries will be cited in the text of the book rather in endnotes. Many citations in the text have appeared in works authored by this writer and previously published in periodicals and conference proceedings. Citations that appear in the text for the first time will be so noted.
- Because of its frequent citations, *Zhuanji Wenxue* (*Biographical Literature*, a periodical published in Taipei, Taiwan) will be cited as *BL*.

Notations on the Text

- For the same reason, Mao Zedong's five volumes of *Selected Works* (New York: International Publishers, 1954) will be cited as *SW*, followed by volume number in Roman numeral, and page number(s). For example, *SW*, I, 13-14.
- *FRUS* refers *to* U. S., *Foreign Relations of the United States*.
- *CMRC* refers to Tai, *Chiang and Mao Ruled China*, a Chinese version of this book, as noted on p. xi, above.

Unless otherwise noted, the author translated Chinese-language materials cited in this book into English.

Terms and symbols:

- The Chinese Nationalist Party will be used throughout the text instead of the Romanized, Kuomintang, excepting that it appears in citations from others' work. Similarly, the term Nationalists or Nationalist will be used throughout the text.
- "Manchu Dynasty" and "Qing Dynasty" are used interchangeably.
- To avoid confusion, the term Beijing will be used throughout the book, not its variant, Peking, Peiping, or Beiping.
- *liang* (or tael), Chinese unit of weight; 1 tael = 1.3 ounces or 50 grams.
- *li*, Chinese unit of length; 1 *li* = 1/3 mile or 500 meters.
- *mu*, Chinese unit of area; 1 *mu* = 0.16 acre or 0.065 hectare.
- $, Chinese dollar
- US$, United States dollar.

PART ONE

UNCANNY SIMILARITIES

Epochal revolutions rarely happen. The American, French, and Russian Revolutions, of 1776, 1789, and 1917 respectively, occurred to the involved nations only once. But in China three monumental revolutions broke out within the 20th century alone: the Republican Revolution of 1911, the Communist Revolution of 1949, and the Cultural Revolution of 1966.

The first of these two revolutions brought Chiang Kai-shek and Mao Zedong to the Chinese political scene. Before they came to power, a string of short-term leaders appeared on the scene. Sun Yat-sen, who led the Republican Revolution to success, served as the Provisional President of the Republic for merely three months in 1912. Succeeding Sun, Yuan Shikai headed the government in Beijing with the Beiyang Army as the main prop and died in 1916, six months into his self-declared emperorship. From 1916 to 1928, while north China came under the rule of the Beiyang-army-spawned warlords, the rest of the country was divided into military fiefdoms headed by still more warlords. China, a great continental empire only a century and a half earlier, was falling to pieces.

Chiang and Mao sought earnestly to reunify the country. When they successively came to power, they became truly the first-generation leaders of the Chinese Republic, exercising power over the entire Chinese territorial domain. However, they waged decades-long internecine wars, harbored deep hatred against each other, adopted different methods for the reconstruction of their country, and sealed alliance with pole-apart foreign powers. Yet, given such personal hostility and political conflicts between the two men, they displayed uncanny similarities in their personal lives, in the way they rose to power and in the goals they pursued.

CHAPTER ONE

THEY COULD HAVE BEEN SWORN BROTHERS

Long back in the Three Kingdoms period in Chinese history, 220-280, three valiant and chivalrous men, not unlike those of *The Three Musketeers*, swore to brotherhood in a Peach Garden. Liu Bei, Guan Yunchang, and Zhang Fei pledged to fight for the creation of one of these kingdoms, later known as the Shu. They solemnly declared: "Though we were born in different years, different months, and different days, we are willing to die in the same year, same month, and the same day." Thus was established one deeply embedded Chinese folklore tradition of the last eighteen centuries.

Chiang Kai-shek was an ardent follower of this tradition, having formed sibling relationship with at least twenty men from different families. Some of these became his lifelong trusted colleagues; others turned into his enemies. Though never finding an occasion to ask Mao Zedong to form such a relationship, Chiang could have done so. For the two men showed close resemblance in their personal lives and convictions.

From Birth to Death

Chiang and Mao were born six years apart, in 1887 and 1893—into times of great turmoil. In 1894 China was severely beaten by Japan in a war that opened the floodgate of Japanese aggressions that left an unsettled Taiwan problem to this day. Then the Boxer Rebellion, the invasion of eight foreign powers, the Republican Revolution, and the chaotic warlordism came in quick succession. From their adolescence to young adulthood, Chiang and Mao agonized over their beloved country in the throes of debilitating internal decay and ferocious foreign aggression.

Chiang and Mao lived to 88 and 83 respectively and shared 82 years of their life in China. Infused with a strong sense of patriotism, they were determined to eradicate the misfortunes their country had suffered over a century's time and to build a prosperous and strong China.

But they died without reaching their lofty goals. And much to their regret, they even failed to realize their last wishes. Chiang could not return to the Chinese mainland he had lost; Mao could not set foot on Taiwan, the island he once attempted to conquer by risking a war with a superpower.

As some Chinese believe in geomancy, they see that Chiang and Mao's wrenching disappointment at the end of their lives must have invoked the wrath of the Old Heavenly God. Violent storms in the Taiwan Strait and thunderous rains throughout the island marked Chiang's death on April 5, 1975. The Tangshan earthquake, the most devastating in Chinese history, shook China six weeks before Mao's passing on September 9, 1976.

The Southerners

Both Chiang and Mao were southerners—a fact of some historical and geographical significance. Historically most great Chinese rulers came from the north. These two men had to break a new path to power by starting their military career in the south. One launched an expedition from Canton, Guangdong; the other hit the hills of Jiangxi to try out rural communism; and both ended up in Beijing when they became China's new rulers.

Geographically speaking, Chiang and Mao's native places were favored with abundant water resources, as southern China is known for. The Chiang family derived its income from a salt trade and was housed in a traditionally styled mansion. The Chiang hometown, Xikou in Zhejiang Province, is cradled by lush hills and segmented by watercourses. Together they endow the town with sceneries of serenity and beautiful vistas. After he came to power, Chiang frequently retreated to this place to pacify his soul and rest his body.

Mao's family, in comparison, was not as well to do but possessed enough paddy fields to qualify as, in the Communist jargon, a middle-class farm family. The village they lived in—Shaoshan, Hunan Province, 550 miles west from Xikou—is situated in the heart of a web of major rivers and small creeks. Mao's ancestral home lies at the end of a valley of fertile fields and faces directly a lotus pond, with another, larger, pond next to it.

The area surrounding Mao's village has a share of charming sights, though not as scenic as those in Xikou. The Di Shui Dong (the Water-Dripping Cavern), situated behind an emerald pond formed from spring water filtering through stone crevices, offers a place of tranquility and seclusion. This and other sceneries lured an occasionally homesick

Mao back to his native place where he composed poems and contemplated on how to launch the tempestuous Cultural Revolution.

Naughty Kids, Studious Adults

Chiang and Mao were first educated in Chinese traditional private schools; both were as indolent in studies as they were energetic in naughty activities. Chiang hated these schools; he regarded them "as prisons" and gleefully exclaimed his release time as "great emancipation."[1] But his mother insisted on educating him this way. From 1892 to 1902, when Chiang was 5 through 15, she sent him to no less than 6 different private schools, each with a Confucian schoolmaster.[2] He feared them "like tigers"; he trembled when recalling his school days even after he rose to a top military leader.[3]

When Chiang was enrolled in a modern high school in the City of Fenghua, he was not any more interested in schoolwork. He once led a student protest, ending up nearly being expelled. When he joined the Zhenwu Military Academy in Japan in 1907-1909, he had poor grades. Upon graduation, his average score was 68 out of 100; he ranked 55 out of 62 graduates.[4]

Chiang's wayward activities were many. When he was 4, he could fancy to measure the length of his esophagus by sticking a chopstick into it, causing him to pass out; when he was 6, he was nearly drown twice, once from swimming in a creek and, another time, from jumping head down into a partially frozen water tank. When he was 7, he liked to act as a general, carrying around "big knife and sword" and treating his schoolmates as soldiers. When he was 16, he gave out orders from his teacher's podium to his classmates, whom he regarded as "playthings." His teacher castigated him as being *"kuang wang bu ke yi shi,"* utterly arrogant and unscrupulous.[5]

Like Chiang, Mao studied the Confucian classics in traditional private schools and detested them. He preferred to read historical novels.[6] Once, when he was 10, he deserted school and roamed in the wild for three whole days before his family caught him. "He was expelled from...at least three schools for being headstrong and disobedient."[7] He frequently changed schools; from 1902 to 1910, at age 9 through 17, he enrolled in 6 different schools as well.[8] In 1911 when he joined a modern middle school in Changsha, the provincial capital of Hunan, he spent more time on political tracts and current events than on school curriculum.

Mao was defiant of social conventions by being disobedient to his father. One day, as his father chastised him as being lazy, he ran away. When cornered by his enraged father, Mao came to his own rescue by threatening a suicidal jump into the pond near his home. When the Republican Revolution occurred in 1911, he quit school to join the army but abandoned his military career a few months later.

In the summer of 1917, Mao and his schoolmate Siao Yu made a weird "experiment" for more than a month in the countryside around Changsha; they pretended to be "beggars...to see if we are equal to solving difficult situations." The two young men ate from handout and slept in the wild or, with good luck, in roadside inns. The most incredible event in their journey was an encounter with an innkeeper, whose reading of Mao's physiognomy proved to be largely clairvoyant. She told Mao,

> You can become...a great officer, a prime minister, or a great bandit chief....You are very audacious and have great ambition, but you have no sentiment at all! You could kill ten thousand or even a hundred thousand people without turning a single hair! But you are very patient....You will have at least six wives, but not many children.[9]

If Chiang and Mao failed to make good grades in their teenager and early adolescent years, they turned around to study assiduously the very Confucian classics they had hated when they reached full adulthood. As will be elaborated in the next chapter, they went far beyond the classics and advanced into many subjects of learning, and they did so throughout their life. It is on the basis of their diligent, extensive learning that they developed their own works with far-reaching impact. Here, Mao's achievement is nothing short of spectacular. Following his principle of "lively study and lively application," he laid down the theoretical foundations of two tasks of worldwide significance: making workers-based Marxist revolution applicable to countries of massive peasantry and crafting a grand strategy for guerrilla bands to defeat modernized army divisions.

Chiang's writings are not as profound. In his 1943-published *China's Destiny*, he made a valid attempt at bridging the Confucian culture with modernity. Had he not been challenged by Mao's works, Chiang's book could have a broader following among the Chinese than it actually did. Chiang's New Life Movement, which was launched nearly a decade earlier, was motivated by the same thought underlying his book.

Chiang also made a nearly lifelong inroad into neo-Confucianism, particularly the theory of one of the most prominent disciples of that school, Wang Yangming.

Wives of Abiding Loyalty

Chiang and Mao both had four wives. At 15, Chiang married his first spouse, Mao Fumei, his mother-chosen bride, who was senior to him by 6 years. His second mate, Yao Yecheng, more of a concubine than a wedded wife, came from Suzhou, a city famed for its beauties. His third betrothed wife, Ch'en Chieh-ju, a 15-year-old high school student (19 years his junior), he married after a two-year passionate pursuit conceivable only to the world's most determined lovers. She became a prominent persona in the early Whampoa Military Academy years but was cajoled to study in Columbia University in New York to make room for Chiang's marriage to his fourth wife, Soong May-ling, the America-educated international celebrity.

One remarkable feature of Chiang's marital life is that his wives, perhaps with the exception of the bitterly disappointed Ch'en Chieh-ju, were consistently devoted to him. Mao Fumei lived and died in the Chiang home in Xikou in spite of the divorce she was imposed upon. Yao Yecheng took care of Chiang's second son, Wei-kuo, during his childhood, followed Chiang to Taiwan, and died in Taichung on the island. Soong May-ling, who passed away in 2003 at the age of 105, never wavered in her love for him in their forty-eight years' married life.

In 1908 Mao, at 15, married his first spouse, a family-chosen Ms. Luo, who was senior to him by four years. They never lived together. In 1920 he married his second wife, Yang Kaihui, daughter of a professor at Beijing University who had befriended Mao, then a library assistant at the university. Yang Kaihui, a neophyte Marxist, was executed in 1930 by an anti-Communist governor of Hunan Province, He Jian, while Mao fought in the hills in the neighboring Jiangxi Province to start his rural Communist movement. While in Jiangxi, Mao fell in love with a young fellow revolutionary, He Zizhen, and their union lasted to the late 1930s when He Zizhen, suffering schizophrenia, went from Yan'an to the Soviet Union for treatment. In the meantime, a movie-actress-turned revolutionary, Jiang Qing, beguiled Mao with such charm and devotion that he could not resist consorting with her.

Likewise, Mao's wives were fiercely loyal to him. Luo died early. Yang Kaihui had professed before their marriage that "I was…living for him…and…would die with him."[10] She, indeed, died for his cause. He

Zizhen was nearly bombed dead in a battle in Jiangxi and was seriously wounded when she went on the Long March with Mao while pregnant. She passed her old age in Shanghai, with the memory of her revolutionary and romantic fervor in the Jiangxi days still gripping her sickly mind; she died in 1984. And, of course, Jiang Qing was the case célèbre of all. She shouted "Long Live the Revolution" during the Gang of Four trial in 1980-1981 when the last spark of the Cultural Revolution had extinguished with her husband's death in 1976. She apparently committed suicide in 1991 after having served years in the infamous Qin Cheng Prison, without ever regretting being "the Chairman's devoted student."

The Petered-out Political Posterity

Chiang had two sons. He had long thought of having his elder son, Ching-kuo, carry his political line, but did not seriously groom him as his successor until he retreated to Taiwan. Ching-kuo held a series of high administrative positions on the island, including Defense Minister and Premier, before he served as president, from 1978 to 1988. Chiang's younger son, Wei-kuo, led a long military career and served as Secretary-General of the National Security Council in Taiwan in the last years of his public life. Ching-kuo and Wei-kuo, died in 1988 and 1997 respectively while their stepmother, Soong May-ling, was still alive. She had to witness the Chiang family's painstakingly-built Taiwan enterprise in an inglorious and precipitous decline when the Opposition forces took over the government.

Ching-kuo had three sons, Hsiao-wen, Hsiao-wu, and Hsiao-yung, all of whom lost battle to serious illnesses in the prime of their lives while, in an unbelievable repetition, their widowed mother—Chiang Fang-liang, the former Faina Epatcheva Vahaleva, a Russian orphan Ching-kuo had married—was still alive. Their tragedy is summed up poignantly in the saying, "The silver-haired mother sends off her black-haired sons."

With two exceptions, all other Chiang's offspring are as of this writing totally out of politics. Elizabeth Chiang, Hsiao-yung's widow, once serving on the Central Committee of the Nationalist Party, remains active in the party affairs. So does John Hsiao-yen Chiang, Ching-kuo's out-of-wedlock son, a former Foreign Minister and a former member of the Legislative Yuan.

Mao's offspring fared no better. He had three sons. Anying, a dedicated military officer, was killed in the Korean War in 1950 at the young age of 28. Anqing, who worked as a Russian-language translator in the Academy of Military Science and, later, in a party agency, died in 2007 after having suffered a decades-long mental illness. Another son, Anlong, disappeared during the civil war in the 1930s. Mao had two daughters, Li Min and Li Na, with He Zizhen and Jiang Qing as their respective mothers, live in obscurity in China after retiring from public services, without ever assuming Mao's family name.

Chiang and Mao, the two tempest-like personalities of 20th-century China, are fading from people's memory at the dawn of the 21st century, seemingly having no one to carry their mantles.

Still Other Coincidences

Richard M. Nixon, who could justifiably claim to be a friend of both Chiang and Mao (at different times, one supposes), observed that the two Chinese leaders had many things in common:

> I detected something of the Emperor in the way both spoke of their country.... [E]ach man had come to identify his country's fate as his own....
> Mao left China only twice, to meet with Soviet leaders in Moscow in 1949 and 1957; Chiang traveled outside of Asia only twice, once to go on a mission to Moscow in 1923 and once to meet as one of the Big Four in Cairo in 1943. Both often withdrew for long periods of solitude. Mao took this time to write poetry; Chiang spent it...in the mountains. Both were revolutionaries.[11]

Other sources of information indicate more coincidences, particularly in the matter of familial relations. Chiang and Mao were devoted to their mothers but were indifferent at best to their fathers. In his diaries, Chiang wrote numerous times about the emotional bond of the mother and the son, with scanty reference to his father. The diaries recorded many touching episodes. For instance, Chiang had a strange dream one night in May 1921 while he was in the military service in Canton; he took it to be an omen of his mother being seriously sick. He rushed home, more than a thousand miles away, and found her, indeed, on the verge of death. He took care of her day and night until she died the following month. In a eulogy, Chiang expressed his sorrow: "There is nothing sadder than a separation because of death;...there is nothing more painful than being left as an orphan...."[12] Following her death,

Chiang made a point of not taking breakfast on her death anniversary throughout his life.

"My mother was a kind woman," Mao told Edgar Snow in 1936, "generous and sympathetic.... She pitied the poor and often gave them rice...during famines. But she could not do so when my father was present. He disapproved of charity....There were two 'parties' in the family. One was my father, the Ruling Power. The Opposition was made up of myself, my mother, my brother and sometimes even the labourer."[13] When his mother died in 1919, Mao wrote a couplet with a brush pen and an ink mixed with water and tears. Then he composed a long eulogy in the form of classic poem, in which he recalled the difficult times she had in raising him and his siblings.[14]

Now turning attention to Chiang and Mao's relation with their children, we find interesting parallels too. Chiang's son, Ching-kuo, resided in the Soviet Union from 1925 to 1937 and Mao's sons, Anying and Anqing, did the same from 1937 to 1946/1947 (and Mao's daughter, Li Min, came in the 1940s, too).[15] None of them received anything like a royal treatment as appropriate to their status as offspring of two vitally important Chinese leaders. Instead, they at times suffered ignorance and ostracism. Ching-kuo was exiled to Siberia to work in a factory; Anying fought the Germans as a soldier of the Soviet army during the Second World War. All of them were, in a sense, held as hostages by the Soviet leaders, who maneuvered to achieve political advantages over their fathers.

Chiang and Mao appeared to very much care for their sons' studies. Chiang repeatedly emphasized this point in his diaries and in his letters to his sons. For example, in one of the letters to them in 1922, Chiang said he took their practiced calligraphy, which he had received, "as a trove of treasures." Yet in another letter, to Ching-kuo, Chiang wrote, "Your calligraphy still does not look good [enough]. You must practice it every other day for one to two hundred words so that you can improve it....In your next school term, you will [begin] a class in English. Try to study hard. Nowadays, if you don't know English, you would be like a dumb. You can't get anywhere and will fall behind in any profession you are in."[16]

Mao was in touch with Anying and Anqing while they were in Moscow. In one letter to them, in January 1941, he commented on their studies: "You have made progress, and I am pleased with it.... Anying's calligraphy is pretty good....One thing I'd like to suggest to both of you is this. When you are young, study more natural sciences and talk less about politics. Well, you will talk about politics, but not now. You should delve into natural sciences as the primary subject and social sciences as a secondary subject. You can reverse that order in the future." Mao twice sent over books from China to the Soviet Union for them to read. One shipment contained as many as 60 books, on 21 different subjects.[17]

Aside from in familial relations, Chiang and Mao showed another similarity. They wore the same style of clothing. For many years, Mao always donned a jacket with a flapped and buttoned collar and four flapped and buttoned pockets, quite similar to a military uniform. It became known as the Mao Jacket. The fact is that Chiang had worn this type of jacket long before Mao did and did so in most of his life. The jacket was, in reality, first popularized by Sun Yat-sen; it is known today as the Sun Jacket among the Nationalist followers.

One final coincidence concerns Chiang and Mao's physicians. Chiang's private doctor for 33 years, Xiong Wan, and Mao's personal doctor for 22 years, Li Zhisui, received their medical education in the late 1930s from the same institution in Chengdu, Sichuan Province: the West China Union University Medical College that was founded by the Canadian missionaries in the 19th century.[18] Both of them did not at first wish to be the Chinese leaders' personal physicians, but their wish was ignored, with their desire to be surgeons never fulfilled.

NOTES

[1] Chiang noted in his diaries for the year of 1917.

[2] For Chiang's six schoolmasters, see, Tai, *CMRC*, p. 42.

[3] Mao Sicheng, ed., *Minguo Shiwunian Yiqian zhi Jiang Jieshi Xiansheng* [*Mr. Chiang Kai-shek prior to 1926*] (Hong Kong: Longmen Shudian, 1965; reprint of the 1936 edition), pp. 8-16. Mao Sicheng, the last of Chiang's childhood schoolmasters and, later, a member on his military staff, compiled this work as a chronology of Chiang's life from his birth in 1887 and to 1926, when he turned 40. The work, with a rich collection of Chiang's diary notes, correspondences, and statements, is considered the most comprehensive and authoritative of all works of this kind up to the mid1920s.

[4] Huang Zijin, *Jiang Zhongzheng Xiansheng Liu Ri Xuexi Shilu* [*Factual Record of Mr. Chiang Kai-shek's Studies in Japan*] (Taipei: Zhong Zheng Wen Jiao Ji Jin Hui, [2001]), pp. 746-52.

[5] Mao, *Chiang Kai-shek prior to 1926*, pp. 8-16.

[6] These included *On the Water Margin, Romance of the Three Kingdoms, Journey to the West,* and *Biography of General Yue Fei.*

[7] Jung Chang and Jon Halliday, *Mao, The Unknown Story* (New York: Alfred Knopf, 2005), p. 6.

[8] For Mao's six schoolmasters, see Tai, *CMRC*, p. 42.

[9] Siao Yu, *Mao Tse-tung and I Were Beggars* (New York: Collier Books, c1959), pp. 98 and 154.

[10] Quoted in Chang and Halliday, *Mao*, p. 23.

[11] Richard M. Nixon, *Leaders* (New York: Warner Books, 1982), p. 241. Nixon also noted that both Chiang and Mao cut off their queues earlier in their life as an act of defiance against the Manchu Dynasty, under which a man without a queue was subject to a summary penalty of decapitation. See also Li Yong and Zhang Zhongtian, *Jiang Jieshi Nian Pu* [*Chronology of Chiang Kai-shek*] (Beijing: Zhonggong Dang Shi Chu Ban She, 1995), p. 16; and *Mao Zedong Zi Zhuan* [*Mao Zedong's Autobiography*] (Beijing: Jie Fang Jun Wen Yi Chu Ban She, 2001), p.19.

[12] Zhou Shengying, *Sun Zhongshan he Jiang Jieshi Jiao Wang Ji Shi* [*Record on the Social Contacts of Sun Yat-sen and Chiang Kai-shek*] (Hebei: Hebei Ren Min Chu Ban She, 1993), p. 60.

[13] Edgar Snow, *Red Star over China* (New York: Random House, 1938), p.114.

[14] Sun Baoyi, *Mao Zedong de Du Shu Sheng Ya* [*Mao Zedong's Lifelong Reading Activities*] (Beijing: Zhi Shi Chu Ban She, 1993), pp. 6-7.

[15] Chiang Ching-kuo's stay in the Soviet Union is widely known. For the Mao children's stay in the Soviet Union, see Li Min, *Wo de Tongnian yu Lingxiu Fuqin* [*My Childhood Years and the Leader, My Father*] (Chengdu: Sichuan Shaonian Ertong Chu Ban She, 2003), pp. 42ff; and Chang and Halliday, *Mao*, pp. 260-62.

[16] Mao, *Chiang Kai-shek prior to 1926*, pp. 144 and 146.

[17] Lin Ke, *Mao Zedong de Ren Jian Xiang: Da Ke Wen* [*The World of Mao Zedong: Questions and Answers*] (Hong Kong: Li Wen Chu Ban She, 1996), pp. 140-41. Lin served as Mao's secretary at one time.

[18] Xiong Wan, *Wo Zuo Jiang Jieshi "Yu Yi" 40 Nian* [*I Served as Chiang Kai-shek's "Royal Physician" for Forty Years*] (Beijing: Tuan Jie Chu Ban She, 2006), pp. 32-36, 171-72; and Li Zhisui, *The Private Life of Chairman Mao* (New York: Random House, 1994), pp. 36-37 and ff. Following Chiang Kai-shek's death, Xiong's service was extended, as personal physician for Chiang Ching-kuo. Xiong's service for the Chiangs totaled forty years.

CHAPTER TWO

THE SAME PATH TO POWER

Chiang and Mao, of course, never became sworn brothers, and the similarities in their lives appear coincidental. What is not coincidental is that they chose the same path to power, and as they advanced on that path, they shared similar experiences that exerted a controlling influence on their political future.

The Starting Point

In 1924 in the southern city Canton (Guangzhou), Guangdong Province, Chiang and Mao crossed their paths for the first time. Chiang came to assume the post of Commandant of the Whampoa Military Academy that was freshly created by the Kuomintang or the Chinese Nationalist Party. Mao was sent over by his Communist comrades in his home province, Hunan, as a delegate to the Nationalist Party's First National Congress. At that time, the Communists held membership in the Nationalist Party.

How did Chiang and Mao all end up in Canton? For more than a dozen years, they had been wandering in the political wild, following a drifting career that took them to nowhere. The only thing they were certain of was their support of the Republican Revolution led by Sun Yat-sen to topple the Manchu Dynasty. On October 10, 1911, the Uprising in Wuchang in Hubei Province brought victory of the Revolution in sight. Upon hearing the news, Chiang immediately aborted his military training in Japan and rushed back to China. Within weeks, he joined a suicide squad to assault the provincial government of Zhejiang in Hangzhou and captured its Manchu governor, Zeng Yun. As the uprising rapidly spread to other provinces, the Qing (Manchu) Dynasty collapsed and was replaced by the Republic of China on January 1, 1912, with Sun Yat-sen elected its provisional president. The Republican Revolution finally triumphed.

However, the revolutionaries' fortunes fell precipitously within months, as Yuan Shikai, the last premier of the Qing monarchy, seized power in March as the new president and went on to revive the monarchy with himself as the new emperor. Backed by the Beiyang Army (the Manchus' belatedly-created modern army) he had trained, he realized his ambition in 1916 as the new sovereign in Beijing but died in the same year. From then to 1928, China was in effect a dismembered nation. Yuan's government fell to the hands of a succession of Beiyang generals, including, among others, Duan Qirui, Wu Peifu, and Zhang Zuolin. They exercised authority primarily in north China, with the rest of the country controlled by other warlords, including Feng Yuxiang, Yan Xishan, Sun Chuanfang, Li Zongren, and still other strongmen.

In these years, Chiang joined the Second Revolution launched by Sun Yat-sen to preserve the Republican system and, following Yuan's death, to fight the Beiyang warlords to unify the country. He participated in a series of rebellious acts, including an assault on the Jiangyin Fortress in Jiangsu Province and random attacks on the Yuan forces in other places. He also joined several splinter armies in a vain attempt to coalesce them into a major fighting force.

In 1918, after the Second Revolution faded as a credible movement, Chiang joined an army in east Guangdong Province under the command of Chen Jiongming, a general then in support of Sun's effort to unify the country. Chiang's association with the Chen army lasted to 1921, and from then to 1924 he performed several short military assignments for Sun. Chiang's military services from 1918 to 1924 were full of irregularities, with frequent unauthorized leaves and resignations and, then, resumption of posts. One Chinese historian tabulated that Chiang left his posts fourteen times, often without approval from his superiors. Other researchers have similar observations.[1] When he was away from the army, Chiang stayed mostly in Shanghai. Though not giving up his dedication to the revolution, he frequented brothels and indulged in gambling and feasts; he also ventured to stock market business, with substantial losses.

In spite of his unsteady military career, Chiang's talent for battle planning had impressed Sun, to whom he had demonstrated an unswerving loyalty since he joined the Sun-sponsored Tong Men Hui—the predecessor of the Nationalist Party—in Tokyo when he was receiving military training in Japan from 1907 to 1911. One episode showed his steadfast devotion to Sun. In June 1922 he rushed from his hometown to be on Sun's side on the Yongfeng warship off Canton, when the Nationalist leader was under a month-and-a-half siege by the Chen Jiongming army then in revolt. Thus earning Sun's trust, he was dispatched by the Nationalist leader in 1923 as head of a mission to the Soviet Union to study the country's military system and received the

Whampoa assignment in the following year. From then on he rapidly advanced in power, never again wavering in his military career.

If Chiang had an unpromising start in his early public life, so did Mao. The Wuchang Uprising of 1911 found the 18-year-old Mao so excited for the Republican Revolution that he dropped out of high school to join an army in Changsha to fight the Manchus. But he quit in the following February and returned to school. In the fall of 1912 he left school again to pursue "self-study" in the provincial library. A year later, he enrolled in the Provincial First Normal School, and following graduation in 1918, he wandered to Beijing to work as a library assistant at Beijing University. With exposure to works on socialism and anarchism in the library, he developed a taste for communism; he held the job for five months before returning to Hunan in 1919.

There he pursued a myriad of activities: joining a movement to drive Governor of Hunan Zhang Jingyao out of office; founding a short-lived Xinmin Xuehui (The New People Study Society), assisting Chinese students to go to France for study; participating in anti-imperialism demonstrations, and traveling to Qufu, Shandong Province, hometown of Confucius, to pay homage to the ancient sage.

In a decisive turn in his young life, he participated in the First National Congress of the Chinese Communist Party in July 1921 in Shanghai as one of the 12 delegates representing a nationwide membership of 53 people. In the following month, he returned to Hunan where he, never being a college student himself, was audacious enough to found a "Hunan Self-Study University." He did not devote much time to the university but became a teacher in the Provincial First Normal School, his alma mater. Before the year was out, he established a Hunan branch of the Communist Party; in the next three years he went on to organize labor unions, sponsor strikes, agitate for student demonstrations, and participate in a movement against Zhao Hengti, another Governor of Hunan.

Mao became increasingly radical in his activities, but as he told Edgar Snow, "just now I was still confused, looking for a road, as we say."[2] He truly was. In 1922 as he went to Shanghai to attend the Second National Congress of the Chinese Communist Party, he forgot "the name of the place where it was to be held, could not find any comrades, and missed it."[3]

The Soviet Factor

Two years later, in 1924, as he participated in the First National Congress of the Nationalist Party, Mao seemed to have finally grasped the handle of a steadier career. For the Congress, which marked the beginning of an alliance of the Nationalist Party and the Communist Party through Soviet brokerage, espoused an anti-warlordism-and-anti-imperialism platform that Mao firmly embraced.

At that time, the newly established Soviet Union proved to be of enormous appeal to the political and intellectual leaders of China. To those Chinese with a Leftist orientation, Marxism and Leninism, the force that brought the Bolshevik Revolution to success in the Soviet Union in 1917, represented a refreshing approach to the problems plaguing their country: elimination of perennial poverty by abolishing China's feudalistic class structure and fighting imperialists' aggression through the concerted action of the exploited nations. In the latter regard, Leninism was especially alluring, as it prognosticated that the Communist movement would eventually shake off the yoke the capitalist Western powers had imposed on Asian nations. This was so because capitalism, in its final stage of its development, would drive these powers inevitably to mutually destructive ventures in the exploited nations, leading to its demise.

Other than its ideological appeal, the Soviet Union also pledged several times to China—in 1918, 1919, and 1920—to renounce the imperialist privileges Russia enjoyed in China and to abolish its unequal treaties with the country.[4] This Soviet gesture of friendship made a striking impression on the Chinese as it was timely contrasted to an act of hostility of the Western powers toward China. At the Treaty of Versailles in 1919, these powers endorsed Japan's forceful grab of Germany's special interests in Shandong, China, in spite of the fact that China was an ally of Britain and France in defeating Germany in the First World War. Such egregious act by these powers and Japan incensed the Chinese enough to launch the May Fourth Movement in 1919—spontaneous massive anti-imperialism protests in Beijing and, later, other cities in the nation.

It was in such atmosphere, Chinese Leftist intellectuals under the leadership of Li Dazhao and Chen Duxiu (two professors of Beijing University), with the active assistance of the Soviet Union via the Third Communist International (Comintern), founded the Chinese Communist Party. At the party's First National Congress in July 1921 in Shanghai, Comintern representative H. Maring served as advisor, working with

Chinese Communist delegates to adopt a constitution, a political program, and an organizational structure of the party. As noted earlier, Mao was one of the delegates.[5]

While the Soviet Union exercised a decisive influence on the formation of the Chinese Communist Party, it also exerted a powerful impact on the Chinese Nationalist Party. In the early 1920s, Nationalist leader Sun Yat-sen had become disillusioned with the future of the Republican Revolution he was leading and frustrated with the Western nations' lack of sympathy for his movement to create a democratic government in a united China—a movement that was ideologically attuned to the Western libertarian tradition. He also found it amazing that Western nations refused to participate in his program for international development of China through joint ventures in industrial and construction projects. Moreover, he became deeply conscious of the fact that his revolution had faltered because the Nationalist Party never maintained a disciplined organization and possessed a strong army to carry out its revolutionary missions.

Sun was heartened by the Soviet friendly gestures to China and highly receptive to the idea of Soviet assistance to the Nationalist Party first broached to him in 1921 by the Comintern representative Maring. In 1923 Sun sealed an agreement with another Comintern representative, Adolf Yoffe, on a set or principles guiding the Soviet-Chinese relations. In it, they stressed, among other things, communism as inappropriate to China and reaffirmed Soviet renunciation of imperialist privileges in China and Soviet "people's... willingness to lend support" to China.[6]

The support that the Soviet Union agreed to provide to the Nationalist Party included Soviet help in reorganizing the party along the Leninist line and in creating a Nationalist army. For these purposes, the Soviet Union sent to Canton in 1923 Mikhail Borodin as a political representative and General Galen (Blücher) as a military advisor.

The reorganization of the Nationalist Party, which was consummated in the party's First National Congress in 1924, consisted of essentially two features. One was the establishment of a two-hierarchy political regime, one of the party and the other of the government; each hierarchy composed of three levels of organization: national, provincial, and local, with the lower level answerable to the higher one; and the government hierarchy was subordinate to the party at each of the corresponding levels of organization. The other feature was that the party maintained direct control of the governmental, social, economic, and cultural organizations and the army of the country and that within the units of all these organizations and the army, party members formed the "cells"—the core groups playing a leadership role in these units. These Leninist features were designed to create a totalitarian party system dominating the government and the masses.[7]

The Soviet Union not only helped shape the structures of the Nationalist and Communist parties but also shepherded the two parties into a common front against warlordism and imperialism. For this purpose, Maring persuaded the Communist Party's Central Committee, over the objection of one of the party's founders, Chen Duxiu, to adopt a resolution in 1922 to allow the Communists to join the Nationalist Party as individuals.[8]

When the First National Congress of the Nationalist Party took place, it consisted of a total of 165 delegates, of whom more than 20 were Communists, including the head of the Communist Party, Li Dazhao, and Mao Zedong. It elected a number of Communists to the Nationalist Party's Central Executive Committee, with Mao as an alternate member. Later, Mao held a number of other Nationalist positions, including Acting Director of the Propaganda Department, membership of the executive committee of the Party's Shanghai branch, and director of a school to train the peasants for political action. Soon Soviet financial and military assistance came in full force, and more Soviet personnel arrived in Canton, some of whom joined the Whampoa Military Academy as advisors and instructors.[9]

Thus, in 1924, as Mao made his debut in the Nationalist Party, Chiang accepted Sun's assignment as head of the party's Whampoa Military Academy. They now belonged to the same party, worked for the same programs, and started to march onto the same path to power.[10]

History-Mandated Goals

As Chiang and Mao marched on the same path to power, it is important to point out what motivated them in their drive to seize power and what means they used to attain power. Chiang and Mao wanted to seize power because they needed it to realize their vision for creating a prosperous and strong China—an objective all Chinese leaders had since the latter part of the 19th century consistently advocated but repeatedly failed to make true. Their vision was, in turn, deeply influenced by their sense of history. From their private school years, Chiang and Mao had learned to take China as an organic entity with a life of continuous growth from the ancient time to the present and into the future. In their adult years, as seen later in this chapter, they reinforced this view with a heavy reading of Chinese history works and dynasty chronicles. They perceived the growth of China in two dimensions: territorial expansion and population growth.

The Silk Road may present some physical evidence on the Chinese territorial expansion. At a fountain, crystal clear water bubbles up from an urn-like stoneware on a bed of pebbles. Some fifty feet away to the south, statues of soldiers lined up in formation; to their left stood a gigantic statue of a marshal in full battle gear raising high a wine cup to his soldiers. What is seen here is a park dedicated to Huo Qubing in Jiuquan, Gansu Province in northwest China. Huo was a young general of the Western Han Dynasty (206 BC-25 AD) who excelled in surprise attack on his enemy with a lean, fast-moving cavalry. Upon one decisive victory against the Xiongnu—a powerful nomadic tribe north of China—one year in the second century BC, Huo received a royal-dispatched jug of wine from Emperor Han Wu to congratulate him for his great deed. Unable to share it with so many of his soldiers, Huo poured the wine into a fountain and let everybody have a drink. That is how Jiuquan has since became known, the Wine Spring.

Jiuquan is located toward the west end of the Hexi Corridor, China's passageway to the Western Territories (*Xi Yu*), a vast region of kingdoms and principalities beyond the reach of China until the early Han Dynasty. To break into this region, the Han Court sent over not only generals and soldiers but diplomats and scholar officials as well. In 139 BC, Zhang Qian, a top Chinese civilian official, journeyed to the region to promote diplomacy and trade, with the routes he traveled on becoming subsequently known as the Silk Road. In the first century AD, Ban Chao, a scholar-turned-general, led an elite force into the Western Territories, where he forged alliances with such chiefdoms as Yiwu, Shanshan, Shache, Wusun, and Kashi—places that still bear these names to this day.

The Silk Road story merely marks one link of the long chain of territorial expansion of China. The first major expansion from the Chinese core area, which centered today's Henan Province stretching to Shaanxi and Shanxi provinces in the west and Shandong Province in the east, occurred in the Qin Dynasty (221 BC-207 BC). The dynasty built the Great Wall to ward off the invasion of the Xiongnu from the north while pushing China's territorial expansion to the south, reaching out to parts of today's southern China and northern Vietnam. Succeeding the Qin, the Han Dynasty shifted direction of expansion by going to the Western Territories, which constitute China's Xinjiang Autonomous Region today.

Four centuries following the Han, the Tang Empire rose to prominence, controlling an area roughly the same as that of the Han. The next expansion occurred in the Yuan Dynasty (1279-1368) when it incorporated Tibet as one of its thirteen provinces. The Qing Dynasty (1644-1911) consolidated all Chinese territorial gains achieved over the centuries. From the Qin to the Qing Dynasty, Chinese territorial expansion lasted twenty-one centuries. It was accomplished through numerous wars, diplomatic entanglements, heavy material costs, and enduring hardship to the people; the expansion also suffered numerous setbacks as well, as China was frequently dominated or conquered by tribes from the peripheral lands. Hence, the Chinese people (more so for the Han than the non-Han minorities) value deeply the end result of the territorial expansion and regard the preservation of Chinese territorial integrity as a sacred mission, something to be achieved at all cost.

However, from the 19th century on China had lost its peripheral lands to the imperialist powers. Russia grabbed Chinese lands east of Manchuria and west of Xinjiang; Britain seized Hong Kong and Kowloon, Portugal acquired Macao; and Japan wrestled away Taiwan. In addition, China had lost its former Tributary States in Indochina to Britain and France and Korea to Japan, and it had to concede its border territories—Manchuria, Xinjiang, and Tibet--as spheres of influence of foreign powers. Moreover, following the Opium War of 1839, it was imposed upon a number of "unequal treaties." Under the terms of these treaties, foreign concessions were created in several major Chinese cities, where foreign powers exercised extraterritorial jurisdiction and stationed troops; foreign companies dominated Chinese fledgling industries; a foreigner headed Chinese Customs Office; foreign powers fixed the tariff rates; and the Chinese were burdened with ruinous war reparations to the foreign nations that had defeated their country.

It was such a China that Chiang and Mao had inherited. As Chinese nationalistic leaders, the more they took pride in the Chinese territorial growth prior to the 19th century, the more they felt humiliated with their country having lost so many of its lands. They avowed to restore Chinese territorial integrity and to remove the unjustified privileges imposed on China by foreign powers. In short, anti-imperialism became an irrepressible force motivating them to march onto the path to power and an unshakable plank of their revolution's platform.

If the territorial factor motivated Chiang and Mao for political action, so did the population factor. In the Northern Song Dynasty (960-1126), an unknown Confucian scholar compiled a book called *Bai Jia Xing* or *One Hundred Family Names*. A collection of Chinese family names, the book consists of, in fact, more than 500 names, with additional ones added on later. The text is written in the form of four-word, rhyming verses, each word being a particular family name.

Considered as the national genealogy of China, *One Hundred Family Names* was among the very first books Chiang and Mao were committed to memory during their study in private schools. It is supposed to trace the Chinese people to a common ancestry of Yan Emperor and Huang Emperor times (about 27th century BC). Though provable documentary evidence and archeological finds about these legendary times were never found, the Chinese (mainly the Han) have over the centuries persistently claimed themselves as the Yan-Huang descendants. The Chinese, thus, call their nation *guo jia,* a familial nation and address each other as *tong bao,* literally, people of the same parentage, and consider themselves, in a folksy way, *Lao Bai Xing,* or members of the One Hundred Family Names.

The earliest count of Chinese population took place in 2 AD in the Han Dynasty. As recorded in that dynasty's chronicle, *Han Shu,* the population then totaled at 57.7 million, which was more numerous than that of the contemporaneous Roman Empire, the then largest political entity outside of China.[11] "From the time when the Roman Empire broke up," Patricia Buckley Ebrey has observed, "China was never seriously rivalled as the world's most populous country. Indeed, China regularly had a greater population than all of the countries of Europe put together."[12] In post-Han times, Chinese population had ranged from 50 to 60 million, until 1100 in the Song Dynasty, when it reached 100 million. In 1851 it jumped spectacularly to 432 million, with China becoming inexorably the world's most populous nation to this day.[13]

The bulk of Chinese population consists of the Han people, those who originally settled in the Chinese core area. But the Han people have over the ages absorbed a substantial number of ethnic minorities outside the core area—on the great arc of territories stretching from Manchuria to Tibet. In the two millennia since the early Han Dynasty, wars, interracial marriage, and Sinicization of minorities (minorities assuming Han names and adopting Han culture and economic pursuits) extensively altered the composition of the Chinese population. In the Yuan Dynasty (1279-1368) and the Qing Dynasty (1644-1911), the entire China was ruled by ethnic minorities, the Mongolians and the Manchurians respectively. Today, the Han Chinese comprise an overwhelming majority of the Chinese population (92 percent, or 1.2 billion, out of a total of 1.3 billion), but many of them are of mixed blood of the Han people originally settled in the Chinese core area and the ethnic minorities in the peripheral lands.

The metamorphosis of Chinese population composition was intensified by the cycle of political union and disunion that appeared in the country's long history. Evidence shows that wars, rebellions, natural calamities, enfeebled emperors, among other factors, normally led to dismemberment of the country. The rise of masterful rulers at the juncture at dynasty turnovers generally united China. This cyclical pattern can be seen in the following table.[14]

Union	*Disunion*
Qin Dynasty, 221-207 BC	Three Kingdoms, 220-280
Han Dynasty, 206 BC-220 AD	Jin Dynasty 265-420
Sui Dynasty, 581—618	Sixteen Kingdoms 304-436
Tang Dynasty, 618-907	North-South Division, 420-589
Yuan Dynasty, 1279-1368	Five Dynasties/Ten Kingdoms, 907-979
Ming Dynasty, 1368-1644	Song Dynasty/Liao, Jin Empire, 960-1279
Qing Dynasty, 1644-1911	The Republic of China, 1912-1928

The disunion times, which frequently saw the domination of north China by ethnic minorities and large-scale southward migration of the people, furthered mixing the Han and ethnic minorities; and the union times saw, in most cases, deepened integration of the populace.

These developments in Chinese population have injected in the minds of the Chinese people (or the much altered, enlarged Han populace) a strong sense of empathy for each other and a desire for unity as a basis for the emergence of a strong and prosperous China. However, when Chiang and Mao were searching for power in the early 20th century, they saw China mired in the last historical period of disunion as the warlords divided the country into regional strongholds. Confronted with such a division, both Chiang and Mao sought earnestly to re-create order out of chaos and to bring the world's largest national population under one government.

To sum up, China's historical experiences with territorial and population growth exerted on Chiang and Mao an overwhelming weight; they mandated the two Chinese leaders to achieve the following goals: to eradicate imperialism and warlordism as the immediate objectives and to build a prosperous and strong China in the long run.

Resorting to Arms

How would Chiang and Mao seize power and accomplish these goals? They quickly realized that the only way to grab power was to resort to arms. They were reminded of Sun Yat-sen's tumultuous experiences with the Republican Revolution. He successfully led the Republican Revolution to overthrow the Manchu Monarchy but failed to defend it when challenged by Yuan Shikai and the warlords. By the early 1920s Sun painfully recognized that his failure had everything to do with his lack of a military force. His failure was made especially obvious in view of the Bolshevik Revolution in Russia. The Bolsheviks formed the Red Army in 1918 out of the rebellious workers and soldiers, with which they successfully defended the Soviet government they had created and, later, defeated the White Russian army in the civil war.

Sun's decision to create the Whampoa Military Academy in Canton to forge a Nationalist army proved to be a decisive opening for Chiang's rise to power. Chiang fully supported Sun's decision but confronted an immediate question. Could he use the army to carry out the anti-warlordism-and-anti-imperialism double mission at the same time? Chiang soon concluded that defeating the warlords had to take the priority, for without a united country, he could never muster enough strength to engage the militarily and economically far stronger foreign powers.

Chiang was a young general in a hurry. In 1925, just one year following his Whampoa assignment, he proposed to take steps to start the Northern Expedition. Yet, without an army remotely matching the strength of any single warlord, to say nothing of the combined armies of several warlords, Chiang's proposed expedition appeared to many of his comrades to be nothing but a dream. And his Soviet advisors counseled strongly against it, arguing that the Academy needed time to create an adequate corps of cadets so as to expand it to a credible force before engaging the northern warlords.

Chiang had, in fact, something else in mind. He wanted to take on the rebellious Chen Jiongming army, which had retreated to east Guangdong Province following its failing revolt against Sun Yat-sen. He planned to defeat the Chen army before consolidating a military base in Canton whereby he could assemble several provincial armies in southern China into a sizable revolutionary army to fight the warlords in the north.

The central authority of the Nationalist Party in Canton promptly endorsed his plan, for the city was under the threat of an attack from the Chen army. In January 1925, the Party appointed Chiang Commander-in-

Chief of the Eastern Expedition and placed under his command, in addition to the 3,000 cadets of the Whampoa Academy, military units of Guangdong, Guangxi, and Yunnan provinces. With these forces, he started counterattacking the Chen army in the following month.

With detailed battle orders, he charged the four components of his forces for a parallel attack on the target areas of the Chen army. Battling an overwhelmingly large hostile force—reportedly of 100,000 men—with superior firepower, Chiang knew it was an extremely dangerous mission. But he counted for its execution on the high morale of his army units, particularly the Whampoa cadets, for they had displayed "a revolutionary fervor" for the campaign. In addition, he steeled all the men under his command with an extraordinary "Code of Mutual Responsibility" (*Lian Zuo Fa*). The Code proscribed unauthorized retreat by the head officer of any unit—from platoon to division commander—with summary execution.

To live up to the spirit of the Code, Chiang went on to the frontline in the battlefield to mix himself with his soldiers. In one chaotic engagement with the enemy, when he found he was totally surrounded, he raised his pistol to shoot himself to avoid capture. One officer of the cadet army jumped to stop him and carried him away on the cadet's shoulders. The cadet, named Chen Geng, rose years later to a top general of the Chinese Communist army.

In several month's fierce fighting, his forces thoroughly routed the Chen army, occupying its two key base areas in east Guangdong: Chaozhou and Meixian. When he returned to Canton in the fall, Chiang received a rousing welcome as a war hero for achieving an incredible victory. The Expedition demonstrated for the first time his quality as commander of a large military operation. With detailed battle orders he issued, he achieved maximal coordination of his cadet army with the disparate Guangdong, Guangxi, and Yunnan armies, which had never collaborated before. He took steps to integrate these armies into "The National Revolutionary Army" with him as the chief commander and others as field commanders. This development reflects a strategic plan he had formulated years ago, as to be elaborated on in the next chapter.

Chiang's victorious performance in the Eastern Expedition not only elevated him to the top military leader in south China but also earned him a seat in the Central Standing Committee of the Nationalist Party, marking his entry to the political center of the Party. More importantly he won confidence of the Party leadership in his ability to carry on the Northern Expedition that he had advocated.

In 1926, the Nationalist Party authorized the commencement of the Northern Expedition. Chiang started the campaign in July, thrusting the then National Revolutionary Army of 85,000 men against a conglomerate of warlord armies of reputedly 1,000,000 men. Like a torrent of lava blazing north from Canton, his force decimated the army divisions of one warlord after another; he stunned the nation by completing the expedition in two years' time, when his army occupied Beijing in June 1928. On October 10, he reached the pinnacle of power when he became Chairman of the National Government. In 1932 the Nationalist Party formally appointed Chiang Chairman of the Central Military Commission, confirming his position as the head of its military arm since 1926.

While Chiang was in the limelight in 1925-1928 with his victorious Eastern and Northern Expeditions, Mao was not directly involved in any of these military actions. He played a subordinate role by engaging in propaganda activities and attempting to mobilize the peasants as an auxiliary political force of the Nationalist revolution without any substantial consequence. When Chiang in the midst of the Northern Expedition purged the Communists from the Nationalist rank in April 1927 and killed many of their comrades in the area under his control, the Communist Party suffered a most crippling setback since its creation.[15]

Yet precisely in that year two strains of thoughts crystallized in Mao's mind that decisively shaped his strategy to acquire power and profoundly affected the Communist Party's future course of evolution. In April he submitted the widely known "Report of an Investigation into the Peasant Movement in Hunan," in which he declared that the Chinese peasants possessed the greatest potential to carry on the Communist revolution to success. Based on a three-month observation in his home province, he found that the peasants had wrestled land from landlords, refused to pay exorbitant rents, and defended their position by organizing themselves into peasant associations, whose membership grew from 300,000 to more than 1.3 million in the year of 1926 alone. He asserted that if the peasant power was fully activated, it would "send all imperialists, warlords, corrupted officials…and bad gentry to their graves."[16]

Mao also developed the concept that the army was critical to the existence of any political regime, making the renowned statement that "political power comes from the barrel of the gun." The union of the peasants and the gun, thus, epitomized Mao's means of acquiring power. But he had very, very few guns at this time. While in Hunan, he started agitating for rural rebellion with splinter armed peasants, but they were hunted down by the authorities. Mao soon saw the hills in the neighboring Jiangxi Province offer the best topographic advantage for his armed band to take root. In November 1927 he and his some 1,000 men trudged to the forested Jinggang Mountain where, through bargain and trade, he absorbed bandit gangs into his force. There he settled down and got an inspiration for survival from, of all people, a brigand chief, Zhu Longzi—the Deaf Zhu. The chief had been dodging successfully the pursuit of the government security force by *da quaner*, meaning "running in circles." Mao practiced it against the Nationalist army chasing after him. In time, he honed the practice to perfection to be known as *youjizhan*, the guerrilla warfare. It was that warfare that enabled the Communists to withstand the repeated onslaughts of the Nationalist army in the 1930s, known as the encirclement campaigns, to be elaborated in the next chapter.

Mao complemented his guerrilla war with a free distribution to the peasants of land that his armed band forcefully grabbed from the landlords. As more land was distributed, more peasants joined his army to defend their vested interest, thus giving momentum to his rural revolution. This kind of strategy, however, was repudiated by the Communist Party's central authority then in underground operations in Shanghai. Under the control of Li Lishan and, later, Wang Ming and the so called 28 Bolsheviks (Moscow-trained Chinese Communists), the central authority considered Mao's strategy running counter to Marxism's emphasis on the urban proletariat as the principal force to carry out the Communist revolution. For a period of time, the Chinese Communists followed the Li Lishan Line and organized labor strikes in major cities such as Nanchang, Changsha, and Canton. All resulted in failures.

For his unorthodoxy approach to communism, Mao was stripped from his position as an alternate member of the party's Politburo. Undaunted, Mao, having earlier joined forces in Jiangxi with an army unit under Zhu De, persisted in his rural communism strategy in the province. In 1931 he set up a Soviet government there, with himself elected chairman of its Executive Committee and vigorously pushed for land redistribution. In 1933 the Communist central authority, unable to survive in Shanghai, moved to Jiangxi. It was then under the control of Wang Ming who, with the help of a military advisor, Li De (Otto Braun, a German national), rejected Mao's hit-and-run tactics and favored frontal engagements with the Nationalist army. The Wang Ming Line, as it was known later, played into the hands of the Nationalist army, which tightened the encirclement campaign in 1934 to the extent of threatening an annihilation of the Communist army.

To break out from the encirclement campaign, Mao and his army made an arduous and long escape. They ran away from Jiangxi to the rugged hills of China's southwest and wound through snow-capped mountains and uninhabited highlands and swamps to northern Shaanxi Province where they set up camp to continue the war with the Nationalists. Earlier, in 1935, en route this cruel and dangerous journey, subsequently known as the Long March, the top leaders of the Communist Party held a crucial meeting in Zunyi, Guizhou Province to discuss the future of the party. With the Li Lishan Line and Wang Ming Line discredited at the Jiangxi battlefield, Mao's senior comrades endorsed his rural communism strategy as the only way to combat the Nationalists and to advance the cause of Communist revolution. They subsequently affirmed Mao's position as the party's leader. In 1936 the Communist Party made Mao Chairman of the Central Military Commission—head of the party's army—a position he never relinquished until his death in 1976.

With the gun firmly in his hand, Mao set out to create the Communist regime thirteen years later.

Chiang attained the Nationalist military power in 1928, at age of 41; Mao achieved the Communist military power in 1935, at 42. At roughly the same age, they started charting out in separate ways the future course of China.

Reading Books

Though Chiang and Mao immersed most of their adult life in military affairs, it would be a mistake to assume that resorting to arms was their only means to acquire power. From their early life on, they were seriously and continuously devoted to self-studies, which helped them acquire as well as exercise power. Though resenting the Confucian studies in their private school years, they did absorb the essentials of the Confucian texts through continuous recitations. Later in their life, they returned to these texts many times and made selective use of them to furnish substance to their political thoughts and, in the case of Chiang, policies. These texts consist of the Four Books and Five Classics.[17]

Beyond these Confucian texts, Chiang and Mao read a great variety of other books, include the following identical Chinese and Western titles.[18] Among the Chinese works, both paid heavy attention to historical studies and dynastic chronicles, especially *The Records of*

History (*Shiji*), *History of the Twenty-four Dynasties* (*Ershisi Shi*),[19] *Complete Mirror for Aid in Government* (*Zizhi Tongjian*), and *An Outline of [Chinese]History* (*Gang Jian*). Other titles ranged from collections from philosophers and scholars, theories on war, biographies, novels, and popular journals.[20] Western titles (translated) include *Hegel's Works*, *Darwin's Works*, *On War* (by Carl von Clausewitz), John Dewey's Speeches in China, *Marx's Works*, *Lenin's Works*, and the Christian *Bible*.[21]

Chiang and Mao often foraged into each others' favorite subjects of studies. A staunch anti-Communist for much of his life, Chiang had in the 1920s an abiding interest in the Marxist and Leninist and other leftist works.[22] His diary entries in September and October 1923 showed that he was reading *Summaries of Marxist Theories* (*Makesi Xueshuo Gaiyao*). He could not comprehend the first half of it but persisted with the second half; he was so absorbed in the book that he could not let it go. He also read *The Communist Manifesto* in the same year. Two years later, he read Lenin's works and found the Bolshevik leader's organizing techniques instructive. In these years, he perused with a great deal of interest *The History of German Social Democrats*, *The History of Russian Revolution*, *The History of Russian Communist Party*, and *New Youth*, a periodical once edited by Chen Duxiu, a founder of the Chinese Communist Party.

Early in his life Mao delved into books that were Chiang's favorites. These include Zeng Guofan's *Works* and Wang Yangming's *Works*. Later, however, he repudiated them. He took Zeng as an enemy of the Taiping Tianguo movement, which he regarded as a sort of rural revolution predating the Chinese Communists'. He rejected Wang's work for its advocacy of metaphysical theory, which contradicted Marxist's concept of materialism.

Both Chiang and Mao led a rough-and-tumble life amidst wars, travels, and flights. Yet their devotion to learning never wavered. Chiang read books at home, in office, and during vacation. He did not give up reading while in the battlefield. During the Northern Expedition he once read a book while riding on a military vehicle (CKSD, 6/3/28). In a battle against the Communists in 1931, he read *Zhuangzi* (a treatise of one of the philosophers who founded Taoism) on a boat (CKSD, 7/26/31). He perused Sun Yat-sen's works while riding a battleship (CKSD, 9/18/31). On December 10, 1949—in what must be regarded as his darkest hours—he was observed to be reading a book on the Chinese classics. He was then on board of a plane in a hurried flight from

Chengdu to Taiwan, his last one out of mainland China, as the Communist army was on the verge of conquering the entire country.

Chiang was a military man living up to the reputation, in a Chinese expression, of "the hand never lets go a book," though he was never so reputed during his lifetime, perhaps even today.

Chiang was not a casual reader. He used a Chinese brush pen to sketch out *dian* (dots) and *quan* (circles)—common practices of serious Chinese readers—next to passages of a given text to emphasize their significance. Frequently he went back to previously-read works for re-reading. Once, chancing upon Zeng Guofan's works that he had read before, he exclaimed with joy, "Reading the Zeng collection is like meeting a good old friend" (CKSD, 4/29/21).

Chiang, of course, read many other books than those listed above. One study on Chiang's early career indicates that during the period from 1917 to 1931, he covered at least eighty-seven different titles, many of which were multi-volume works.[23] A research on his reading experiences tabulated that from 1919 to 1945, Chiang perused close to two hundred subjects, many of which were not mentioned above.[24]

Mao was even more studious than Chiang. Like Chiang, he read books anytime he found a chance to: in the battlefield during the Jiangxi days, on horseback during the Long March, and, after moving to Beijing in 1949, in his bookshelf-lined reception room and on his specially constructed bed with bookshelf attached to it.[25] He maintained a private library containing thousands of volumes; he borrowed books from public library and private individuals.[26] During his travels, he was often accompanied by two large crates of books. He practically lived amidst his books—and, then, died with them. He once said if he had ten years to live, he would read until the day before his death. Incredibly, he made good of this promise. The last book he read was on September 8, 1976 at 5:50 PM after he was resuscitated to life in an emergency operation; he read for seven minutes before falling to a coma and died the next day.[27]

Like Chiang, Mao was a serious reader. He used dots and circles, too, to mark important passages of his books. He reread his books. He went over, he said, at least seventeen times *Complete Mirror for Aid in Government (Zizhi Tongjian)*.[28] He spent 24 years, 1952-1976, on reading *History of the Twenty-four Dynasties (Ershisi Shi)*, a collection of 800 volumes, with 40 million words; he read many of these volumes several times.[29] And he saw the utility of learning English, taking time to study the language with his secretary and his physician and practiced it on his foreign visitors such as the former British Marshal Bernard Montgomery.[30]

Why were Chiang and Mao so thirsty for learning? They offered different answers. Chiang stated simply, "I'm ashamed I was not well-educated. I can never spare enough time for reading" (CKSD, 3/13/28). He believed that "pursuing studies without letup will improve my moral character. If I want to be a man of strength and integrity, I must obtain learning from studies" (CKSD, 12/20/30). Indeed, his effort at moralizing his political leadership, as will be analyzed in Chapter Four, rested squarely on his reading experiences. More pragmatically, he viewed reading as a necessary means to broaden his knowledge so as to sustain his effort to carry on the revolution and to govern a nation deep in the throes of domestic turmoil and foreign exploitation. It was for this reason, he once condemned himself "for failing to do reading today" (CKSD, 9/3/28).

A man with learning was like one standing on the top of a mountain, Mao said in 1939 in Yan'an; it allowed him to see many things over the distance. A person without learning was like, he continued, someone walking in a dark alley, groping with difficulties.[31] What was the specific learning Mao found it enabling him to see things farther and clearer? It was the mixture of Chinese history and Marxism. In a 1935 essay on "Study," he wrote:

> Our task is to study our historical heritage and use the Marxist method to sum it up critically. Our national history goes back several thousand years and has its own characteristics and innumerable treasures. But in these matters we are mere schoolboys.... We should sum up our history from Confucius to Sun Yat-sen and take over this valuable legacy.[32]

His reading preference was clearly with Chinese history, rather than Marxism and other Socialist writings. In his *Selected Works* he cited from Chinese history and Chinese classics four times as many as he did from Marxism.[33]

Rising above Others

If Chiang and Mao battled each other to attain power, how did they beat their contenders for power within their own ranks? For Chiang, he was rather a junior leader in the Nationalist hierarchy at the time of the death of the party's leader Sun Yat-sen in 1925. According to an account of Chiang's wife at the time, Ch'en Chieh-ju, Chiang was ranked seventh in the race for succession, after Wang Jingwei, Hu Hanmin, Xu Chongzhi, Liao Zhongkai, Liu Zhenhuan, and Wu Zhihui.[34] Wang Jingwei, Hu Hanmin, and Liao Zhongkai were Sun's closest comrades in arms, working together for the longest time during the revolution. Liao died of an assassin's bullet in 1925. Xu Chongzhi and Liu Zhenhuan, two military leaders, lost out in the race during the Eastern Expedition because of incompetence and failed mutiny respectively. Wu Zhihui, a scholar and theoretician involved in the Nationalist revolution back to the Tokyo days, dropped out on his own.

The only persons wielding a greater political influence within the Nationalist Party than Chiang were Wang Jingwei and Hu Hanmin. But both were civilian administrators without the military competence to meet the requirement of the time: defeating the warlords. With the army firmly lodged in his hands, Chiang did not hesitate to scuttle Wang Jingwei's political clout during the Zhongshan Warship Incident in 1926, and Hu Hanmin was implicated in the case of Liao Zhongkai's assassination.[35] Though both men survived the crises, their political strength was severely undercut; they were no longer serious contenders for the party's top leadership position. Thus, Chiang's military prowess constituted the critical factor for his rise to the top of the Nationalist hierarchy.

For Mao, his position in the Chinese Communist Party in the early 1930s was even more inferior than Chiang's in the Nationalist Party in the mid1920s. He had then succeeded in establishing rural base areas in Jiangxi and withstood Chiang's encirclement campaigns. But he was not yet able to make a full member of the Politburo, the highest ruling organ of the Communist Party.

Like Chiang, Mao was hoisted to the power pedestal through the process of elimination. Li Dazhao and Chen Duxiu, the two founders of the Communist Party, were removed from the scene in 1927, one being executed by the warlord Zhang Zuolin and the other expelled from the party because of his anti-Comintern position. Then the Soviet-trained Communist leaders Li Lishan and Wang Ming fell out the leadership lineup for following erroneous political and military strategies.

By 1935 the only Communists rivaling Mao for power were Zhang Guotao, Zhou Enlai, and Zhu De. Zhang Guotao, owing to a strategic error over the Communists' retreat route during the Long March, suffered crippling military setbacks for the forces he had led; he eventually defected to the Nationalist side. Zhou Enlai had by this time embraced Mao as the new party leader; speaking for his senior comrades at the time, he declared Mao's "ideas" as constituting "the party line of Chinese Communism"—as to be discussed later. He had since remained satisfied as the number two man of the Communist hierarchy. Zhu De excelled in the conduct of guerrilla warfare but showed no all-embracing strategic vision in that warfare, and he was purely a military man without political ambition.[36]

In the decades since their rise to power, Chiang and Mao had seen challenges to their leadership positions within respectively the Nationalist and Communist hierarchies from people other than those noted above. But Chiang and Mao experienced only temporary setbacks, holding fast to their positions to the end of their political journeys.

NOTES

[1] See Li Ao, *Jiang Jieshi Yanjiu* [*Research on Chiang Kai-shek*] (Taipei: Tianyuan Tushu Company, 1986), pp. 86-126; Zhang Xianwen and Fang Qingxiu, *Jiang Jieshi Quan Zhuan* [*Complete Biography of Chiang Kai-shek*], (Zhengzhou, Henan: Henan Ren Min Chu Ban She, 1996), pp. 40-41; and Pichon P. Y. Loh, *The Early Chiang Kai-shek: A Study of His Personality and Politics, 1887-1924* (New York: Columbia University Press, 1971) p. 31.

[2] Snow, *Red Star over China*, p. 135. Snow's interviews with Mao, taken in 1936, constituted the only autobiographical work on Mao's early life, from which several Chinese works were derived and annotated. See, for example, *Mao Zedong Zi Zhuan* [*Mao Zedong's Autobiography*], Qingdao: Qingdao Chu Ban She, 2003.

[3] Snow, *Red Star over China*, p. 142.

[4] Emmanuel C. Y. Hsü, *The Rise of Modern China*, 2nd ed. (New York: Oxford University Press, 1979), p. 620; and Harold R. Isaacs, *The Tragedy of the Chinese Revolution*, 2d rev. ed. (Stanford: Stanford University Press [1966, c1961]), p. 47.

[5] Zhong Gong Zhong Yang Zu Zhi Bu, Zhong Gong Zhong Yang Dang Shi Yan Jiu Shi, and Zhong Yang Dang An Guan, eds., *Zhongguo Gong Chan Dang Zu Zhi Shi Zi Liao* [*Materials on the History of the Chinese Communist Party Organizations*], Vol. 1 (Beijing: Zhong Gong Dang Shi Chu Ban She, 2000), p.18. Chang Kuo-t'ao, *The Rise of the Chinese Communist Party: The Autobiography of Chang Kuo-t'ao*, Vol. 1 (Lawrence: University Press of Kansas [1971-72]), pp. 137-47. For the party's early history, see Arif Dirlik, *The Origins of Chinese Communism*, New York: Oxford University Press, 1989; and Benjamin I. Schwartz, *Chinese Communism and the Rise of Mao*, Cambridge: Harvard University Press, 1961 [c1951].

[6] Conrad Brandt, Benjamin Schwartz, and John K. Fairbank, eds., *A Documentary History of Chinese Communism* (London: Allen & Unwin, 1959), pp. 70-71.

[7] In subsequent decades the Nationalist Party retained essentially these Leninist structural features, but the party had gone through so many changes in actual operations that it had become vastly different from the Soviet model—a subject we shall return to later, in Chapter Seven.

[8] Brandt, *A Documentary History of Chinese Communism*, p. 52. For citation of other relevant works, see Tai, *CMRC*, p. 63, note 8.

[9]A detailed study of Soviet advisors in China from 1923 to 1927 showed that more than 100 of them served with the Nationalist Party and the Whampoa Military Academy. Zhou Xingliang, "Su Lian Gu Wen Tuan yu Sun Yat-sen Huang Pu Jian Jun Shi Ye di Kai Chuang he Fa Zhan" [The Soviet Advisory Group and the Development of an Army at Whampoa under Sun Yat-sen], Shanghai Sun Yat-sen Soong Ching Ling Wen Wu Guan Li Wei Yuan Hui, ed., *Sun Yat-sen & Soong Ching Ling: Archive & Research*, Vol. 3 (Shanghai: Shanghai Su Dian, 2011): 55-80. See also *Soviet Volunteers in China, 1925-1945: Articles and Reminiscences*, translated from the Russian by David Fidlon, Moscow: Progress, c1980.

[10]It should be pointed out in this connection that Soviet gesture of friendship to China and Soviet assistance to the Nationalist and Communist parties were not merely prompted by a desire to forge a Soviet-Chinese common front against Western imperialism or by an altruistic motivation. There was also an underside of Soviet actions. As Bruce A. Elleman has pointed out, the Soviet Union intended to use its negotiations with China as leverage to regain the country's privileges in Manchuria and Outer Mongolia. Bruce A. Elleman, "Soviet Diplomacy and the First United Front in China," *Modern China*, Vol. 21 (October 1995): 450-80.

For this purpose, the Soviet Union actually first negotiated with Beijing's warlord government; only after the warlord government rebuffed the Soviet effort did the Soviet representatives start negotiation with the Nationalist Party. Similarly, in promoting the Nationalist-Communist alliance, as John King Fairbank and Merle Goldman have pointed out, "the ulterior objective of the Comintern was to develop the Chinese Communist Party and get it into a strategic position within the Guomindang (GMD) so as eventually to seize control of it." John King Fairbank and Merle Goldman, *China: A New History*, 2nd and enlarged ed. (Cambridge: Belknap Press of Harvard University Press, 2006) pp. 281-82.

[11]*Han Shu* was edited by the historian Ban Gu (32-92AD). For the evolution of the Chinese population, see Ge Jianxiong, *Zhongguo Ren Kou Fa Zhan Shi* [History of the Development of Chinese Population], Fuzhou: Fujian Ren Min Chu Ban she, 1991.

[12]Patricia Buckley Ebrey, *The Cambridge Illustrated History of China* (Cambridge: Cambridge University Press, 1996), p. 246.

[13]Ibid., pp. 73, 141, and 246; Fairbank and Goldman, *China: A New History*, pp. 167-68.

¹⁴This table is based on "Table 1, Eras of Chinese History," in Shuhsi Hsü, *Understanding Chinese History,* edited and revised by Hung-chao Tai (Carlsbad, CA: American Society of China Scholars, 2004), p. 3.

¹⁵According to one study, the purge resulted in the killing of over 300 communists, imprisonment of over 500, and disappearance of over 5,000. Wang Jianhua, *Hong Se Kong Bu de Tie Quan* [*The Iron Fist of Red Terror*] (Beijing: Ren Min Zhong Guo Chu Ban She, 1993), pp. 16-17. Chiang took this drastic action because he believed that the Communists were then resorting to unban insurrection tactics in Shanghai in the fashion of the Bolshevik Revolution in an effort to supplant the revolution he was leading.

¹⁶Mao, *SW*, I, 22, 34. Peasant movements also occurred in Hubei and Jiangxi provinces during the Northern Expedition. Membership of the peasant associations there numbered at tens of thousands. Some of the associations appeared Communist inspired, but most of them took place under their own initiative. Within the Communist Party, division of opinions over the activities of the associations occurred. Some deemed them helpful to the prosecution of the Northern Expedition. Some others considered that if the party endorsed the extreme violent activities that the associations were known to engage in, such endorsement would jeopardize the party's cooperative relations with the Nationalist Party. Zhang Xianwen, et al., *Zhonghua Minguo Shi* [*A History of the Republic of China*], Vol. 1 (Nanjing: Nanjing Da Xue Chu Ban She, 2005), pp. 572-79; and Philip Short, *Mao: A Life* (New York: Henry Holt, 2000), pp. 165-78.

¹⁷The Four Books consist of *The Analects* (*Lunyu*), *The Great Learning* (*Daxue*), *The Doctrine of the Mean* (*Zhongyong*), and *The Works of Mencius* (*Mengzi*); and The Five Classics, *Classic of Odes* (*Shijing*), *Ancient Records* (*Shujing*), *Classic of Changes* (*Yijing*), *Record of Ceremonies and Proper Conduct* (*Liji*), and *Spring and Autumn Annals* (*Chunqiu*).

¹⁸The sources of information on Chiang Kai-shek's reading titles are his diaries and Mao, *Chiang Kai-shek prior to 1926*. The sources of information on Mao's reading titles include Gong Yuzhi, Pang Xianzhi, and Shi Zhongquan, *Mao Zedong de Du Shu Sheng Huo* [*Mao Zedong's Reading Activities*], Beijing: Sheng Huo, Du Shu, Xin Zhi San Lian Shu Dian, 1996; Sun Baoyi, *Mao Zedong's Lifelong Reading Activities*; and Jiang Dongran, *Bo Lan Qun Shu de Mao Zedong* [*Wide-Ranging Reading Activities of Mao Zedong*]. Changchun: Jilin Ren Min Chu Ban

She, 1998. It should be noted that the Chiang and Mao's reading titles as listed here are far from exhaustive.

[19] Chiang read only *The Essentials* edition; Mao read the complete series.

[20] For a full citation of these works, see Tai, *CMRC,* pp. 64-65, notes 20, 21.

[21] The sources of information on Chiang and Mao's reading lists, as identified on these pages, did not always spell out the exact titles of the citied books.

[22] Cf. Yang Tianshi, *Jiang Shi Mi Dang yu Jiang Jieshi Zhen Xiang* [*Secret Archive on Chiang and the Inside Story of Chiang Kai-shek*] (Beijing: She Hui Ke Xue Wen Xian Chu Ban She, 2002), pp.12-15.

[23] Paul H. Tai, "Chiang Kai-shek's Rise to Power: Reflections from His Recently Released Diaries," *American Journal of Chinese Studies,* Vol. 16 (April 2009): 54.

[24] Wang Qisheng "Jiang Jieshi Yuedu Shi—Yi 1920-1940 Nian Dai Wei Zhong Xin" [Record on Chiang Kai-shek's Reading List, around 1920-1940], a paper presented at the Conference on "Political Change and Leadership of Nationalist China, 1911-1949," sponsored by the Institute of Modern History of the Chinese Academy of Social Sciences and the Hoover Institution, Stanford University, November 2008, Beijing, China.

[25] Mao's bed had a platform-like shelf attached to it lengthwise. On the shelf were laid mostly Chinese books in classical binding.

[26] From 1949 to 1966 Mao borrowed from the city and university libraries in Beijing more than 5,000 volumes.

[27] Gong Yuzhi, *Mao Zedong's Reading Activities,* p.16.

[28] Sun Baoyi, *Mao Zedong's Lifelong Reading Activities*, p. 111.

[29] Ibid., p. 110.

[30] Lin Ke, Mao's secretary from 1954 to 1966, taught Mao English off and on in these years. Li Zhisui, Mao's private physician, occasionally did so too. See Lin Ke, "Yi Mao Zedong Xue Yingyu" [Recalling Mao Zedong's Study of English], in Gong Yuzhi, *Mao Zedong's Reading Activities,* pp. 242-50; Li, *Chairman Mao,* pp. 68 and *passim.*

[31] Jiang Dongran, *Wide-Ranging Reading Activities of Mao Zedong*, p. 362.

[32] Mao Zedong, "Study," in Mao Zedong, *Mao Tse-tung on Literature and Art* (Peking: Foreign Language Press, 1977), p. 49.

[33] Xiao Yanzhong, "Shilun Wannian Mao Zedong Yanjiu de Sige Ceng Mian" [A Discussion of the Four Aspects of Research on the Mao Zedong Thoughts of His Last Years] Http://www.chinastudygroup.org. Cf. Jiang Dongran, *Wide-Ranging Reading Activities of Mao Zedong*, pp. 158-59.

[34] Ch'en Chieh-ju, *Chiang Kai-shek's Secret Past: The Memoir of His Second Wife, Ch'en Chieh-ju* (Boulder: Westview Press, 1993), p. 157.

[35] The Zhongshan Warship Incident occurred in March 1926. As the military leader in Canton, Chiang suspected that the Chinese Communists on that warship in the Canton area were, at the instigation of the Soviet advisors, attempting to kidnap him and to ship him out to the Soviet Union. He promptly arrested the implicated Communists and placed the Soviet advisors under house arrest. Since Wang Jingwei was closely allied with the Soviet advisors, he was under suspicion too. He went abroad to avoid the political storm.

[36] Michel Oksenberg has provided a penetrating analysis of Mao's techniques and mechanisms to safeguard his leadership position within the party in Michel Oksenberg, "Chapter 3: The Political Leader," in Dick Wilson, ed., *Mao Tse-tung in the Scales of History: A Preliminary Assessment* (New York: Cambridge University Press, 1977), pp. 70-116.

PART TWO

WIELDING THE TWO BARRELS

The Political Man

Aristotle has said, "Men are political animals." Chiang and Mao were probably more political than most of their countrymen. They possessed the type of personality, in Harold D. Lasswell's terms, "characterized by an intense and ungratified craving for" power.[1] And if they desired for other things of value, such as wealth and knowledge, they would make use of these to enhance their power.

Chiang and Mao seldom sought financial gains throughout their political life. Now, four decades following their death, never has there been a revelation of any substantial personal estate they left for their heirs. In the case of Chiang, this fact takes on special significance, for his regime has been widely criticized for corruption. As will be discussed later, he did spend government funds liberally on warlords to achieve national unity and on his colleagues and subordinates for meritorious conduct.

Chiang and Mao had an insatiable thirst for learning, but their focus centered primarily on politics. Chiang was frequently immersed in Neo-Confucianism; his venture in this school of philosophy, however, was intended to shape up a personality enduring the vicissitudes of political life and to help him act as an exemplary leader. Mao was fond of composing poems, but he had hardly composed any that was unrelated to politics since he embarked on the path of revolution.

Chiang and Mao had few hobbies and very few intimate friends late in their life. Chiang was fond of retreating to mountains; more often than not he used the occasion to ponder how to cope with a political crisis. Mao enjoyed swimming. On July 16, 1966, at the start of the Cultural Revolution, he swam across the Yangzi River near Wuhan. A news dispatch, which flashed throughout China, claimed that the Chairman had set a swimming speed record—one that would shame the best of the Olympian meets[2] He intended to serve notice to his domestic opponents that he, at age 73, had enough physical prowess to launch the

Cultural Revolution and to dispel speculation of his foreign detractors that he had suffered an incurable disease.

Two Suns in One Sky

If Chiang and Mao shared the traits of political personality, it is in politics they differed sharply. Perhaps summing up this reality is a remark Mao made to the reporters in August 1945, upon his arrival in Chongqing for peace talks with Chiang. He said, "Mr. Chiang always believes that 'there cannot be two suns in the sky, and there cannot be two sovereigns in one country.' I just don't believe it. I will show him two suns can exist in one sky."[3] What Mao meant was that he challenged Chiang's claim as the sole ruler of China and that two different but contemporaneous rulers, in fact, existed in China. History appears to agree with Mao. As noted in "Preface," for nearly a half of a century, Chiang and Mao governed China together. From the late 1920s to the late 1940s, Chiang ruled much of the country but not the territories successively under the Communist control (Jiangxi, Yan'an, and pockets of land in the Japanese occupied areas during the Chinese-Japanese war).[4] From 1950 to the mid-1970s, Mao reigned supreme in continental China but not in Taiwan and the offshore islands under Chiang's tight grip.

The Two Barrels of Power

Chiang and Mao possessed—in Mao's graphic terms—two "barrels" in their arsenal of power.[5] One was *qiang gan zi*, the barrel of the gun, symbolically represented by the rifle. They relied on the gun to battle each other and their enemies and to control the people under their governance. The other is *bi gan zi*, the barrel of the pen. The Chinese pen is shaped like a slender barrel with a supple brush at its end. Chiang and Mao used this instrument to pour out messages to assure a massive following and to contest for power with their foes. In the use of these two instruments of power, they differed vastly over how and when to use the gun and what messages they gave out.

NOTES

[1] Harold Dwight Lasswell, *Power and Personality* (New York: Viking Press, 1948), pp. 17, 38, and 54.

[2] Li, *Chairman Mao*, p. 463.

[3] Xin Ziling, *Mao Zedong Quan Zhuan* [*Complete Biography of Mao Zedong*], Vol. 4, 1945-1949 (Taipei: Shu Hua Chu Ban Shi Ye You Xian Gong Si, 1993), p. 2. Mao first made this remark in a conversation with Zuo Shunsheng, a leader of the China Youth Party, during the latter's visit with Yan'an in July 1945. Http://blog.sina.com.cn/s/blog_49afd4c50 1000ciw.html.

[4] As of 1930, the Communist-controlled area in Jiangxi consisted of thirty-four counties, with a population over two million. See Huang Yunsheng, *Mao Zedong San Luo San Qi: Kai Pi Zhongguo Ge Ming Dao Lu de Jian Nan yu Qu Zhe* [*Mao Zedong's Triple Falls and Rises: The Difficulties and Twists in the Opening of the Path of Chinese Revolution*] (Beijing: Zhong Yang Wen Xian Chu Ban She, 2006), pp. 197 and 265. At that time, the total number of counties in China was over 2,000, with a population about 450 million. In the 1940s, the Communists occupied portions of Shaanxi, Gansu, and Ningxia provinces. According to the estimate of Lin Beiqu, Communist finance minister at the time, these areas totaled about the size of Austria or England. See Snow, *Red Star over China*, pp. 226 and 261. The present author is not aware of any precise estimate of the total size of Communist-controlled areas in Japanese-occupied territories during the Chinese-Japanese war.

[5] In his "Talk at the Yan'an Forum on Literature and Art" in May 1942, Mao said, "In our struggle for the liberation of the Chinese people...there are the fronts of the pen and of the gun." Mao Zedong, *On New Democracy; Talks at the Yenan Forum on Literature and Art; On the Correct Handling of Contradictions among the People. Speech at the Chinese Communist Party's National Conference on Propaganda Work* (Beijing: Foreign Languages Press, 1967), p. 72. In 1958, he repeated this point in a talk with the Communist cadres: You "should hold the barrel of the pen in one hand and the barrel of the gun in the other. [You are men] of culture and also of war." Mao Zedong, *Mao Zedong Wai Jiao Wen Xuan* [*Mao Zedong's Selected Works on Diplomacy*] (Beijing: Zhong Yang Wen Xian Chu Ban She, 1994), pp. 347-48.

CHAPTER THREE

THE BARREL OF THE GUN

Use the Gun to Change Destiny

On Monday mornings, people assembled in auditoriums or public grounds in front of an image of Sun Yat-sen, flanked by a couplet with these words: "The Revolution Has Not Succeeded; Comrades Must Continue to Strive for It." Below the image, an inscription of Sun's testament began, "I have devoted forty years to the revolution...." The assemblage would recite the testament and bow their heads three times to the image in unison. Such a ritual was uniformly observed by all government organs, schools, and the armed forces in much of the Chiang-ruled China and Taiwan. For fifty years since Sun's death in 1925, Chiang, more often than any other Nationalist leader, faithfully presided this service.

The Chinese Communist Party observed no similar ritual. Yet it takes strong pride as a revolutionary party as well. In its political lexicon, "revolution" and "counter-revolution" take on signal significance, differentiating honor from disgrace, freedom from imprisonment, and, at times, life from death. Likewise, Mao showed a strong and persistent devotion to revolution. In the very first document of his *Selected Works*, he asked in March 1926, "Who are our enemies, and who are our friends? This question is one of primary importance in the revolution."[1] In the next selection, the "Report of an Investigation into the Peasant Movement in Hunan," he declared a year later, "A revolution is not the same as inviting people to dinner, or writing an essay, or painting a picture.... [It is] an act of violence whereby one class overthrows another."[2]

For a term of such importance, what does "revolution" mean? The Chinese words for "revolution" are literally "*ge ming*," change of destiny. To Chiang and Mao, two vital questions immediately arose. First, how was a destiny to be changed? To Mao, the answer was simple and clear cut: It was one class overthrowing another class by violence. Chiang, on the other hand, rejected class struggle as the defining characteristic of revolution but agreed with Mao on the use of force to change destiny. In short, to both of them, military power, symbolized by the gun, constituted the vital means of revolution.

Another question concerned what the new destiny the revolution was supposed to bring about. In the early 1920s when Chiang and Mao marched together onto the path to revolution, they wanted to change China from a country dominated by warlords and imperialist powers to a nation free from warlordism and imperialism. In 1927 when Chiang and Mao parted company, they differed in regard to other changes the revolution should effectuate. Mao began promoting socialism; he also advocated abolition of feudalism—an institution that was based on the existing land tenure system and sustained by Chinese cultural traditions. Chiang considered socialism ill-suited to China and believed feudalism had been abolished in historical times. He deemed Chinese cultural traditions as the immutable social foundation of the nation under all circumstances; he was committed to defend them.

When Mao started advocating his brand of rural communism in the Jiangxi hills with his little arm band, he likened it to a spark that would set a prairie fire. Chiang countered with encirclement campaigns to contain the fire, for he realized what Mao intended to do was nothing short of toppling the political order he had created. Thus, beginning in the late 1920s the two revolutionary comrades fell into armed foes. They fired the gun at each other, often and on, for nearly fifty years.

Chiang's Barrel of the Gun

How did Chiang use the gun to change the destiny of China? His attempt to master the gun started out with a brief study in the Manchu-created Baoding Military Academy in Hebei Province; then he went on enrolling in 1907 in the Zhenwu Military Academy in Japan, an institution created by the Japanese government at the request of the Manchu government to develop an officer corps for the Chinese modern army. Upon graduation in 1909, he joined a Japanese artillery unit for two years' practical training before returning to China to participate in the Republican Revolution. In all his Japanese military education and training, positional warfare received continuous attention, with a heavy emphasis on Germany's military theories and practices going back to Bismarck days.

As noted earlier, Chiang's military career in China started with random rebellious activities against the Manchus in 1911. From 1918 to 1925 he first served in the Chen Jiongming army as Staff Director of War Operations and then turned around to defeat the Chen army in the

Eastern Expedition when Chen revolted against Sun Yat-sen. He commenced cadets training in the Whampoa Military Academy in 1924 and formed the National Revolutionary Army two years later, with which he completed the Northern Expedition in another two years. He fought a major battle against Feng Yuxiang and Yan Xishan and vanquished their combined forces in 1930 and engaged the Communist guerrilla army in five encirclement campaigns from 1930 to 1934. He led China in a war against Japan from 1937 to 1945 and lost mainland China to the Communists in the civil war from 1947 to 1949; he retreated to Taiwan in 1949, where he remained until his death in 1975.

In his early military career, especially in the period from 1925 to 1928, Chiang made spectacular gains. In four short years, he completed the Eastern and Northern Expeditions and defeated various warlord armies totaling more than ten times the size of his army. He rose from a general commanding a few thousand men to the military and political leader of the nation, with over one million men answering his call. He brought a new destiny to China, a deeply divided country on the way to national union.

Several factors account for Chiang's military successes: bravery in action, talent for strategic planning, and adroit employment of positional warfare. At age 18, he cut his queue as an act of defiance of the Manchu Dynasty, and he did so in no other place than the Baoding Military Academy. As the only cadet in his unit without a queue, he drew the stern attention of the Manchu officers in the Academy. When in the military services later, he often expressed the belief that a man in arms had to have the courage to defy death. Upon reading *The Collected Works* of Hu Linyi—a general in the late Manchu Dynasty—he discovered that the general had a piece of advice for army commanders: "Hang the word of 'death' by the bedside. Only then might he have a chance to survive." "What a truthful saying!" Chiang exclaimed (CKSD, 11/7/18).

Chiang always wrote down a will when undertaking a dangerous mission or facing a life-threatening situation. He did so on November 2, 1911, when he joined the suicide squad to attack the Manchu governor of Zhejiang; on March 1, 1920, when he was ordered to fight a hopeless battle during his service with the Chen Jiongming army; on June 20, 1922, when he was on his way to join the beleaguered Sun Yat-sen during the Yongfeng Warship Incident; on September 28, 1931, when he was anticipating that the Japanese army would launch a total war against China following the Manchurian Incident. And during the Xi'an Incident in December 1936 when he was kidnapped by mutinous generals, he wrote down three wills, one each to the Chinese people, his wife Soong May-ling, and his two sons, Ching-kuo and Wei-kuo.

Chiang repeatedly demonstrated his valor in the battlefield. For example, in an engagement with a warlord army in Fujian in 1918, he thrust his lonely force of several hundred soldiers more than two hundred miles (700 *li*) into the enemy territory while riding in a sedan chair during the attack because he was ill. In the Eastern Expedition in 1925, he was on the frontline and issued as many as 60 battle orders to his cadet army. He showed "self-confidence verging on fanaticism."[3] In the Northern Expedition, he braved bullets and cannon shots from warlords as well as the Japanese army, which threw a roadblock to his army in Jinan, Shandong.[4]

Though considering intrepidity a required trait of a militarist, Chiang believed that "the essence of a commander is his strategic vision, not his bravery" (CKSD, 7/30/22). True to his belief, he formulated no less than thirty-three plans for all the battles and armed clashes he was engaged in, from 1914 to 1931.[5]

One of these particularly merits attention. In a "Plan for Fighting the Northern Army" submitted to Sun Yat-sen on September 20, 1917, Chiang assessed the strength of the warlords in the north, devised ways to assemble troops in the south, and charted out routes of attack. The entire document was written with clarity and precision and full of operational details. Half a year later, on March 10, 1918, he updated this plan with an "Assessment of the Present and Future Operations of the Northern and Southern Armies."[6]

What is most striking of this plan is that it was formulated when Chiang was still an unknown quantity. Yet when the Northern Expedition actually took place nine years later, the operations were consistent with the plan.[7] The National Revolutionary Army (NRA) was formed with military units from Guangdong, Guangxi, Yunnan, and Hunan provinces, totaling 85,000 men. From Canton the army marched northward, facing the combined army of one million men under the command of several major warlords: Wu Peifu in north-central China, Sun Chuanfang in central-eastern China, Zhang Zuolin in northeastern China (Manchuria) and Beijing; and Feng Yuxiang and Yan Xishan in northwestern China. The NRA first assaulted the Wu Peifu-controlled Hunan Province in July 1926, capturing its capital, Changsha, within the month; it conquered the pivotal city of Wuhan in Hubei Province in October, thereby finishing off the Wu army. It then turned eastward to engage the army of Sun Chuanfang and, within four months, from November 1926 to March 1927, took over several vital cities successively: Nanchang, Nanjing, and Shanghai. It routed the Sun army within the year and marched into Beijing on June 8, 1928, marking the successful completion of the Northern Expedition.

During the Northern Expedition, Chiang took advantage of the divisions among the warlords, most of whom had fought each other previously. When he started attacking Wu Peifu, Chiang was able to neutralize Sun Chuanfang by offering him the possibility of a Nationalists-Sun alliance. Thus Sun took no action when Wu took a severe beating during his engagement with the NRA. Sun had an additional reason for not intervening, for he regarded Wu as posing a greater challenge to him than did Chiang, whose fighting capacity he at first belittled. When Chiang, after having defeated Wu, turned against him, Sun had no one to come to his aid. In the meantime, Chiang's fast breaking advances impressed Feng Yuxiang and Yan Xishan enough that the two hitherto wavering warlords joined the NRA in December 1926. Chiang took time to deal with Zhang Zoulin. Through several emissaries he persuaded Zhang not to get involved in the fighting. He let Zhang know that he had no intention to attack Zhang's well-defended territory, Manchuria; he also sweetened his persuasion with generous monetary compensations. Zhang cooperated. Indeed, on June 4, 1928, just four days before the NRA occupied Beijing, Zhang evacuated his force from that city to Manchuria. Viewed from a historical perspective, Chiang's strategy for the Northern Expedition was consistent with the well-known stratagem of the Kingdom of Qin for conquering other kingdoms in the last stage of the Warring States Period (475-221 BC). That stratagem was known as *"Yuan Jiao, Jin Gong"* (Negotiate with the Enemy Afar, Attack the Enemy nearby).

Chiang's strategic talent also came to light during the Chinese-Japanese war when he initiated the Shanghai Battle in August 1937 in order to achieve his twin war objectives: "Trade Space for Time" and multi-nationalizing the conflict. As will be elaborated in Chapter Ten, it was this strategy that saved China from being conquered by Japan.

Chiang's effective use of positional warfare is another factor contributing to his battle successes against the warlords, many of whom received Japanese military training in the same type of warfare as Chiang did. Positional warfare is conducted with the deployment of one combatant's field army arrayed against another. On each side, infantry divisions are placed on the frontline, with the support of armored units and warplanes if available; the artillery field is set up on the second line; and the command headquarters and supply base are situated at the rear. Each side would maneuver against the other, using superior tactics and firepower to occupy strategically important terrain, expand area of control, and defeat the enemy. Chiang employed all these tactics with considerable skill and frequently went into the artillery field to observe and direct the fighting.

Chiang's fortunes in all the wars he fought saw a dramatic reversal in the year of 1930, when he defeated the warlords Feng Yuxiang and Yan Xishan then in revolt against him. In that year and earlier, he proved to be an invincible commander, winning nearly every battle he was in. Following that year, he lost most of the battles he fought, especially those against the Communists.[8] In the Chinese-Japanese war, he scored momentary victories in Taierzhuang, Changsha, and other places, but he was on the whole losing to the Japanese continuously until 1945 when, with American military assistance and equipment, his modernized army scored victories in the India-Burma theater and in southwest China. His repeated setbacks in that war can be attributed to the significant disparity in weaponry between his army and his Japanese counterpart and, from his critics' perspective, the incompetence of his entire military establishment. The causes of his defeat in the civil war of 1947-1949 will be examined later.

Mao's Barrel of the Gun

In 1927 when Mao and his armed band fled to the forested Jinggang Mountain in Jiangxi, he was far from certain as to how to take root there. For the area was infested with brigands, who had no reason to yield it to him. He made a calculated move to win over the bandits rather than to wrest the area from them. He offered to two bandit chiefs, Yuan Wencai and Wang Zuo, the most precious gifts they coveted, 100 and 70 rifles respectively—something he himself was in short supply. Thus securing the bandits' gratitude, he went on persuading them to spread out his grab-land-from-the-landlord message. Yuan Wencai, a sort of local Communist once leading peasants for uprising, agreed. Gradually Mao absorbed the bandits into his rank and attracted more and more landless peasants to his fold.[9] By the following year, Mao had enough men to declare himself commander of the First Division of the Red Army.

Mao's strategy of rural communism, thus, had set a spark, which, over time, did ignite a prairie fire that eventually consumed the massive Nationalist army. As evolved over the years, this strategy consists of three features: politics takes command, the guerrilla war, and the people's war. The first of these features was derived from the Soviet experiences, and the other two were of Mao's invention, improvised from the battling experiences that he had gone through.

Mao cited Clausewitz's dictum that "War is the continuation of politics" with wholehearted approval. He believed that "there has not been a single war since ancient times that does not bear a political character," and he put forward a dictum of brutal clarity of his own: "Politics is bloodless war, while war is the politics of bloodshed."[10]

He emphasized to his followers that he totally agreed with a point made by Chiang Kai-shek, "Whoever has an army, has [political] power." Therefore, he urged, "Every Communist must grasp the truth: 'Political power grows out of the barrel of a gun."[11] However, he warned that the army was only *a* means of the Chinese Communist Party to accomplish its political tasks. For this reason, he exhorted his comrades, "Our principle is that the Party commands the gun, and the gun will never be allowed to command the Party."[12]

Adhering to this principle, the Communist army maintains a double command of its troops, patterned after the Soviet model: a field commander to direct battle operations and a party representative—the Commissar—to provide political guidance. This system operates in the entire armed forces, from the defense ministry down to the basic field units.

One central political task the Party had to accomplish was to create a Communist regime. While doing so, Mao warned, the Party had to guard against its being inured to fighting, thereby becoming a warlord regime.[13] Another major task was to recruit peasants to fill the Communist army. The Party had to insure that the recruits accept communism as their faith and to provide them with incentive to fight an expected long and harsh war. This meant the recruits had to be indoctrinated in communism; it also meant a forceful transfer of land from the landlord class to the landless peasants so as to give the peasant recruits a vital stake in the Communist revolution. "Red soldiers are volunteers," discovered Edgar Snow in an interview with a Communist army unit in 1936. In contrast, "White [Nationalist] soldiers are conscripts."[14] Volunteers were motivated to fight for themselves; conscripts were forced to fight for others.

As mentioned in Chapter Two, Mao's guerrilla war concept was first inspired in 1927 by the "running-in-circles" tactics of a bandit leader, the Deaf Zhu, in Jinggang Mountain. Later he adapted from the tactics of other bandits. On the basis of these tactics, with close attention to the local topography (steep and crisscrossing hills with heavy wood covers), Mao developed a sixteen-word dictum of guerrilla warfare:

Enemy advances, we retreat;
Enemy encamps, we harass;
Enemy exhausted, we hit;
Enemy retreats, we pursue.

Later, in 1938, he issued six directives to guide the Communist guerrillas to fight the Chinese-Japanese war.[15] In 1947, he expanded these into what were widely regarded as the canon of guerrilla warfare, as excerpted below:

> Attack dispersed, isolated enemy forces first; attack concentrated, strong enemy forces later.
>
> Take small and medium cities and extensive rural areas first; take big cities later.
>
> Make wiping out the enemy's effective strength our main objective; do not make holding or seizing a city or place our main objective.
>
> In every battle, concentrate an absolutely superior force (two, three, four and sometimes even five or six times the enemy's strength), encircle the enemy forces completely, strive to wipe them out thoroughly and do not let any escape from the net.
>
> Fight no battle unprepared; fight no battle not sure of winning.
>
> Replenish our strength with all the arms and most of the personnel captured from the enemy. Our army's main sources of manpower and matériel are at the front.[16]

It is of interest to note that while Mao devised these principles from his battle experiences, he must have drawn considerable inspiration from the Chinese classics on warfare he perused with diligence.[17] Of particular relevance to the guerrilla war was *Sun Bin Bing Fa* (*The Art of Warfare* by Sun Bin), which has this to say: "If we avoid the enemy's strong points and attack him where he is most vulnerable, and if we change the overall circumstances and control the strategic advantage, the situation will resolve itself...."[18]

In the opinion of Robert T. Ames, another work, *Huai Nanzi* (a collection of essays by a scholar in the early Western Han Dynasty, 206 BC-25 AD), which summarized in an essay the "military strategies" as practiced in ancient China, must have influenced Mao's thinking as well:

> In military preparations there are three kinds of strategic advantage....There is the advantage of morale, the advantage of terrain, the advantage of opportunity.
> 1. When the general is full of courage and regards the enemy with contempt, when his troops are steeled in their resolve...when their morale is like a tempest and their battle cries ring like thunder—this is called a morale advantage (*qi shi*).
> 2. Precipitous passes, narrows, high mountains, known strategic locations, spiraling approaches, basins, snaking roadways, bottlenecks, places where one man can hold a thousand enemies at bay—this is called a terrain advantage (*di shi*).
> 3. Taking advantage of the enemy's fatigue, their ill-preparedness and disorder, their hunger and thirst, their exposure to the elements, pressing upon them where they are unsure of themselves and giving them no ground where they are most vulnerable—this is called an opportunity advantage (*yin shi*).[19]

An analysis of Mao's theory of guerrilla war would not be complete without a discussion of the methods he adopted to unite the guerrillas with the people. As noted earlier, land reform provided the incentive for the landless peasants to join his army and for their families to cover the guerrillas' trails. Mao and his comrades also developed over the years an army's civilian relations program for the soldiers to follow. It consists of "Three Great Disciplines": "Obey orders in all your actions. Don't take a single needle or piece of thread from the masses. Turn in everything captured." In addition, the soldiers have to observe "Eight Points for Attention."[20]

This program, it should be emphasized, applied to only the people in the Communist base areas, and the definition of "the people" was quite fluid. It included landless farmers or small landowners as specified by the Communists at specific times. Medium-sized and large-sized landowners and merchants were generally not considered "the people." In short, the Communists divided the people into two categories: the peasants and their families, and all others. To the former, the Communist army applied its civil relations program, not taking "a single needle or piece of thread" from them and "paying fairly what you buy." To the latter, the program did not apply. These people could be subject to torture or execution, with their crops, property, and land confiscated.

The purpose of the program was to make the guerrilla army a "People's Army" so that the people would perform functions essential to the army's operations. Mao's "fish in the water" analogy vividly illustrates this point. Guerrillas, he said, were fish; the people, water. Fish was in constant motion; water nourished fish and hid it from view.

In a 1938 essay on the Chinese-Japanese war then in progress, Mao formulated a doctrine of the protracted war.[21] The war, he proposed, would go through three stages: "The first stage is one of the enemy's strategic offensive and our strategic defensive. The second stage is one of the enemy's strategic defensive and our preparation for the counter-offensive. The third stage is one of our strategic counter-offensive and the enemy's strategic retreat." In these stages respectively, he pointed out, the guerrilla warfare, the mobile warfare, and the positional warfare would apply and would assume different degrees of importance. The characteristics of the guerrilla warfare and the positional warfare have been described on previous pages. The characteristics of the mobile warfare, as Mao saw them, included the use of large army corps for offensive campaigns, fluidity in military operations (allowing frequent advance *and* retreat), and the possession by the army of a numerical strength superior, or equal, to that of the enemy.[22]

Though this essay was Mao's prescription for how China was to fight the war against Japan, it can be accepted as his all-inclusive war doctrine—applicable to both the civil war and international war that the Communist army was involved in. Mao's staged warfare is generally subsumed under the name of "the people's war."[23] It stressed fluidity in operations, prolonged conflict, and battle outcome dependent on men rather than on weapons. The first two points are evident from discussions on previous pages. The last point requires explanation.

Mao long held the view that "weapons are an important factor in war but not the decisive one; it is man and not material that counts." This is so because "the contest of forces is not only a contest of military and economic power, but also one of the power and morale of man."[24] The power and morale of man, as viewed from the Communist experiences, could be enhanced through persistent indoctrination or what the Americans have called "brain washing." This point is most strikingly illustrated in the Korean War. The Chinese army was incomparably inferior to the American army in weapons but managed to end the war in a draw. It did so because the "fanatic" fighting spirit and the overwhelming size of the Chinese soldiers overcame their weapon deficiency.[25]

In the final stage of Mao's protracted war, the size of the Communist army as well as of the people under its control would grow larger than that of the enemy. The Communists army would amass so large a force as constituting what the Nationalists called "a human sea." This force would form the frontline, with waves of attack from the countryside on the cities that the enemy possessed, and with a still much larger number of people, the civilian population, forming the second line to perform supportive functions for the frontline. Eventually the enemy in the cities would be strangled to surrender.

Beyond the people's war doctrine, Mao fathered no new military theories. But he was known to have regarded the people's war doctrine as applicable to the Korean War and the Vietnam War—two major international wars China was involved in during Mao's times (China's 30-day war with India in 1962 was of no comparable magnitude). In a 1965 essay titled "Long Live the Victory of the People's War," Lin Biao summed up Mao's theory of war as "the encirclement of the cities from the rural areas and the final capture of the cities." He declared that this theory "is of outstanding and universal practical importance for the present revolutionary struggles of all the oppressed nations." He went on to proclaim: "Taking the entire globe, if North America and Western Europe can be called 'the cities of the world,' then Asia, Africa, and Latin America constitute 'the rural areas of the world'.... In a sense, the contemporary world revolution also presents a picture of the encirclement of cities by the rural areas."[26] Given the fact that Lin was rapidly rising at this time in military and political stature in the Communist power hierarchy, soon ascending to the position as Mao's designated successor, Lin's essay was widely viewed as an authoritative statement of Mao's people's war doctrine.

How Did Mao Win

How did Mao apply his theories on war to the battlefield? How did he start out in a rebellion with only a thousand men in an obscure corner of Jiangxi and end up beating millions of Chiang's troops and conquering the entire continental China? To answer these questions, we will focus on three instances of battles he fought against Chiang: the Nationalists' five encirclement campaigns from 1930 to 1934, the battle of Yan'an of 1947, and the civil war of 1947-1949.

During the Nationalists' encirclement campaigns, 1930-1934, Chiang mobilized increasingly larger forces to destroy the Communist guerrillas in southern Jiangxi. In the first campaign that started in 1930, 100,000 Nationalist troops swooped down on the Communist base area in a cluster of counties with a radius estimated no longer than 100 miles, where some 30,000 guerrillas concentrated. The Nationalist army rapidly penetrated the area, meeting no resistance. It found the guerrillas hidden in the mountains' forests, leaving no one in sight; the guerrillas might also be dispersed among the people, following what Mao called a "fisherman's net" tactic—"casting it wide to win over the masses and draw it in to deal with enemy."[27]

One Nationalist divisional commander in the attack, Gong Bingfan, recalled his experiences. He noticed that the area through which his army advanced was "not showing one soul. The houses were all cleared out, not even with any kitchen utensils left." On the other hand, "The guerrillas fired their rifles here and there to intimidate" the invaders. "Well acquainted with the local terrain, they hid themselves in not easily discoverable, advantageous spots. They waited until the opportunity came to hit the head of a column of the invading force or to cut off the column's tail and to catch the soldiers falling behind." The Nationalist soldiers very often "got confused," not knowing which direction they should fire their rifles. Often, they fell to the traps set by the guerrillas and suffered tremendous casualties. Gong's division was thus defeated, and he had to disguise to escape.[28] By the end of the first campaign in January 1931, the guerrillas had routed more than 15,000 Nationalist troops and captured some 12,000 rifles and more than one million rounds of bullets.[29]

In the second campaign that started in May 1931, Chiang doubled his attacking force, to 200,000. But within two months, it quickly lost out to the guerrillas again. Mao composed a poem to celebrate the occasion, which read in part as follows:

> Again an army of 200,000 entered Jiangxi,
> With waves of dusts and smokes rising to half of the sky.
> Rousing tens of thousands of proletariats and peasants,
> To fight on with solidarity.
> Soon the Red flags burst out below the Buzhou Mountain.[30]

At a meeting with other Communist leaders, Mao identified three reasons for their victory:

> Though our military strength is relatively inferior, we had several advantages: First, the Red Army is good. Our soldiers had a high morale for the struggle...eagerly rubbing their fists for a fight. Second, the masses, who are benefited from our agrarian revolution and have been constantly persecuted by the enemy, are naturally passionate for the fight, giving the Red Army every

possible support. Third, the terrain is good. We...can perch on advantageous spots to fire at the enemy.[31]

In his third and fourth encirclement campaigns, Chiang did not modify his basic strategy but relied on a larger force—with 300,000 and 250,000 soldiers respectively—and superior weapons to overwhelm the guerrillas.[32] Both of these campaigns also ended in failure. During the third campaign, the Red army routed 75,000 Nationalist troops, took 46,000 prisoners, and captured 36,000 weapons and 5,000,000 rounds of bullets.[33] The Red Army paid a heavy price for its gains. In one battle one commander, Huang Gongluo, was killed, and Mao's wife He Zichen was nearly bombed dead.[34]

In the fifth campaign, in 1934, Chiang adopted the advice of his German advisors, radically altering his strategy. Instead of advancing his army—now with 400,000 men—into the Communist base area, he kept his attacking units in close coordination with each other and moved forward at a deliberate speed while building fortifications along the way, thus allowing the guerrillas no chance to ambush his units.

On the Communist side, a dispute over the strategy on how to fight the Nationalist army had been brewing. Wang Ming, the Moscow-trained Chinese Communist Party leader, preferred the Bolsheviks' "city-centered" strategy of revolution to Mao's rural revolution approach. In disagreement, Mao took a sick leave twice from the Communist base area.[35] Following Wang's strategy, the Communist guerrillas once laid a 33-day siege to Ganzhou, the largest city in southern Jiangxi, but failed to conquer it.[36]

When confronting the Nationalists' fifth campaign, Wang ordered the Red Army to engage frontally with the invading force. Soon overpowered by the Nationalist army, the Red Army faced an imminent danger of annihilation if it were to fight on; in the end, it had to break out the encirclement by escaping from the Nationalists' southern flank. It survived through the Long March and regrouped in Yan'an, where it steadily expanded its area of control.

Thirteen years later, in the Battle of Yan'an in 1947, the Nationalist army had a commanding lead over the Communist army in the size of forces. It possessed 4.3 million men against the Communists' 1.27 million.[37] Of the Nationalist army, 250,000 troops had been deployed since 1937 in the area south of Yan'an to block Communists' possible incursion into the Nationalist area. They were under the command of General Hu Zongnan.

Immediately following the Chinese-Japanese war, the Communists rushed the bulk of their forces to eastern and northeastern China where they intended to seize control in the Japanese-surrendered territories. That move left Yan'an overexposed, with only 27,000 troops to guard the Communists' wartime capital. Chiang took advantage of the situation by ordering the Hu Zongnan army to attack Yan'an. On March 11, 1947, Hu amassed a force of 140,000 troops, supported by 75 planes, and spearheaded toward Yan'an.[38]

Facing the Nationalist onslaught, Mao decided to abandon Yan'an, but many of his comrades disagreed. They argued that the Communist army could not afford losing its headquarters city at a time when the Communist army was to wage the largest civil war with the Nationalist army. They also had a strong feeling for Yan'an, for the city had been built up painstakingly in the previous ten years from an isolated, desolate town to a vital and bustling revolutionary base attracting young patriots all over the country to its embrace. Mao had long talks with his comrades, persuading them to accept his view, ending with a curt statement: "If we save our men but lose the city, we can recover it [later]. If we try to save the city by losing our men, we will lose both."[39] He gambled with this decision and stayed in Yan'an until the dusk of March 18—the eve of the Hu army's occupation of the city—when he dispersed his force away in the surrounding mountains.

Entering the city, the Hu army found it was entirely emptied out except for stacks of books on Marxism and Leninism that Mao ordered to leave for the Hu troops to read. The Hu army immediately ran after the Communists, who dodged the fight with a *"ge-shan-xing-jun"* tactics. That is, when the Hu army pursued on one side of a mountain, the Communists would elude it by running to the other side of the mountain. When the Hu army rushed to switch side, the Communists would run to the side of another mountain—and on and on. They followed a battle plan like a plate of spaghetti of twists and turns and maneuvered to achieve a numerical advantage over a Hu unit at a particular spot and unleashed a sudden and concentrated attack on their enemy. In 40 days' fighting, the Communists managed to score victories around three spots: Qing Hua Bian, Yang Ma He, and Pan Long. They routed 14,000 of Hu's troops, took thousands of prisoners, and captured 12,000 bags of flour.[40] With these setbacks to the Hu army and with the Communist reinforcement coming from east of the Yellow River, the Battle of Yan'an dragged on for a year until the Communists reoccupied the city in 1948.

The Battle of Yan'an marked the beginning of the ensuing civil war of 1947-1949. The year 1947 saw a significant transition of the Communist war strategies. Early in the year, the Communist army continued its guerrilla war tactics that it had honed to perfection in the defeat of sizable Nationalist troops and vastly expanded area of control east of Yan'an. By the latter part of the year, it had acquired enough men and weapons to adopt what Mao had called the mobile warfare. Its regular force, organized into four Field Armies, swung into full action, actively seeking after the Nationalist army, now centered in major cities in eastern, northern, and northeastern China, for continuous engagements. After one major battle, it rapidly moved on to another, even abandoning the cities it had wrested from the Nationalist army. Its purpose was to seek the Nationalist forces to destroy. As Mao pointed out,

> In seventeen months of fighting (from July 1946 to November 1947; December figures are not yet available), we killed, wounded and captured 1,690,000 of Chiang Kai-shek's regular and irregular troops—640,000 killed and 1,050,000 captured. Thus we were able to beat back Chiang Kai-shek's offensive, preserve the main territories of the Liberated Areas and go over to the offensive.[41]

The dramatic reverse of fortunes of the Communist and Nationalist armies accelerated in 1948.[42] According to the Nationalist government's estimate, the Communist army swelled to 2,600,000 men in June 1948, exceeding for the first time the strength of the Nationalist army, then standing at 2,180,000.[43] In that year, the Communist army entered the final phase of Mao's "Protracted War" by mounting the strategic offensive. The Fourth Field Army under the command of Lin Biao laid siege to Changchun and Shenyang in Manchuria with decidedly larger forces than the defenders and strangled the enemy to surrender. In the following year, the Fourth Field Army joined other field armies to congregate on Beijing, winning over the city without much of a fight, and the Third Field Army together with the Second Field Army battled the Nationalist forces around Xuzhou in central eastern China and routed several Nationalist best-equipped corps under the command of Huang Baitao, Qiu Qingchuan, and Huang Wei. In each battle, the Communist field armies, following exactly Mao's "Protracted War" dictates, "encircle the enemy forces completely, strive to wipe them out thoroughly and do not let any escape from the net." By the year's end, the Communists had effectively controlled all territories north of the Yangzi River.

Facing these disastrous defeats, Chiang stepped down in January 1949 as president of the Nationalist government, leaving his vice president, Li Zongren, to make a futile attempt at peace with the Communists. In the following October, with the Communist army having crossed the Yangzi River and mopping up the remaining Nationalist army in south China, Mao announced in Beijing the establishment of the People's Republic of China. At the year's end the Nationalist government retreated to Taiwan, signaling the end of its rule on the mainland.

The Communist army had by now fully implemented the war doctrine enunciated by Mao in his "Protracted War" essay: it conducted a guerrilla war for strategic defensive in the period from 1927 to 1946; a mobile war in preparation for offensive in 1947; and a positional war for strategic offensive from late 1947 to 1949. Capping his two-decade long campaign of "surrounding the city from the countryside," Mao called the Communists' victorious march into Beijing as "Entering the City." Mao's revolutionary experiences gave substance to a perceptive observation by Samuel P. Huntington, an eminent American political scientist, in his analysis of Western and Eastern revolutions. "In the Western revolution [as seen in the American, French, and Russian examples]," Huntington wrote, "the revolutionaries come to power in the capital [city] first and then gradually expand their control over the countryside. In the Eastern revolution [as exemplified by the Chinese experiences], they…establish a base area of control in a remote section, struggle to win the support of the peasants…slowly expand the scope of their authority….The last phase of the revolutionary struggle is the occupation of the capital [city]."[44]

A summary of how Mao defeated Chiang in the two decades' epic battles can be seen in the following points.

In most of the battles Chiang fought against Mao, he used the positional warfare tactics against Mao's guerrilla operations. Chiang's army was larger in size and better equipped than his Communist counterpart. In the encirclement campaigns in the 1930s and in the early civil war of 1940s, his army was on the offensive, chasing after the Communist guerrillas. But the guerrillas, following the dictum "When we can win, fight; when we can't, run," placed Chiang's army in a phantom war. It could not find the enemy until the guerrillas maneuvered to their advantage and suddenly mounted a devastating attack. Chiang's army failed in the engagements with the guerrillas because it lost initiative to them.

In Chiang's military writings, he did emphasize the importance of initiatives and mobility in battle operations.[45] And he had constantly and painstakingly examined Mao's tactics of guerrilla warfare; he personally prepared manuals on how to combat the Communist guerrillas for distribution among his military academy cadets as well as the Nationalist troops (see, for instance, CKSD, 5/17/47, 2/27/48, 8/1/49). But the Nationalists cadets and troops were mentally and physically less conditioned to the guerrilla warfare than the Communist soldiers, who fought the hit-and-run war everyday in the hills and rivers. Once a tale, perhaps apocryphal, went its round in the Nationalist army that spoke of this reality. A brilliant Nationalist military theoretician was appointed a field commander to fight the Communists in a battle but lost miserably. Upon Chiang's inquiry as to why he lost the battle, the commander remarked, "The Communists did not fight battles according the rules we teach in classrooms."

Among his first order of business in force deployment, Chiang staged sufficient logistics—food and ammunition—in the rear of the battlefield to insure their delivery to the troops. Starving and bullet-less soldiers cannot win battles. But the guerrillas took advantage of the situation by attacking the logistics depots and cutting off the supply routes. As a result, Chiang had to divert some of his troops to guard the depots and supply routes, thus reducing the strength of the combatants. On the other hand, Mao's guerrillas were not burdened with setting up bases for food and ammunition; they grabbed these supplies from the enemy.

In regard to the degree of importance of manpower, weapon, and city to war, Chiang's view was precisely opposite of Mao's. Chiang had to give top priority to controlling the city because it symbolized his capacity for maintaining a functioning national government and public order. In addition, the city provided the resource base—revenue and materiel—to sustain the war effort. Chiang regarded adequacy of weapons as a critical factor affecting the conduct of a battle if other considerations being equal. He believed that as long as he possessed the cities, he would have financial resources to either manufacture or purchase weapons. He, of course, considered manpower as vital to troop strength. But since the completion of the Northern Expedition in 1928, he was never short of manpower. If anything, with his army absorbing the forces of former warlords and with his unlimited authority for conscription, he at times found it necessary to reduce his force levels, as in the aftermath of the Northern Expedition and of the Chinese-Japanese war.

Mao's war experiences indicate that Chiang's order of priority was misplaced. As Mao said during the Yan'an Battle of 1947, if an army lost a city but retained its men, it had the chance to recover the city. If, on the other hand, it lost its men, it lost everything. As for weapons, they came or went, depending on whoever held upper or lower hand in the battlefield. As seen in the civil war of 1947-1949, Chiang lost an enormous number of troops in his stubborn defense of many cities. In the end, he lost the cities as well. Again, Mao's soldiers followed Mao's "Protracted War" dictates to the letter: Before the final stage of the war, "make wiping out the enemy's effective strength our main objective; do not make holding or seizing a city or place our main objective."

If Mao invented the grand concepts of "rural communism," "surround the city from the countryside," and "the guerrilla warfare," Chiang developed no counterpart of an integrated political-military program relevant to the Chinese social and economic conditions of his times. In a prolonged contest for power, Chiang lost in the battlefield because of lack of military agility and failed in the political arena because of lack of public appeal.

A relatively unknown factor that contributed significantly to Mao's military victory was the spy warfare he employed against the entire Nationalist military establishment. This warfare was so massive and persistent and effective that it deserves an extensive investigation, as to be seen in Chapter Eight.

An even more unknown factor than the spy warfare was the deliberate atrocities committed by the Communist army in order to seek battlefield victory. It was not until 2009 that some of the atrocities surfaced in the Western press. On the occasion of the 60th anniversary of the People's Republic of China in 2009, *The New York Times* reported on a hitherto unaccounted for tragedy during the Communist siege of Changchun in Manchuria in 1948: "What the [Communist] official story line does not reveal is that at least 160,000 civilians also died [of starvation] during the siege…from June to October of 1948." *The Times* pointed to a book from a Communist lieutenant colonel, Zhang Zhenglu, who recorded his impression of the battle: "'Changchun was like Hiroshima…. The casualties were about the same. Hiroshima took nine seconds; Changchun took five months.'"[46] The Communist army also committed many other acts of monstrous brutalities against the civilians.[47]

NOTES

[1] *SW*, I, 13.
[2] Ibid., p. 27.
[3] Ch'en, *Chiang Kai-shek's Secret Past*, p. 176.
[4] See Tai, "Chiang Kai-shek's Rise to Power," pp. 51, 54; and Zhou Shengying, *Social Contacts of Sun Yat-sen and Chiang Kai-shek*, p.114.
[5] Li Yong and Zhang Zhongtian, *Jiang Jieshi Nian Pu* [*Chronology of Chiang Kai-shek*] (Beijing: Zhonggong Dang Shi Chu Ban She, 1995), pp. 26ff; Mao, *Chiang Kai-shek prior to 1926, passim*.
[6] Mao, ibid., pp. 41-44; 50-52.
[7] For a narration of how the Northern Expedition actually proceeded, see The Second Historical Archives of China, Nanjing, *Guo Min Zheng Fu Dang An* [*Archive of the National Government*], "Guo Min Ge Min Jun Zhan Shi Ji Yao," Di Er Bian, "Hui Shi Wu Han" [Summary Record of the War History of the National Revolutionary Army], Volume Two, "Join Forces at Wuhan." Microfilm 16J0104, Item #630.
[8] In post-1930 years, Chiang did win other battles. In the fifth encirclement campaign in 1934, he defeated the Communists in Jiangxi, but they escaped through the Long March and turned around to vanquish the Nationalist army fifteen years later. In November 1949, the Nationalist army annihilated an entire Communist invasion force, of more than 9,000 men, against the offshore island Quemoy. The scale of the battle was rather insignificant as compared with the gigantic battles he lost on the mainland.
[9] Huang Yunsheng, *Mao's Triple Falls and Triple Rises*, pp. 30-33. Another source indicates that Mao became a sworn brother of the bandits' and married one of their sisters. See Xiaobing Li, *A History of the Modern Chinese Army* (Lexington, KY: University Press of Kentucky, c2007), p. 50. The integration of the bandits' men into Mao's army often took complicated and dangerous turns. After joining Mao's army, the bandits continued, on occasion, to loot the civilians, murdered Mao's political workers, and some of them even tried to defect to the Nationalist army. But eventually they were totally absorbed into the Red Army. See Agnes Smedley, *China's Red Army Marches* (Westport, Conn.: Hyperion Press, c1934), pp. 94-109.

[10] *SW*, II, 203. Most citations of Mao's writings on war in the present book can also be found in Mao Zedong, *Selected Military Writings of Mao Tse-tung*, Peking: Foreign Languages Press, 1963.

[11] *SW*, II, 271-72.

[12] Ibid., 272.

[13] *SW*, I, 106.

[14] Snow, *Red Star over China,* p. 292.

[15] For the six directives, see *SW*, II, 122-23.

[16] Mao, "The Present Situation and Our Task," *SW*, V, 161-62.

[17] Mao was thoroughly familiar with the now world-famous *Sun Zi Bing Fa* (*The Art of Warfare* by Sun Wu) but did not actually read it until 1936.

[18] Quoted in Robert T. Ames, *The Art of Rulership: A Study in Ancient Chinese Political Thought* (Honolulu: University of Hawaii Press, 1983), p. 66. Sun Bin (c380-320) was a descendant of Sun Wu (c544-496 BC).

[19] Quoted in ibid., p. 71.

[20] These points are: "Speak politely [to civilians]. Pay fairly what you buy. Return everything you borrow. Pay for anything you damage. Don't beat or swear at people. Don't damage crops. Don't take liberty with women. Don't ill-treat captives." Mao, "On the Reissue of the Three Main Rules of Discipline and the Eight Points for Attention," *SW*, V, 155.

[21] For the complete text of "On the Protracted War," see *SW*, II, 157-243.

[22] Ibid., 183-84; 222-26.

[23] For Western analysts' perception of the people's war doctrine, see Andrew J. Nathan and Robert S. Ross, *The Great Wall and the Empty Fortress: China's Search for Security* (New York: W.W. Norton, 1997), pp. 139-41; for other relevant works, see Tai, *CMRC,* p. 95, Note 23.

[24] *SW*, II, 192.

[25] In a study on the Chinese army's performance in the Korean War, Alexander L. George cited two quotations to underscore this point. The first of these was from an American field officer during the war, in 1950: "You can't fight millions and millions of *drugged fanatics*, and it's not worth the waste of life to try. What are we here for, anyway?" [italics added] The second is from Mao, "A revolutionary army must have discipline.... [But it] must be self-imposed, because only when it is, is the soldier able to understand completely why he fights and how he must obey." Alexander L. George, *The Chinese Communist Army in Action:*

The Korean War and Its Aftermath (New York, Columbia University Press, 1967), pp. 1, 25.

Thus, ideological indoctrination instilled in the Chinese soldiers' consciousness a sense of something like the holy war. They fought like drugged fanatics against the overwhelming American firepower. In contrast, American soldiers did not know what they were fighting for and did not think it worthwhile to die for. Their superior firepower could not subdue the drugged fanatics.

For Mao Zedong's observation on the Chinese army's reliance on its large manpower and high morale to contest American army's superior firepower, see Li Yongtai, *Mao Zedong yu Mei Guo* [*Mao Zedong and the United States of America*] (Kunming: Yunnan Ren Min Chu Ban She, 1993), p. 446.

[26] The essay was widely publicized in Chinese media at the time and was subsequently printed in a pamphlet by Beijing's Foreign Language Press. The text can be found in http://www.marxists.org/reference/archive/ lin-biao/1965/09/peoples...

[27] *SW*, I, 124-25; and Snow, *Red Star over China*, pp. 154, 163.

[28] Yang Shubiao, *Jiang Jieshi Zhuan* [*Biography of Chiang Kai-shek*] (Beijing: Tuan Jie Chu Ban She, 1989), p. 216.

[29] Huang, *Mao's Triple Falls and Triple Rises,* p. 203.

[30] Ibid., p. 207.

[31] Ibid., p. 209. Here, the first and third reasons for the guerrillas' victory in the second encirclement campaign, as identified by Mao, correspond precisely to the first and second "strategic advantages" described in *Huai Nanzi*, as cited earlier.

[32] According to Mao, as recorded by Edgar Snow in an interview in 1936, the Nationalists deployed approximately the following number of troops in the five encirclement campaigns: The first campaign, December 1930 to January 1931, 100,000 troops; the second, May to June 1931, 200,000; the third, July to October 1931, 300,000; the fourth, April to October 1933, 250,000; and the fifth, October 1933 to October 1934, 400,000. Snow, *Red Star over China,* pp. 163-67. The strength of Communist guerrillas grew from about 1,000 men in 1927, to about 30,000 at the first encirclement campaign, and to about 80,000 at the beginning of the Long March in 1934.

[33] Huang, *Mao's Triple Falls and Triple Rises,* p. 220.

[34] Ibid., pp. 219-20.

[35] For a full account of Mao's plight at this time, see John E. Rue, *Mao Tse-tung in Opposition, 1927-1935*. Stanford: Stanford University Press, 1966.

[36] Huang, *Mao's Triple Falls and Triple Rises,* p. 237.
[37] Chen Guanren, *Mao Zedong de Dou Zheng Yi Shu* [*Mao Zedong's Art of Struggle*] (Beijing: Zhong Yang Wen Xian Chu Ban She, 2003), p. 116.
[38] Xin Ziling, *Mao Zedong Quan Zhuan* [*The Complete Biography of Mao Zedong*], Vol. 6 (Taipei: Shu Hua Chu Ban Shi Ye Gong Si, 1993), p. 78.
[39] Chen, *Mao's Art of Struggle,* p. 151.
[40] Ibid., p. 158. For a vivid account of Mao's activities during the Yan'an Battle, see a description by his bodyguard, Yan Changlin, in *Jing Wei Mao Zedong Ji Shi* [*A Factual Account on Safeguarding Mao Zedong*] (Changchun: Jilin Ren Min Chu Ban She, 1992), pp. 30-236. For a Nationalist account of the battle, see Hu Zongnan Shang Jiang Nian Pu Bian Zuan Wei Yuan Hui, *Hu Zongnan Shang Jiang Nian Pu* [*Chronology of General Hu Zongnan*] (Taipei Xian, Taiwan: Wen Hai Chu Ban She, 1978), pp. 205-08.
[41] *SW*, V, 160. Though Mao tabulated the Nationalist casualties from the year of 1946 on, only skirmishes between the Nationalist and Communist forces occurred in that year. A full-scale civil war started in 1947.
[42] For a lucid analysis of the significance of the year 1948 in the Nationalist-Communist civil war by a researcher at the Chinese (Communist) Academy of Military Science, see Liu Tong, *Zhongguo de 1948 Nian: Liang Zhong Min Yun de Jue Zhan* [*The Year 1948 in China: A Battle for Two Destinies*], Beijing: Sheng Huo, Du Shu, Xin Zhi San Lian Shu Dian, 2006.
[43] F. F. Liu, *A Military History of Modern China, 1924-1949* (Princeton: Princeton University Press, 1956), p. 254. Cf. Xin, *Biography of Mao Zedong,* p. 246.
[44] Samuel P. Huntington, *Political Order in Changing Societies* (New Haven: Yale University Press, 1968), pp. 271-72.
[45] See Deng Wenyi, *Xian Zhongtong Jiang Zhongzheng Zhi Bing Yu Lu* [*Quotations from the Late President Chiang Kai-shek on Military Training*] (Taipei: Gu Lao Chu Ban She, 1978), pp. 162, 178, 185.
[46] *The New York Times,* October 2, 2009, p. A4. Zhang's book, titled *Xue Bai Xie Hong* [*White Snow, Red Blood*], was published in China in 1989 but was promptly banned.
[47] Lung Ying-tai, a once University of Hong Kong professor, documented eyewitness accounts on other traumatic events in the civil war in 1949 in her 2009-published, widely acclaimed book *Da Jiang Da Hai* (*Big River, Big Sea—Untold Stories*).

The author of the present book can add personal observations on the Communist atrocious treatment of the civilians during two battles in Henan Province in 1948. In one battle over the city of Luoyang in March, a machine gunner of the Nationalist army's 206th Division told the author afterwards on how the Communists conquered the city. Facing a city best known for its strong fortifications, the Communist army forced unarmed civilians to swarm the fortifications in waves of attack. They fell to the deeply dug trenches in front of the pillboxes, where the Nationalist soldiers fired their machine guns. As their bodies eventually filled the trenches and blocked the view of the machine gunners in the pillboxes, the Communist regular soldiers swarmed in and overwhelmed the defenders. In the following June, this author learned from several eyewitnesses about a battle east of the city of Kaifeng. One Nationalist tank force found itself suddenly surrounded tightly by a mass of unarmed villagers. The Nationalist soldiers had to swerve and spin their tanks to repel the attackers but had to surrender in the end because they could not extract themselves from the enclosing human sea.

CHAPTER FOUR

THE BARREL OF THE PEN, I: INSPIRING TRUST

Instrument and Style

Chiang and Mao used the pen as much as wielded the gun in the exercise of leadership. Writing out millions upon millions of words, both of them preferred to use the Chinese brush pen to any other writing instrument. Chiang followed the style of ancient calligraphy masters who stressed balanced, uniform, and formalistic strokes. He often carefully composed words in a square form and aligned them neatly both horizontally and vertically.

Mao followed a calligraphic style of his own, which favored the cursive type. The strokes are dispersed, irregular, and often condensed—exactly opposite of Chiang's. When in good mood, he poured out words in a form like *long fei feng wu*—flying dragon and dancing phoenix. When written in a hurry, his words look like crumpled weeds blown up by gusty wind; they would require a writing connoisseur to decipher their meaning.

In their writings, Chiang and Mao not only used different calligraphic style but also varied in linguistic form. Chiang favored the traditional form, distinguished by laconic expressions with rich connotations and by, mostly, the absence of punctuation marks. It is used by the educated elite familiar with the Chinese classics. In some of his public statements and speeches, Chiang often used the vernacular or common language. Mao used the classic language to compose poems but preferred the vernacular language for his other writings, often with man-on-the-street expressions and sprinkled with humors and anecdotes.

Both employed secretaries to produce their formal statements and treatises. Chiang's secretaries included the widely known literary talent Chen Bulei. On Chiang's staff for twenty-two years, Chen not only did the writing for Chiang but also served as his closest advisor on political as well as linguistic matters. Many of Chiang's important messages have been speculated to have come exclusively from Chen's pen. The reality is that Chiang and Chen had developed a close literary kinship that their styles of writings were not clearly differentiable—not unlike the common thread in the writings of John F. Kennedy and his special counsel and speechwriter Theodore Sorensen in the White House years. Chiang also retained scholars on his staff, including notably Tao Xisheng, Xu Fuguan, Xu Daolin, and others.[1] These were highly respected historians and philosophers from prominent colleges.

Mao's secretaries included Chen Boda, Hu Qiaomu, Li Rui, Lin Ke, among others. Chen was for a long time the chief ideologue of the Chinese Communist Party until he fell to disgrace in the early 1970s when he was alleged to be associated with Lin Biao in opposition to Mao. Others were later to become political leaders or middle-level administrators. Mao preferred to do his own writing and even to write statements in others' name or anonymously, especially for the editorials of the party's opinion organs such as *The People's Daily* and *the New China News*.[2] He made use of his secretaries primarily for purpose of researching, proofreading, and copying. By no means belittling these men's talents, he reduced their role to that of the scribe.

The writing output of Chiang and Mao is enormous. Both authored books and essays; collected their speeches, communications, and statements into multi-volume works; and maintained their unpublished works in extensive archives. In comparing how the two men used their pens to influence others, we shall focus on their writings or ideas that significantly impacted on Chinese politics and that the people still associate the two Chinese leaders with today. They consist of three categories: Those that inspire trust, establish political orthodoxy, and offer policy guidance. In the remainder of this chapter, the first category will be discussed; the next chapter will cover the second and third categories.

Chiang: Moralizing Leadership

On the morning of December 25, 1936, Soong May-ling was getting ready to fly to Nanjing from Xi'an, where her husband, Chiang Kai-shek, had been kidnapped since December 12 by mutinous troops, numbered at hundreds of thousands. Through painstaking negotiations by her and her brother T. V. Soong with the rebellious leaders, Generals Zhang Xueliang and Yang Hucheng, she had obtained their consent to release her husband. A devout Christian, she regarded the peaceful conclusion of the Xi'an Incident, which had gripped the attention of a shocked nation for two weeks, as the best Christmas gift she ever received. Two planes at the Xi'an airport stood ready for the arrival of the Chiang party for takeoff.

But the party could not leave the city, for they confronted a last-minute hurdle. The rebellious leaders had consented to let Chiang go on the basis of an agreement they had reached with the Soongs. The agreement stipulated that Chiang stop fighting the Chinese Communists and prepare for war with Japan, which had wrested Manchuria away from China in 1931. Chiang only gave a verbal consent that he would carry out the agreement after he returned to Nanjing but adamantly refused to put his signature on the agreement while in Xi'an. He said he would rather die than sign the agreement.

Chiang's refusal was anything but a recantation. Early in the Incident he had indicated in his diary several times his readiness to die rather than to accede to the rebellious generals' demand. He believed that tolerating the existence of the revolting Communist Party would harm the nation and accepting the generals' demand under duress would impair his character as a principled national leader (CKSD, 12/12-16/36). Demonstrating his uncompromising stand, he wrote out three wills, one each to the people, his wife, and his sons. He emphasized that if the generals would not release him unconditionally, he "is determined to sacrifice my life for the sake of the nation" (CKSD, 12/15/36). These wills were later given to T. V. Soong for delivery (CKSD, 12/20/36).

Then, why did Chiang change his mind? Many explanations have been offered by the voluminous publications on the Incident. In this author's opinion, Chiang changed his mind because of T. V. Soong's persuasion. In his meeting with Chiang on December 20, Soong warned him that if Chiang died under the present circumstances, "the country would break up, with civil war everywhere rampant." That is, wars among the Nationalist Central army, the forces commanded by the rebel leaders, the Communists, and warlords would all likely to break out. In such an event, Soong implied, the Japanese army would take advantage of the chaos to conquer the country. Thus, Chiang's acceptance of the rebels' demand would be detrimental to his position as the national leader, but his rejection of it would do much harm to the nation. Soong advised Chiang to take the former option.[3] Chiang fell silent but ruminated for days before heeding Soong's advice. But he never explained to the public that this was the real reason for him to accept the rebels' demand. Only in his diary entry one year later did he admit it.[4]

Yet he adamantly refused to sign the Xi'an agreement, for he believed such an action would give the appearance that he was coerced to do something that he had prepared to die for not doing so. He explained,

"Once I [do] that, I would be doing something unlawful, as well as against the revolutionary principles of the [Nationalist] Party, and it would amount to betraying the trust which the people have placed in me."[5]

In the end, Zhang and Yang yielded and let Chiang depart on the Christmas Day without signing the document.

This episode illustrates a point that was central to Chiang's concept of rulership. He considered effective political leadership contingent upon people's trust, which, in turn, owed to a clear sense of morality of the leader. This concept reflects a Confucian prescription for best governance by Chinese imperial rulers in the past: "*Qi shen zheng, bu ling er cong; qi shen bu zheng, sui ling bu cong.*" That is, if the ruler is an upright person, the people will follow him without being ordered to. If the ruler is not an upright person, the people will not follow him even being ordered to. As John K. Fairbank put it succinctly, "Right conduct gave the ruler power."[6] Indeed, Chiang had explicitly embraced this Confucian adage in a statement on September 23, 1928 before assuming the position of chairman of the National Government.[7] Later He elaborated on this concept in a treatise on *Zhengzhi de Daoli* (*The Principles of Politics*), with citations from many Confucius' works.[8]

Though Chiang placed a high premium on morality in the exercise of leadership, his behavior in the early years of his revolutionary career was not beyond reproach. On the contrary, in the late 1910s and the early 1920s, as noted before, he frequented brothels and socialite houses to no end; he indulged excessively in feasts, drinks, and poker and mahjong; and he possessed a temperament given to impetuosity and rages. He was far from being a person with exemplar conduct appropriate to a national leader.

Yet, he had long harbored an ambition to succeed Sun Yat-sen as the Nationalist leader. To realize his ambition, he was convinced, he had to reshape fundamentally his behavior pattern so as to form a model personality. Such an undertaking would require a Herculean effort over a long time to achieve result. But he took the challenge with determination. He first identified, as thorough as possible, his character flaws and then developed and followed a rigid regimen for improvement of his behavior. He persisted with strenuous effort; he frequently expressed pain for failing to make progress; but in the end he purged most of his flaws and regulated his behavior with a code of rightful conduct (See the Appendix, "Chiang Kai-shek's Confession and Redemption").

The documentation that recorded Chiang's character transformation and his attempts at moralizing political leadership is his diaries. They constituted a single longest—the earliest as well as the latest—of all Chiang's personal writings. They were daily journals from 1917 to 1972, lasting for fifty-six years. The daily entries were filled with details on his thoughts and activities and on the important events of the day and then complemented with weekly, monthly, and yearly working plans as well as reviews. They enclosed his startlingly frank evaluation of his personal conduct and commentaries on others. Though writing them as his private papers, Chiang disseminated his diary entries, in excerpts, among the public to explain his policies and his thoughts. They appeared in several well-publicized, large collections.[9]

From Chiang's diaries, three sources of his concept of morality can be identified: Confucianism, Neo-Confucianism, and Christianity. Over his adult life, he made numerous references to his concept of morality as the underpinning of his personal conduct and political style. Yet he never went on for any lengthy articulation of it, taking it as a matter of truism, without the necessity for explanation.

Chiang's education in the traditional private schools and subsequent reading of ancient classics provided him with a firm grounding of Confucianism, and he considered the moral exhortations of Confucianism as embodying the spirit of the Chinese nation. In 1935, he noted, "I feel I very much benefited from *Daxue* [*The Great Learning*] and *Zhongyong* [*The Doctrine of the Mean*] [two of the four standard Confucian works], with a deepened belief in them as time goes on" (CKSD, 4/11/35).[10] *The Great Learning*, he noted particularly, has set three tasks for the political leader to perform: "To promote morality, to serve the people, and to strive for the ultimate good." He recorded these as his motto in his diary (See, for example, CKSD, 5/4/34; 7/30/36).[11] Gleaned from the Confucian text, the moral precepts he was dedicated to promote consisted of what are known as the "Four Principles and Eight Virtues," to be discussed in the next chapter.

Neo-Confucianism—a derivative of Confucianism—is a system of thought prevailing in the Song (960-1279) and Ming (1368-1644) dynasties. It represents a revival of what might be called the orthodoxy Confucian theories in the face of challenges of two different systems of thought: Buddhism and Taoism. For our purpose, we need merely to identify two strands of its content. One is its proposition of a union of nature with humanity though the mind (reasoning power). The other is the idea that *qi* (the right spirit or moral force) permeates the natural and human worlds. In its concrete manifestation, Neo-Confucianism requires its believers to pursue morality-based missions. Insofar as Chiang was concerned, Neo-Confucianism was basic to his meditation practice and the mottos he adhered to.[12] His expositions on this subject can be seen in the following citations from his diaries: "The heavenly mandate is a manifestation of nature; in other words, it is the principle behind the natural world. It is something that humans can explore and understand through reason" (CKSD, 2/21/36; see also 9/2/34; 9/15/35). "The right spirit is omnipresent and omnipotent..." (CKSD, 6/16/36; 9/20/38).

Chiang came to accept Christianity later than his embracing Confucianism and Neo-Confucianism; yet, he referred to Christianity in his diaries more frequently than Confucianism and Neo-Confucianism. Chiang accepted Christianity as personal faith as seen in the following citations: "I must model after Jesus" (CKSD, 6/12/36). "I am determined to accept the burden of guilt for the sake of salvation of all" (CKSD, 9/16/36). "My faith in God has deepened. I never missed a prayer" (CKSD, 12/31/38).

He sought guidance from God to his public policies. During the critical American-Japanese negotiations over the matter of war or peace in November 1941, just before the Pearl Harbor Incident, Chiang thought he succeeded in convincing the American government not to compromise with Japan at China's expense because of the divine intervention: "I cannot achieve this result without God's blessing and guidance" (CKSD, 11/29/41).

In July 1944, when China was fighting a major battle against Japan in Hengyang in central China, Chiang prayed "to God to let me win this battle. I promise to establish on my 60th birthday a big iron cross on the peak of the Nanyue Mountain [nearby]" (CKSD, 7/25/44). He promised to do the same on the summit of the Yu Mountain in Taiwan on his 80th birthday if he could then defeat the Communists on the Chinese mainland (CKSD, 2/17/59). In August 1945, following Japanese surrender to the allied powers, Chiang wrote: "[The] blessing God has given us and the wisdom he has demonstrated to us are so enormous as to defy explanation. This is seen especially in Psalm, Chapter Nine. Every verse of it has come true" (CKSD, 8/15/45).[13]

He went so far as to father the idea of making China a Christian nation: "Only after Christianity replaces Buddhism as the [dominant] Chinese religion can China contend for equality with the nations in Europe and America. Only then can we promote our national spirit and revive our traditional morality with half of the effort to achieve a doubled result" (CKSD, 2/15/36). "I pledge that after we win this war against Japan [1937-1945], we will make the Republic of China a Christian nation. Let the Bible be studied in all schools so that all can comprehend the holy scriptures" (CKSD, 9/18/37).

Mao: Empowering Poems

In the fall of 1945, the Chinese were overjoyed as they turned attention to Chongqing, the nation's wartime capital, where Chiang and Mao held talks for peaceful cooperation of the Nationalist and Communist parties in the aftermath of the devastating Chinese-Japanese war. In the midst of excitement, the people were surprised to learn that Mao—a man Chiang had long despised as a bandit chief of a collection of illiterate peasants—turned out to be a poet, a masterful one. On one November day one Chongqing newspaper published "Snow," a poem Mao had written years ago, whose powerful and elegant verses captivated the intellectual circle of the city and, soon, of the nation. The uncouth bandit chief was after all a literary man.

It happened that Mao had long before engaged in the romantic pursuit of poem writing. Though he hated in his youth to study the Chinese classics, Mao found traditional poetry particularly alluring. As a poet, he set himself apart from many famed Chinese poets in historical times. His poems do not belong to the genre of "moaning without being sick" or "spring flowers and autumn moon." They gush forth words of force, destiny, and hope.

Chinese traditional poetry is in two forms. One is *shi,* a form developed in pre-Confucius times that stresses strict schemes of lines and words in specified tonal patterns of rhyme. It flowered into its golden era in the Tang Dynasty (618-907). The other form, *ci,* is understood to have originated in the Tang Dynasty but flourished in the Song Dynasty (960-1279). It developed from theatrical songs of specified tonal pattern of rhyme and rhythm with fixed number of lines and words of varying length. Fond of both forms of poetry, Mao used them as a literary device to manifest his deeply impregnated feelings and to activate the dreams and yearnings of his followers.[14] A few citations of Mao's poems will show how he used this device to achieve his purposes.

The Barrel of the Pen, I: Inspiring Trust

"Snow"
To the Tune of Qin Yuan Chun, 1936

[*Background:* Mao used this poem to manifest an extraordinary vision of what he was expected to become. He wrote this poem in a cave dwelling in northern Shaanxi in the deep winter of 1936. It was a few months after he wound up the exhausting Long March that had thinned his Red Army to a skeleton of its former self, less than one-third of what it was when the March started. Short of food and ammunition, living on a barren land, relentlessly pursued by the Nationalist army, Mao was in his darkest hour. Yet he could master an artist's pen to paint the desolate landscape into splendid scenery and lively imageries. Defying the danger of annihilation, he could harbor the thought that the land might turn Red. In a desperate situation, he could exude an unbounded optimism by comparing, implicitly, himself with a parade of China's greatest imperial rulers.[15] At the nadir of his revolutionary career, Mao dared to scale the impossible height.]

The sweeping northern lands,
    Frozen in ice over a thousand miles.
    Snow swirls over the unending landscape.
Inside and outside the Great Wall,
    All turns to a white immensity;
Up and down the Yellow River,
    The waves suddenly disappear.
Mountains dance like silvery snakes,
Highlands gallop like wax-hued elephants,
    All vying with the heaven for height.
Awaiting a sunny day,
    The Red is wrapped in white,
    Looking especially enchanting.
The magnificent rivers and mountains are so captivating,
    Countless heroes have bowed in homage.
Alas, Emperors of Qin Huang and Han Wu,
    A little short of literary talent;
Emperors Tang Taizong and Song Taizu,
    Without much grace and flair;
The epic hero Genghis Khan,
    Only knew how to shoot eagles with a bow.
All gone.
For the truly great heroes,

Look only now.[16]

[*Commentary*: Mao pointedly recited this poem in 1945 when meeting Chiang in Chongqing. He was, not without subtlety, hinting that he was a truly great hero in the perspective of Chinese history, throwing a literary gauntlet to Chiang. Only a man madly arrogant could entertain such a notion. Indeed, he was so viewed by many of his countrymen at the time. Yet in four short years he had triumphed over all odds to become the ruler of the most populous nation of the world and had drawn unquestioned adulation of millions of his comrades and the grudging acceptance of hundreds of millions more of his countrymen as The Red Sun of the East. The poem had since been cited and recited over and over in China and elsewhere in the world. Arguably it was the single most politically significant poem of 20th-century China.]

"Swimming"
To the Tune of Shui Diao Ge Tou (Excerpt), 1956

[Background: Here, Mao manifested another vision: how an unprecedentedly large construction project could emerge in a Socialist China. In a visit to Wuhan in Hubei Province on a June day of 1956, Mao swam across the nearby Yangzi River against all the caution of his aides, who regarded the river as too broad and its currents too turbulent for a 63-year old man to test his mettle. He defied the risk and plunged into the river, out-swimming many of his bodyguards following him. Celebrating this adventure with a poem, he expressed a desire to see a gigantic dam to be built in the Yangzi River's Three Gorges west of Hubei. He was capturing an idea of Sun Yat-sen, who first proposed the project in 1919. During his Wuhan visit, he consulted with the staff of Yangzi Valley Planning Office and urged them to undertake the gargantuan project.[17] Fifty years later the world's largest dam loomed over the site.]

> Swimming across the mighty Yangzi River,
> I gaze at the distant horizon of western Hubei.
> Care less about the lashing wind and surging waves;
> More pleasant than strolling in a courtyard.
> Sails flutter with the wind;
> Tortoises and snakes fall silent.[18]
> A great plan afoot:
> With a bridge flying over the nature's chasm,

A thoroughfare runs from the south to the north.
Stone walls rise over the river's west,
Holding back the Wu Mountain's clouds and rains,
A tranquil lake emerges from the gorges.
Should the mountain goddess turn alive,
Would be wonderstruck over the changed world.

"To Comrade Guo Moruo"
To the Tune of Man Jiang Hong (Excerpt), 1963

[*Background:* Though infrequently doing so, Mao did use poem to project his perception of the power constellation of the world. In 1963, as China and the Soviet Union had split apart, Mao wrote this satirical piece—addressing to his friend Guo Moruo—to mock at the Soviet leaders for intimidating China and to assert his power in reshaping the world. Later he wrote more poems to denounce the Soviet Union, the United States, and Great Britain for colluding to contain China.[19]]

On this rather small globe,
A few flies banging their heads against the wall.
They buzz and moan and scream.
Ants take the locust tree they climb on as a big kingdom,
What nonsense for them to think of shaking the tree.
Many great deeds awaiting,
Ten thousand years are too long;
Seize the day, seize the hour;
We have to contend for the present.
Roaring waves surging in the Four Seas;
Powerful winds and thunders shake the Five Continents.
All pests are swept away,
The invincible will prevail.

"To Li Shuyi"
To the Tune of Die Lian Hua (Excerpt), 1957

[*Background*: Mao used poem as a device to establish emotional bond among his comrades-in-arms. He wrote this piece in response to Li Shuyi's poem in memory of her lover Liu Zhixun. Li was a close friend of Mao's second wife, Yang Kaihui, who as mentioned in Chapter One, died young in the cause of communism. So did Liu Zhixun. In his poem, Mao adroitly mixed metaphors, fairytales, similes to express the survivors' mourning of their lost lovers in verses that are, at once, nostalgic, sad, and uplifting. It happens that Yang and Liu, as Chinese words, also mean poplar and willow trees, two highly popular plants in China, whose fallen leaves are feathery light often seen riding on the wind to a distance. "Chang O," a legendary figure residing on the moon, is considered to be a talented dancer. "The tiger" refers to enemies of the Chinese Communists.]

> I lost my proud Yang and you, your Liu;
> Soaring to the Ninth Heaven were Yang and Liu.
> The lonely Chang O spreads out her loose sleeves,
> In a dance to console the martyrs' souls.
> Suddenly tamed was the tiger;
> Sputtering tears turn into a downpour.

[*Commentary:* This poem establishes an intimate camaraderie between Mao and Li and, vicariously, an esprit de corps among all Communists that survived the harsh, prolonged revolution. Even many non-Communist Chinese who understand the connotation of the verses cannot but regard this short poem as hauntingly beautiful and deeply moving. The perfect rhyme of the verses especially accentuates their sentimental appeal. The English translation here cannot do full justice to the original version in terms of linguistic elegance and emotional impact.]

"The Loushan Pass"
To the Tune of Yi Qin O, 1935

[*Background*: In his poems, Mao had the knack of enmeshing battle scene in the context of nature. He wrote this piece in February 1935 in the Long March as he and his comrades threaded through the Loushan Pass against the blustering wintry elements. Short, with repetitive verses, this poem enlivened his comrades by depicting scenes of an uplifting dawn following a reddening sunset.]

> Gusty wind lashing from the west,
> Wild geese shriek in the vast sky under a frosty morning moon.
> A frosty morning moon,
> Horse hooves clatter,
> Bugles sound low.
> The path along the Pass hardened like iron,
> In great stride we cross over it.

We cross over it,
Gray hills roll like the sea.
The setting sun looks bloody red.

"The Long March," 1935

[*Background*: Mao composed this piece to transform the treacherous mountains and rivers the Communists marched through into lively landscapes. In symmetrical verses that balance mountains against rivers, warmth against chill, joy against trial, Mao used this poem to build into the survivors' psyche a sense of boundless optimism, courage, and strength.]

The Red Army fears not the Long March's tribulations,
Easily passed over thousands of mountains and waters.
The Five Great Ranges winding forward like sea waves,
The majestic Wumeng undulates like running globules.
The Golden Sand River warms its banks with lapping water.
The Dadu Bridge chills with its iron chain.
Looking at the snow-capped Min Mountain.
Our soldiers were exuberant for having crossed it.

[*Commentary*: Both "The Loushan Pass" and "The Long March" poems are most frequently recited in Chinese schools and army and are often found in inscriptions chiseled into rocky cliffs in scenic Chinese mountains. "The Loushan Pass" seems more inspiring in impact, for it embraces a more noble and more subtle *yi jing* (idealized scenes)—something classical poets value the most--than does "The Long March", which merely depicts the scenes and travails that the Red soldiers had marched through].[20]

Among 20th-century Chinese political leaders Chiang and Mao poured out from their barrel of the pen something truly unique. No one else is known to have written diaries lasting as long as Chiang's; nor anyone else composed as many poems as did Mao. They used their unique literary devices to persuade their countrymen to trust their leadership. Chiang propagated a set of moral principles and projected an image of the rightful ruler. Mao shaped up common destinies, impassioned camaraderie, and eternal optimism.

NOTES

[1] In the 1930s Chiang retained what became known as the "Eight Great Secretaries": Luo Gonghua, Xu Qingyu, Gao Chuanzhu, He Fangli, Fu Rui, Xu Daolin, Zhang Yiding, and Li Yujiu. Most of them were first-rate scholars, having studied abroad; three in Japan, one each in Britain, the Soviet Union, France, Germany, and the United States. "When consulting them on policy matters," Chiang's aide Ju Yiqiao has observed, "Chiang always listened with respect, did not interrupt, nor took a point of view, and let them finish their talk; he then analyzed the merits and demerits of their suggestions." Ju Yiqiao, *Gen Sui Jiang Jieshi Shi Er Nian* [*Serving under Chiang Kai-shek for Twelve Years*] (Changsha: Hunan Ren Min Chu Ban She, 1988), pp. 20-21.

[2] See observation on this point by Lin Ke, who served as Mao's secretary, in Lin, *The World of Mao*, pp. 84-85.

[3] Soong kept a diary, in English, on the Xi'an Incident from December 20 to 25, 1936. See T. V. Soong Files, Box 62, File 1. Stanford University, Hoover Institution Archive. Quotations appeared in his diary entries of December 20 and 21.

[4] On the first anniversary of the Xi'an Incident, Chiang wrote in his diary, "If I died because of the Incident, the Communist Party would have usurped national power, the warlords in the provinces would have divided the rest of the territory, the National Government would have been toppled, and the Japanese army would have invaded China. If the Incident resulted in such a situation, saving my life to pick up the pieces is better than having died for it" (CKSD, 12/12/37).

[5] Chiang's experiences during the Xi'an Incident were recorded in English in May-ling Soong, *General Chiang Kai-shek, the Account of the Fortnight in Sian [Xi'an]: Extracts from a Diary...and Mme Chiang Kai-shek, Sian: A Coup d'État*. Garden City, NY: Doubleday, Doran & Co., 1937. Citation is from *The Fortnight in Sian,* p. 170. Chiang also recorded what transpired during the Incident in his diary, from December 12 to 25, 1936.

[6] John King Fairbank, *The United States and China*, 3rd ed. (Cambridge: Harvard University Press, 1972), p. 55.

[7] For Chiang's September 23, 1928 statement, see Wang Zhenghua, ed., *Jiang Zhongzheng Zongtong Dang An. Shi Luo Gao Ban* [*President Chiang Kai-shek Archive, Preliminary Manuscript on [His] Deeds*], Vol. 4 (Taipei: Guo Shi Guan, 2003), p. 168.

[8] Chiang Kai-shek, *Zhengzhi de Daoli* [*The Principles of Politics*]. Taipei: Zhong Yang Wen Wu Gong Ying She, 1971. This treatise was based on a speech Chiang delivered in 1939; it was revised in 1969 for publication.

[9] These include Mao, *Chiang Kai-shek prior to 1926*; Qin Xiaoyi, Chief Compiler, *Zongtong Jiang Gong Da Shi Chang Bian Chu Gao* [*President Chiang Kai-shek's Chronology of Major Events, Preliminary Edition*], 8 volumes, published in Taipei, Taiwan, 1978; Wang, *President Chiang Kai-shek Archive,* 61 volumes. The Second Historical Archives of China, Nanjing, contains copied Chiang's diary, classified by subjects, from 1917 to 1949. The Japanese newspaper *Sankei Shimbun* published in 1974-1976 a serial on *Sho Haiseki Hiroku* (a declassified *Chiang Kai-shek Secret Archive*), which also contains many excerpts from Chiang's diary.

[10] In his *The Principles of Politics*, Chiang also stated that "*the Great Learning* and *the Doctrine of the Mean*... constitute the fundamental principles of Chinese political philosophy." See p. 1.

[11] See also ibid., p. 19.

[12] For Chiang's Neo-Confucianism-based mottos, see Appendix.

[13] What struck Chiang the most were these verses: "O Lord...When my enemies turn back, they shall fall and perish at Your presence. For you have maintained my right and my cause; you sat on the throne judging in righteousness.... You have destroyed the wicked." In his diary, Chiang constantly maintained that China, as a victim of the Chinese-Japanese war, fought the war for righteousness and that Japan, as the aggressive nation, was wicked and cruel. The words "righteousness" and "wicked" rang especially resonant in his mind and ears.

[14] For two standard collections of Mao's poems, in Chinese and English versions, see *Mao Tse-tung Poems.* Beijing: Shang Wu Yin Shu Guan, 1976; and Willis Barnstone, *The Poems of Mao Tse-tung.* New York: Harper & Row, 1972.

[15] The origin of the list of great Chinese emperors in "Snow" may be traced to Mao's conversation with his high school friend Siao Yu one summer night in 1917. Siao, *Mao Tse-tung and I Were Beggars*, p. 132.

[16] In a 1958 note appended to "Snow," Mao claimed that he was not comparing himself, as an individual, with China's great emperors. Rather, he was comparing the Chinese proletariat with the past imperial rulers. See Liu Jikun, *Mao Zedong Shi Ci Quanji* [*Complete Collection of Mao Zedong's Poems*] (Taipei: Hai Feng, Inc., 1992), p. 131. But judging by the content of the poem and the timing of its presentation in

1945, this author believes that Mao's intent was to present a personal challenge to Chiang as to who should be considered the greatest contemporary Chinese ruler.

[17] See Li, *Chairman Mao*, pp.166-67.

[18] "Tortoises and snakes" may also refer to the two mountains in Wuhan that are named as such. See Mao's poem, "Huang He Lou (Yellow Crane Pavilion), to the tune of Pu Sa Man, 1927," in Liu, *Complete Collection of Mao's Poems*, pp. 55-57, 178.

[19] For example, see his poem, "Birds' Talk" (1965), in *Mao Tse-tung Poems*, pp.102-05.

[20] Wang Guowei (1877-1927), one of the greatest contemporary Chinese classicists, spoke of the mind of many accomplished Chinese poets when he said that "idealized scene is the highest standard a poet can aspire to achieve." He went on to say, "The scene created by master poets must conform to nature and approach a high ideal." See Wang Guowei, *Ren Jian Ci Hua* [*Observations on Ci*] (Taipei: Kai Ming Shu Dian, n. d.), p. 1.

CHAPTER FIVE

THE BARREL OF THE PEN, II: ORTHODOXY AND GUIDANCE

Establishing Orthodoxy

In the third century BC, the founding emperor of the Qin Dynasty (221-207 BC) confiscated all books then in existence—except those on the Qin history, medicine, and other specialized subjects—and burned them to ashes. The emperor, later known as Qin Shihuang, destroyed in one stroke much of the written heritage of ancient China, including many works of the Hundred Schools. He rounded up some 460 dissenting scholars and had them buried alive.

Qin Shihuang took these atrocious actions because he sought to establish one political orthodoxy for the whole nation; he was determined, in particular, to root out the Confucian School of thought, whose adherents were opposed to his effort at building a tightly organized empire. Thus, he created a millennium-old tradition in China: the imperial ruler, acting as the sage king, was the single source of political wisdom. The emperors of each subsequent dynasty would establish or reaffirm a political orthodoxy that all of their subjects had to uphold. Ironic as it may seem, the orthodoxy embraced by Emperor Wu (143-87 BC) of the Han Dynasty—the dynasty succeeding the Qin—and observed by subsequent Chinese emperors was derived from Confucianism, the very system of thought Qin Shihuang was bent to destroy.

Performing their role of dispenser of political wisdom, many Chinese emperors explicated the orthodoxy as a set of rules of conduct for their subjects to follow. For example, Emperor Zhu Hongwu of the Ming Dynasty—a man of little education—issued a *Sacred Edict* (*Sheng Yu*) *of Six Maxims*, and Emperor Kangxi of the Qing Dynasty, an accomplished scholar conversant with Chinese classics as well as Western science, issued a *Sacred Edict of Sixteen Maxims*.[1]

In 20th-century China, Chiang and Mao inherited the tradition that the ruler had the right to impart political knowledge to their citizens. They took upon themselves to create anew their respective orthodoxies for the nation; they also adopted shortened linguistic expressions to guide the public to observe the policies they initiated.

Chiang: To the Right of Sun's Ideology

The intellectual works authored by Chiang from which he sought to create a political orthodoxy are relatively few. The most important of these is *China's Destiny,* published in 1943. Anticipating the end of the Chinese-Japanese war, he charted out in this book a path for postwar reconstruction of the country; more significantly, he concerned himself with an endeavor to reinvigorate Chinese traditional culture and to amalgamate it with the Western culture.

Chiang's attempt at such amalgamation represented one of a long series of efforts of the Chinese political and intellectual leaders to bridge Chinese tradition with modernity. The efforts began in the mid19th century when China suffered a decisive defeat in the Opium War of 1839-1842—a war that led to a century-long Western domination of China. The Chinese leaders at first perceived China's loss to the West as resulting from Western nations' science-based industrial and military might. Their response to the West's challenge was the Self-Strengthening Movement of the 1860s-1880s. It aimed at creating a "Prosperous Nation, Strong Army" (*Fu Guo Qiang Bing*) by infusing China with Western science and technology for purpose of industrialization. However, they regarded Chinese culture as superior to the Western and strove to preserve it at all cost. An expression catching the Chinese sentiment of the time was enunciated by Zhang Zhidong, a major leader of the Movement: "Chinese learning for the essence; Western learning for the utility" (*Zhong Xue Wei Ti; Xi Xue Wei Yong*).

The failure of the Self-Strengthening Movement, which was glaringly demonstrated by the crushing defeat of China's modernized naval fleet and land army by the Japanese forces in a war between the two countries in 1894, dawned on the Chinese leaders that importing Western science and technology alone would not help China become a rich and strong nation. They realized that what was needed, in addition, was the acceptance of Western ideology and government institutions. Such a realization provided a powerful stimulus for radical political changes; these included the One-Hundred-Day Reform of 1898, the Republican Revolution of 1911, and the May Fourth Movement of 1919.

The May Fourth Movement heralded new trends of change. Certain Chinese intellectuals began to repudiate the Confucian orthodoxy, considering it the root cause of China's misfortunes in modern times.

Some of these intellectuals were in favor of wholesale embracing Western democracy and science, while others, disappointed with the West's domination of China, advocated Marxism as the salvation of their country.

At this moment of great intellectual and political ferment, Sun Yat-sen proposed still another direction of change. In his lectures on *The Three Principles of the People* delivered in the early 1920s, he offered a three-part program for a merge of selected elements of Chinese and Western cultures. In "The Principle of Nationalism," he advocated the adoption of Western idea of national independence and the revival of Chinese moral tradition. In "The Principle of Democracy," he proposed to create a five-branch government for China—the legislative, executive, and judicial branches (from the Western political tradition) and the Examination and the Control branches (from the Chinese political tradition). In addition, he endorsed the Western concept of civil rights and civil liberties. In "The Principle of the Peoples' Livelihood," he favored adoption of the Western market system, moderated with a good dose of state intervention to assure the people a decent living.

In his *China's Destiny*, Chiang accepted Sun's *The Three Principles of the People* as an article of faith and was committed to its implementation. Yet on two points Chiang's stance was at variance with Sun's. With respect to Western democratic ideas, Chiang favored the adoption of constitutional government but spurned an unquestioned acceptance of the West's libertarian tradition that underpinned the concept of civil liberties and civil rights. He stated,

> After the May Fourth Movement, two types of thought—individualistic Liberalism and class-war communism—were suddenly introduced among the educated classes and spread throughout the whole country….[They] adopted the superficial husks of Western culture and lost…their confidence in Chinese culture….[They] adopted the theories and interests of the imperialists as their own….This is the greatest single danger of cultural aggression, and the greatest threat to the nation's spirit.[2]

In contrast, Sun did not see that Western Liberalism had such a baneful effect.

As for the revival of the Chinese moral tradition, Chiang placed a greater emphasis and elaborated more on the subject than did Sun. He believed the long Chinese history was sustained by the Confucianism-based "inherent moral character" of the people. He went on to say, "We know that the ethical tenets of a Chinese citizen are loyalty, filial piety, benevolence, love, faithfulness, righteousness, peace, and harmony [*Zhong, Xiao, Ren, Ai, Xin, Yi, He, Ping*], and that the basic principles on which the Chinese state is founded are propriety, righteousness, modesty, and honor [*Li, Yi, Lian, Chi*]." Together, these precepts were known as the eight virtues and four principles.[3] In 1934 he introduced the New Life Movement as a way to apply these virtues and principles directly to the life of the Chinese people. To insure the success of the Movement, he issued a citizens' code of conduct that consists of twelve guidelines—the equivalent to the Sacred Edict of Maxims of Emperors Zhu Hongwu and Kangxi—for recitation and memorization by the people.[4]

Chiang's another major work is *Soviet Russia in China*, first published in 1957. As its subtitle appropriately indicates, this is "*a Summing up at Seventy*" of his age about his anti-Soviet activities and policies since the early 1920s.[5] His distrust of the Soviet Union began in his three-month observation mission in Moscow in 1923. "The Russian Communist Party, in its dealings with China," he stated, "has only one aim, namely, to turn the Chinese Communist Party into an instrument for its own use."[6] But as Sun Yat-sen had then initiated a policy of collaboration with the Soviet Union and of acceptance of the Chinese Communists into the Nationalist Party, Chiang did not openly oppose such policy, owing to his respect for Sun. Following Sun's death in 1925, Chiang had a running dispute with the Soviet advisors while he headed the Whampoa Military Academy and, later, commanded the forces for the Northern Expedition. He purged the Chinese Communists from the Nationalist Party in 1927 and severed relations with the Soviet Union later. In the subsequent civil strives with the Chinese Communist Party, Chiang firmly believed that the Party remained a Soviet instrument for domination of China. In the 1950s as he retreated from mainland China to Taiwan, he blamed the Soviet assistance to the Chinese Communists as one principal reason for his loss of the mainland.

Chiang's book restated these developments without adding anything substantially new. It listed historical events and illustrated with maps to enhance its credibility to his followers in Taiwan and to win sympathy from the anti-Communist nations in the Cold War era. Chiang did not have other intellectual works, excepting, perhaps, a booklet published as a supplement to Sun's "Principle of the People's Livelihood;" it dealt with the educational and recreational activities of the people (*Min Sheng Zhu Yi Yu Le Liang Pian Bu Shu*).

Claiming as Sun's political and intellectual heir, Chiang created a political orthodoxy to the right of Sun's ideology. It incorporated

Sun's thought on the revival of Chinese moral tradition, substantially diluted Sun's Western concept of political liberalism, and rejected Sun's notion of a Nationalist-Communist alliance.

Mao: To the Left of Marxism

In 1935, after eight years of battles with the Nationalists and factional disputes with his Communist rivals, Mao finally rose to the top of the Communist hierarchy, as his senior comrades first affirmed at the Zunyi Conference his guerrilla war strategy as the party's chosen military policy and later endorsed him as the leader of the party. Eight years later, in 1943, he saw his position within the Communist Party further strengthened when Zhou Enlai declared on behalf of the rank and file of the Party: "Our party's twenty-two-year history has proven that the ideas of Comrade Mao Zedong …have made Marxism applicable to China. They form the party line of Chinese Communism."[7] Two years later still, he found his thoughts were formally incorporated into the Party's constitution. And after the founding of the People's Republic of China in 1949, the thoughts of Mao Zedong, along with Marxism and Leninism, were enshrined in the several successive constitutions as the ideology of the state.

The most authoritative publication on Mao's thoughts is his *Selected Works*, and analysis of Mao's ideas by Western scholars can be found in many published works, with Stuart R. Schram's books as standard references.[8] Mao's writings are mostly in the form of essays, with his key ideas interspersed in several essays. Summarized below are the ones that are of profound and enduring influence.

The Theory of Contradictions.—Fundamental to Mao's conception of revolution, and, in fact, to all of his political thoughts is his theory of contradictions, which he expounded on in an extended essay in August 1937.[9]

Mao opened the essay by saying, "The law of contradiction in things, that is, the law of the unity of opposites, is the most basic law in materialist dialectics." He rested his claim on a perception of the universe as a dynamic entity in constant motion. Motion is impelled by internal contradiction, that is, a combination of positive and negative forces. Based on the writings of Engels and Lenin, he went on to show that contradiction exists in all natural as well as human conditions:

For example, positive and negative numbers in mathematics; action and reaction in mechanics; positive and negative electricity in physics; decomposition and combination in chemistry; productive forces and relations of production, classes and the struggle between the classes in social science; offence and defence in military science; idealism and materialism; the metaphysical outlook and the dialectical outlook in philosophy.

Adopting Marx's class struggle theory, he saw the driving forces in the progression of human history as follows: "The contradiction between the proletariat and the bourgeoisie is solved by the method of socialist revolution; the contradiction between the great masses of the people and the feudal system is solved by the democratic revolution; the contradiction between colonies and imperialism is solved by the method of national revolutionary war." And insofar war is concerned, "offence and defence, advance and retreat, victory and defeat are all contradictory phenomena. Without the one, the other cannot exist."

Rural Communism.—While contradiction exists universally, Mao noted, it has a peculiar characteristic at each stage of historical development. The peculiar characteristic of the Chinese history of his times was that China was an overwhelmingly rural country, with industrialization at an infant stage. As he told Edgar Snow in 1936, "there are scarcely 4,000,000 industrial workers in China"—less than one percent of the country's total population of 450 million. In such a country, a revolution by the industrial proletariat stood no chance of success.[10] The failure of the Communist-sponsored uprisings in Nanchang and Canton in 1927 only proved this point.

Mao believed that the principal contradiction in Chinese society was the irreconcilable conflict between the landed class and the landless peasants. He boldly predicted in 1927, "In a very short time, in China's central, southern and northern provinces, several hundred million peasants will rise like a tornado or tempest, a force so extraordinarily swift and violent that no power, however great, will be able to suppress it."[11] "Agrarian Revolution" or rural communism was, therefore, the call of the day.

In Mao's opinion, the numerous rural rebellions in Chinese history showed that the peasants had a revolutionary potential. He emphasized, "The gigantic scale of such peasant uprisings and peasant wars in Chinese history is without parallel in world history." And casting the Chinese peasants' role in a Marxist mold, he continued, "These peasant uprisings and peasant wars alone formed the real motive force of

China's historical evolution."[12] To carry out rural revolution in contemporary China, Mao considered it imperative for the Chinese Communist Party to provide leadership to the peasants. It had to incorporate them in military units, train them to fight, indoctrinate them with correct ideology, and give them incentive to fight on by giving them land grabbed from the landlords.

Mao's idea of rural communism represented his innovation in Marxism for the sake of, as Zhou Enlai has said, applying it to China. Marx had argued that communist revolution could occur only in advanced industrialized nations. The proletariats in these nations constituted the majority of the people, and as a severely oppressed class, it was bound to rise up to overthrow the bourgeois class. Marx belittled the peasants' capacity for communist revolution, for they were illiterate, conservative in outlook, lacking class consciousness, and difficult to mobilize because they lived in scattered areas. But Mao rejected this notion of Marx's and proved that a communist-led peasant revolution could succeed in China.

The Guerrilla Warfare.—The success of rural communism in China could not be achieved without the seizure of political power by the Communist Party, which, as Mao has vigorously argued, required the pursuit of the guerrilla warfare. This subject is largely of Mao's invention, something Marx had never contemplated. The significance of Mao's writings on this subject goes far beyond the boundary of China. They fill the curriculum of military academies of the West; they have been since the mid1950s applied in many parts of the Third World, as will be discussed later.

Since this subject has been extensively treated in Chapter Three, no further reference to it is necessary here.

"On Practice."—In an essay under this title, Mao described the process of acquisition of knowledge in fairly simple terms: "The first step is ...perception [of the objective world]. The second step is the synthesis of the data of perception...[to form] conception, judgment and inference."[13] Knowledge thus acquired is of perceptual and judgmental types.

He went on to say that correct and valuable knowledge must derive from and be verified by practice: "Knowledge starts with practice, reaches the theoretical plane via practice, and then has to return to practice." Claiming that communism was a scientifically-based truth, he asserted, "Marxism-Leninism is considered true not only because...Marx, Engels, Lenin and Stalin scientifically formulated it but also because it has been verified in the subsequent practice of revolutionary class struggle and revolutionary national struggle."

Mao's proposition that knowledge must be based on practice is not, by itself, of any significance. The importance of the essay lies in the fact that the essay provided a justification for the need of adjustment of Marxism when it was applied to China. Moreover, the essay proved to be especially valuable to Mao in his exercise of political leadership, for he treated the long history of China as a rich record of practices and frequently made use of this record to substantiate his policy initiatives.

New Democracy.—One more important element of Mao's thoughts is his notion of "New Democracy." Writing an essay on this subject in 1940, Mao perceived the modern world to have gone through two fundamental revolutions.[14] One was "the democratic revolution" initiated by the bourgeoisie in the West in the 18th century, which Mao called the old democratic revolution. The other was "the socialist revolution" launched by the Soviet Bolsheviks in 1917.

Mao considered the Chinese Republican Revolution of 1911 as a bourgeoisie-sponsored movement, similar to that of the West. Beginning in 1927, as the Chinese Communists launched armed insurrections, a socialism-inspired revolution appeared. But the prevailing conditions in China did not permit a *full-fledged socialist revolution* to come to fruition because, as Mao had diagnosed, the Chinese society was dominated by semi-feudal and semi-colonial forces. Under the circumstances, the Chinese revolution had to proceed in two steps. "The first step is to change a society that is colonial, semi-colonial and semi-feudal into an independent, democratic society. The second stage is to develop the revolution further and build up a socialist society. In the present Chinese revolution, we are taking the first step." The first step led to establish a New Democracy, where "a coalition of several revolutionary classes" had to form a united front to accomplish the mission. The revolutionary classes meant proletarian forces—workers and peasants—*and* national bourgeoisie (capitalists in support of national independence). Thus, New Democracy was a stage between the old democratic revolution and a full-fledged socialist revolution; it was a stage at which Mao intended to draw as many non-communists as possible to the side of the communists.

The Great Leap Forward.—If Mao considered New Democracy as a system of government functioning only in a pre-socialist state, he had since 1949 proceeded at full speed to construct a socialist society. And with the introduction of the Great Leap Forward Movement in 1958, he even wanted China to leapfrog to a communist society—something neither the Soviet Union could then achieve nor Marx would have thought possible under the existing conditions of China. Yet, employing the crudest and harshest means conceivable, he attempted to reach that goal with the Great Leap.

It should be noted that though the Great Leap is a subject falling in the category of "policies" to be discussed in the next section of this chapter, it marks as a conspicuous part of Mao's political thoughts. And viewed as a whole, Mao's thoughts are radical enough to stand to the left of Marxism on the ideological spectrum.

Guidance through Sloganeering

Both Chiang and Mao were intimately involved in the formulation of policies for their regimes. To carry out their policies, they often used catchy phrases to capture and retain the attention of the people. These phrases were short, pointed, and rich in connotation. They functioned as slogans designed to guide the people to carry out the two leaders' policies. The slogans were frequently repeated in political pronouncements; etched out on government buildings, street walls, public monuments; or recited in political gatherings. Some of these phrases have formed the political vocabularies that the Chinese or even foreigners are familiar with today.

Chiang preferred to use four-word idioms—often in rhyme—to strike an impression on his countrymen. Some major examples are as follows:

"*Securing Domestic Unity before Resisting Foreign Aggression*" (*An Nei Rang Wai*).[15]—Soon following the Northern Expedition, China fell to a disunited country again while Japan stepping up unrelenting aggression against the country. As leader of the National government in Nanjing, Chiang adopted this phraseology to reveal his policy on how to handle the twin crisis.

Within the country he faced then military challenges from five directions. In the northwest, Yan Xishan and Feng Yuxiang, two prominent warlords once collaborating with him in the Northern Expedition, posed renewed threat to the Nanjing government; in Henan in north central China, the warlord Shi Yousan was plotting for revolt; in Jiangxi in south central China the Communists had been in rebellion; in Canton in south China, Chiang's opponents within the Nationalist Party had set up a rival regime to challenge his rule; and in Hunan, the province next to Jiangxi, the authorities were wavering in their loyalty to Nanjing (CKSD, 8/16/31). The threat from Japan, in the meantime, was serious and aggravating. Since it defeated China in the war of 1894, it had occupied Korea (a China-protectorate), grabbed Taiwan, seized a portion of Shandong, stationed forces in Manchuria, and harbored an ambition to conquer the entire country.

Under the circumstances, Chiang reasoned that his domestic foes posed an imminent threat to his regime while Japan's drive to conquer the entire country remained a distant possibility. He further reasoned that if his regime fell to his domestic foes, the country would sink to a total chaos without a new government capable of coping with the Japanese threat. If, on the other hand, he could reestablish unity of the country by first defeating his domestic opponents, he would gain time to prepare for war with Japan later. He opted for taking on his domestic enemy before fighting Japan and revealed his choice to the nation in a speech in July 1931.

Many of Chiang's countrymen, however, sharply differed with him. They believed that the Chinese should not fight each other while foreign aggressors threatened the existence of the country. The public sentiment against Chiang's policy rose sharply after the Japanese army forcefully wrested away Manchuria from China in the Mukden Incident of September 18, 1931.

Believing that his policy choice was in the best interest of the nation, Chiang persisted in fighting his domestic foes, particularly the Communists, for several years until the occurrence of the Xi'an Incident in 1936 forced him to change course, as described in the previous chapter.

"Propriety, Righteousness, Modesty, Honor" (Li Yi Lian Chi).—These four Chinese words constituted the behavioral guide that Chiang would like his countrymen to follow when he launched the New Life Movement in 1934. His adoption of this guide owed to his conviction that Western nations' century-long aggression against China had caused a persistent spiritual decline of the Chinese people. The salvation of the country did not lie merely in modernizing the country's economy and army but also in strengthening the moral fiber of the Chinese people. That could be done only with a revival of the traditional moral precepts, of which *"Propriety, Righteousness, Modesty, Honor"* were the epitome. This idiom appeared in many of Chiang's speeches and, also, in the form of inscription—in his calligraphy—on government and school buildings during Chiang's rule on the mainland and Taiwan.

"Fight the War of Resistance to the End" (*Kang Zhan Dao Di*).—When the Chinese-Japanese war broke out on July 7, 1937, Chiang

was for a time uncertain as to whether Japan intended to seize only north China or to conquer the entire country (CKSD, 7/8-12/37). But as he soon concluded that Japan was pursuing the latter objective, he decided that China had to resist such an attempt with a total war. On July 19 he issued a statement at Lu Shan, Jiangxi in which he used the expression "*Fight the War of Resistance to the End*" to convey to the Chinese people that this was the policy they had to follow unequivocally.

Chiang wanted his countrymen to grasp two important connotations of this expression. First, if Chiang had attempted to avoid war with Japan before July 1937, he now saw war as the only solution of the long broiling conflicts between the two nations. Chiang took his stand on the war not easily, for he faced at this critical juncture opposition within and without his government. Several top Nationalist leaders believed that China could not win the war and, hence, argued for a pursuit for peace. Among these were, surprisingly, Yu Youren, head of the Control Yuan, and Ju Zheng, head of the Justice Yuan; both were known as highly patriotic to the nation (CKSD, 12/26, 27, 29/37). In the academic community, prominent scholars such as Hu Shih and Jiang Menglin also expressed reservation about the war. Chiang's fighting-the-war-to-the-end expression was intended to neutralize the opposition and to rally all Chinese behind him in what appeared to him a life-or-death struggle with Japan.

Second, as to be seen in Chapter Ten, Chiang's policy was anchored on a "Trade Space for Time" strategy as a way to deal with a superiorly-armed Japan. With China's vast landmass, Chiang thought his country could afford to lose its territories gradually to the enemy so that it could win time for two possible advantages. One, foreign powers might join China to fight Japan; and two, Japan might give up fighting because of exhaustion from a prolonged war.

"*Meet Injustice with Magnanimity*" (*Yi De Bao Yuan*).—Japan's defeat at the war in August 1945 brought enormous joy and relief to the Chinese. Yet the war had caused China damages unprecedented in the country's history. Tens of millions of soldiers and civilians had died and wounded, uncountable value of properties had been lost, and millions of families had been dislocated. It was at this time that Chiang asked his countrymen to forgive Japan's misdeeds. With this expression serving as a guide to China's post-war policy to Japan, he saw to it that Japanese soldiers and residents in China rapidly and completely repatriated to their homeland; in addition, he renounced Chinese claim against Japan for war reparations. This policy immediately caused considerable anguish to those Chinese suffering from the Japanese wartime atrocities, such as the

Nanjing Massacre in 1937. And, today many Chinese still question the wisdom and appropriateness of the policy in view of Japanese government's subsequent denial of responsibility for the aggressive war and adulteration of school textbooks to cover up war crimes.

"*Anti-Communism and Resisting Russia*" (*Fan Gong Kang E*).—In the 1950s, as the Nationalists were driven out of the mainland to Taiwan, Chiang coined this expression to enunciate a fundamental policy of his exiled government: He was committed to continuing the fight against the Chinese Communists; and since he regarded the Chinese Communists had been operating under Russia's direction, he treated Russia as an enemy nation as well, whose aggressive actions in China had to be resisted. This expression, together with another expression he adopted, "*Counter-attacking the Mainland*" (*Fan Gong Da Lu*), was the slogan most frequently appearing in his speeches and policy statements at the time.

"*Forget not [We Are] in the City of Ju*" (*Wu Wang Zai Ju*).—In the Warring States Period of ancient China (475-221 BC), the Kingdom of Qi lost most of its territory to the Kingdom of Yan but held on to only two cities, one of which was Ju. Using it as a base for recovering the lost land, Qi's general Tian Dan took five years' laborious preparations to drive Yan's army out of Qi. Chiang likened his plight in Taiwan to this historical event. He inscribed this idiom on the summit of Mountain Tai Wu in Quemoy—Taiwan's forward base against the Communists on the mainland—as a constant reminder to his followers that they should never forget their mission to recover the mainland.

"*Meet Fateful Change with Equanimity*" (*Chu Bian Bu Jing*).—In November 1971 when U. S. President Richard Nixon stunned the world with his announcement of seeking normalization of relations with China, Chiang received the news only hours in advance. For most of the previous three decades, the U. S. had been a staunch supporter of the Chiang regime. Yet, Nixon, a persistent, strong anti-Communist American leader, could so drastically reverse American policy by reconciling with the Chinese Communists and implicitly dumping Taiwan as an ally.

Such a reversal of American policy threw the future of Taiwan to uncertainty and increased the possibility of a Communist takeover of the island. Chiang invoked the phrase, *Meet Fateful Change with Equanimity* to calm down the dispirited public on the island. Chiang also paired this expression with another one, "*Be Self-respectful, Be Self-reliant*" (*Zhuang Jing Zi Qiang*), as a way to cope with the crisis. The people in Taiwan, however, have since subsumed the second expression under the first as Chiang's response to the unsettling international relations.

Some of Chiang's idioms stirred up controversies lingering for decades (for example, *Securing Domestic Unity before Resisting Foreign Aggression*); others won enthusiastic support of his countrymen (*Fight the War of Resistance to the End*); still others generated no policy consequences but evoked sympathy from devoted friends and sarcasm from determined foes (*Meet Fateful Change with Equanimity*). But regardless of how people reacted to these idioms, Chiang had persistently invoked them for the enforcement of the policies they encapsulated. As a result, they faithfully reflected what he stood for during his rule in China and in Taiwan; they were better remembered by his countrymen than were his numerous policy speeches and statements.

Chiang's choice of classical words to form his policy directives is contrasted to Mao's preference for lively, colorful, and, at times, earthy expressions to grab public attention, as seen in the examples below.

"*Revolution Is Not the Same as Inviting People to Dinner*" (*Ge Ming Bu Shi Qing Ke Chi Fan*).—In defining the meaning of revolution, Mao came up with this graphic phraseology in 1927. He followed this expression with a statement: "A revolution is an uprising, an act of violence whereby one class overthrows another. A rural revolution is a revolution by which the peasantry overthrows the authority of the feudal landlord class.... To put it bluntly, it was necessary to bring about a reign of terror in every rural area...."[16] This statement provided a sure justification for Mao and his followers to embark on a bloody path to power.

"*Political Power Comes from the Barrel of the Gun*" (*Qiang Gan Zi Li Chu Zheng Quan*).—In April 1927 the Chiang Kai-shek regime in Nanjing purged the Communists from the Nationalist Party in the area under its control. In the following July Chiang's rival regime in Wuhan under the leadership of Wang Jingwei also expelled the Communists, which had been hitherto in alliance with it. Thus ostracized and driven to underground, the Communist Party held an emergency meeting on August 7, 1927 in Wuhan to decide upon the future course of action. At the meeting, Mao used this expression to explain why he decided to resort to arms to gain power. He believed that the Communists' agitation tactics—propaganda, demonstrations, sporadic uprisings, and strikes—

would not help them gain power. They had to use the gun to topple the Nanjing government and to create another one. The expression speaks of the historical truth of how the founding government of nearly every nation comes into being.

"*When We Can Win, Fight; When We Can't, Run*" (*Neng Da Jiu Da, Bu Neng Da Jiu Pao*).—As elaborated on in the previous chapter, Mao's guerrilla strategy was one principal reason, among others, for the success of his 22 years' drive to create the Communist regime in China. In this period of time, his guerrilla fighters grew from a thousand to several million under extraordinary difficult circumstances; they were for most of the time short of ammunition and food, outnumbered by better equipped enemy forces, and, very often, scattered and isolated over wide areas of mountains and hills. As a result, each guerrilla band had to rely on its own resources and its own judgment to decide upon whether to carry out a military engagement. Mao's shorthand expression cited here constituted the most vital tactical guidance he offered to his guerrillas. With the expression drilled into their consciousness through repeated combat, the guerrillas became masters of their own destiny in the battlefield.

"*25,000-li Long March*" (*Liang Wan Wu Qian Li Chang Zheng*).—In 1934 when the Communist army broke out of the Chiang's fifth encirclement campaign to escape from annihilation, Mao and his army were really beating a humiliating retreat. Yet Mao could use the expression of "Long March" to convert the public perception of what was a military disaster to a courageous mission. He explained:

> The Long March is...a manifesto. It proclaims to the world that the Red Army is an army of heroes.... The Long March is also an agitation corps. It declares to the approximately two hundred million people of eleven provinces [along the route of the Long March] that only the road of the Red Army leads to their liberation....The Long March is also a seeding-machine. It has sown many seeds in eleven provinces, which will sprout, grow leaves, blossom into flowers, bear fruit and yield a harvest in the future. To sum up, the Long March ended with our victory and the enemy's defeat.[17]

"*Paper Tiger*" (*Zhi Lao Hu*).—Perhaps no expression of Mao's has received as much attention in the West as this three-worded folksy remark Mao made in an interview with American correspondent Anna Louise Strong in 1946. He asserted with relish, "The atom bomb is a paper tiger which the U. S. reactionaries use to scare people. It looks terrible, but in fact it isn't. Of course, the atom bomb is a weapon of mass slaughter, but the outcome of a war is decided by the people, not by one or two new types of weapon."[18] He affirmed this people-over-weapon idea by citing the Chinese civil war experiences: "Take the case of China. We have only millet plus rifles to rely on, but history will finally prove that our millet plus rifles is more powerful than Chiang Kai-shek's aeroplanes plus tanks."[19]

In a 1958 speech at the Politburo of the Communist Party, Mao talked further on this point. Calling "imperialism, feudalism and bureaucratic capitalism in China" as reactionaries, he pointed out that the Chinese people took more than a century's time and sacrificed tens of millions of lives to defeat them all. "Were these [reactionaries] not living tigers, iron tigers, real tigers?" he asked. "But in the end they changed into paper tigers, dead tigers, bean-curd tigers."[20]

Mao addressed two audiences with his "paper tiger" expression. He was telling the Chinese not to be afraid of atomic bomb; he was implicitly calling upon America not to intimidate China with the weapon.

"The Chinese Have Stood up" (*Zhong Guo Ren Zhan Qi Lai Liao"*).—On September 21, 1949, Mao declared to the more than six hundred delegates of the Chinese People's Political Consultative Conference: "Accounting for one quarter of the population of the world, the Chinese have now stood up." Ten days later, on October 1, he stood on the Tiananmen Square to proclaim to a massive audience of 300,000 the founding of the People's Republic of China. He used this expression to mark the triumph of the Chinese Communists' decades-long struggle against his "reactionary" enemies: imperialism, feudalism, and bureaucratic capitalism. But many Chinese have taken it as more of a manifestation of a patriotic sentiment: the Chinese have risen up as a truly independent and robust people, being finally rid of the foreign domination and domestic decay.

"Resist America, Help Korea" (*Kang Mei Yuan Chao*).—Mao's "The-Chinese-Have-Stood-up" expression was immediately put to test in Korea. In June 1950 the North Korean army crossed the 38th Parallel to launch a surprise attack on South Korea. In response, the Japan-based American army came to the assistance of South Korea under the aegis of the United Nations. In October, fearing an American invasion of Manchuria, Mao threw a Chinese "Volunteer Army," numbered at 380,000 troops, to the Korean battlefield. And the war went into a stalemate that persisted to 1953 when an armistice agreement was signed by both sides.

The West has for years perceived the Korean War as a coordinated move of the Soviet Union, China, and North Korea to expand the Communist sphere in Asia. As to be seen in Chapter Eleven, a revisionist view suggested that China participated in the war really under the duress of Joseph Stalin, and that China sent its army to Korea as a preemptive defense of Manchuria from possible American invasion. Reading the Chinese history, one may find a number of precedents of Chinese military involvement in the Korean peninsula. In 1592, the Chinese imperial court of the Ming Dynasty dispatched as many as 200,000 troops to Korea to help it repel the invasion of Japan under the Hideyoshi regime. The war lasted to 1599 when the Japanese army was forced to withdraw. In 1894 the Chinese imperial court of the Qing Dynasty sent an army to Korea to help it resist, again, the Japanese invasion. But this time, the Chinese army was defeated, and Korea went under Japan's control.[21]

In the light of these precedents, Mao came up with the Resist-America-Assist-Korea slogan in 1950 to portray his policy as a patriotic, defensive move. With it, he summoned the Chinese to undertake the most dangerous task of battling the world's mightiest power.

"*The East Wind Prevails over the West Wind*" (*Dong Feng Ya Dao Xi Feng*).—In his December 1949 visit with the Soviet Union, Mao reaffirmed his "lean to the one side" statement that he had made in the previous June. That statement marked his acceptance of the Soviet Union as the leading nation in the Communist camp in the emerging Cold War. In November 1957, Mao went to the Soviet Union for a second time—to attend meetings celebrating the 40th anniversary of the Bolshevik Revolution. At this time, the revolts against the Communist rule in Poland and Hungary had been put down, and the Soviet Union had astounded the West by outpacing the United States in space exploration by launching the world's first satellite, the Sputnik. In the meantime, China had registered considerable progress in its massive Socialist reconstruction program. Speaking with unbounded euphoria, Mao expounded on his East-Wind thesis. He upheld again the leadership position of the Soviet Union in the Communist camp, evinced a sense of solidarity among all Communist parties, whether they were in power or not, and offered the prospect of an eventual establishment of a Communist order all over the world and the demise of capitalism in the West.

"*Let One Hundred Flowers Bloom*" (*Bai Hua Qi Fang*).—By the mid-1950s, the Chinese Communist Party had been firmly planted in power, weathered the tough test of the Korean War, and registered impressive progress in economic reconstruction. Yet, at the same time, China had experienced what Mao called serious "contradictions," as evidenced by numerous labor strikes in the country in 1956. At a meeting of provincial party secretaries in Beijing in January 1957, Mao proposed the "Let One Hundred Flowers Bloom, Let One Hundred Schools Contend" campaign as a way to handle the contradictions. Subsequently known as the "Two-Hundred" Movement (or best remembered as "One Hundred Flowers Bloom" campaign), this term came from an expression that was current in the Spring and Autumn times (770-476 BC). At that time, China's intellectual community enjoyed unprecedented freedom and productivity, with the existence of one hundred schools, each of which advanced a distinct line of thought.

Mao used the expression to initiate a two-sided campaign: one was intended to rectify three problems of the Communist cadres: Subjectivism, Sectarianism, and Bureaucraticism, and another was to solicit the non-Communists public, particularly intellectuals and minority political parties, to identify the Communist Party's faults, errors, and failures. He invited the public to criticize the party as "sharply as possible" and repeatedly assured the critics of their exemption from any retribution.

But the invited criticisms became sweeping, severe, and even threatening to the Communist regime. Mao halted the campaign and turned around to initiate a new one—the anti-Rightists campaign, which will be discussed in Chapter Nine.

"The Great Leap Forward" (*Da Yao Jin*).—The Great Leap has two connotations. Mao used the expression as an ideological statement, asserting boldly that communism was realizable in China of his time. He also saw it as an instrument to tame the masses, as will be discussed in Chapter Nine. Here, we will focus on Mao's use of the expression to reveal the means by which China could establish a communist society. He believed that a country could create a communist society only when it possessed as well as equitably distributed abundant material supplies of life to its people. In his view, Britain and the United States possessed sufficient material supplies for establishing communist societies but failed to do so because of their lack of equitable distribution of these supplies to the people. Thus, he set as goals for China to match the national output of Britain and the United States in some twenty years and to advance from its existing system of egalitarian economic distribution (relative equal pay and rations of living necessities) to a higher plane.

"The Cultural Revolution" (*Wen Hua Da Ge Ming*).—In the aftermath of the Great Leap, Mao became a very discontented man. He

condemned the contemporary Chinese culture for still retaining feudalistic features. He fell out with many of his senior colleagues for their following the Soviet Revisionist policy of reconciliation with the West and for their revival of the capitalist way of economic development. Above all, he agonized for having lost power to his rivals—Liu Shaoqi and Deng Xiaoping and their followers. In 1966 he initiated the Cultural Revolution as a clarion call to summon the Red Guards for random destruction of the old Chinese culture and restoration of his political supremacy.

A More Powerful Communicator

Both Chiang and Mao wiggled the bamboo-barrel pens to write down shortened or extended messages to their countrymen. They differed vastly in the way of delivering their messages as well as in the content of their messages.

Using a formalistic language, Chiang tended to address his audience in a manner of providing instructions or exhortations in a top-down style of communication. His favorite expressions such as, for example, "Propriety, Righteousness, Modesty, and Honor," "Meet Fateful Change with Equanimity," and "Forget not [we are] in the City of Ju" look like composition topics assigned to students from their teachers. They sound abstract, their meaning being liable to different interpretations by different people. But Chiang was a tenacious person. Through constant repetition of his messages, he tried to drill his intended meaning into the consciousness of his subordinates, civilian and military alike. For others, particularly the illiterate public, he relied on his subordinates to constantly verbalize his messages to them—whether or not they could fully comprehend them.

Mao favored the vernacular language in most of his writings. His messages, therefore, were easily verbalized and understood by the illiterate public. When addressing his audience, he seemed to be engaged in a two-way conversation. The political terms or slogans he coined were expressive, colorful, able to strike a lasting impression on his listeners. Indeed, who among his guerrilla fighters could forget "When we can win, fight; when we can't, run"? And who among his domestic as well as foreign foes could fail to be struck by such terms as "the Great Leap Forward" and "Paper Tiger"? Mao was, no doubt, more effective in communicating his ideas to his audience than was Chiang—perhaps more effective as well than the Great Communicator that Ronald Reagan was known to be.

Taking the content of Chiang's and Mao's writings as a whole, we may see that they centered on two different themes. Chiang's writings focused on the principle of morality. To himself, his subordinates, and the general public, Chiang exhorted incessantly the need for restoration of the traditional moral precepts; he believed that only with these precepts faithfully followed by the Chinese could they proceed to build a modern, prosperous, and strong nation. In contrast, Mao's writings concentrated on the search for political wisdom necessary for the solution of the problems at hand, with little concern for the issue of morality.

It is of interest to point out that one popular Chinese expression is especially pertinent to the discussion here: "The moral man loves mountain; the wise man loves water" (*Ren Zhe Le Shan; Zhi Zhe Le Shui*). Chiang had a penchant for sojourns in mountains. His early life in the Siming Mountain around his hometown; his frequent visits to Lu Shan in Jiangxi in the 1930s and 1940s; his prolonged residence in Yangming Mountain in Taiwan—all these are well-known facts. Mao swam in the Xiang Jiang around his hometown in his youth years; he plunged into the stormy sea near Beidaihe in Hebei to "battle the wind and waves" in 1956; he kept a swimming pool in his Beijing residence beginning in 1958; he swam crossed the Yangzi River near Wuhan in 1966—all these have become celebrated events as well.

Chiang pondered on morality in the mountains; Mao groped for political wisdom around water. How uncannily this popular expression applies to the thought patterns of the two Chinese political leaders!

NOTES

[1] Fairbank and Goldman, *China, a New History*, pp. 155-56.

[2] Chiang Kai-shek, *China's Destiny and Chinese Economic Theory* (New York, Roy Publishers [1947]), pp. 99-100.

[3] Ibid., p. 40.

[4] The citizens' code of conduct consists of: "1. Loyalty and bravery are fundamental to patriotism; 2. Filial piety is fundamental to a sound family; 3. Benevolence and love are fundamental to rightful personal conduct; 4. Faithfulness and righteousness are fundamental to one's professional achievement; 5. Harmony and peace are fundamental to proper social relations; 6 Propriety is fundamental to the rightful work attitude; 7. Obedience is fundamental to discipline; 8. Diligence and frugality are fundamental to public service; 9. Tidiness and cleanness are fundamental to good health; 10. Being helpful to others is fundamental to happiness; 11. Scholarship is fundamental to service to the humanity; and 12. Persistence is fundamental to success." These guidelines were at first applied to members of the Nationalist Party.

[5] Chiang Kai-shek, *Soviet Russia in China, A Summing up at Seventy*. Taipei: China Publishing Company, 1969.

[6] Ibid., p. 26.

[7] Ye Yonglie, *Mao Zedong yu Jiang Jieshi* [*Mao Zedong and Chiang Kai-shek*] Vol. 2 (Taipei: Feng Yun Shi Dai Chu Ban Gong Si, 1993), p. 371. For the transition of power from Zhou Enlai to Mao Zedong in the crucial year of 1935, see Gao Wenqian, *Wan Nian Zhou Enlai* [*Zhou Enlai's Later Years*] (New York: Ming Jing Chu Ban She, 2003), pp. 53-60.

[8] Stuart R. Schram, *The Political Thought of Mao Tse-tung*. New York, Praeger, 1972, c1969; and Stuart R. Schram, ed., *Mao's Road to Power: Revolutionary Writings 1912-1949*, 7 volumes, Armonk, NY: M. E. Sharpe, 1992. Secondary sources on Mao's thoughts may be found in the Chinese-Communist-Party-compiled *Zhong Gong Zhong Yang Wen Jian Xuanji, 1921-1949* [*Selected Documents of the Central Committee of the Chinese Communist Party, 1921-1949*], 18 volumes; *Jian Guo Yi Lai Zhong Yao Wen Xian Xuan Bian* [*Collection of Selected Important Documents since the Founding of the State, 1949-1966*], 20 volumes; and *Jian Guo Yi Lai Mao Zedong Wen Gao, 1949-1976* [*Mao Zedong's Manuscripts since the Founding of the State, 1949—1976*], 13 volumes.

[9] "On Contradiction," *SW*, II, 13-53. All citations from "On Contradiction" below are from this essay except otherwise noted.

[10] Snow, *Red Star over China*, p. 439.

[11] Mao, "Report of an Investigation into the Peasant Movement in Hunan," *SW*, I, 21-22.

[12] Mao, "The Chinese Revolution and the Chinese Communist Party," quoted in Schram, *Political Thought of Mao*, p. 262.

[13] *SW*, I, 282-97. All subsequent quotations from "On Practice" on these pages are from this essay.

[14] *SW*, III, 106-56. All subsequent quotations from "New Democracy" on these pages are from this essay.

[15] In its Chinese version, this expression originally consists of six words: *Rang Wai Bi Xian An Nei*. The four-word version has been in popular use.

[16] *SW*, I, 27.

[17] *SW*, I, 161-62.

[18] *SW*, V, 100. Mao made the point that people, rather than weapons, decided the outcome of war as early as 1938. See *SW*, II, 192.

[19] *SW*, V, 100-01.

[20] *SW*, V, 98-99.

[21] See, Hsü, *Understanding Chinese History*, pp.146, 164, 218-19.

PART THREE

THE ART OF THE POSSIBLE

Chiang Kai-shek and Mao Zedong used the gun and the pen as their principal means of governance of the nation. They also used a great variety of other, supplemental means in the exercise of power. Grouped as the art of the possible, these means included manipulation of others' emotions, desires, and preferences; methods assuring the allegiance of the people, especially their subordinates; spy warfare; and managing contradictions of different groupings. Some of these means are endemic to the Chinese culture; others may have been invented by these leaders; still others are used by all types of political leaders. These means shall be treated in the following four chapters, with two chapters devoted to each of the two leaders' art of the possible.

CHAPTER SIX

CHIANG, APPEAL TO EMOTIONS

Chiang Kai-shek frequently formed family-centered relationships with people not linked to him by blood or marriage; he often made elaborate effort to pay respect to people on their birthdays or at their funeral services. By actively engaging in these kinds of activities, he created an emotion-bonded social network with which he attempted to secure people's acceptance of him as the rightful national leader, to strengthen his rule of the country, and to enlarge the scope of his political following.

All in the Family

Sworn Brotherhood

As mentioned in Chapter One, Chiang was fond of forming sworn brotherhood with his friends or political associates.[1] Sanctioned by a long Chinese tradition dating back to eighteen centuries ago, sworn brotherhood is formed through a ritualistic ceremony in which the participants exchange the required protocols (called *Jinlan Pu* or Gold-Orchid Covenant).[2] The protocols contain the participants' biographical information and their signed oaths, pledging friendship and mutual assistance throughout their lives.

Listed below are Chiang's sworn brothers, the purposes he had in mind when engaging them, and the evolution of their relationship afterwards.

Ten Brothers of Fenghua.—While a teenager, Chiang swore to brotherhood with at least nine other youths from their native county, Fenghua, Zhejiang Province. Most of these were unknown to the public, but some did participate in the anti-Manchu or anti-Yuan Shikai movement and served in middle-rank or lower positions in the Chiang regime.

Chen Qimei and Huang Fu in 1911 in Shanghai.—Chen was a prominent leader of the Republican Revolution under whom Chiang served as a military officer in the early 1910s. Huang was also a military officer involved in the Republican Revolution. The three people exchanged protocols in Shanghai in the year the Wuhan Uprisings occurred; they pledged to "live and die together and help each other whether in safety or in danger" for the cause of the Revolution. Chiang was fiercely loyal to Chen, and when Tao Chengzhang, another revolutionary leader, challenged and severely criticized Chen, Chiang was so enraged that he hired men to have Tao assassinated. In 1916 Chen was himself assassinated, as widely suspected, by agents of Yuan Shikai.

After Chiang came to power, Huang became his top diplomat. Often engaging in difficult and treacherous negotiations with Japan in the 1930s, he received much public condemnation for the concessions he had to make to the Japanese militarists under Chiang's then appeasement policy. Being faithful to Chiang, he silently accepted the blame and died in 1936 with regret for the diplomatic role he had played. When the Chinese-Japanese war occurred in 1937, Chiang issued a proclamation posthumously honoring Huang as a national hero.

Huang Fu and Zhang Qun in 1911 in Shanghai.—Huang Fu participated in a sworn brotherhood ceremony with Chiang a second time within the year of 1911, now with Zhang Qun as the third participant. In the early 1900s Zhang and Chiang were cadets in both the Baoding Military Academy in north China and the Zhenwu Military Academy in Japan. After Chiang became the national leader in 1928, Zhang served on a series of high posts in Chiang's government, including Foreign Minister and Prime Minister. For nearly seventy years, Zhang remained one of Chiang's closest friends and confidants.

Zhang Jingjiang and Xu Chongzhi in 1916 in Shanghai.—Zhang was a financier, having made his fortunes in China and France; he provided Sun Yat-sen with critically needed funds during the Republican Revolution. He came to know Chiang in 1911 and persuaded Chiang and Xu Chongzhi to form sworn brotherhood with him in 1916 for the cause of the anti-Yuan Shikai Movement. He immediately became one of Chiang's most trusted confidants, with timely, shrewd advice during Chiang's spectacular rise in the Nationalist leadership rank in the 1920s. He also provided Chiang with financial assistance and formed a stock brokerage house with Chiang in Shanghai. In the late 1920s he served on several key posts in the Chiang regime, including governor of Zhejiang Province. But he stepped out of politics in the 1930s and died in New York in 1950.

Xu Chongzhi was a follower of Sun Yat-sen and once served as his Military Minister. He subsequently became the commander of the

Second Army in Guangdong, under whom Chiang served as a staff officer. In 1925 when Chiang, as Commandant of the Whampoa Military Academy, launched the Eastern Expedition, Xu, then still a commander of the Guangdong army, joined the campaign. In 1926, Chiang took over all of Xu's troops on account of Xu's dereliction of duties and sent Xu to Shanghai for retirement. In the late 1920s, Xu joined the rank of Chiang's opponents but remained in the periphery of the political arena; he died in Hong Kong in 1965.

Chen Zhaoying in 1916 in Zhangzhou, Fujian Province.—A participant in the Republican Revolution and the Anti-Yuan Shikai Movement, Chen struck friendship with Chiang when both served in the army in the 1910s in Fujian. In the Chiang regime, Chen served on several high-level positions, mainly in the Nationalist Party. Beginning in 1948 Chen served as a member of the Control Yuan, a branch of Chiang's government with power to discipline public officials for wrongful acts. He stayed on that post until 1977 when he died in Taiwan.

Dai Jitao in 1920 in Shanghai.—Like Zhang Qun, Dai was a life-long friend and confidant of Chiang's. They became acquainted in 1908 in Tokyo and became sworn brothers in 1920 in Shanghai. When Chiang was languished in the military service in the late 1910s and the early 1920s, Dai constantly furnished him with advice on how to advance in his career; he also often reprimanded Chiang for untoward personal behavior. Later, he became an ideologist, authoring treatises to re-interpret Sun Yat-sen's political philosophy, decisively leaning to the right. In 1928 Chiang appointed him head of the Examination Yuan in charge of civil service examination; Dai held that post for the following twenty years. In 1949 he stunned Chiang and many Nationalists with a totally unexpected suicide. He took the drastic action as an expression of his ultimate loyalty to his sworn brother, then on the verge of losing mainland China to the Communists.

Dai was widely known as the biological father of Chiang's second son, Wei-kuo, who was born to a Japanese woman unmarried to Dai. Unable to acknowledge the parentage of Wei-kuo, reportedly because of his wife's objection, Dai entreated Chiang to adopt the child as his son. On account of his friendship with Dai, Chiang agreed.

Wu Zhongxin in 1921 in Guilin, Guangxi Province.—A follower of Sun Yat-sen since the early 1910s, Wu participated in the Republican Revolution and the Anti-Yuan Shikai Movement as a military officer. In 1921 he formed sworn brotherhood with Chiang, witnessed by Xu Chongzhi. After Chiang became the national leader in 1928, he served on several administrative positions in the Chiang government, including governorship of Anhui and Guizhou provinces. In 1936 he was appointed Chairman of the Commission on Mongolian and Tibetan Affairs and had since actively extended the influence of the Chiang government to the tribal territories in the northwestern and southwestern parts of China. In 1940, he represented the Chiang government in the enthronement ceremony of the 14th Dalai Lama—the one exiled to India since 1959—in Lhasa, Tibet. He died in 1959 in Taiwan, being then a presidential counselor to Chiang.

Shao Yuanchong in 1923 in Moscow.—Shao made acquaintance with Chiang in the 1910s during the anti-Yuan Shikai movement. In 1923, when Chiang headed a military mission to the Soviet Union, Shao came from Great Britain, where he was on a political tour, to join the mission. There, in Moscow, the two swore to brotherhood with an exchange of protocols (for the text of the protocols, see Note 2 of this chapter). Since the late 1920s Shao served on several administrative positions in the Nationalist Party and in the Chiang government, including Acting Head of the Legislative Yuan. During the Xi'an Incident in 1936 he was with Chiang and was shot dead by the mutinous soldiers in his failed attempt to escape.

Li Zongren in 1926 in Changsha, Hunan Province.—Head of a military faction based in Guangxi Province, Li pledged allegiance to Chiang during the Northern Expedition in 1926. In that year, at Chiang's solicitation, Li formed sworn brotherhood with him; they signed an oath, stating, "As comrades and as compatriots, we have identical political orientation, being willing to live and to die for it."

Both Chiang and Li had ulterior motives in forming sworn brotherhood. Chiang intended to use the brotherhood to induce Li to place his troops in the army under Chiang's direct command. Li wanted to use his connection with Chiang to expand his political influence. In 1927, during the Northern Expedition, Li fell out with Chiang and joined other commanders that forced Chiang to step down as Commander-in-Chief of the National Revolutionary Army. After Chiang's resumption of his post in 1928, Li fought battles against Chiang in 1928-1930 either alone or in alliance with two other warlords, Feng Yuxiang and Yan Xishan. In 1937, on the eve of Chinese-Japanese war, he returned to the fold of the Chiang government, and in the following year his army won a major battle against Japan in Taierzhuang, making him a famous national hero.

In 1948 Li campaigned for the position of vice president of the Nationalist government. The campaign signaled his undeclared intention to rally a political following in opposition to Chiang. He won the election in spite of Chiang's determined objection. In the following year, as Chiang stepped down as president in consequence of Communists' military victory in north China, Li served as acting president in charge of peace negotiations with the Communists. Unsuccessful in the negotiations, Li went into exile in the United States in 1949, where he remained until 1965 when he returned to China to pledge allegiance to the Communists. He died in Beijing in 1969.

Feng Yuxiang in 1928 in Kaifeng, Henan Province.—A warlord deeply entrenched in northwestern China, Feng fought battles against other warlords in the 1910s and early 1920s. In 1927 Chiang cut a deal with Feng in Xuzhou, Jiangsu Province, whereby Chiang provided the Feng troops with 500,000 silver dollars of financial assistance in return for their participation in the Expedition and Feng's support of Chiang's purge of the Communists from the Nationalist Party then in progress.

In 1928, in a ceremony held in Kaifeng, they signed an oath in which Feng declared, "We are forming sworn brotherhood to promote an ideology [Sun Yat-sen's *The Three Principles of the People*]. We are willing to do so even we have to die with our bodies dismembered." Correspondingly Chiang pledged, "We will help each other while in safety or in danger; we will share pleasure and hardship. We will never change our mutual commitment in our lives even when the sea goes dry and the rock turns rotten."

The reality was that they abandoned their mutual commitment right afterwards. In 1930 Feng and Chiang fought against each other in "the Great War of Central China"—a fiercely fought battle that also found Yan Xishan, another warlord, on Feng's side. Aided by far superior firepower and manpower, and with the critical and timely assistance of Zhang Xueliang, the warlord in Manchuria, Chiang totally routed Feng's army within the year while Yan was forced to retreat to his home province, Shanxi. From then on Feng became an opponent of Chiang's but served off and on in the Chiang government, gradually leaning to the left. In 1949 he died in a fire accident on a ship in the Black Sea following a tour in America and Europe.

Zhang Xueliang in 1930 in Nanjing.—Son and successor of Zhang Zuolin, the Manchuria-based warlord who died from a reportedly Japanese-plotted accident in 1928, the Young Marshal, as Xueliang was popularly known, pledged token allegiance to Chiang within the year. In 1930, when Feng Yuxiang and Yan Xishan fought Chiang in the Great War of Central China, the two warlords as well as Chiang assiduously courted for the Young Marshal's alliance. In the end Zhang took Chiang's side—for two reasons. One was that Zhang considered Chiang the most likely Chinese leader to unite the war-torn country, a prerequisite for war with Japan to avenge his father's death. No less important than this consideration was the fact that Chiang made very generous offer to the Young Marshal, via Zhang Qun, that the two warlords could not match. It included 1. Supply of $5 million to Zhang's army units for deployment from Manchuria to north China; 2. Issuance of a $10 million-bond by the Chiang government for monetary reform in Manchuria and other purposes; 3. Authorizing Zhang to exercise administrative control of north China; and 4. Subsidies to Zhang's troops for stationing in Beijing and Tianjin.[3]

Accepting these offers, the Young Marshal sent some of his army units to north China, posing a threat to Feng and Yan at their back while they were battling Chiang on the front. Though never participated in the fighting, Zhang's army contributed to Chiang's victory in the Great War. Grateful for the Young Marshal's critical assistance, Chiang welcomed him to Nanjing in 1930, and there they exchanged protocols for sworn brothers.

Chiang and the Young Marshal almost immediately fell to a prolonged, fateful, and turbulent relationship. In 1931, while the Japanese army forcefully seized Manchuria, the Young Marshal hurriedly withdrew all his troops there to north China without a fight. The Chinese public vociferously condemned him for his ignominious retreat, and he and Chiang went into an acrimonious argument as to who should take the blame for the disaster. In 1936 the Young Marshal, together with General Yang Hucheng, staged the Xi'an Incident to force Chiang to abandon his appeasement policy toward Japan and to stop fighting the Communists. In the aftermath of the Incident, the Young Marshal was placed under house arrest under Chiang's orders for military insubordination. Released in 1990, he had been in detention for 54 years, considered the world's longest-confined political prisoner of his time. He migrated to Hawaii and died there in 2001 at the age of 100.

Altogether Chiang formed sworn brothers with more than twenty people in the period from the early 1900s to 1930. He apparently stopped doing so with others since. Aside from his *Ten Brothers of Fenghua,* twelve of Chiang's sworn brothers were men of great prominence. Of these, eight were basically high civilian administrators, with a brief stint in the army in their early careers: Chen Qimei, Huang Fu, Zhang Qun, Zhang Jingjiang, Chen Zhaoying, Dai Jitao, Wu Zhongxin, and Shao

Yuanchong. Of these eight, Chen Qimei, Zhang Jingjiang, Dai Jitao, and Zhang Qun served over different periods of times as Chiang's closest political associates and steered him to the right path to power: to introduce him to Sun Yat-sen, to induct him to the Nationalist Party, to persuade him to accept the offer of the position of Commandant of the Whampoa Military Academy—an offer he was initially reluctant to take. They also furnished counsel critical to the resolution of a number of crises Chiang was involved in: The Zhongshan warship crisis of 1926, his split with the Communists in 1927, his forced resignations from Nationalist leadership position in 1927, 1931, and 1949. In return, Chiang appointed them to high-ranking positions (prime ministers, cabinet ministers, and provincial governors).

The other four sworn brothers were of strong military background, each having commanded tens of thousands or troops: Xu Chongzhi, Li Zongren, Feng Yuxiang, and Zhang Xueliang. In forming sworn brotherhood with them, Chiang was motivated by a specific objective at a specific time, as noted above. But Chiang won their friendship or allegiance only temporarily, with all of them turning against him later in their lives and seriously threatening his leadership position or even his life. In contrast, his association with the eight civilian sworn brothers had stood the test of time. They were unswervingly loyal to him to the end of their lives.

Pseudo-Family Relations

Sworn brotherhood is a formal and ritualized extra-familial relationship Chiang had formed. He also sought to forge informal pseudo-familial relations with a vast number of his political and military associates by treating them as if they were his relatives. His treatment of these people was often manifested in the way in which he addressed them.[4] For his associates senior to him by one generation, he would address them uncles or use similar salutations. For instance, he called Sun Yat-sen as "Teacher Zhong," considering himself Sun's student (Zhong is Sun's middle name; in Chinese custom, a teacher is accepted as a person belonging to the parental generation of the teacher's students). In a letter to his son Wei-kuo, dated January 28, 1922, Chiang referred to Sun as Wei-kuo's granduncle.[5]

For most of his associates who were senior to him in age (not in generation), Chiang would address them, in correspondence or in oral expression, as "My Elder Brothers." Occasionally he would address his associates even junior to him in age in the same way. In such case, the salutation was intended as an expression of politeness. For subordinates who were junior to him in age, he might address them as "My Younger Brothers." When addressed as such, the individuals concerned would feel deeply satisfied and honored, for such an expression manifested Chiang's acceptance of them as part of his extended family.

Chiang treated many of his cadets at the Whampoa Military Academy, when he served as its Commandant in the 1920s, as if they were his family members of a younger generation. During the Eastern Expedition 1925 he composed a poem stating that he was "leading personally three thousand family soldiers" (*qin shuai sanqian zidi bing*). For cadets who graduated from the Academy afterwards, he was fond of characterizing their relationship as one of "principal and students" (*xiaozhang yu xuesheng*). Many of these cadets respected him like a fatherly figure; and he trusted them as if they were his sons. And when they failed to carry out his orders in the battlefield, he scolded and harangued them but seldom levied harsh disciplinary actions against them unless they betrayed his trust by defecting to the enemy.

Honoring the Dead[6]

More so than any other Chinese political leader of his time, Chiang took very elaborate actions to honor prominent or worthy individuals on their "life and death occasions." An Suping, who has extensively studied Chiang's practice in this regard, aptly summarized it:

> To show favors to his subordinates, to ingratiate with his colleagues, to win over his opponents, Chiang Kai-shek paid close attention to their "life and death" occasions. "Life" refers to the occasions when these individuals and/or their parents celebrate their birthdays; Chiang would send over congratulatory messages and favor them with gifts. "Death" refers to these individuals' funeral services, at which he would make elaborate arrangements to honor them....Thus, other people's life and death occasions would provide him with opportunities to gain political advantages.[7]

For people steeped in traditional Chinese culture, they all showed great respect to their friends, associates, and even some opponents on the occasion of their birthdays or funeral services. For Chiang, he appeared to take more seriously how to honor the dead than how to celebrate the living. He did so because of a cultural preference of the Chinese society. Honoring the dead at the end of a person's life allows the society to make a final expression of appreciation of the deceased. A person's funeral service is often conducted like a religious rite, which can last from one day to several days or even more than one month. Birthday of an individual, on the other hand, marks only a milestone in the person's life, not the end of it. Birthday celebration is the occasion for conviviality and can be renewed in the future.

To honor the dead, Chiang offered eulogies as the first order of business, which took a variety of forms: "eulogy statements, mourning telegrams or letters, short condolence messages, eulogistic couplets, eulogistic plaques, elegiac poems, stele statements, posthumous order of merit, posthumous order of commendation," and so on. In Chinese cultural practices, eulogistic couplets and eulogistic plaques are the most important forms of expression by the living to the dead. Couplets are composed of two short statements that denote the accomplishments of the dead and the sentiments of the living toward the deceased. Plaque is invariably inscribed in four words that capsulate the deceased's status from a historical perspective. The composition of both couplets and plaque inscriptions demands a great deal of literary skills.

No complete tabulation of the number of eulogies—in various forms—from Chiang is available, but An Suping has collected texts of Chiang's eulogies for more than 300 persons and has estimated that the total number of Chinese individuals being honored with Chiang's eulogies at 1,200 and foreign dignitaries, at 1,000.

Chiang honored the dead for various purposes. The most conspicuous one was for recognition of patriotism and bravery of military personnel. Since Chiang was involved in wars most of his life, he was continuously and passionately involved in the military memorial services at the end of each war and also on the Nationalist Memorial Day, March 29, each year. Particularly worth noting was his recognition of top military commanders dying in action. On May 1, 1940, Lieutenant General Zhang Zizhong perished in the battlefield in Hubei Province, the first casualty of such high ranking officer in the Chinese-Japanese war. Chiang ordered to have Zhang's coffin ship to the war capital Chongqing, nearly 1,000 kilometers away. Upon its arrival, Chiang crouched over it and bitterly cried. On May 28, he presided the funeral services, with his hand-written eulogistic plaque bearing the inscription, *Zhonglie Qianqiu* (loyalty and valor shining for a thousand years) prominently displayed. At the time of Zhang's death in 1940, his wife, Li Minhui, reportedly did not immediately learn about it. When she did, she committed suicide by stopping eating for seven days as a way to honor him. The event shocked the nation, and an elaborate memorial service for her was also held in the nation's war capital, at which Chiang had his personally-written eulogistic plaque bearing the inscription "*Xiangcheng Zhongjie*" (twice demonstrated loyalty and heroics) displayed in the center of the service platform.

Chiang never failed to honor the death of his senior military officers whenever he learned about it. In 1964, he issued an Order of Commendation to the family of General Tang Yisheng, who died in a battle with the Chinese Communists eleven years earlier, in 1953. In 1969, he issued an Order of Commendation to the family of General Tai Minchuan, Commander of the Fifth Guerrilla Column, who had died in the war with Japan 29 years ago, in 1940!

"Honoring the dead" was a practice Chiang could use to win over his opponents. For instance, when Zhang Zuolin, the Manchuria-based warlord, died in 1928 from a reportedly Japanese plot, Chiang immediately dispatched a personal representative, Fang Benren, to participate in Zhang's funeral services. On that occasion, Fang persuaded Zhang's son and successor, Zhang Xueliang, to pledge allegiance to Chiang on the ground that a united China under Chiang would provide the Young Marshal with the best chance to avenge against the Japanese for his father's death. Fang's persuasion made an emotional impact on the Young Marshal, who loved his father dearly. This was one factor contributing to the Young Marshal's conversion to the Nationalist cause.

Speaking of the Young Marshal, we may note one related episode that reveals how seriously Chiang treated the dead from war. Prior to the Xi'an Incident, the Young Marshal took extraordinary care in preparation for kidnapping Chiang, who was protected by hundreds of best-trained, heavily armed bodyguards. Aside from assigning a large unit of assault force for the mission, the Young Marshal deliberated for days on selecting the most suitable officers to lead the unit. He ended up with two officers, one of whom was Liu Guiwu, a regiment commander known to be a sharpshooter. He administered a series of improvised tests to see if Liu was fit for the job and was satisfied with his selection.[8] As it happened, Liu successfully executed the mission, with Chiang's bodyguards nearly completely wiped out and Chiang captured. Zhang promoted Liu subsequently to a general in commander of a cavalry division.

Following the Xi'an Incident, Chiang did not punish Liu but, instead, let him keep his job. Two years later, in 1938, as Chiang learned of Liu's death in the battlefield in the Chinese-Japanese war, he wrote a highly touching eulogistic couplet to honor the general at the funeral services. His magnanimity toward a former rebel, who might have killed him, earned the admiration of the public.

Another major warlord Chiang dealt with was Yan Xishan, the Shanxi-based military chieftain who lost to Chiang in the Great War of Central China in 1930. Following Yan's retreat back to Shanxi with his forces firmly entrenched there, Chiang took a special trip in 1934 to visit Yan to appease his former enemy. He also made a point to pay a courtesy call on Yan's father, Shutang, who resided in a village. There Chiang took off his hat, bowed three times to the senior Yan, and addressed him as uncle. Shutang, a villager being so much honored by the national leader, was overcome with emotion. He humbly requested Chiang to "provide guidance to Xishan." As Shutang soon died, Chiang ordered a solemn funeral service in 1935, authorized $100,000 to fund the rite, and issued a eulogistic couplet to honor him.

Being a filial son, Yan Xishan was deeply grateful to Chiang for showing such respect to his father. He was never to fight Chiang again. Instead, he let many of his top military and civilian aides, including Fu Zuoyi, Shang Zhen, Xu Yongchang, Jia Jingdei, and others serve in the Chiang government—as field commanders or cabinet ministers. In 1960 as Yan died in Taiwan, Chiang personally presided Yan's funeral services and issued a eulogistic plaque.

Chiang paid special attention to the death of preeminent scholars, who command high respect in Chinese society, and of other important personalities. Over several decades academic luminaries such as Cai Yuanpei, Hu Shih, Qian Mu, and many others all received upon their death prompt and fitting eulogistic plaques from Chiang, who, in most cases, attended their funeral services. In 1933, when Dalai Lama the 13th died in Tibet, Chiang dispatched to Lhasa a delegation of high-ranking officials to pay attribute to him. In 1951, as Du Yuesheng died in Hong Kong, Chiang promptly sent off to the Du family a eulogistic plaque. This was an unusual move on the part of Chiang, for Du had gained domestic and international notoriety as head of the Green Gang in Shanghai from the 1920s to 1940s. He was reportedly to having helped Chiang in 1927 in the purge of Chinese Communists and assisted prominent personalities in the 1940s to escape from Japan-occupied areas to Chongqing. In awarding Du a eulogistic plaque, Chiang considered it less important to keep his own reputation as an upright national leader than to give appropriate recognition of Du's political deeds. The plaque bore the inscription, *Yi Jie Yu Zhao*, (chivalry and fidelity deserving recognition).

As expected, Chiang sent well-scripted condolence messages to foreign leaders such as U. S. presidents Franklin D. Roosevelt and Dwight Eisenhower at their deaths. What was totally surprising was that Chiang responded in 1946 with respect and feeling to the death of Joseph Stilwell, who had blatantly sought to replace Chiang as the military leader of Chinese armed forces during the Chinese-Japanese war. Chiang sent off a condolatory telegram to the Stilwell family, presided Stilwell's memorial service in Nanjing, wrote a eulogistic couplet, and issued an Order of Commendation, detailing the general's contributions in the China and Burma war theaters.

Chiang's response to the death of Mahatma Gandhi in 1948 provides another illustration of the careful attention he paid to the passing of an important foreign personality. Chiang first sent off to India's Prime Minister Jawaharlal Nehru a condolatory message and attended a memorial service in Nanjing at which he honored the Indian national hero with a eulogistic plaque. On the plaque was his handwritten inscription, *Nai Sheng Nai Ren*. These simple four words aroused much discussion as well as praise in China and India. They meant literally "being saintly, being benevolent," but the Chinese words *sheng* and *ren* have a much richer connotation than the translated words in English. To erudite Chinese classicists, this inscription met three criteria for the best-composed eulogistic plaque: being literary and artistic, being fitting to the life and deeds of the dead, and being in rhyme.

Indian scholars familiar with Chinese classics rated the inscription as better written than the thousands of eulogies Gandhi received from his own countrymen. One China hand in India regarded the inscription as best exemplifying the essence of Confucianism as well as of world humanism, and he coined a four-word Chinese phrase to pay tribute to the Chinese leader, which reads, in Chinese, *Nai Wen Nai Wu* (being scholarly, being soldierly).

Though seeing a political utility in his services for honoring the dead, Chiang always showed extraordinary care and, on many occasions, deep sincerity in rendering the services. In spite of the huge volume—in the thousands—of various forms of eulogies he delivered, he often took a personal hand in drafting the messages himself. He then went through the drafts again and again, revising them word by word as necessary, until he was fully satisfied that they conformed to the correct literary style as well as were appropriate to the status of the individuals concerned.

Sometimes Chiang became intensely emotional at funeral services. He could cry out loud and wail long when sighting the coffins of the dead. He did so uncontrollably at the services of Chen Qimei (Chiang's mentor and sworn brother) in 1916, Sun Yat-sen in 1925, General Zhu Peide in 1937, and General Zhang Zizhong in 1940. His emotional outbursts, which often came unexpectedly, evoked a spontaneous response of sobs and tears from many others at the services.

Celebrating the Living[9]

Chiang paid close attention to birthdays of his colleagues, subordinates, and prominent personalities—and their relatives. In 1948 General Lei Wanting, Deputy Commander of the 12th Army Corps became distressed over a job reassignment ordered by Chiang. In a subsequent meeting with the Nationalist leader, he heard Chiang say, "I understand your mother is younger than I by two years. Her 60th birthday is soon coming up." Stunned and moved by Chiang's knowledge of his mother's birthday, Lei expressed deep appreciation to Chiang, who in turn said, "Go on with your new job and take care. I'll pay my respect to your mother when the occasion comes." And he did. In 1949 while deep in a gigantic battle of Huai-Hai (in eastern China) with the Communists, Chiang personally ordered a birthday party to be held for the mother of General Du Yuming, commander in chief of the Nationalist troops in the battlefield. Du was likewise surprised by Chiang's knowledge about his mother's birthday and fought the battle with ferocity, ending up with him being captured by the Communists.

Chiang handled many warlords to his advantage with birthday activities. The case of General Han Fuqu is illustrative. Han, once served under Feng Yuxiang, defected to the Nationalists, and Chiang rewarded him by placing Shandong and Henan provinces under Han's control. Yet, never sure of Han's loyalty to him, Chiang took steps to win over one key general under Han: Sun Tongxuan. He granted Sun tax collection authority in part of Shandong. Then, at the 70th birthday of Sun's father in 1933, Chiang sent over a felicitation message inscribed on six panels, together with a gift of $5,000 and his photo image with an inscription addressing Sun's father as his uncle and calling himself a nephew. Deeply touched by Chiang's gestures, Sun had since become a commander fiercely loyal to Chiang.

Two years later, Chiang took a further action to isolate Han. The occasion was the birthday of the mother of General Song Zheyuan, who, like Sun Tongxuan, once served under Feng Yuxiang and had ostensibly pledged allegiance to Chiang. Known to be deeply attached to his mother, Song hosted an elaborate birthday party for her in Beijing in 1935. Chiang and his colleagues in Nanjing took the occasion to forward numerous felicitation messages and gifts, making the party a national event. In the following year, when the military chiefs of Guangdong and Guangxi provinces mounted an opposition movement against Chiang, they attempted to persuade Song to join their side. Song not only rejected the request but also prevailed upon Han Fuqu, his former colleague under Feng Yuxiang, not to flirt with the opposition movement.

Chiang took time to honor the birthdays of Chinese and foreign dignitaries. What is unusual is he could repeatedly honor certain leaders with felicitation messages, gifts, or personal visit over a long period of time. He did so toward Yu Youren—head of the Control Yuan of the Nationalist government—every year from 1953 to 1964; toward Syngman Rhee, president of South Korea, from 1952 to 1960; and—to set a record—toward Japanese Emperor Hirohito from 1951 to 1968.

Prominent personalities, in all walks of life, also received Chiang's attention on their birthdays. Scholars like Hu Shih and Lin Yutang; Chiang's former schoolmasters such as Zhou Zhenqin and Mao Sicheng—all received "longevity plaques," gifts, or felicitation messages. And at the risk of tarnishing his reputation as a national leader, Chiang honored Shanghai's prominent gang leaders on their birthdays with "longevity plaques" and gifts: the 60th birthday of Zhang Xiaolin in 1936, the 60th birthday of Du Yuesheng in 1947, and the 80th birthday of Huang Jinrong in 1947. On each of these occasions, many of Chiang's government colleagues as well as Shanghai's citizens participated in the festivities, involving tens of thousands of people.

Whether acting as head of China as a familial nation or as an individual, Chiang pursued the four kinds of tradition-laden activities described above with diligence, persistence, and intensity. He projected an image of himself as a warm and concerned national leader in the Chinese familial nation. He created a vast social network that was cemented by reciprocal emotional bonds between him and others. He retained many of his sworn brothers as his closest political associates, with a life-long unswerving loyalty. He converted some of the warlords to his subordinates and neutralized the opposition of some other warlords.

NOTES

[1] Two principal sources of information are relied upon for this section: Yan Ruping, ed., *Chiang Kai-shek yu Jiebai Xiongdi* [*Chiang Kai-shek and Sworn Brothers*], Beijing: Tuan Jie Chu Ban She, 2002; and Yan Ruping, et al., "Chiang Kai-shek he Ta de Baxiongdi [Chiang Kai-shek and His Sworn Brothers]" *Zhongguo Gushi* [*Chinese Stories*], No. 162 (March 2004).

[2] Among the protocols of sworn brotherhood Chiang Kai-shek had signed, only the one he did with Shao Yuanchong is known to the public in its entire text, as follows:

"Chiang Zhongzheng, Kai-shek, 37 years old, born at noon on September 15, 1887 [Lunar Calendar], [in my] native place Xikou, north of Fenghua County. As signers of this protocol, Zhongzheng [and Shao Yuanchong] observe same moral principles, find our character compatible, follow traditions set by ancient sages, and now form an alliance of brotherhood. We will exhort each other on matters of morality and help each other while in safety or in danger, even under the most trying circumstances. Our bond is solid like gold or rock. Mountains and rivers can be changed but not our bond. If the signer violates this oath, he will be severely punished by God. This is our oath of alliance.

"To my younger sworn brother [Shao] Yuanchong

"Signed in Moscow, Chiang Zhongzheng, on November 16 in the 12th year of the Republic of China [1923]."

See, Yan, *Chiang Kai-shek and His Sworn Brothers*, p. 214.

[3] "Chiang Kai-shek and His Sworn Brothers," p.79.

[4] Chiang addressed his associates as "comrades" if they were not close to him.

[5] Mao, *Chiang Kai-shek prior to 1926*, p.144.

[6] Sources of information for this section of this chapter consist of two series of articles published in *Zhuanji Wenxue*, as follows: An Suping, "Chiang Kai-shek Leici Shuoxiao" [The Odds and Ends of Chiang Kai-shek's Eulogistic Messages] *BL*, No. 519 (August 2005): 4-21; No. 521 (October 2005): 47-59; No. 523 (December 2005): 54-71; No. 524 (January 2006): 48-66; No. 526 (March 2006): 112-31; No. 527 (April 2006): 53-73; No. 529 (June 2006): 51-66; No. 531 (August 2006): 84-100; No. 533 (October 2006): 74-89; No. 538 (March 2007): 102-18; and An Suping and Sheng Changwang, "Chiang Kai-shek de Renji Shijie" [Chiang Kai-shek's Social Activities], *BL*, No. 543 (August

2007): 19-41; No. 544 (September 2007): 41-59; No. 545 (October 2007): 111-22; No. 546 (November 2007): 88-109; No. 548 (January 2008): 94-108; No. 549 (February 2008): 81-100; No. 552 (May 2008): 102-10; No. 553 (June 2008): 95-109; No. 554 (July 2008): 76-88; No. 555 (August 2008): 108-19.

These articles, together with other materials, were later published as a book, when this author had already completed research on this subject: An Suping and Wang Changsheng, *Chiang Kai-shek Leici Shuoxiao* [*The Odds and Ends of Chiang Kai-shek's Eulogistic Messages*], Taipei: Zhuanji Wenxue She, 2009.

[7]An Suping, "Chiang Kai-shek Leici Shuoxiao," *BL*, No. 524 (January 2006): 58.

[8]One day the Young Marshal showed Liu a box he had just accidentally picked up. Suddenly the Young Marshal exclaimed that he suspected that the box contained a bomb, as a wisp of smoke was curling up out of it. Liu grabbed the box from the Young Marshal's hand and threw it away, which turned out not to be a bomb. The Young Marshal asked why Liu did not run away when sighting the smoke. Liu said he would never abandon his boss to his own devices in such a crisis. On another occasion, the Young Marshal unleashed a powerful thrust of his fist at Liu's chest. Liu did not dodge but asked why he did that. The Young Marshal said he wanted to see whether his officer could remain calm when being hit without provocation. Satisfied with Liu's loyalty and calmness, the Young Marshal confided to Liu that he wanted him to lead a force to kidnap Chiang. Shocked speechless for a moment, Liu said he would do it. The Young Marshal felt with his hand Liu's heart to see whether there was a burst of heartbeat and also Liu's legs to see whether they were trembling. Finding none, the Young Marshal took Liu to meet with Chiang so as to scout the national leader's temporary residence in a sprawling mountain retreat east of Xi'an. In the meeting with Chiang, the Young Marshal introduced Liu as one of his most meritorious officers who wished to see the national leader he had long admired. Then he excused himself, leaving Liu and Chiang alone to carry on the conversation. Following the meeting, Liu expressed gratitude to the Young Marshal for the trust his superior had placed in him, believing that Liu would not betray the kidnapping plot to Chiang.

Another officer selected for the mission was Sun Mingjiu, commander of Zhang's security guards, who gained national notoriety for having personally captured Chiang.

[9]For sources of this section, see Note 6, above.

CHAPTER SEVEN

CHIANG, WHAT IS MEANT BY CUNNING

In his earliest diary entries, Chiang Kai-shek repeatedly agonized over a character flaw he strove unsuccessfully to get rid of. That was *"ji zha,"* which means "opportunistic and deceiving"—or being cunning (CKSD, from January 1918 to April 1920). Indeed, viewing his political activities throughout his adult life, one has to agree with this self-characterization of his. In practicing the art of the possible, Chiang would make calculated moves to take advantage of every opportunity for political gains. He would use material incentives to convert adversaries to cooperative colleagues or subordinates, take resolute action to remove the most recalcitrant opponents, play the divide-and-rule game to assure his supremacy over those staffing his administration, party, and army, practice dictatorship in the guise of democracy, and manage insurmountable crises with a political withdrawal-and-comeback scheme.

Loyalty for Purchase

In politics, as in any other human undertakings, people are invariably susceptible to the influence of money. Aware of this human weakness, Chiang was fond of using the monetary resources he controlled to win over his opponents and to strengthen the allegiance of those serving in his regime. Numerous of his opponents were warlords, and it was to them Chiang dispensed the largest sums of money.

In 1925 when Chiang fought his first major battle as a Nationalist military leader against a revolutionist-turned-warlord Chen Jiongming, he had only 3,000 cadets from the Whampoa Military Academy directly answering his call. In 1926 as he started the Northern Expedition, he commanded a conglomerate army of 85,000 men. Within the year, two wavering warlords, Feng Yuxiang and Yan Xishan, threw their armies to his side, swelling his forces to 264,000 men. In the following two years, his army absorbed large chunks of forces from the defeated warlords, and in 1929, Zhang Xueliang pledged allegiance to Chiang's government in Nanjing, increasing the size of the Nationalist army to over one million men. Thus, Chiang's army grew from 3,000 men to one million in just five years.

The spectacular growth of Chiang's military power, however, did not allow him to fully integrate the troops of the former warlords into the army he commanded. He quickly realized that many former warlords not only craved for power but also had an insatiable thirst for wealth. He made numerous references to the subject in his diaries.

On August 19, 1929, Chiang indicated that his "subordinates"—including the former major warlords and their division commanders—constantly "asked for additional troops and money" to be placed under their control. On February 16, 1931, he complained, "All those coming to see me are asking for nothing but money. All those sending me telegrams are demanding nothing but to deliver the funds [I promised them]. Indeed, I have become our nation's greatest debtor. By owing them debts, I have become their slave." On February 16, 1936, he further observed, "What warlords and politicians are so greedy for is money." Yet, he felt, "As long as they ask [for money], it won't be a problem to handle." On August 13, 1937, he repeated this point by stating, "Giving out liberally small sums is the best way to satisfy others' unending thirst for money."

With the rich coastal provinces in eastern China under his control, Chiang was ready to use the resources he possessed to purchase these warlords' loyalty. He paid out to the warlords in various sums of silver dollars and, since 1935, *fa bi*, the legal tender issued by the Nanjing government.[1]

To Feng Yuxiang.—As previously mentioned, in December 1926 Chiang induced Feng's participation in the Northern Expedition with a supply of 500,000 silver dollars to his troops. In the following year, he "promised to authorize a $2 million monthly allowance to [him]" (CKSD, 6/21/27). In June 1929, he, aware of Feng's plan to move against him, contemplated, "I'm willing to offer him $5 million to go overseas" (CKSD, 6/12/29).

To Yan Xishan.—For years since Yan joined the National Revolutionary Army in 1926, Chiang subsidized the Yan army, which remained in Yan's home province Shanxi and northern China, never coming under Chiang's direct control. Chiang did not reveal the specific amount of the subsidies, merely noting that he regularly "authorized release of funds to Yan" (CKSD, 3/20/36). One would assume the amount not to be substantially different from that provided to Feng, since the two warlords possessed then comparable military power.

To Li Zongren.—Head of the Guangxi army, Li joined the National Revolutionary Army when the Northern Expedition started in July 1926. Like Feng and Yan, he retained practically complete control of his army and exercised dominant political influence in his home province, Guangxi. Until 1937, he had alternatively fought against and then pledged allegiance to Chiang, who subsidized him with funds off and on accordingly:

Li "accepted payment but refused to assume the post [offered to him]" (CKSD, 5/6/33).

Chiang: "Released funds to the Guangxi [Army]" (CKSD, 11/19/34);

"Provided the Guangxi Army with additional funds of $1 million, now totaling $3 million" (CKSD, 9/8/36); and

"Sent T. V. Soong a telegram for releasing funds for the Guangxi [Army]" (CKSD, 10/20/36).

To Shi Yousan.—Once under the command of Feng Yuxiang, Shi commanded an army centered in Henan Province and rebelled against Feng and defected to Chiang in 1929. In June, Chiang awarded the Shi army with $3 million and logistic supplies and, in addition, provided Shi personally $500,000.[2]

To Han Fuqu.—Another subordinate of Feng Yuxiang, Han was the military chief in Shandong Province; he received a check of $100,000 in 1929 from Chiang and defected to him in the following year.[3] In 1931, Chiang "sent a telegram to T. V. Soong to provide Han with $500,000" (CKSD, 7/21/31).

To Zhang Xueliang.—As previously mentioned, the Manchuria-based warlord received from Chiang a financial assistance package of $5 million in subsidies to Zhang's army and $10 million in bond for monetary reform in Manchuria.

To Chen Jitang's Air Force.—Chen headed the military and political authorities of Guangdong Province from 1929 to 1936. First collaborating with Chiang, Chen fought him in indecisive battles in the mid1930s on the southern flank of Chiang's forces. Chiang could not afford engaging major confrontations with Chen while facing more serious challenges from Feng Yuxiang and Yan Xishan in the north. Instead, he worked behind the scene to unseat Chen from power. In 1936 Chiang successfully persuaded—reportedly with a handsome amount of money—Chen's air force personnel, with 48 planes, to defect to the Nanjing government. In addition, Yu Hanmou, a major commander in the Chen army, defected as well. Chiang was elated:

"Thoroughly took over Guangdong's air force, thus doubling ours. This is a great achievement" (CKSD, June 1936, Month-end Review)!

Other generals also received payment from Chiang. For instance, Xu Chongzhi—commander of the Guangdong army—received from Chiang a gift of $300,000 in 1925 when he was packed off to Shanghai for retirement.[4] Duan Qiri, the general-turned prime minister of the warlord government in Beijing, received in 1928 "$20,000 as living allowance."[5] Chen Mingshu, a Guangdong-based general, received $1 million in 1931 for the expansion of the 19th Route Army then under his command.[6] In 1942, Sheng Shicai, a warlord-turned-governor of Xinjiang Province who had long resisted Chiang's rule in the province, received $100,000 before Chiang eased him out as governor.[7]

Many civilian leaders in rivalry with Chiang also were awarded with cash payment. Wang Jingwei, the top Nationalist leader losing out in power struggle to Chiang in the early 1930s, was generously subsidized by Chiang for several years in regular intervals. When Wang stopped by Hanoi in 1939 on his way of defection to the Japanese side during the Chinese-Japanese war, Chiang offered him via an emissary $500,000 to go overseas instead of defection.[8] Wang rejected the offer.

Chiang provided his faithful subordinates, military or civilian, with monetary incentives in addition to their regular pay. A sampling of the recipients may be listed: He Chengxun (a top general in the Northern Expedition and Governor of Hubei) (CKSD, 3/23/34), Chen Cheng (another Governor of Hubei, minister of war) and other provincial governors (CKSD, 12/23/34); Gu Zhenggang (a top Nationalist Party official) (CKSD, 12/28/40); Chen Bulei (Chiang's most trusted secretary and confidant) (CKSD, 12/5/42); Wu Zhongxin (Chiang's sworn brother, a top Nationalist administrator) (CKSD, 9/24/44); Yu Youren (Head of the Control Yuan) (CKSD, 11/16/45).

Chiang's "liberal" dispensing of largess to so many people understandably caused financial difficulties. From the late 1920s to the mid-1930s, he exercised effective control of the most affluent Chinese provinces, but these constituted only one third of the total. "In a discussion with T. V. Soong on the military expenditure," Chiang learned that "only $12,600,000 was available per month, with a shortfall of more than $3 million" (CKSD, 3/23/28).

As the finance minister of the Nationalist government from 1928 to 1933, T. V. Soong made strenuous effort to increase revenue. However, as an America-educated economist with attention to accounting rules, Soong was frequently at odds with Chiang on dispensing public funds, especially Chiang's free spending for courting his opponents. One million dollars to this, three million to that, they amounted to inordinate sums month after month. He at times asked Chiang to account for his expenditure and even refused to release requested funds, causing unending anguish to Chiang.

"T. V. Soong is a sly fellow, dodging his financial responsibilities," Chiang castigated in 1926 his future brother-in-law in no uncertain terms. "Under his pressure, I cannot do what I wish. It's an unbearable pain" (CKSD, 12/26/1926). In the next few years, Chiang and Soong constantly argued over financial matters, even after Chiang married Soong's sister, May-ling, in 1927. In 1930 as Chiang was battling with Feng Yuxiang and Yan Xishan while ingratiating with Zhang Xueliang for military assistance, May-ling jotted down a note on how she persuaded T. V. Soong to release the urgently needed funds to her husband:

> My husband was at pains requesting funds for military operations, but T. V. would not raise and release the funds. I talked to his [T. V.'s] face, "If you don't supply the funds, I will give you all my real estates and other savings for sale to raise the funds. For I am fully convinced that Kai-shek would die for his cause if he loses the battle because of lack of funds....In that case, I would die with him...." Deeply touched, T. V. released the funds (Quoted in CKSD, 7/19/30).

Chiang replaced T. V. Soong with H. H. Kung as finance minister in 1933, who served on the post until 1944. Kung, another brother-in-law of Chiang's, was compliant with Chiang's wishes, providing funds to Chiang whenever or whatever amount as asked. Yet, convinced that "success or failure in both politics and military affairs all depends on control of the finance" (CKSD, 3/17/31), Chiang was determined to have direct access to funds without a finance minister as intermediary. In July 1945 he told T. V. Soong, when the Director of the Central Bank of China became vacant, the successor "must absolutely follow my orders and be entirely trusted by me. This is something I learned from the bitter experiences of the last twenty years, which frustrated my military, political, and diplomatic policies" (CKSD, 7/25/45). Indeed, Chiang had since made all future directors of the bank directly answerable to him.

Chiang was initiated to the world of power and money early in his political and military career. From the Northern Expedition in 1926 to the onset of the Chinese-Japanese war in 1937 he learned that the growth of his power resulted from not only battlefield victories but also purchase of his opponents. Compared to military operations, conquering the enemy by money was perhaps preferable to battles, which involved bloodshed, uncertainty, and enormous expenditure. So in this sense, purchase is a cost-effective proposition, something that, as Robert T. Ames noted, has long been practiced in ancient China: "Political authority and purchase are the carriage of the ruler; rank and emoluments are the harness and bit of the minister."[9]

From Chiang's perspective, loyalty was to be purchased if possible or to be exacted by war if necessary. Chiang's concept of loyalty was personally focused, i. e., submission to his rule and avoidance of defection. Because he was unable to differentiate personally-directed loyalty and nation-directed loyalty, he considered his under-the-table monetary operations entirely legitimate and necessarily secretive. Such perception of the fusion of power and money is perhaps one factor accountable for the widely known corruption in his regime even though he himself was free from grafts as the political ruler.

Action of Removal

If an opponent could not be conquered by purchase or by battle, would Chiang be susceptible to method of surreptitious removal of him? Assassination is practiced in many societies—and as long as politics. In Western societies Julius Caesar of ancient Rome, Abraham Lincoln of the civil-war torn America, and John Kennedy of a vibrant modern democracy all died at assassins' hands. In early Republican China, several Nationalist political leaders were assassinated, including Chen Qimei, Liao Zhongkai, Song Jiaoren, and Zhu Zhixin. In the jargon of the Nationalist Special Service, assassination was known as *xing dong,* or action of removal.

As for Chiang, he was subject to numerous close-call assassination attempts, and it was a miracle that he survived them all.

One day in July 1925, as he was riding in a car in Canton with the Nationalist Party's flag on it, he ran into engine trouble and sped away in another car. After the chauffeur restarted the troubled car and rushed to catch up with him, a fusillade of shots hit the car, killing two bodyguards inside. The shooters assumed Chiang was still in the car. A few days later, Chiang ran into another incident, in which two individuals on the street tried to shoot at him when he was riding a car home, but Chiang's Chief Bodyguard, Mi Xi, shot first, killing one of them, with the other one apprehended.[10]

Still more incidents occurred. Walking in the hallway of the Nationalist Party's headquarters in Canton one day in 1925, Chiang, with his second wife, Ch'en Chieh-ju, at his side, came down to face a young uniformed officer. The officer drew a revolver from a folded newspaper and shot pointblank at Chiang, screaming, "You stole my cousin's army and shot his two best generals in cold blood; so take this!" Chiang's bodyguard jumped on him and deflected the bullet. The officer was identified as Xu Qi, cousin of Xu Chongzhi, commander of the Guangdong army.[11] Deep in the night of August 27, 1929, while staying at the residence of his mother-in-law, Mrs. Soong, in Shanghai, two men sneaked into his bedroom, aimed their guns at the sleeping Chiang, and were ready to pull the triggers. But Chiang's cough somehow scared them away. The attempted assassins were no other than his bodyguards, Chen Pengfei and Pang Yongcheng (CKSD, 8/27, 28/29). In June 1930, Chen Jitang, the Guangdong chieftain referred earlier in this chapter, sent three men to assassin Chiang in Nanchang, Jiangxi Province. Unsuccessful in their attempt, they were apprehended and executed.[12] In June 1931, Chiang was vacationing in Lu Shan, a mountain retreat in Jiangxi Province. One day as he was riding on a sedan chair to savor the scenery, one young man jumped out of a wooded area and opened fire, with the bullet hissing past Chiang's right ear. His bodyguards shot back, killing the man. Later the man was identified as belonging to an assassination gang headed by Wang Yaqiao, a labor union activist with a Leftist tendency, who faulted Chiang for following an appeasement policy toward Japan.[13]

Chiang was also target of foreigners' assassination plots. In 1943 Colonel Carl F. Eifler, an officer of the United States Office of Strategic Services (an American intelligence agency) attached to General Joseph Stilwell's staff in China, was under Stilwell's orders to find way to kill Chiang. Eifler went back to Washington, D.C. to experiment with a food poisoning method that could not be identified in an autopsy.[14] In the following year, General Stilwell authorized preparation for another plan to have Chiang killed, which was revealed 27 years later by the very person in charge of the plan, Frank Dorn. A senior American military aide to Stilwell, Dorn worked out a plan code-named "Blue Whale," based on the general's authorization following the Cairo Conference in 1943. Stilwell quoted President Franklin Roosevelt as telling him at the conference, "If you can't get along with Chiang, and can't replace him, get rid of him once and for all. You know what I mean. Put in someone you can manage."[15] The plan, as developed by Dorn, would involve dispatching an American military aircraft to fly Chiang to India in 1944 to inspect Chinese troops under training by Americans there. And the plane would run into "a faked accident," sending Chiang down to death over the Himalaya.[16] Both the Eifler and Dorn plans were not executed as the order for carrying them out never came.

If Chiang had been subject to so many assassination attempts, did he resort to the same tactics toward his opponents? Records indicate that he certainly did. As mentioned in the previous chapter, he personally planned out a plot to assassinate Tao Chengzhang—a rival of Chiang's mentor and sworn brother Chen Qimei.

After he rose to power, Chiang is said to have authorized assassination of a variety of political foes, as described in detail in a book by Wen Jun et al. A number of cases, which bear close scrutiny later on, are summarized below.[17]

Yang Xingfu.—A Harvard University-educated scholar, Yang established a reputation as one of the earliest advocates of human rights in modern Chinese history and constantly criticized Chiang as a dictator. He was killed in 1933 at Academia Sinica—the highest national research institute of the Nanjing government—where he served as a principal researcher.

Shi Liangcai.—A top journalist and owner of a Shanghai newspaper, *Shen Bao*, Shi frequently published essays to oppose Chiang's policies of suppressing the Chinese Communists and appeasing the Japanese militarists. In 1934, he was shot dead in his car on the way to Shanghai from Hangzhou, Zhejiang Province.

Zhang Jingyao.—A former governor of Hunan Province, Zhang was actively involved in the Japanese effort to create the puppet Manzhouguo in Manchuria. He was assassinated in a hotel in Beijing in 1933.

Ji Hongchang.—A general in the Feng Yuxiang army, Ji participated in the Northern Expedition; he opposed Chiang's policy of compromise with the Japanese militarists. He joined the Chinese Communist Party in 1932 and was shot and wounded in Tianjin in the French Concession in November 1934; he was extradited to Beijing, where he was executed.

Wang Yaqiao.—As noted earlier, he headed a group of professional killers and was involved in the plot to assassinate Chiang in Lu Shan in June 1931. In April 1932, he instigated a Korean Youth, Yoon Bong-Gil, for a bombing attack at a party celebrating Japanese emperor's birthday in Shanghai. Mamoru Shigemitsu, Japan's minister to China, was wounded, losing a leg. In 1933, he masterminded a plot to shoot Wang Jingwei in Nanjing, who was wounded and survived. In 1936 Wang Yaqiao was killed in an ambush by the Nationalist Special Service agent in Wuzhou, Guangxi Province.

Xuan Xiafu.—A Communist Party member since 1923, he was a graduate of the Whampoa Military Academy and rose to Lieutenant General during the Northern Expedition. Going open with his Communist identity, Xuan differed sharply with Chiang on many policy matters and actively promoted Communists' United Front policies. In 1937 he was kidnapped in Xi'an by the Nationalist Special Service and was subsequently killed.

Tang Shaoyi.—Educated at Columbia University, Tang served in 1912 as China's first prime minister in the Beijing government following the Republican Revolution. In 1937, the Japanese militarists courted him to organize a collaborationist cabinet during the Chinese-Japanese war. He was axed to death in Shanghai by a Nationalist Special Service agent, Li Ada.

Wang Tianmu.—In pre-Chinese-Japanese war years, Wang headed the Nationalist Special Service's station in Tianjin, undertaking underground work against the Japanese in north China. In 1939, two years following the outbreak of the Chinese-Japanese war, he defected to the Japanese side when heading the Shanghai station of the Nationalist Special Service. The Nationalist Special Service soon retaliated by killing him in Shanghai.

Wang Jingwei.—While Wang was in Hanoi in 1939 on his way of defection to the Japanese side during the Chinese-Japanese war, several Nationalist Special Service agents sneaked into his temporary residence at night and attacked. Wang escaped death but one of his principal aides, Zeng Zhongming, was killed.

Fu Xiaoan.—A businessman and banker, Fu collaborated with the Japanese occupation authorities by serving as mayor of Shanghai in 1938. In 1940 Zhu Shengyuan, Fu's decades-long servant, killed him with a kitchen knife while he was asleep at night.

Shi Yousan.—Shi was an army man working under warlords Feng Yuxiang, Yan Xishan, and Zhang Xueliang at one time or another; he also joined the Nationalist and Communist armies successively. He defected them all one by one, earning the epithet "the Defection General." In 1940 while he was collaborating with the Japanese army, General Gao Shuxun of the Nationalist army, a sworn brother of Shi's, trapped him at a meeting and buried him alive by the bank of the Yellow River.

Li Gongpu and *Wen Yiduo*.— In the mid1940s both Li and Wen were leaders of the Democratic League (*Minzhu Tongmeng*), a leftist organization opposing the Nationalist monopoly of power and Chiang's foreign and domestic policies. On July 11, 1946, Li was shot on the street in the city of Kunming, Yunnan Province and died soon afterward. Wen was a well known poet and literary figure serving on the faculty of a number of prominent universities. On July 15, at Li's memorial service in Kunming, he delivered an impassioned eulogy under the title "The last speech" to condemn the Nationalists. He was shot dead right after the speech.

Yang Jie.—A participant of the Republican Revolution of 1911, Yang served on many high military and diplomatic posts under Chiang, including President of the Army College and Chinese Ambassador to the Soviet Union. After the Second World War, he leaned gradually to the left and started to form a political force with other Nationalist dissidents in opposition to Chiang. On August 23, 1949, while in Hong Kong reportedly on the way to join the soon-to-be-established Communist regime, he was shot dead in his temporary residence.

Wen Jun and his associates identified in their book the Nationalist Special Service agency to have carried out most of these assassinations. The agency has a checkered history, emerging from such informal organizations as the Lanyi She, the Fu Xing She, and the Li Xing She.[18] In 1932, a formal organization was established in the Central Military Commission, known as the Secret Investigation Bureau (*Mi Cha Zu*). In 1938 the Bureau was reorganized and enlarged into the Military Investigation and Statistical Bureau (popularly known as the Jun Tong), with Dai Li as its head. A separate agency, the Investigation and Statistical Bureau of the Nationalist Party (known as the Zhong Tong), was also created as part of the organization of the Nationalist Party. The Jun Tong, was renamed as Bao Mi Ju (The Security Agency) in 1946 and placed under the jurisdiction of the National Defense Ministry. The Zhong Tong was renamed as Diao Cha Ju and placed under the jurisdiction of the Ministry of Internal Affairs following the Nationalists' retreat to Taiwan.

The book by Wen and his associates claimed that Chiang authorized all these cases of assassination and other ones. Judging by other works on the Nationalist secret service agencies, one may challenge the claim. Some of the assassinations were carried out as part of Nationalist military operations, with or without Chiang's authorization.[19] These include Zhang Jingyao, Tang Shaoyi, Wang Tianmu, Wang Jingwei, Fu Xiaoan, and Shi Yousan.

As for the cases of assassination of Chiang's intellectual critics, such as Yang Xingfu, Shi Liangcai, Li Gongpu, and Wen Yiduo, the Nationalist secret services might have taken "the action of removal" on their own as a sycophantic measure to please Chiang, who was known to have been enraged by the criticisms from his opponents. Some former members of the Jun Tong and the Zhong Tong have presented evidence to this effect.[20] With regard to the assassination of Li Gongpu and Wen Yiduo specifically, Chiang was outraged by it. Considering it an act of sheer stupidity, he ordered a thorough investigation of the matter. The investigation revealed that Huo Kuizhang, Commander of the Yunnan Garrison Command, authorized the action and that two of Huo's subordinates carried it out. Chiang relieved Huo of his position and had his two subordinates executed.[21]

The way in which Chiang handled the cases of assassination of his intellectual critics raises questions. In the specific case of Li Gongpu and Wen Yiduo, he did not punish the principal culprit, Huo Kuizhang, in a way fitting the seriousness of the crime; in other cases, he did not make an effort to apprehend the assassins. As a result, the suspicion that he condoned the use of drastic means to remove his determined intellectual dissidents lingered in the public mind.

Looking at the ways in which Chiang dealt with his opponents over the years, one may summarize them in the following verses:

> If you can't befriend your opponents, battle them;
> If you can't defeat them, buy them;
> If you can't buy them, remove them;
> If you can't remove them, live with them.

Divide and Rule

The Nationalist Party has been infested with factions almost since its inception in the 1910s; they proliferated in the 1920s after the death of Sun Yat-sen.[22] Ample evidence indicates that Chiang manipulated them, with relish, to facilitate his rule. However, following his retreat to Taiwan in 1949, Chiang banned all factional politics, regarding it as one cause of his loss of the mainland to the Communists. He placed all reins of power gradually in the hands of his son Chiang Ching-kuo as he groomed him as his successor.

During Chiang's rule on the mainland, five principal factions existed: the CC group, the Political Studies group, the Whampoa group, the Kung-Soong group, and the security services group. With one exception, these groups did not have formal structures and tended to center around influential personalities as their leaders. The CC group was named as such as it was derived from the surname in English of Chen Lifu and Chen Guofu, the two brothers heading the group. The Political Studies group was headed by Zhang Qun, with other top administrative and financial ministers such as Wu Guozheng, Weng Wenhao, Chen Yi, Huang Fu, and Chang Kia-ngau as its members. The Whampoa group consisted of high-ranking military officers who were instructors—such as He Yingqin—and early graduates—such as Hu Zongnan—of the Whampoa Military Academy. The Kung-Soong group was headed by H. H. Kung and T. V. Soong—Chiang's two brothers-in-law. And, the security services group was further divided into the Military Investigation and Statistics Bureau and the Central Investigation and Statistics Bureau of the Nationalist Party—the Jun Tong and the Zhong Tong, as described earlier. From the 1930s to 1946, the Jun Tong was headed by Dai Li, and the Zhong Tong, by Xu Enzeng and his successors. Only the Jun Tong and the Zhong Tong possessed formal structures as apparatus of, respectively, the Central Military Commission and the Nationalist Party.

These groups maintained a functional division of—with occasional overlapping—responsibilities. The CC group was in charge of organization of the Nationalist Party and the civilian administration. In addition, its members dominated two electoral organs of the national government: the National Assembly and the Legislative Yuan. The Political Studies group, much less cohesive and smaller in its political reach than the CC, furnished candidates for high-level administrative, diplomatic, and financial posts. The Whampoa group normally concerned itself with appointment of corps, army, division commanders and established fellowship and camaraderie among themselves on the basis of classmate relationship. The Kung-Soong group controlled public banks and government-managed corporations, with a say in foreign affairs. Kung and Soong were often in rivalry, with clearly separate entourages staffing the key positions of the banking and business institutions they respectively dominated. And the security services group maintained its presence within all units of the Nationalist regime: administrative, diplomatic, military, and intelligence. The function of intelligence was broadly defined, covering wide-ranging activities such as intelligence gathering, counter-intelligence, political action (assassination), police, and anti-smuggling. The Jun Tong grew a far more powerful agency than the Zhong Tong and maintained extensive underground network in Japanese-occupied Chinese territory during the Chinese-Japanese war.

Chiang made use of a number of devices to insure that these groups serve as his compliant instruments of governance. Foremost of these was to keep the power of appointment of important positions to himself, never allowing the head of any group to usurp it. While he would not permit one group to spill into the function of another group, he might himself appoint members of one group to positions in another group's purview. For instance, H. H. Kung and T. V. Soong of the financial group both served as prime ministers; Weng Wenhao of the Political Studies group was appointed prime minister in 1948 specifically in charge of monetary reforms.

Juggling appointments required a delicate hand. Two episodes illustrate Chiang's skillful manipulation of the factions to achieve his objectives. Both episodes concern one key Nationalist official, Wu Guozheng, a Political Studies member who joined Chiang's staff in the 1930s and had since then risen, successively, to Mayor of Hankou, Chongqing, and Shanghai; Vice Minister for Foreign Affairs; and Governor of Taiwan.

In 1941 as Mayor of Chongqing, the wartime Chinese Capital, Chiang assigned him responsibility for air defense of the city, intruding into the jurisdiction of the army. In a heavy air raid on June 5, Japanese warplanes bombed shut the air vents of a huge bomb shelter, causing thousands of deaths from suffocation. Upon hearing the news, Wu was seriously worried for being charged for dereliction of duties because the shelter was not well built to withstand the attack. When facing a crisis of this kind, Wu normally resorted to a superstitious practice for divination of what was in store for him. It was known as *cezi*: telling one's fortune from clues of a chosen Chinese word. Wu asked his wife to say a word. Then in bed, she fortuitously mentioned the word "*zhang*," 帳, or bed curtain. Wu was astounded and blurted out, "It is a terrible omen. It means the mayor will lose his head." "Mayor" in Chinese is written as 市長. And 帳 consists of two components, 巾長. 巾 differs from 市 in that it is short of a top part; hence, it could mean the mayor was to lose his head. Wu's wife was equally astonished and hurriedly asked him to think over the word again. Wu pondered and then said he might escape from the disaster unscathed. For 帳 could be interpreted to mean that the city, 市, was losing its top, but that the mayor, 長, remained intact.

Chiang summoned Wu the following day and angrily chastised him for not properly maintaining the bomb shelter and issued an order to strip Wu from the position of mayor but kept him on the job—until the order was lifted. Chiang knew the army was actually in charge of air defense, and Wu could not perform his job with complete discretion. To pacify Wu, Chiang later invited him as a guest to a banquet Chiang hosted in honor of some personality; he also allowed Wu to continue as mayor.[23]

The second episode occurred a year later. At that time Chiang had in mind to appoint Wu as vice foreign minister but knew the appointment would be opposed by H. H. Kung, the then prime minister, and might not be endorsed by T. V. Soong, the foreign minister, either. This was so because both Kung and Soong had their preferred candidates. Meeting with Soong one day on the subject of appointment, Chiang did not say he favored Wu for the position but instead offered Jiang Tingfu—a highly respected historian—as the candidate. As Chiang had expected, Soong would not agree, for Jiang was Kung's candidate. In a subsequent meeting with Soong, Chiang raised the issue of appointment again. Before Soong had a chance to recommend his preferred candidate, Hu Shizhe, a professional diplomat, Chiang suggested Wu for the post. Uncomfortable with the idea of twice rejecting Chiang's candidates, Soong accepted Wu; and Kung expressed no objection either, for he knew Chiang had suggested Jiang Tingfu first.[24]

Chiang used devices other than the power of appointment to manage the factions. He kept his security services penetrate deep and wide into all spheres of Chinese politics, including the factions. Intimately informed about the factions' activities, he was able to take initiative to meet their demands, to reconcile their differences, and to pacify a disaffected faction. At the same time, he deliberately separated the security services group into two hierarchies—the Jun Tong and Zhong Tong—so that they would compete with each other for allegiance to him.

Chiang, of course, also kept the factions under tow by exercising the power of the purse. His first priority was to provide the military with as much budgetary support as he could, often leaving it short for the civilian administration. Accepting Chiang's financial preference for the military because the Nationalist regime was continuously involved in wars, factions other than the Whampoa group had to compete for the relatively meager financial resources Chiang allocated to them.

Chiang's manipulation of the factions was not always successful. In the waning days of his rule on the mainland, he suffered a serious setback on the formation of a new leadership team at the highest level of the government. In 1948 the National Assembly was about to elect a president and vice president of the Nationalist government. All factions unanimously accepted Chiang as their presidential candidate. But they differed on the Nationalists' choice of the vice presidential nominee. Li Zongren, head of the Guangxi faction often in rivalry with Chiang, decided to run for the position, while Chiang announced Sun Fo—the son of Sun Yat-sen—as his choice. The issue resulted in an open breach between Chiang and Li. Chiang was confident that his choice would easily receive a majority vote in the National Assembly, which was under the control of the CC faction—a faction that had always been abiding by Chiang's wishes. But Li surprised him by winning the hotly contested election because Sun Fo was not popular with the CC faction. This episode enraged Chiang enough that he, after retreating to Taiwan, forced the CC faction to disband and sent its leader, Chen Lifu, to the United States in 1950 for retirement. For years, Chen raised chickens in New Jersey for living and returned to Taiwan later without ever getting back to the power center of the Nationalist Party.

Dictatorship in the Guise of Democracy

While pulling all strings to insure an authoritarian rule, Chiang liked to maintain an image that he adhered to faithfully Sun's *The Three Principle of the People*, including the idea of democracy. He also followed Sun's prescription of a three-stage political development in the Republic of China: military government, political tutelage, and constitutional rule, with a fully democratic government established at the last stage. Yet, deep at heart Chiang had an insatiate desire for perpetuation of his position as the supreme Chinese leader. How did he reconcile his commitment to democracy and his dictatorial predilection?

He devised several measures to bridge the dichotomy. One of these was to make a persistent effort at upholding constitutionalism. In 1931 he proposed to adopt a Covenant (*Yue Fa*) of the Republic of China as the fundamental law of the land but failed in the move because of a determined opposition from Hu Hanmin, an eminent political leader then serving as head of the Legislative Yuan of the Nationalist government. He broke with Hu, a once political ally, and stunned the nation by placing Hu under house arrest for eight months. Within the year he had his government adopt a "Provisional Constitution of the Political Tutelage Period." In 1936 he endorsed a Draft Constitution of the Republic of China formulated by the Nationalist Party. But no permanent constitution was adopted until 1947, when the National Assembly approved the Constitution of the Republic of China, the basic law of his government since then.

In upholding constitutionalism, Chiang attempted to demonstrate his support of the idea of democracy, for all the constitutional documents mentioned above were committed, in varying degrees, to a popular rule of the government and to respect for civil liberties and civil rights of the people. Yet, when the 1947 constitution set a term limit on his position as president and inhibited his authority to prosecute the civil war because of civil liberties concerns, he maneuvered to have the National Assembly amend the constitution to suspend the provisions unacceptable to him. He was elected president in 1948 and reelected four times afterwards, for a total service period of thirty years, from 1948 to 1978 (he died in 1975).

The second measure he adopted to resolve the dichotomy was to make use of the Nationalist Party to control the government. As described in Chapter Two, the party was organized along the Leninist line, which required the government at the national, provincial, and local levels to be subordinate to the party at every corresponding level.[25] As leader of the party with untrammeled power, Chiang could thus assure himself as the government leader with the highest authority as long as he retained his position as the party leader.

While in Taiwan, Chiang adopted a third measure to show his commitment to democracy. In 1950 he approved the initiation of provincial and local elections for the administrative and legislative positions of the government. But he kept the Nationalist Party candidates dominating these elections by prohibiting the formation of new political parties. Campaigning for electoral positions was, therefore, largely confined to competition between Nationalist and non-Nationalist candidates. With the significant institutional and financial resources of the party available to them, Nationalist candidates won continuously an overwhelming majority of the contested seats, usually about 70 percent, against the unorganized non-Nationalist candidates. Beginning in 1969, supplementary elections were held at the national level, including those of the National Assembly and the Legislative Yuan. Nationalist candidates commanded even larger shares of seats there.[26]

Chiang could be ruthless in the application of naked power to suppress his opponents and dissidents if he deemed them as thwarting his favored policies or threatening his regime. As noted earlier, he put Hu Hanmin under house arrest because Hu refused to lend him legislative support for constitutional reform. In 1936 he ordered to take into custody several well-known intellectuals for criticism of his policy of compromise with Japanese aggressors; he did not set them free until after the start of the Chinese-Japanese war in 1937.[27]

On February 28, 1947, massive riots occurred in Taiwan because of widespread discontent of native residents with the Nationalist rule on the island. The rioters assaulted government agencies and attacked at random the Chinese mainland residents there. In response, Chiang dispatched troops from the mainland to Taiwan for extensive arrests and killings of the rioters. According to a recent study, a total of 2,084 native Taiwanese were killed, wounded, or imprisoned. In addition, according to other sources, 2,601 mainland Chinese were killed, missing, or wounded from the attack of the rioters.[28] The casualties estimated by other sources varied from 10,000 to 30,000. A scrutiny of several recent publications on the incident suggests that the number of total casualties is likely in the thousands, not more.[29]

The 228 Incident became the single most divisive issue between the Nationalist government and the natives in Taiwan, with unsettling consequences for several decades. It triggered recently a debate on Chiang's personal responsibility for the event. Many of the Nationalists' opponents charged that Chiang was the principal culprit, having ordered troops to the island that massacred uncountable civilians. Others claimed that Chiang was not personally involved in the handling of the incident, being preoccupied with the civil war on the mainland. In a dispassionate analysis of this fiasco and with extensive citation of Chiang's diary entries during the incident, Yang Tianshi reached what appears to be a fair assessment: In ordering the troops to Taiwan, Chiang had cautioned them not to take retaliatory measures against the rioting Taiwanese, but the troops did engage in extensive shooting and killing. Chiang must bear an indirect responsibility for the tragedy.[30]

When dealing with the incident in 1947, Chiang suspected a Chinese Communist complicity in the case, though only circumstantial evidence existed. As he retreated to Taiwan in 1949, he became much more sensitive about Communist spying activities on the island. In the following year he authorized an island-wide search and arrest of people—both mainland and native residents—suspected of having any remote connection with the Communists. This hunting of the Red spies became known to the Nationalists' critics and opponents as "the Reign of White Terror." Under the direction of Chiang's son, Ching-kuo, who took charge of all of Taiwan's security agencies, the "White Terror" lasted into the early 1960s, with even sporadic arrests in the 1970s. Acting under the Martial Law of 1949 and the Sedition Act of 1950, Taiwan's security agencies arrested, imprisoned, and killed not only

Communist spies but also advocates of Taiwan-independence movement and other dissidents. The scale of persecution in the White Terror appears much broader in scope than that of the 228 Incident. According to one researcher, the security agencies arrested about 10,000 people and put more than 1,000 to death in 1950 alone, and decades later the Ministry of Justice revealed that the total of all arrests under martial law from 1949 to 1986 numbered at 29,407.[31]

These arrests involved several prominent dissidents. The most celebrated case concerned the imprisonment of Lei Chen, a former Nationalist Party official and publisher of a magazine *Ziyou Zhongguo* (Free China), who urged the government to fully respect civil rights of the citizens and to remove the ban on formation of new political parties. Li Ao, publisher of the magazine *Wen Xing* and a gadfly constantly critical of Chiang's policies, was twice imprisoned, with the magazine closed down. Guo Yidong, with Bai Yang as pen name, received prison terms for writing satirical pieces ridiculing Chiang's avowal of recovery of the mainland as unrealistic. These and other cases of political imprisonment can be seen in a number of publications.[32]

The measures Chiang adopted to facilitate his dictatorial rule in the guise of democracy showed his constant struggle to bridge the conflicts of the two irreconcilable concepts. And on the occasions when his struggle failed, he would not hesitate to preserve the former at the expense of the latter. Symbolizing his struggle is a revealing semantic device he adopted in his Taiwan days when he characterized the Nationalist Party as a "revolutionary democratic party." A revolutionary party is supposed to engage in massive violence to change the political order; as such, it requires concentrated authority in the leader of the party who commands the rank and file of the party, like in a military organization. A democratic party is committed to a rotation of power through electoral competition; as such, its leadership and policies must rest on the consensus of the membership of the party. Chiang devised this contradictory term but never indicated how it was operationalized.

Mao Zedong confronted the same dilemma as Chiang did. He proclaimed the establishment of the People's Republic of China in 1949 and pledged in the constitution of his government to uphold the principles of democracy. Like Chiang, he preferred dictatorship to democracy. With his forever fertile mind, Mao also invented a semantic device to reconcile the irreconcilables. In June 1949 he fathered the idea of "the People's Democratic Dictatorship" to characterize the Communist government that was to emerge four months later.[33] "The People", Mao explained, consisted of primarily the proletariats (workers and farmers), who had to exercise dictatorship over their oppressors: the landlords, the bourgeoisie, and other "enemies of the people." These latter groups, Mao continued, could not enjoy democratic rights. And, as will be seen in the next Chapter, when the persecution of these groups took place in the People's Republic, its scope was far greater and its measures of punishment were much more severe than in the case of persecution of dissidents in the Republic of China under Chiang.

The Art of Withdrawal

While maintaining a dictatorial rule, Chiang was alert to the possibility of losing it; hence, he often took a subtle and preventive measure to perpetuate it. Like many of his countrymen, Chiang subscribed to two popular Chinese proverbs: *"wu ji bi fan"* and *"ju gao lin wei."* He took these notions as a warning to himself that he had be to be constantly prepared for cyclical changes in human fortunes (CKSD, 12/8/41). The first notion means that when the evolution of an event reaches its extremity, an opposite event will inevitably occur. The second suggests that when staying at a high point, one has to think of the danger of fall.[34] He summed up these notions by stating: "All events are [governed by the idea of] contradiction" (CKSD, 5/31/44). Ironically, Chiang's metaphysical proposition on human events coincided with Mao's dialectical perspective of the world.

Since the 1910s Chiang was bent to seek the highest office of the land; while in office, he was fully cognizant of the reality that the longer he held power, the more likely he would generate an opposition force. Thus, the accumulation of power in his hands over time might engender so much opposition that would jeopardize his political future. A timely withdrawal from office might so soften the opposition as to allow him to come back to it later.

During his rule on the Chinese mainland and Taiwan, Chiang did precisely that kind of cyclical exercise of withdrawal and comeback—not once but several times. In the summer of 1927, Chiang's swift and decisive victories in the first phase of the Northern Expedition had allowed him to set up a government in Nanjing, expelled the Communists from the Nationalist Party, and took control of the richest provinces on the east coast. Yet, a convergence of circumstances unexpectedly drove him to a corner. A rival, left wing regime headed by Wang Jingwei in Wuhan, in alliance with the Soviet advisors and the Chinese Communists in areas out of Chiang's control, rallied all Chiang's distracters to its side and waged a determined fight to oust him as Commander-in-Chief of the National Revolutionary Army. Then, Chiang's army suffered a setback in a battle with warlord Sun Chuanfang. And added to these woes, several of his subordinate generals, including Li Zongren and one of his closest Whampoa associates, He Yingqin, staged what might be called a mild coup. They asked him "to take a rest."

On August 14, Chiang announced his resignation as army chief, using the Chinese expression *xia ye*, or "going to the countryside" to characterize his move. He went back to his hometown, Xikou, the rural town tucked in mountains and watercourses. There he immersed himself in the natural scenes, easing into a retreat life distant from the tumultuous political and military conflicts elsewhere. Within the month, he decided to ask the hand of his future wife Soong May-ling by sending her a letter. In it he wrote, "I have decided to stay away from politics, but I have to say you are the only lady I have been adorning [for a long time]....I am now nothing but a man of the countryside...having lost interest in everything except that I could not forget for a moment your talent as well as elegance as a graceful lady. I wonder how you would look on this retired soldier."[35]

In late September, Chiang went to Japan where he held a series of meetings with his acquaintances, including Prime Minister Giichi Tanaka. In the meantime, a momentum for calling him back to his post had been built up in China. Chiang's departure left the Northern Expedition stalled, and a substitute chief commander could not be found in either Nanjing or Wuhan or anywhere else. Now two-thirds on its way to completion, the Expedition risked failure at its final phase. Then the Wang Jingwei regime in Wuhan discovered through a series of revealing documents that the Soviet Union's "real intention [was] to destroy the KMT [Nationalist] left wing and turn the Wuhan regime into a Communist puppetry."[36] It expelled the Soviet advisors, ousted the Chinese Communists from the regime, dissolved itself, and conceded to the Nanjing government to be the sole governing authority.

The Nanjing government urgently asked Chiang to resume his post, with many of Chiang's former opponents making similar pleas. In November Chiang returned to China; in December he married Soong May-ling in a spectacular ceremony; and on the following January 7, he became the Commander-in-Chief of the National Revolutionary Army again. In February his army resumed the northward march and successfully completed the Expedition on June 8.

On the following day, June 9, Chiang surprised many, including his closest confidant Zhang Jingjiang, by resigning from his military position again. On June 14, he went with his bride to the countryside—Xikou. It turned out that this was his subtle gesture to accentuate his achievement of a great deed. Understandably, at the request from the Nanjing government, he resumed his position a few days later, on June 17. On October 10, he assumed the chairmanship of the National Government—a singular, highest political office of the nation. For the first time in seventeen years, China was united, and Chiang was its new ruler—a goal he had sought to reach in as many years.

Chiang was immediately facing a series of other challenges. In 1927, the Chinese Communists already took to the hills of Jiangxi to start a rebellion. In 1930, he had a five-month war with Feng Yuxiang and Yan Xishan. Though defeated, Feng and Yan held a grudge against Chiang, seeking every opportunity for revenge. On September 18, 1931, the Japanese army brazenly attacked Manchuria and soon forcefully seized the entire territory.

Blamed for not resisting the Japanese aggression in Manchuria, Chiang faced massive student protests in major Chinese cities. Elsewhere, in Guangdong, Chen Jitang, with the endorsement of Chiang's old nemesis, Hu Hanmin, set up a rival government in Canton and forged an alliance with the Guangxi-based Li Zongren faction in demand for Chiang's stepping down from power. Never before had Chiang encountered such widespread opposition in all directions, the Japanese in the nation's north, the Communists in the middle, the Canton government in the south, and the students in the metropolitan areas all over the country.

On December 15, 1931 Chiang resigned all his military and political posts and returned to Xikou a week later—the third time in five years. Yet, just as in his two previous resignations, the Nationalist Party passed resolutions requesting him to take back his resignation, a request that was made all the more urgent by the Japanese army's threat of a possible invasion of north China from Manchuria. Even Chiang's former arch enemies pleaded with him for return. Wang Jingwei, in a meeting with Chiang in Hangzhou, urged him to resume his military position while Wang would be in charge of the civilian administration.[37] Feng Yuxiang, who battled Chiang only a year ago, even knelt down in front of some senior Nationalist leaders, urging them to request Chiang's early return to Nanjing (CKSD, 12/30/31). Chiang agreed and resumed his posts on January 18, 1932.

Thirteen years later, on V-J Day 1945, Chiang rose to the apogee of his political career. Praised by his countrymen and many foreign sympathizers as a heroic figure of historical magnitude for leading China to victory over Japan in eight years of hard fight, Chiang commanded a shining prestige like the sun at high noon. Yet in a relative short time of four years, his fortune vaporized. In January 1949, exactly seventeen years after his last comeback to office, he had to leave his office again and to go back to Xikou again so that his vice president, Li Zongren, could sue for peace with the Communists, to whom Chiang had suffered sweeping military losses. As Li's peace attempt fizzled and the Communists took over the entire Chinese mainland within the year, Chiang shored up all his resources in Taiwan, where he resumed the presidency on March 1, 1950.

From 1927 to 1950, Chiang experienced four cyclical withdrawal-comeback exercises. His withdrawals from office appear to be motivated by several considerations. First, he attempted to vitiate the anger of his opponents that had accrued over a period of time. In 1925 he fell out with Wang Jingwei, the then top Nationalist leader; in 1927 he purged the Communists, his previous comrades; in the same year he had frictions with Li Zongren, the warlord who joined his army only the year before. The bitterness of his opponents reached a boiling point by 1927, when he saw his resignation as the best way to ease the tension with them all, and he went to the countryside. In 1931, his opponents—Wang Jingwei, again, Hu Hanmin, Chen Jitang, Li Zongren, the Communists, and the students—each had a specific agendum but all were united in demanding his resignation. By accepting their demand, he made them feel satisfied for being able to remove their most powerful foe. In 1949, the Li Zongren-led opposition was particularly elated with Chiang's resignation, for it fulfilled its avenge for Chiang's strenuous objection to Li's running for the vice president earlier. The opposition was even more delighted because Chiang's absence removed a stumbling block to its hope for a co-governance of China with the Communist Party—one controlling the south of the Yangzi River and the other, the north.

In most of these cases, it is important to note, Chiang could exercise the option of fighting it out against his opponents, for he possessed a far stronger military might than many of them. But he did not, because a bitter fight to the end could ruin his chances of a comeback.

Second, by stepping out of office and letting his opponents run the government, Chiang could expose their weaknesses as political leaders so that they might fall on their own weight. Wang Jingwei and Hu Hanmin commanded enormous prestige in the Nationalist Party and proved to be competent civilian administrators, but they never possessed any military power—the crucible of politics in 20th century China.

Chiang's other major opponents within the Nationalist Party, Li Zongren and Chen Jitang, could not grow out of their regional power base to acquire the stature of a truly national leader; nor did they possess a political acumen comparable to Chiang's in the contention for power. None of Chiang's opponents could endure for long when power was actually devolved to their hands.

Third, letting the opponents run the government, Chiang posited a hope for comeback because he sensed they would experience significant failures during their tenure. In 1928 Wang Jingwei, Li Zongren, and He Yingqin could neither organize an effective government nor push forward the Northern Expedition, risking the loss of Nationalists' mandate for continuing its rule. In 1932 Wang Jingwei, Hu Hanmin, Chen Jitang, and Li Zongren could not recover the lost Manchuria or cope with the rising Japanese threat to north China. In 1949 Li Zongren failed to bring a peace settlement with the Communists or to carry on the fight with his own military might. In all these cases, the failings of Chiang's opponents made it logical to let Chiang handle the problems they could not.

Chiang's recovery of his office was not merely based on what happened to his opponents when they took over the reins of the government. He also made preparations for comeback upon his departure from office. Central to his preparations was to hold on to the army whenever he could. "If I control the army," he confessed to his wife Ch'en Chieh-ju in 1924, "I will have the power to control the country. It is my road to leadership."[38] His control of the army started in the days when he was the Commander-in-Chief of the National Revolutionary Army in the mid1920s. As Hans J. Van de Ven has succinctly pointed out, he used several devices to insure his control of the army: appointment of unit commanders, allocation of logistic supplies to army divisions, and financial support of the forces.[39] He continued to use these same devices in subsequent years.

In his diaries, Chiang indicated several times the importance of keeping the army in his hands, On June 5, 1928, four days before resigning as the Commander-in-Chief of the National Revolutionary Army, he told his closest associates that he would not mind resigning but "will never give [military] power away" (CKSD, 6/5/28). In 1931 when he was once again contemplating resignation, he pondered,"I can stay away from party affairs and politics and let others handle them as they wish. But I must make proper arrangement for the armies so that they would not fall apart" (CKSD, 8/6/31). In January 1949, before he left office as president, he kept a tight control of two groups of massive armies in southeastern and southwestern China under the command of, respectively, Tang Enbo and Hu Zongnan, Chiang's most trusted corps commanders. Elsewhere, he made preparations for sending some 600,000 Nationalist soldiers to Taiwan. In each case, the army he kept in control served as the most potent force for his staged comeback.

Chiang's manipulation of financial resources to his advantage was of equal importance to his holding on to the army in the recovery of office, though it was a game less conspicuously played out. In the 1920s and 1930s, the Nanjing government was perennially in debt, and Chiang depended on T. V. Soong to float high-interest government bonds among Shanghai industrial and banking interests to meet the shortfall. In 1927 when Chiang made his first resignation, Sun Fo became prime minister. At that time the government had a monthly budget of $20 million, but Sun was able to raise only $8 million. When he made appeal to the banking community for purchasing government bonds, he received only token support. Tottering on the verge of bankruptcy, Sun gave up running the government and let Chiang pick up the pieces. With T. V. Soong serving as his intermediary with the Shanghai business community, Chiang received the community's financial backing of the Nanjing government.[40]

Chiang's resignation in 1931 led to a repetition of the 1927 financial woes for his successor. Sun Fo, who became prime minister the second time, had no better luck than four years ago in securing financial support from Shanghai. In addition, T. V. Soong resigned as finance minister, thus depriving the Nanjing government a crucial linkage to Shanghai.[41] Sun resigned on January 18, 1932, having been in office for less than three weeks. When Chiang returned to Nanjing, he again regained Shanghai's financial support without problem.

In early December 1948, several weeks before announcing his intention to vacate the office of the presidency, Chiang made elaborate preparations for shipping out from Shanghai the financial assets of the Central Bank to Taiwan. He assigned the mission to three of his most trusted subordinates: Yu Hongjun, Director of the Central Bank; Wu Songqing, Director of Military Budget; and Tang Enbo, Shanghai Defense Commander. In an extensively documented research, Wu Sing-Yung—son of Wu Songqing—estimated that nearly 2,960,000 taels of gold (close to 90 tons); 34,000,000 silver dollars, more than 100 million taels of silver, and US$74 million were shipped from Shanghai to Taiwan over a six-month period, from December 1948 to May 1949 (a tael is slightly less than an ounce).[42] The operations, which must be ranked as the largest gold rush in modern history of the world, were conducted in secrecy and successfully carried out. With these massive resources at his disposal in Taiwan, Chiang was financially more solvent than any of his political foes, Communist or Nationalist. He used these assets to support monetary and financial reforms in Taiwan that were crucial to the island's rapid economic transformation in the 1960s.

In addition to managing his military and financial resources to his political advantage, Chiang also paid close attention to personnel matters before his departure from office. Prior to his resignation in 1931, he appointed his faithful followers Gu Zhutong, Lu Diping, Xiong Shihui, and Shao Lizi as governors of four key provinces then under the control of the Nanjing government: Jiangsu, Zhejiang, Jiangxi, and Gansu.[43] In 1949 before he left Nanjing, he appointed Zhang Qun, his sworn brother, Director General of the Southwestern Military Administration in Sichuan in preparation for continuing battles with the Communists on the mainland; and he named Chen Cheng, considered Chiang's alter ego, Director General of the Southeastern Military Administration in Taiwan to prepare the island as the future anti-Communist bastion. He kept the Nationalists' party apparatus under his control while he remained as the party's head.

In his four cyclical resignation-and-comeback exercises, Chiang kept three vital elements of power in hand: the army, finance, and appointment. Thus, he always possessed enough political capital for the continual contention for power. It is of interest to note that when withdrawing from office in these exercises, he intended only to expose the weaknesses of his opponents. Moreover, when resuming office, he did not try to eject them from power forever or to destroy them altogether. Indeed, he sought out his opponents to collaborate with him. In 1928, when he resumed the commandership of the National Revolutionary Army, he retained Li Zongren and He Yingqin as his subordinate generals without retribution; and he compromised with Wang Jingwei by letting him take charge of the civilian administration. In 1932, when Chiang came back to his office, Wang Jingwei willingly took the second spot in the Nationalist power hierarchy. In early 1950 when Chiang was contemplating to resume his office as president, he asked Li Zongren to remain as vice president. Thus, reconciliation with opponents characterizes Chiang's art of withdrawal.

Under Chiang's rule on the mainland, he never allowed a rotation of power between him and his opponents through election. Nevertheless, rotation of power between them did take place. Chiang's artful exercises of withdrawal seem to serve as the functional equivalent of election.

NOTES

[1] From the late 1920s to the mid1930s, the value of Chinese currency was relatively high and stable; one Chinese silver dollar or one *fa bi* was worth about US$0.30. The regular pay for the Nationalist army officers ranged from $40 a month for a second lieutenant to $320 for a general. See Hu Zhiwei, "Bei Fa Kang Ri Shi Qi de Jun Ren Dai Yu" [Military Pay during the Northern Expedition and the War against Japan], *BL*, No. 555 (August 208): 123-24.

[2] An Suping, "Chiang Kai-shek Leici Shuoxiao" [The Odds and Ends of Chiang Kai-shek's Eulogistic Messages], *BL*, No. 533 (October 2006): 79.

[3] An Suping and Sheng Changwang, "Chiang Kai-shek de Renji Shijie" [Chiang Kai-shek's Social Activities], *BL*, No. 543 (August 2007): 20-21.

[4] Zhang Fuxing and Wang Shaojun, *An Suan Jiang Jieshi: Guo Min Dang Nei Bu de Pai Xi Dou Zheng* [Chiang *Kai-shek's Conspiracies: Factional Disputes in the Party*] (Beijing: Jun Shi Ke Xue Chu Ban She, 2000), p. 106.

[5] An and Sheng, "Chiang Kai-shek de Renji Shijie" [Chiang Kai-shek's Social Activities], *BL*, No. 546 (November 2007): 97. Part of a series, same authors and title as in Note No. 3.

[6] Yan Ruping, *Chiang Kai-shek and Sworn Brothers*, p. 400.

[7] Hsiao-ting Lin, "From Rimland to Heartland: Nationalist China's Geopolitics and Ethnopolitics in Central Asia, 1937-1952," *The International History Review*, Vol. 30 (March 2008): 57.

[8] An and Sheng, "Chiang Kai-shek de Renji Shijie" [Chiang Kai-shek's Social Activities], *BL*, No. 546 (November 2007): 102.

[9] Ames, *The Art of Rulership*, p. 185.

[10] For details of the two incidents in Canton, see Ju Yiqiao, *Serving Chiang Kai-shek for Twelve Years*, pp. 26-27.

[11] See Ch'en, *Chiang Kai-shek's Secret Past*, pp. 198-99. The two generals mentioned by the would-be assassin were Liang Hung-k'ai and Yang Kam-lung. They showed displeasure with Chiang by refusing to take orders from him following Chiang's takeover of the Xu army. Chiang had them arrested and executed for insubordination. Ibid., p. 164. See also, Zhang and Wang, *Factional Disputes in the Party*, pp. 104-05.

[12] Zhang and Wang, ibid., pp. 163-70.

[13] Ibid., pp. 168-69.

[14]Thomas N. Moon and Carl F. Eifler, *The Deadliest Colonel* (New York: Vintage Press, 1975), pp. 145-46. See also Jay Taylor, *The Generalissimo, Chiang Kai-shek and the Struggle for Modern China* (Cambridge: Harvard University Press, 2009), pp. 258-59.

[15]Frank Dorn, *Walkout with Stilwell in Burma* (New York: Pyramid Books [1971]), p. 117.

[16]Ibid., pp. 117-22.

[17]See Wen Jun, Zheng Xin, Zhu Wenqi, and Li Xiuyuan, *Chiang Kai-shek de Shi Qi Ci An Sha Xing Dong* [*Seventeen Instances of Assassination by Chiang Kai-shek*] (Changchun: Jilin Ren Min Chu Ban She, 1999). The summary of these instances in the text above does not include three assassination attempts described in the book: against Vice President Li Zongren in 1949, Mao Zedong in 1949, and Zhou Enlai in 1955. In the opinion of this author, the allegation that Chiang was personally involved in these cases is less than plausible.

[18]See Gan Guoxun, *Lan Yi She, Fu Xing She, Li Xing She* [*The Blue Shirt Society, the Revival Society, the Positive Action Society*], Taipei: Zhuanji Wenxue Chu Ban She [1984].

[19]For instance, Xu Enzeng, *Xishuo Zhong Tong Jun Tong* [*A Detailed Discussion of the Zhong Tong and the Jun Tong*], Taipei: Zhuanji Wenxue Chu Ban She, 1992; and Liang Xiong, *Dai Li Zhuang* [*Biography of Dai Li*], Taipei: Zhuanji Wenxue Chu Ban She, 1990; Shen Zui, *Jun Tong Nei Mu* [*Inside Story of the Jun Tong*], Beijing: Wen Shi Zi Liao Chu Ban She, 1984. Xu was a former head of the Zhong Tong, and Shen, a ranking officer of the Jun Tong.

[20]See Gan, *The Blue Shirt Society*, pp. 208-10; and Shen Zui, *Shen Zui Yu Zhong Qu Wen* [*The Interesting Stories Shen Zui Learned in the Prison*] (Beijing: Zhongguo Wen Shi Chu Ban She, 2002), pp. 81-82 and 296-300. Shen was for years a prisoner of war in the Chinese Communist detention center, where he met many captured ranking Nationalist officers.

[21]See Tang Zong, *Zai Chiang Kai-shek Shen Bian Ba Nian: Shi Cong Shi Gao Ji Mu Liao Tang Zong Ri Ji* [*My Eight Years with Chiang Kai-shek: Diaries of a High Counselor at Chiang's Secretariat*] (Beijing: Qun Zhong Chu Ban She, 1991), pp. 630ff. Tang, Chief of the National Police Administration at the time, was in charge of the investigation of the Li and Wen case under Chiang's order. See also CKSD, 7/17, 24/46 and 8/10, 17/46.

[22]For references to the Nationalist factional politics, see Jin Yilin, *Guomindang Gao Ceng de Pai Xi Zheng Zhi* [*The High-Level Factional Politics of the Nationalist Party*], Beijing: She Hui Ke Xue Wen Hsian

Chu Ban She, 2009; Hung-mao Tien, *Government and Politics in Kuomintang China, 1927-1937* (Stanford: Stanford University Press, 1972), pp. 45-76; Tien-wei Wu, "Contending Political Forces during the War of Resistance," in James C. Hsiung and Steven I. Levine, eds., *China's Bitter Victory: The War with Japan, 1937-1945* (Armonk, NY: M.E. Sharpe, c1992), pp. 51-78; Zhang and Wang, *Factional Disputes in the Party*; Quan Guo Zheng Xie Wen Shi Zi Liao Wei Yuan Hui Bian, *Ji Zha Quan Bian: Jiang Jieshi yu Ge Pai Xi Jun Fa Zheng Dou Nei Mu* [*Cunning and Scheming: Inside Story of Chiang Kai-shek's Power Struggle with the Cliques and Warlords*], Beijing: Zhongguo Wen Shi Chu Ban She, 2001; and Liu Hong, *Jiang Jieshi Dazhuan* [*A Major Biography of Chiang Kai-shek*] (Beijing: Tuan Jie Chu Ban She, 2001), Vol. 2, pp. 362-74; and Vol. 3, pp. 721-27.

[23]The whole story of the air raid disaster and Wu's response to it was widely circulated in Chongqing at the time. Its authenticity was confirmed more than half of a century later, in Wu Guozheng, *Wu Guozheng Zhuan* [*Biography of Wu Guozheng*] (Taipei: Zi You Shi Bao, 1995), pp. 327-33.

[24]Hua Ping Kang, "Chong Wu Guozheng Zhuan Kan Chiang Kai-shek de Zhi Shu [A Look at Chiang Kai-shek's Political Craftsmanship from a Reading of the Biography of Wu Guozheng]," *BL*, No. 403 (December 1995): 82.

In 1966 Chiang wanted Yan Jiagan, a relatively young financial administrator, to succeed the deceased Chen Cheng as the vice president of the Nationalist government in Taiwan, but Chiang's senior colleagues were in favor of a veteran Nationalist leader as the candidate. Chiang in the end selected Yan but managed not to offend the sensibilities of his senior colleagues. He did so in a similar circuitous way as the appointment of Wu as vice foreign minister. See Ruan Daren, "Chen Cheng Yan Jiagan Tuo Ying Er Chu Zhi Jing Guo" [The Story of How Chen Cheng and Yan Jiagan Rose above Others]," *BL*, No. 536 (January 2007): 6-10.

[25]The Nationalist Party retained the structural features of the Leninist model well into the late 1980s. However, a number of researchers have noticed that the party underwent during Chiang's time so many transformations that it no longer conformed to the original model. For a citation of their works, see Tai, *CMRC*, pp. 186-87, Note 25.

[26]Hung-chao Tai, "The Kuomintang and Modernization in Taiwan," in Samuel P. Huntington and Clement H. Moore, eds., *Authoritarianism in Modern Societies: The Dynamics of Established One Party Systems* (New York: Basic Books, 1970), pp. 416-23; and Linda

Chao and Ramon H. Myers, *The First Chinese Democracy: Political Life in the Republic of China on Taiwan* (Baltimore, Md.: Johns Hopkins University Press, c1998), pp. 40-42.

[27] The seven leaders included Shen Junru, a legal specialist; Li Gongpu, a journalist; Sha Qianli, a Leftist activist; Shi Liang, a painter and calligrapher; Wang Zhaoshi, a college professor; Zhang Naiqi, a college professor; and Zou Taofen, a journalist.

[28] Yang Tianshi, "228 Shi Jian yu Jiang Jieshi di Dui Ce" [The 228 Incident and Chiang Kai-shek's Response], *BL,* No. 561 (February 2009): 8, 18.

[29] See Academia Sinica, Institute of Modern History, *228 Shi Jian Zi Liao Xuan Ji* [*Selected Materials on the 228 Incident*]; 2011 Report of the 228 Memorial Foundation. http://www.228.org.tw/pages.aspx?v=82D4F7824F7815C6; Zhu Hongyuan "228 Shi Jian Zhen Xiang Huan Yuan" [Return to the Truth of the 228 Incident]. http://www.wretch.cc/blog/ rainbow2/5435457; and Lai Zehan, *228 Shi Jian Yan Jiu Bao Gao* [*A Research Report on the 228 Incident*], Taipei: Shi Bao Wen Hua, 1994.

[30] Yang, "The 228 Incident and Chiang Kai-shek's Response," pp.18-19. For a comparable view from a native Taiwanese—a dissident who was once a Chiang's follower—see Li Xiaofeng, *Taiwan Ren Ying Gai Ren Shi de Jiang Jieshi* [*The Chiang Kai-shek the Native Taiwanese Should Know*] (Taipei: Yu Shan She Chu Ban Shi Ye Gu Fen You Xian Gong Ai, 2004), pp. 49-100.

[31] Taylor, *The Generalissimo,* p.412, 423, 464, 679; Jay Taylor, *The Generalissimo's Son: Chiang Ching-kuo and the Revolutions in China and Taiwan* (Cambridge: Harvard University Press, 2000), pp. 211-13.

[32] Chao and Myers, *The First Chinese Democracy,* pp. 5, 52-56, 70, 73; Taylor, T*he Generalissimo*, pp. 465, 544; and Li Xiaofeng, *The Chiang Kai-shek the Native Taiwanese Should Know*, pp. 124-32. For a witness' account, see Chen Jianjie, "Taiwan Bai Se Kong Bu Kai Jia Zheng Zhi An Jian: Miao Li Hu Haiji Zhi Ge An Yan Jiu" [The Political Case of Kai Jia in Taiwan's White Terror: A Case Study of Hu Haiji in Miao Li], *BL,* No. 573 (February 2010): 100-11.

[33] "On the People's Democratic Dictatorship: In Commemoration of the Twenty-eighth Anniversary of the Communist Party of China," *SW,* V: 411-24.

[34] This proverb is originally written as *"ju an si wei,"* meaning that when one is secure, think of danger. Chiang modified it in his diary entry of December 8, 1941.

[35] Li and Zhang, *The Chronology of Chiang Kai-shek*, p. 158.
[36] Hsü, *The Rise of Modern China*, p. 637.
[37] Li and Zhang, *The Chronology of Chiang Kai-shek*, pp. 201-02.
[38] Ch'en, *Chiang Kai-shek's Secret Past*, p. 155.
[39] Hans J. Van de Ven, *War and Nationalism in China 1925-1945* (London: Routledge, 2003), p.125.
[40] Parks M. Coble, Jr., *The Shanghai Capitalists and the Nationalist Government, 1927-1937* (Cambridge: Harvard University Press, 1980), pp. 42-45.
[41] Quan Guo Zheng Xie Wen Shi Zi Liao Wei Yuan Hui, *Chiang Kai-shek's Power Struggle with the Cliques*, p. 64.
[42] Wu Sing-Yung, *Huang Jin Dang An: Guo Fu Huang Jin Yun Tai, Yi Jiu Si Jiu Nian* [*The Archive on Gold: Shipping Gold to Taiwan by the Nationalist Government in 1949*] (Taipei: Shi Ying Chu Ban She, 2007), pp. xviii-xix.
[43] Quan Guo Zheng Xie Wen Shi Zi Liao Wei Yuan Hui, *Chiang Kai-shek's Power Struggle with the Cliques*, p. 64.

CHAPTER EIGHT

MAO, THE SPY WARFARE

As noted earlier, central to Mao Zedong's political thoughts is his concept of contradictions. He divided contradictions into two kinds: one concerns contradictions between "the people and the enemy of the people;" the other, contradictions among "the people," that is, Chinese citizens under his control. Using this art of the possible, Mao intended to hold absolute sway over both the people's enemy and "the people" themselves. In this chapter we shall discuss how he handled the contradictions of the first kind, targeting the Nationalists as the people's enemy. In the next, we shall see how he dealt with the contradictions among the people under his control, including his closest comrades.

A Man Devoid of Emotions[1]

In the management of contradictions, we need to note first how Mao applied this art of the possible with extreme ruthlessness and cruelty so as to assure uttermost success.

On March 18, 1947, as General Hu Zongnan's assaulting force of 140,000 troops was rapidly approaching Yan'an, Mao was sitting in his cave dwelling, refusing to leave. He had earlier decided to abandon the city, for he could muster no more than 27,000 soldiers to defend it. Yet he not only rejected the urgent appeal of many of his comrades, including Peng Dehuai, to run away to the countryside but also insisted that his six-year-old daughter Li Na to stick out with him in spite of the plead of her desperate mother, Jiang Qing, for early evacuation. Mao said he wanted the child to taste the war that was closing in by listening to the gunfire. In the end, his aides had to, literally, pull them away to a waiting car.

Mao's treatment of his daughter only epitomized his cool relations with his family members. When he was a teenager, he characterized the relation between his father and himself as one of "party in power" and "party in opposition." Toward his wives, he behaved just as dispassionately. In 1930 he led a small guerrilla band from Jiangxi to make a daring attack on Changsha, Hunan, knowing well such a rash action would endanger his wife Yang Kaihui, then imprisoned in that city. The attack ended in disastrous failure, and Yang was executed by the Nationalist Governor He Jian. Prior to the attack Mao had been consorting with He Zizhen in the Jinggang Mountain; He Zizhen later went through with him the harsh and cruel Long March. But Mao abandoned her in the late 1930s in favor of Jiang Qing, changing wife as if savoring one flower after another. Mao banned Jiang Qing from political involvement for three decades until he needed her as a henchman to push forward the Cultural Revolution in the 1960s. Yet during that revolution, she, having been earlier ejected from his residence in Zhongnanhai, had to "apply for an appointment" to see him.

Mao had two sons, Anying and Anqing. Anying died in 1950 as a staff officer of the Chinese Communist army in the Korean War. As reported in the press, when the news reached him, Mao said, "Ah, who asked him to be Mao Zedong's son!?"Anqing served in the army in Manchuria and then worked as a Russian-language translator in a party organization; he died a mentally deranged man in March 2008.

As for Mao's relations with his comrades, the following was what Li Yingqiao, Mao's long-time chief bodyguard, said:

> Mao Zedong seemed to restrain himself deliberately from developing any personal friendship with the people in charge of party, administration, and army affairs; he would not maintain any relationship with them beyond that of comrades-in-arms.... For instance, Zhou Enlai worked with him for decades and even took extraordinary care of his daily life....their relationship must be considered very, very close. But in my fifteen years with Mao Zedong, I never heard him say to Zhou Enlai even one sentence revealing his private feelings—beyond their relationship as comrades.[2]

Viewing these all too familiar episodes of Mao's life, one cannot but gather the impression that the man was largely devoid of emotions. With a few exceptions, he showed no sentiments toward others.[3] Affection, tenderness, gaiety, sympathy, and sadness seem to be absent from his stony heart. Another inescapable impression is that Mao frequently politicized social relations. Personal interactions among the people should be governed by the dictates of the party—and of himself.

If Mao behaved as an emotionless man, it is appropriate at this point to contrast his personal trait with that of Chiang Kai-shek. In appearance Chiang looked stern and impassive, but he was a deeply impassioned man. He was devoted to his mother all his life; he loved his wife Soong May-ling with passion throughout their forty-eight years' marriage, and he had a parental affection for his two sons, Ching-kuo and Wei-kuo, in the best of Chinese tradition. And his relations with his colleagues such as Zhang Qun, Dai Jitao, Chen Bulei, Yu Youren, Huang Fu, and Wu Zhongxin can be characterized, as the Chinese would say, a matter of "life-and-death" mutual commitment.

Chiang painstakingly built up an emotion-based web of relations through sworn brotherhood, pseudo-familial network, reverence for the dead, and celebration of the living. With his intense and repeated emotional appeal toward others, Chiang sought to strengthen his political hold of them.

Mao rarely followed these practices. He did not appear to have sworn brothers; he addressed his colleagues not as brothers but as comrades; he seldom participated in birthday parties or funeral services. Mao did attend Joseph Stalin's 70th birthday party in December 1949 in Moscow. But it was a pure and simple political event, in which Communist leaders all over the world gathered to pay attribute to the head of the Communist movement. In 1953 when Stalin died, Mao wrote a eulogy to mourn a Soviet leader whom he found politically disagreeable while alive but acceptable while dead. As for this eulogy of his, let Mao speak for himself: "As a rule, I do not like to felicitate others, nor do I like others to felicitate me....Upon his [Stalin's] death the Soviet Union needed our support, and we wanted to support the Soviet Union; therefore, that eulogistic article was written. It did not eulogize Stalin as an individual but eulogized the Soviet Party."[4]

On January 10, 1972 Mao attended the funeral service of Chen Yi, a field marshal, in Beijing on the spurt of the moment. Wearing an overcoat to hide his pajama-like robe and a pair of leather slippers, he braved the blustering wind to rush to the scene for one important reason. He sought to ingratiate with the many veteran commanders in attendance, whom he had alienated because of his scheming to have the disgraced Lin Biao as his successor. He was also known to have sent birthday congratulatory messages to Anna Louise Strong (the leftist American journalist who interviewed Mao in 1946) and a few others. But these are about all the instances of Mao's involvement in the functions marking the "life and death" occasions of others.

Compared with Chiang, Mao was extremely stingy in shedding emotions to his acquaintances, social or political. He preferred to take direct, forceful action to score political gains rather than to follow a circuitous route via emotional appeal to reach political goals, as Chiang often did.[5] Grasping this psychological trait of Mao's would allow us to understand why, in the pursuit of supremacy in politics, he could so unfeelingly subject his enemy as well as his comrades to extremely unusual and cruel treatment.

The Massive Underground Network[6]

Mao's bag of art of the possible contained many tools. Toward "the people's enemy", the Nationalists, he used primarily the gun to defeat them, but he also used a supplementary tool, the spy warfare, to penetrate and decimate them from the inside. He commanded an extensive underground network within the entire Nationalist power structure to ferret out enormous amount of intelligence critical to his victories in the battlefield and, further, to instigate massive defections of Nationalist forces to his side.

When Hu Zongnan's army thundered over Yan'an in March 1947, Mao showed extraordinary equanimity by not retreating from the city until the last moment. He was able to do so for one reason. He knew ahead of time precisely every battle move Hu was to take. Earlier, on February 28, Chiang summoned Hu to Nanjing and ordered him to mount a surprise attack on Yan'an in accordance with a carefully prepared secret plan. Three days later, on March 3, the plan was in Mao's hand. He thoroughly studied it well before Dong Zhao and Liu Kan—the two Nationalist army commanders spearheading the assault—learned about it.

The person who stealthily secured the plan for Mao was Xiong Xianghui, a Communist mole long planted in the Hu Zongnan headquarters. Joining the Communist Party eleven years earlier, in 1936, Xiong worked his way to be Hu's confidential secretary in 1939. Being with Hu in Nanjing in March 1947, he secretly copied down Chiang's war plan and forwarded it to Yan'an.

Upon receiving it, Mao exclaimed, "This Xiong Xianghui is as good as ten army divisions!" Mao was not exaggerating, for the plan involved not only the attack operations against Yan'an but also the detailed military moves following the expected fall of the city. Thus equipped with foreknowledge of Hu's battle operations, Mao maneuvered nimbly with his 27,000 men, defeating an enemy five times their size.

It was revealed years later that as Hu arrived in Yan'an on March 25, Xiong was with him and witnessed an event. Hu discovered a note Mao left for him: "After coming to Yan'an, Hu Zongnan is like a man riding on the back of a tiger. Cannot go forward, nor backward. What a pity!" Hu laughed out loud about it. What Mao meant was that Hu would suffer defeat if he pursued the Communists and would face disciplinary action if he stayed put.

Xiong returned to the Communist fold later and served as a ranking officer in the office of the Chief of Staff of the People's Liberation Army, Chinese ambassador to Mexico, and Deputy Director of the United Front Department of the Communist Party. He was a member of the Chinese liaison team meeting with Henry Kissinger and Richard Nixon in Beijing in 1971 and 1972.

The Xiong Xianghui case is perhaps the most celebrated one in the history of the Communists' spy warfare. He was once praised by Zhou Enlai as one of the "Later Three Heroes" (*Hou San Jie*) of the Chinese Communist intelligence service. The other two were Chen Zhongjing and Shen Jian, who together with still other underground agents extensively infested the Hu army. In contrast to these agents, Zhou also identified the "Earlier Three Heroes" (*Qian San Jie*): Li Kenong, Qian Zhuangfei, and Hu Di, who were active in the Nationalist-controlled areas in the 1920s and early 1930s. They infiltrated the Investigation and Statistical Bureau of the Nationalist Party (the Zhong Tong) and gained access to its secret code of radiogram, with which they learned the Nationalist military operation plans for the first two Encirclement Campaigns in the 1930s before the plans were executed.

Zhou Enlai was the founder of the Communist intelligence service in 1927, known as the Bureau of Special Operations (*Te Wu Gong Zuo Chu*); it was reorganized and renamed later as the Central Special Service Bureau of the Chinese Communist Party (*Zhong Gong Zhong Ying Te Ke*); and it operated later under still other names. These organizations have been successively headed by Zhou Enlai, Li Kenong, Kang Sheng, and others.

Mao began exerting influence on the Communist spy warfare in the mid-1930s. In no small measure, he gained inspirations from two influential Chinese classics. One is Sun Zi's *The Art of War*, in which the ancient theorist on war provided an exquisite discourse on the subject:

> The means by which enlightened rulers and sagacious generals moved and conquered others...was advance knowledge.
> Advance knowledge...must be gained from men [spies, intimately familiar with]...the enemy's true situation.
> Thus there are five types of spies to be employed: local spy, internal spy [moles in the enemy camp], turned spy [double

agent], expendable spy [agent sacrificed for providing information], and the living spy [surviving agent with intelligence]....

[To the supreme commander] no relationship is closer than with spies; no rewards are more generous than those given to spies, no affairs are more secret than those pertaining to spies.[7]

Mao also read time and again *The Three-Kingdom Stories*—a book tracing the history of the tail end of the Eastern Han Dynasty (220-280 AD). It describes how each of the Three Kingdoms—Wei, Shu, and Wu—used spies, ruses, disinformation, counterintelligence, and stratagems to gain an upper hand in a triangular game of collaboration, competition, war, and annihilation.

Mao devised a 16-word maxim as guidance to intelligence operations parallel to his 16-word dictum for the guerrilla warfare:

> Hide under cover, be alert and active.
> Lie low for the long run.
> Conserve and accumulate strength.
> Wait for the right moment.

Later, Mao issued a further directive to his underground agents: "Let's grab every piece of information on the power struggles, loopholes, and contradictions inside the enemy camp—lock, stock, and barrel—and put it to use in the fight against our enemy at hand." In the operations of the underground network, Mao emphasized not only intelligence gathering but also, more importantly, making intelligence serviceable to battle operations and securing enemy defections.

Infiltration of the Nationalist Central Command

From the 1930s to the early 1950s, the Chinese Communists placed several key agents in the very center of the Nationalist high command, some with direct access to Chiang's office:

Liu Fei.[8]—Liu joined the Nationalist Military Administration Ministry in 1937 as deputy minister in charge of battle planning. Having earned so much of Chiang's confidence in his performance, he shared office with the Nationalist leader in an underground air shelter in Nanjing during the Shanghai Battle that year. From then to the spring of

1949, he was the ministry's chief battle planning officer, holding the rank of Lieutenant General.

Liu had joined the Communist Party in 1930, well before he entered the nerve center of the Nationalist army. During the civil war in 1947-1949, he leaked vital war intelligence to the Communists during a number of crucial battles, including the battle in Shandong in 1947, where the Nationalist 74th Reorganized Division was routed, with its commander Zhang Lingfu killed. He also revealed Chiang's battle plan against Yan'an to the Communists, separately from what Xiong Xianghui did. In the battle north of the Yangzi River in 1948, Liu's spying work contributed significantly to the defeat of the largest concentration of the Nationalist army up to that time, around Xuzhou, Jiangsu Province.

In 1949 he served as a member of the Nationalist delegation for peace negotiation with the Communists in Beijing. He remained there when the mission failed to reach an agreement. In 1950 he joined the newly established Communist government and served afterward on several high posts, including head of the Water Conservation Ministry and deputy chairman of the Political Consultative Assembly (a quasi-legislative body); he died in 1983.

Guo Rugui.—A Whampoa Military Academy graduate in 1926 and Chiang's protégé, Guo rose through the army ranks rapidly. He served as chief of staff as well as commander of, successively, Division, Army, and Army Corps; head of the Third and Fifth Section of the Defense Ministry for battle operations; member of the Military Conciliation Commission during the George Marshall Mission; and head of the Nationalist Military Mission to the United States.

Guo joined the Communist Party in 1928 and worked as an undercover agent in the Nationalist army until the last days of the civil war. In 1948, while heading the Defense Ministry's Third Section, he was constantly at Chiang's side in the midst of three gigantic battles: in Manchuria, north China, and central China. On November 9, 1948, right after a Chiang-presided meeting of the war council, Guo gathered nine top secret documents pertinent to the battle in central China and delivered them to his conduits, Ren Lianru and Wang Paozhen, to pass on to the Communists. 0The mission failed because the Nationalist intelligence agency had apprehended Wang. Undaunted, Guo continued his spying activities until December 1949 when he, as commander of the Nationalist 72nd Army in southern Sichuan, led his tens of thousands of troops to defect to the Communist army during the Nationalists' last battles on the mainland.

According to one estimate, Guo's spying activities over the years contributed to the defeat and defection of the Nationalist forces totaling at least one and half million men. Following the establishment of the People's Republic of China, he served in the Military Academy in Nanjing and became a member of the Political Consultative Assembly.

The Tang Brothers.[9]—In 1938 Tang Bingyu participated in the Communist New Forth Army in southern Henan through the introduction of his brother Tang Junzhao (a Communist since 1926). In 1946, with the help of his other brother Tang Binglin, who was then a staff officer at the Nationalist Defense Ministry's Third Section (in charge of battle operations), Tang Bingyu joined this Section to start his clandestine activities. He surreptitiously copied several Chiang personally-approved battle plans, including "the National War Plans and Force Deployment during Vital offensive Operations," "Implementation of Major Battle Plans in Eastern China," "Map of Force Deployment and Battle Plan for the Defense of the Yangzi River," and "Plan for Troops Reinforcement at the Second Line [of Defense]" and had them delivered to the Communists through the conduits, Tang Jianhua and Tang Zhongheng (relatives of the Tang brothers).

The Tang brothers also worked together to infiltrate the Jiangyin Fortress Command. Located strategically on the south bank of the Yangzi River between Nanjing and Shanghai, the Fortress was Chiang's most vital defense constellation to prevent the Communist army from crossing the river. Incredibly, the Tang brothers schemed to have nearly all military units of the Fortress headed by Communist agents. In April 1949 when millions of Communist soldiers poised on the north bank of the Yangzi to cross the river, these agents seized control of the Fortress and forced its Commander Dai Rongguang to stop firing at the invaders and to surrender to them. The Communist soldiers were ferried to the south bank without much of a fight and conquered Nanjing and Shanghai within weeks.

Wu Shi.—Joining the National Revolutionary Army in the late 1920s as staff director of battle operations, Wu worked through the ranks of the Nationalist army to the Deputy Commander of the 16th Army Corps, holding the rank of Lieutenant General, in the final days of the civil war.[10]

Available evidence does not show as to whether he had joined the Communist Party, but he was known to be a close friend of Wu Zhongxi, a Communist since 1937. In 1948 Wu Zhongxi, then a Lieutenant General of the Nationalist army at the Xuzhou field command, secretly gathered war intelligence for the Communists. At that time he persuaded Wu Shi to join the "People's United Front," a Communist front organization. In 1949, while in Fuzhou, Fujian Province, Wu Shi was entrusted by the Defense Ministry with the upkeep of the army's archive of classified documents. Later that year, as he was departing for Taiwan to take up his new post as Deputy Chief of Staff of the Defense Ministry, Wu Shi arranged to have the archive's 298 cases of classified documents delivered to the Communists.

In 1950 while in Taiwan, Wu, then code-named by the Communist intelligence service as "Secret Emissary No. 1," kept contact with two Communist undercover agents on the island. After assembling a series of most vital documents on the defense of Taiwan against the expected Communist invasion, Wu delivered them in a microfilm to one of the two agents, Zhu Zhanzhi. These documents consisted of "Map of Defense of the Taiwan War Theater," "Force and Weapon Deployment at Forward Coastal Line," Taiwan area ocean currents, topographical analysis of possible landing sites, and naval and air deployment in Taiwan.

Zhu, a woman, rapidly forwarded the microfilmed documents to the Communist East China Bureau on the mainland via Hong Kong. When the documents were delivered to his hand, Mao remarked with unrestrained joy: "How talented this woman special agent [Zhu Zhanzhi] and that 'Secret Emissary No. 1' are!" He instructed the Communist intelligence service to record their "great merit of service." Anticipating an early conquering of Taiwan with the aid of these documents, he composed a poem to celebrate the event:

> A perilous storm soon to crash on the isolated island.
> Green waves are shining under the morning sky.
> Hiding in the Tiger's Den are our loyal souls.
> Dawning light heralds an early welcome.

In January 1950 the Nationalist intelligence service apprehended the head of the Communist "Taiwan Taskforce Commission," Cai Xiaoqian—the other agent Wu had been in touch with. Cai's confession led to an arrest of 400 Communist agents in Taiwan and also revealed Wu's identity and activities. Chiang was so incensed by the enormous damage to Taiwan's defense inflicted by Wu that he ordered his arrest in March and his execution, along with Zhu Zhanzhi and two other Communists, in June. In 1973 the Chinese State Council officially declared Wu a "Martyr of the Revolution."

Penetration of the Nationalist Field Commands

In his battles with the Communists over the years, Chiang created a number of field commands in various regions of China. Designated under various titles, all these commands, which are referred to in the discussion below by the regions in which they operated, were deeply penetrated by Communist spies as well.

The Northwestern Command in Xi'an.[11]—Created in 1935, the Command was headed by Chiang himself, with its actual operations under the direction of its deputy commander, Zhang Xueliang. The command's task was to mobilize Zhang's forces from Manchuria and, in addition, forces of General Yang Hucheng from northwestern China to combat the post-Long March Communists in northern Shaanxi. At this time Zhang and his troops were homesick, wishing to fight the Japanese to regain Manchuria rather than to fight the Communists.

Aware of Zhang's sentiment, Mao sought to penetrate the Northwestern Command in several ways. In January 1936 he initiated contact with Zhang through several emissaries and proposed collaboration of forces of the two sides. Responding favorably to the overture, Zhang secretly flew on April 9, 1936 to Fushi (later renamed Yan'an, then still under Nationalist control) on a Boeing plane piloted by himself. There he met a Communist delegation headed by Zhou Enlai in a former Catholic church. The two sides quickly agreed to adopt an anti-Japanese policy and to make an effort to persuade Chiang to support that policy. In September, Mao dispatched Ye Jianying, a top Communist general, to Xi'an for discussion of a ceasefire agreement between the Communist and Nationalist forces. Zhang accepted the idea of ceasefire but could not get Chiang's approval. When Ye returned to the Communist base, he carried a generous gift from Zhang—50,000 silver dollars for the Communist army.

These Communist contacts with Zhang took place without Chiang's knowledge, and one of the persons serving as the vital link between the Communist base and Xi'an was Liu Ding. Working first for the Communist Central Special Service Bureau in Shanghai in the early 1930s, Liu, with the help of several intermediaries, joined the Northwestern Command and became Zhang's military aide in 1936.

To avoid the detection by the Nationalist intelligence service, Liu set up a dentist clinic to cover up his clandestine activities. He routinely funneled war intelligence gathered at the Command through a radio transmitter in the clinic to the Communist base. He arranged for delivery of medical supplies provided by foreign Communist sympathizers such as Rewi Alley and Agnes Smedley to Communist controlled territories.

In July 1936 Liu flew in Zhang's plane to northern Shaanxi to meet with Mao and other Communist leaders. When seeing them, he produced a letter from Zhang with an incredible request. Zhang wanted to join the Communist Party with his army to be merged with the Communists'.[12] Mao did not agree to the idea, for the move would precipitate a war between Zhang's army and Chiang's army, damaging the anti-Japanese cause. "Your assignment is," Mao instructed Liu, "aside from collecting intelligence, mainly to work on General Zhang Xueliang so that his troops become a truly anti-Japanese force....As our representative, you must get the assignment done."

On December 12 Zhang staged the Xi'an Incident and kidnapped Chiang. A few days later, Zhou Enlai—with Liu making all the necessary arrangements—arrived in Xi'an to participate in the convoluted negotiations eventually leading to Chiang's release. As a condition of his release, Chiang promised to fight the Japanese instead of the Communists—an elusive goal that Mao had long sought was now realized. Following the Incident, Mao found occasion to observe: "In the Xi'an Incident, Comrade Liu Ding performed a great service."[13]

After the establishment of the Communist government in 1949, Liu served on several important posts, including membership of the Standing Committee of the Political Consultative Assembly and head of the Ministry of Chinese Aviation Industry.

The Northeastern Command in Shenyang.—Created after the Chinese-Japanese war, the Command was headed successively by several Nationalist generals in a short period of two years, from 1947 to 1948. It was during the tenure of General Wei Lihuang, in 1948, that the Nationalist forces suffered disastrous defeats, leading to the loss of the entire area. Wei had been serving under Chiang since the 1920s; during the Chinese-Japanese war, when the Nationalist and the Communist armies were supposed in alliance to fight the Japanese, Wei showed sympathy for the Communists while serving as Deputy Commander-in-Chief of the Second War Zone in 1938. He once visited Yan'an and met Mao.

In that year he appointed Zhao Rongsheng his confidential secretary and entrusted him with the creation of a Battlefield Service Corps. Zhao turned out to be an undercover Communist. The Corps, which was supposed to conduct cultural and entertainment activities for the troops, became in reality an underground network promoting the

Communist cause. In 1938, apparently falling to the Communist propaganda, Wei told Zhao of his wish to join the Communist Party and asked Zhao to forward his wish to Yan'an. The request was rebuffed, for the Communist leaders were uncertain of Wei's intention, suspecting that he might be scheming a ruse.[14]

In August 1947 Wei was on a honeymoon trip with his wife Han Quanhua to Europe; there he met Wang Deizhao, a relative of his wife's, who was a Communist secret operative doing research in the field of atomic energy in France. As Wei came back to China to take over the Northeastern Command in 1948 at Chiang's call, he appointed Wang Director of Secretariat of the Command. With access to all military directives from Nanjing, Wang informed the Communists of all Wei's battle moves, resulting in a series of Nationalist defeats. Chiang angrily removed Wei's position in November 1948, barely nine months after his appointment. By the end of the year, the Communists took over entire Manchuria and routed the Nationalist army of 450,000 men. Years later, in 1955, Wei went to Beijing to pledge allegiance to the Communists after a sojourn in Hong Kong.[15]

The Northern Command in Beijing.—Established in 1947, the Command was headed by Fu Zuoyi, one of Chiang's most loyal generals. In late 1948, the Communist army in Manchuria, fresh from the victory there, joined with other Communist forces to lay siege to Beijing, then being cut off from all physical linkage with Nanjing.

Long before then, in 1942, the Communists, acting in accordance with to Mao's 16-word maxim on intelligence operations, started to build an underground network in the then Japanese-occupied Beijing. By 1948, 3,000 Communist Party members and 5,000 left-leaning activists had established themselves in the Nationalist army, party, and government agencies in the city. When the Beijing battle shaped up, the underground network mobilized its resources to persuade Fu to deliver the city peacefully to the Communists.

Three individuals played key role in this endeavor. One was Liu Houtong, a Major General Counselor at the Command. Liu displayed a left-leaning tendency and made acquaintance with Communists, including Cui Yueli, a major agent in Beijing. At Cui's urging, Liu made ceaseless representation with Fu on the need for disassociation with the Nanjing government and for prevention of the culturally rich city from being ruined by war. Fu became open to such discussions, without reporting Liu's activities to Chiang.

The second person was Fu Dongju, Fu's own daughter. She was a Communist and worked as a journalist. Living in her father's residence, she constantly talked with Fu for a peaceful settlement with the Communists. As Fu's army had in the meanwhile suffered severe losses in the outlying areas, he had to concentrate his forces, some 250,000 strong, in area around Beijing. Fu knew he had fallen into a no-win situation. Yet, as a person steeped in Chinese traditional values, he considered loyalty to one's superior an indispensible virtue. A peaceful resolution of the conflict without Chiang's approval, to him, was nothing but surrender, an event that no honorable military leader could contemplate. Yet, to fight for the defense of Beijing would bring destruction to the historical monuments and imperial buildings that the city was famous for.

The third person was Deng Baoshan, Fu's deeply-trusted Deputy Commander. A top Nationalist general, Deng had shown sympathy for the Communists since the late 1930s and, like Wei Lihuang, visited Yan'an in 1938 and received a warm welcome from Mao. He had since maintained contact with the Communists via his daughter, Youmei, a Communist who had studied in high school and college in Yan'an. In 1948 Cui Yueli approached Deng and asked him to make a direct appeal to Fu for peace. Deng agreed. In a talk with Fu, he pointed out that under the prevailing circumstances, Fu could expect either a destruction of the Fu army and the city through war or a preservation of both through peace. Fu could not resist the persuasion any longer. On January 16, 1949 Deng, on behalf of Fu, and Zhou Enlai signed an agreement for a peaceful delivery of the city, along with all the forces under Fu's command, to the Communists. The Communist army marched into the city within the month.

After the establishment of the Communist government in 1949, Fu became head of Water Conservation Ministry, and Deng served as Governor of Gansu Province and on other high posts.

The Command in Xuzhou.—Created in June 1948, the Command covered northern Jiangsu Province and southern Shandong Province, north of the Yangzi River. No available evidence indicates whether Communist agents had penetrated the Command's headquarters, except that Wu Zhongxi, a Defense Ministry official assigned to the Command, had collected intelligence for the Communists. However, three high-rank Nationalist field commanders were undercover Communists; they worked to the defeat of the Nationalist army in the battle taking place in the area.

One of these was Zhang Kexia, once a junior officer in Feng Yuxiang's army. In 1927 he enrolled in the Sun Yat-sen University in Moscow for a short-term study; in 1929 he joined the Chinese

Communist Party and continued to serve in the Feng army. Later he joined the Nationalist army and moved up through the ranks to Chief of Staff of the 59th Army. In 1945 he was promoted to Deputy Commander of the Third Pacification Zone, which came under the jurisdiction of the Xuzhou Command in 1948.

In November Chiang regrouped all his available forces in the area, totaling 800,000 troops, in a showdown battle with the 600,000 Communist soldiers staged north of the area. He deployed the 59th Army and the 77th Army along a forward defense line in southern Shandong in the Third Pacification Zone to shield the city of Xuzhou from Communist attack from the north. He then placed the 7th Corps a distance to the east of the city and the 2nd Corps and other corps around the city and to the west. The 7th Corps and the 2nd Corps were, in part, heavily mechanized.

A seemingly impregnable iron triangle was formed to test the Communist mettle. What Chiang did not anticipate was the Communists in the north rapidly skipped his forward defense line and ran to the east of the 7th Corps and attacked westward. While the 7th Army Corps retreated slowly toward Xuzhou, Chiang was surprised that the 59th Army and the 77th Army in the north, at the instigation of Zhang Kexia and He Jifeng, went over to the Communist side. Joining the nearby Communist units, they drove a wedge southward to attack the 7th Army Corps from behind. The Communists strangulated the Corps to its collapse, with its Commander Huang Baitao committing suicide.

He Jifeng was another Deputy Commander of the Third Pacification Zone; like Zhang Kexia, he once served under Feng Yuxiang. In 1933 he joined the Nationalist army and advanced to Commander of 179th Division in the 77th Army in 1937. He made a secret visit in Yan'an in 1938 and met Mao and other Communist leaders; he joined the Communist Party secretly in 1939 and continued to serve in the Nationalist army.

The coordinated defection by the 59th Army and the 77th Army not only routed the 7th Army Corps but also threatened Xuzhou with a siege. To avoid such a prospect, the 2nd Corps, along with other corps, rapidly broke away to the west, but they were plagued by heavy equipment and immobilized by snow blizzards; they were quickly surrounded by Communists in the Jiangsu-Anhui-Henan border area. Chiang rushed the 12th Corps from central China to rescue the corps under siege. The 12th Corps' Commander Huang Wei sent forward one division, the 100th, to bore through the Communist interception line. The Division broke through it successfully, but as the 12th Corps' other divisions followed suit, they were suddenly attacked by the 100th Division itself and also by the Communist forces nearby. Thrown into a state of shock, chaos, confusion, these divisions were quickly surrounded by the Communists, who, after an intense fight, forced these divisions to surrender. Chiang's other corps under siege soon surrendered as well. By January 1949 the largest battle of the civil war was over.

What happened was that the Commander of the 100th Division, Liao Yunzhou, led the division to defect to the Communists. Liao joined the Communist Party long ago, in 1927, and his political identity was never known to the Nationalists until the last moment, when he triggered the collapse of the largest concentration of Nationalist troops in the civil war.

Zhang Kexia, He Jifeng, and Liao Yunzhou acted precisely according to what Mao has instructed his spy network to do: "Lie low for the long run," and "wait for the right moment." They hid themselves facelessly in the Nationalist army for two decades before seizing the most critical moments to strike a lethal blow at Chiang's core units, one at a time, causing the 800,000 Nationalist troops to disintegrate like "a mountain crushing down."

Zhang, He, and Liao all served on high government posts after the Communist came to power. Zhang and He were respectively Deputy Minister of Forestry and Deputy Minister of Water Conservation. Liao was appointed Commandant of the Artillery Academy in Shenyang, Manchuria.

The Command in Shanghai.—In the spring of 1949, as the Nanjing-Shanghai battle was shaping up, Chiang placed 450,000 troops, with the support of sizeable air and naval units, under the Nanjing-Shanghai-Hangzhou Command that he had created. He appointed Tang Enbo the chief of the Command, with its headquarters in Shanghai.

Arrayed against Tang's army were over one million Communist foot soldiers north of the Yangzi. To shorten the battle, the Communist Party's underground Shanghai Bureau activated a spy operation to win over General Tang to the Communist side. The Shanghai Bureau set to work on General Tang through Chen Yi, Nationalist Governor of Zhejiang Province, of which Shanghai was physically a part. Chen had served under Chiang since the late 1920s on several key military and civilian posts, including Army Commander, Deputy Defense Minister, and Governor of Taiwan. He had for decades maintained close contact with Tang; Chen acted as the general's mentor, and Tang treated the governor like a fatherly figure.

The Shanghai Bureau approached Chen through Hu Yungong and Shen Zhongjiu—Chen's two senior aides who were long-time Communist moles. Hu and Shen successfully persuaded Chen to send a letter through an emissary to Tang in which the governor asked the general to discuss the procedures with Shen for a peaceful settlement with the Communists. But Tang, more loyal to Chiang than to Chen, informed Chiang of Chen's activities. Incensed by Chen's betrayal, Chiang had Chen arrested in February and executed later in Taiwan.

The Shanghai Bureau then engaged another person to persuade Tang. This was Lu Jiuzhi, a military counselor of Tang's, holding the rank of major general. Lu had an unusual background, being, in a sense, Chiang's son-in-law. He married Chen Yaoguang, the adopted daughter of Chiang's second wife, Ch'en Chieh-ju, and he was a long-time Communist mole too. In April, as the battle loomed over Shanghai, Lu took a great risk to persuade Tang to quit fighting, for the case of Chen Yi just occurred two months ago. In a meeting with Tang, he told the general bluntly that with the overwhelming Communist military power to bear on the city, it was futile to carry on the fight. Tang stopped Lu short, telling him that Chiang had arrived in Shanghai to direct the battle, with the Nationalist leader's son, Wei-kuo, to be staying in Tang's residence. The case ended there.

Though the Shanghai Bureau failed to persuade Tang to quit fighting, it mobilized its other resources to secure the defection of a number of high-profile Nationalist military units, including the 97th Division, the Chongqing Cruiser (the largest of the Nationalist warships), and a number of other warships. In addition, it acquired several classified documents vital to the defense of the Shanghai area. These included map of force deployment in the Shanghai area and the lower reaches of the Yangzi River and map of embargo against the bridgehead ports on the north bank of the Yangzi River.

The Shanghai battle took place in May, and of Tang's 200,000 troops then in Shanghai, 150,000 were entirely routed, with the remaining 50,000 beating a hurried retreat with Tang on naval transport ships out of Shanghai. Tang's other troops farmed out in retreat to other places.

The Southwestern Command in Chongqing.—After conquering Shanghai in May the Communist army rapidly swept over the entire south China in the following summer. Though no longer holding the presidential office, Chiang was nevertheless busy preparing for the final battle on the mainland, now gravitating toward southwestern China, mainly Sichuan. The responsibility for defense fell on the Southwestern

Command in Chongqing that was hurriedly created in 1949, with Zhang Qun as its chief. Because Zhang had long been a civilian administrator without combat experience, Chiang took it upon himself to direct the battle.

Chiang had in his possession several army corps directly answerable to him and several more under the control of three former warlords: Liu Wenhui, Deng Xihou, and Pan Wenhua. The Nationalist strength totaled half of a million soldiers. For battle planning and coordination, Chiang relied on Liu Zongkuan, Acting Chief of Staff of the Southwestern Command. An early Whampoa Military Academy graduate, thus supposedly a student of Chiang's, Liu had long been a Communist spy in the Nationalist military establishment without the knowledge of Chiang or the Nationalist intelligence services.

Liu did two things that critically undermined Chiang's elaborate preparations for the battle. He funneled to the Communists, through his contact men Fang Xianzhi and Huang Kexiao, documents on the Nationalist force deployment of the region, the combat capability of different army divisions, and personal characteristics of the commanding officers.

Liu also recommended to Chiang to concentrate the Nationalist forces in northern Sichuan in expectation of a Communist invasion from there. To the north of Sichuan is Shaanxi Province, where Chiang's most loyal and best-equipped troops under Commander Hu Zongnan had long stationed. Chiang approved Liu's recommendation and deployed the Nationalist troops accordingly. He ordered the Hu army to move to northwestern Sichuan and placed other Nationalist forces in central and southern parts of the province. To Chiang's surprise, the attacking Communists—the Second Field Army under the command of Liu Pocheng—did not come from the north but from the thinly defended eastern Sichuan. In November the Communist army thrust deep into the center of Chiang's defense area and was about to conquer Chongqing, where Chiang had been staying. He escaped under gunfire to fly on November 28 to Chengdu to the northwest, a city guarded by the Hu Zongnan army. On November 30 Liu Zongkuan surfaced in Chongqing as a Communist officer and openly welcomed the Second Field Army to the city. He was praised by Liu Pocheng as the "Greatest contributor to the liberation of southwest China."

Soon following Chiang's flight to Chengdu, he was astonished by a series of defections of the Nationalist units. The three former warlords—Liu Wenhui, Deng Xihou and Pan Wenhua—took the move first; they issued a joint declaration on December 9 to repudiate their loyalty to the Nationalist government and pledged allegiance to Mao Zedong. Then, Guo Rugui, led the 72nd Army to defect, as noted earlier. Two weeks later still, on December 24, Luo Guangwen, Commander of Chiang's 15th Army Corps, at the instigation of Jia Yinhua (deputy Chief of Staff, a Communist sympathizer) and Chen Jisheng (a Communist agent), went over to the Communist side.

This flood of defections left the Hu Zongnan army as the only major force remaining loyal to Chiang. It retreated from Chengdu to Xikang to the west and was annihilated there. The Nationalist-Communist civil war on mainland China was over at the end of 1949.

Dagger in the Heart

When compiling the two volumes of *The True Story of the Chinese Communist Party's Underground Activities*, the editors of *Biographical Literature* likened the Communist spy apparatus to a dagger in the heart of the Nationalist army. That is an apt characterization. Liu Fei, Wu Shi, and Guo Rugui penetrated the very center of the Nationalist high command. Liu Ding, Xiong Xianghui, Wang Deizhao, Fu Dongju, Deng Baoshan, Zhang Kexia, He Jifeng, Liao Yunzhou, Liu Zongkuan, among others, all occupied pivotal positions in the field commands. Together they squeezed out intelligence severely damaging the Nationalist army's fighting capability and drawing droves of Nationalist soldiers to the Communist side. They acted, indeed, like a dagger piercing the heart of the Nationalist military establishment, bleeding it to collapse.

The Communists' spy warfare, despite its extraordinary success, could not substitute actual combat in bringing about Communist victory in China. Its contributions to the victory are nevertheless vital and indispensable. It demoralized the Nationalist troops who, suffering one defeat after another, accepted the invincibility of their Communist counterparts without knowing that they were defeated not because of the inferiority of their combat capability but because of the superiority of their opponents' spy handiwork. The flood of Nationalist defections and surrenders enabled a small and poorly equipped Communists to grow enormously in number and fire power to overwhelm the Nationalist forces in the final days of combat. In all, the spy warfare shortened the time of the civil war. Indeed, reviewing even today the post-Second World War Nationalist-Communist battles, one cannot but be astonished by the fact that the under-one million Communist troops could defeat the Nationalist forces four times as large in less than four years.

Speaking of the effectiveness of the Communist spy warfare, one would wonder to no end why the Communists could place in the Nationalist power structure so many spies who occupied so sensitive positions, worked for so long, and ferreted out so much critical military intelligence as they did without Chiang Kai-shek's knowledge in spite of the two powerful intelligence agencies he had maintained: the Jun Tong and the Zhong Tong.

Viewed from a broad perspective, the Chinese Communist spy warfare may not find a precedent—in terms of its scope, endurance, and effectiveness—in the chronicles of the world's major civil wars: the conflicts of the Three Kingdoms in China in the 3rd century, the American Civil War in the 19th century, and the Spanish Civil War in the 20th century.[16] Much of its success owed to Mao Zedong. Though not the originator of the Communists' spy network, he became the Commander-in-Chief of the soldiering spies in the 1930s—at a time when he assumed the reins of the Communist army. He issued directives to his agents on the conduct of the spy warfare, assigned them to specific missions; made sure they were properly rewarded, and celebrated their gains with poems. Spy warfare was one of Mao's most potent tools to annihilate the Nationalist army.

NOTES

[1] Unless otherwise noted, sources of information for this section of the chapter are from works by people having most intimate relations with Mao and by Mao himself. See Yan Changlin (Mao's bodyguard, 1946-1951), *Guarding Mao Zedong*, pp. 52, 476-77; Li Min (Mao's daughter), *My Childhood Years*, pp. 81-82, 147-48; Li Zhisui (Mao's personal physician, 1954-76), *Chairman Mao*, pp. 382-84, 545-46; and Mao, *Mao Zedong's Autobiography*, pp. 5-6.

[2] Quoted in Quan Yanchi, *Zou Xia Shen Tan de Mao Zedong* [*The No Longer Godly Mao Zedong*] (Huhehaote, China: Nei Menggu Ren Min Chu Ban She, 2001), p. 178.

[3] These included his mother, his second wife Yang Kaihui, his daughter Li Min, and his son Anying. In 1919 Mao composed a long poem eulogizing his mother upon her death (Sun, *Mao Zedong's Lifelong Reading Activities*, pp. 6-7). In 1923, he wrote a tender poem saying farewell to Yang Kaihui (Ye, *Mao Zedong and Jiang Jieshi*, Vol.1, p. 10). As noted in Chapter Four, in 1957, he composed another poem, mourning Yang's death 27 years earlier. When Li Min, his first daughter, was a child, Mao apparently had genuine affection for her (Li, *My Childhood Years*). Mao's private reaction to the news of death of his son Anying was more emotional than what was portrayed in public, as to be described in Chapter Eleven.

[4] Mao Zedong, *Mao Zedong on Diplomacy* (Beijing: Foreign Language Press, 1998), p. 201.

[5] Chang and Halliday put it succinctly: "Chiang consistently let personal feelings dictate his political and military actions. He lost China to a man who had none of his weak spots." *Mao, The Unknown Story*, p. 311.

[6] The primary sources of information for this section of the chapter are the two volumes of *Zhong Gong Di Xia Dang Xian Xing Ji* [*The True Story of the Chinese Communist Party's Underground Activities*], Taipei: Zhuanji Wenxue Za Zhi She, 1991 and 1993, edited by *Biographical Literature* magazine in Taiwan.These volumes consist of numerous articles by writers who were Communist spies themselves. They reminisced about their activities during the civil war years with vivid details. Several supplementary sources of information, which corroborated much of what was reported in these two volumes were

consulted during the research for the present book: Xiong Xianghui, *Wo de Qing Bao yu Wai Jiao Sheng Ya* [*My Career in Intelligence and Diplomacy*], Beijing: Zhong Gong Dang Shi Chu Ban She, 1999; He Yanling, et al., *Hong Yan Er Nü de Zui yu Fa: Zhong Gong Di Xia Dang zhi E Yun* [*The Crime and Punishment of the Hong Yan Cadres: The Deplorable Plight of the Chinese Communist Spies]* Hong Kong: Tian Xing Jian Chu Ban She, 2008; Zheng Yi, "Yi Bai Ge Ou Ran Yan Bian Cheng Yi Ge Bi Ran—Jian Lun Guo Min Dang Wei Shen Me Bai Zou Taiwan" [One Hundred Accidents Make for One Inevitability and a Discussion of Why the Nationalist Party Went to Taiwan in Defeat] *BL*, No. 540 (May 2007): 24-45; Zhou Gu, "Kang Zhan Jiao Gong Qian Hou Gong Die Wu Suo Bu Zai" [The Omnipresent Communist Spies during the War of Resistance and the Battles against the Communists] *Zhong Wai Za Zhi*, Vol. 84, No. 2 (August 2008): 116-24; Chen Guangxiang, "Yi Jiu Si Jiu Nian Nanjing He Yi Xun Su Jie Fang" [How Nanjing Was Rapidly Liberated in 1949]. http://www.jllib. org.cn/interact/y80cntst/ readcnt5.asp.

Two relevant works published by the People's Liberation Army, *Zhong Guo Ren Min Jie Fang Jun Lian Luo Gong Zuo Shi* [*Record on the Liaison Work of the Chinese People's Liberation Army*] and *Zhong Guo Ren Min Jie Fang Jun de Jun Gong Zuo Shi* [*History of the Chinese Liberation Army's Military Works*], are not available to this writer at this writing.

[7]Sun Tzu, *The Art of War*, trans. by Ralph D. Sawyer (New York: Barnes and Noble, 1994), pp. 231-32.

[8]See Ju Yiqiao, *Serving under Chiang Kai-shek*, pp. 31, 145; Zheng Yi, "One Hundred Incidents," p. 37; http://baike.baidu.com/ view/484523. htm; and http://bbs.tiexue.net_1144634_1.html.

[9]See especially a reprint of Tang Bingyu, "Jiangyin Yao Sai Qi Yi Shi Mo" [The Complete Story of the Uprising at the Jiangyin Fortress], and Mei Hanzhang, "Jiangyin Yao Sai yu Zhong Gong Di Xia Dang" [The Underground Communist Party at Jiangyin Fortress] in *The Chinese Communist Party's Underground Activities*, Vol. 1, pp. 425-55.

[10]Zheng Yi, "Wu Shi Wei Shen Mo Qiang Jue Er Shi Shan Nian Hou Cai Zhui Ren Lie Shi" [Why Was Wu Shi Posthumously Declared a Martyr Twenty-three Years after He Was Executed] *BL*, No. 566 (July 2009): 38-47. See also http://boxun.com/hero/2006/xsj12/50_5.shtml and http://baike.baidu.com/view/923196.htm.

[11]*The Chinese Communist Party's Underground Activities*, Vol. 1, pp. 359-74; Vol. 2, pp. 127-51; Ye, *Mao Zedong and Chiang Kai-shek*, Vol. 1, pp. 77-97; 111-12, 147-48.

[12] For details of this meeting, see *The Chinese Communist Party's Underground Activities*, Vol. 1, pp. 368-70; and Ying Hang, "Shao Shuai Ceng Yao Qiu Jia Ru Gong Chan Dang" [The Young Marshall (Zhang Xueliang) Once Asked to Join the Communist Party] in Yu Fengzhi, *Wo yu Hanqing de Yisheng* [*My Life with Zhang Xueliang*] (Beijing: Tuan Jie Chu Ban She, 2007), pp. 108-09. Yu was Zhang's first wife, being privy to his political activities from the 1920s to 1930s.

[13] The Communists infiltrated the Northwestern Command with many other undercover agents than Liu Ding. One of these was Dong Jianwu. Like Liu, he was a member of the Central Special Service Bureau of the Chinese Communist Party in Shanghai and acted as a Christian minister to hide his clandestine activities. He took care for more than four years Mao's sons, Anying and Anqing, in Shanghai while Mao was fighting his guerrilla war in Jiangxi in the 1930s. He traveled to Xi'an to meet Zhang Xueliang for the Communist cause and, once, shepherded Edgar Snow to Xi'an on way to Yan'an. Other Communist agents made extensive contact with General Yang Hucheng, head of a northwestern army acting in concert with Zhang Xueliang in the Xi'an Incident.

[14] Zhao Rongsheng has written extensively on his activities at the Command of the Second War Zone when he served as Wei Lihuang's secretary, see *The Chinese Communist Party's Underground Activities*, Vol. 2, pp. 9-107.

[15] For Wang Deizhao's working relations with Wei Lihuang, see Zhou, "The Omnipresent Communist Spies," pp. 118-19.

[16] The Communist spies identified in this chapter are cited to illustrate the vast scope of their activities. Many other agents, some of whom had access to the innermost power center of the Nationalist hierarchy, are not yet referred to. These include Chen Lian, daughter of Chen Bulei, Chiang's most trusted confidant over twenty years and her husband Yuan Yongxi; Ni Peijun, wife of He Yaozu, the founding director of the Jun Tong and Chief of Secretariat of the Central Military Commission; Duan Beiyu, a Communist agent since 1938 and a senior aide to Chiang Kai-shek holding the rank of major general, who instigated the Third Paratroop Regiment to defect in April 1949 in the crucial battle of Shanghai; and the Sha brothers of Zhejiang Province: Sha Wenhan, Sha Wenqiu, Sha Wenwei, Sha Wendu—all were underground Communists and brothers of Sha Menghai, a confidential secretary of Chiang's. Sha Menghai was not a Communist but gave shelter to his brothers when they were in trouble with the Nationalist intelligence services. The most unexpected story of Communist

concealed underground operations, according to one recent study, concerned Soong Ching Ling, wife of Sun Yat-sen. She worked so closely with the Communist International that she might be considered its agent. For decades, she also promoted the cause of the Chinese Communist Party while living in the Nationalist-controlled area. She was admitted to the Party shortly before her death in 1981 and became an honorable chairman of the People's Republic of China. See Zhang Yaojie, "Soong Ching Ling yu Gong Chan Guo Ji" [Soong Ching Ling and the Communist International], *BL,* No. 543 (August 2007): 4-18; and Chang and Halliday, *Mao, The Unknown Story,* p. 134.

CHAPTER NINE

MAO, THE CAMPAIGNS OF STRUGGLE

Conflict Resolution in the Political Universe

From 1927 to 1949, Mao employed one art of the possible, the spy warfare, to help ransack "the people's enemy": Chiang's four and half million troops. From 1949 to 1976, Mao used another art of the possible—the campaigns of struggle—to subdue the enemies *within* the people. The latter task was by far a much tougher and more sweeping job than the one of defeating Chiang's army. To see how he exercised this art of the possible, we need to grasp fully his concept of contradictions and the ways in which he applied it to politics. We have noted briefly in Chapter Five how Mao treated this concept from a philosophical perspective. Here, we place the concept in a comparative perspective.

It is inherent "in the nature of" the people, James Madison pointed out in *The Federalist*—a collection of essays on the emerging American polity in the 19th century—that they have "different opinions," attach to "different leaders," and look for different "fortunes."[1] In Madison's view, politics is about conflicts of interests and opinions, and the job of a political leader is to resolve the conflicts. In the light of human experiences in all societies, Madison's view constitutes a truth in the political universe, ancient or modern, democratic or non-democratic.

If we confine our attention to modern times, we may say that the conventional Marxists would endorse Madison's view. To them, people are differentiated by classes, hence with conflicting interests. Politics is the business of the property-less class to overthrow the propertied class and to safeguard the interests of the property-less people. But these Marxists would take one exception to the Madison maxim: people will no longer have conflict of interests in a Communist society because in such a society classes cease to exist. Mao accepted the Marxist idea of class struggle. However, as a man with a more realistic view of politics than the conventional Marxists, he would endorse Madison's view that political conflicts exist *in any society at any time*. Mao argued vigorously and persistently that political conflicts existed in pre-Communist as well as in Communist societies.[2] But he also differed with Madison. To

Madison, conflicts *are inherent in the nature of the people*. To Mao, conflicts *can also be defined, created, and manipulated by political leaders*.

In Mao's phraseology, conflicts mean, of course, contradictions. In an essay on this subject written in 1957, Mao identified two types of contradictions: those between the people and the enemy and those among the people themselves. He continued,

> To understand these two different types of contradictions correctly, we must first be clear on what is meant by "the people" and what is meant by "the enemy." The concept of "the people" varies in content in different countries and in different periods of history in the same country....
>
> The contradictions between ourselves and the enemy are antagonistic contradictions. Within the ranks of our people, the contradictions among the working people are non-antagonistic, while those between the exploited and the exploiting classes have a non-antagonistic aspect in addition to an antagonistic aspect.[3]

Thus, Mao's notion of "the people" and "the enemy of the people" was fluid and changeable, and judging by the reality of politics of his time, these terms were defined by no one except himself. Since contradictions varied in content according to time, place, and issue, the nature of contradictions was changeable as well, from antagonistic to non-antagonistic, and vice versa.

In his 1957 essay, Mao summed up twelve types of contradictions.[4] In another essay written a year later, he focused on contradictions that were derived from what he called "The Ten Great Relationships."[5] The contradictions identified by Mao in these essays were by no means exhaustive. Notable in the absence was the contention for power between him and his castigated top comrades, as to be seen later in this chapter.

Mao followed a formula to manage contradictions. First, he initiated major policies—for example, a land reform program. Then, he divided people into two camps, those supporting his initiated policy versus those opposing it. Next, he cast the differences in the two camps as ideological disputes. Still next, he reduced the ideological disputes as conflicts between the Party and the anti-Party group. And finally he banished the anti-Party group and subjected the group's elements to hellish treatment. The entire exercise was intended to impose on the

Chinese society his preferred ideology and policies and to secure himself as the nation's supreme leader.

How did Mao proceed to conduct the exercise? He did so by subjecting the people to what he called *dou zheng yun dong*—the campaigns of struggle. Campaigns were numerous in frequency and varied in content, and they could aim at any of the following four target groups: *the masses, the cadres, the intellectuals, and Mao-designated rivaling comrades*. The techniques of struggle included self-criticism, mutual criticism, rallies, street demonstrations, public trials, intimidation, torture, hard labor, imprisonment, and execution.

A List of the Campaigns

During his reign, Mao conducted the following major campaigns of struggle among the people—with no less energy and concentrated attention than his military campaigns against the Nationalist army. The scale of the campaigns of struggle was stupendous, involving, frequently, tens or even hundreds of millions of Chinese.[6]

> The Suppression of Counter-Revolutionaries(*zhenfan*) Campaign, 1950-1953.
> Land Reform Campaign, 1950-1953.
> The Three Anti/Five-anti Campaigns,1951-1952.
> The Hundred Flowers Campaign, initiated 1957.
> The Anti-Rightist Campaign, initiated 1957.
> The Great Leap Forward Campaign, 1958-1961.
> The Socialist Education (Four Cleanups) Campaign, 1963-1966.
> The Cultural Revolution, 1966-1976.

These campaigns, though numerous, spawned many secondary ones.[7] Most of them had overlapping targeted groups, notably in the case of the Cultural Revolution, which rolled all four target groups into one.

Taming the Masses

Of the campaigns listed above, several were aimed at the masses or the population in general. In March 1950, just a few months after the civil war ended, Mao launched *the Suppression of the Counter-Revolutionaries Campaign*. It aimed at two types of culprits. The first included individuals committing counter-revolutionary crimes, that is, activities against the newly established Socialist order or promoting the causes of the Nationalist Party, feudalism, or imperialism. The second included those individuals committing ordinary crimes—banditry, robbery, murder, sabotage, destruction of public property, and the like—with the effect of undermining the new political order. All these were designated as counter-revolutionaries. Without a modicum of legal exactitude, the victorious Communists defined the crimes in any way as they pleased, thus causing a widespread fear among the masses.

To insure a vigorous implementation of the campaign, Mao directed that a quota of counter-revolutionaries at $1/1,000^{th}$ of the population be set up and that among these people 700,000 be executed, 1,200,000 imprisoned, and 1,200,000 reformed under supervision.[8] The quota numbers revealed clearly the artificiality of the contradictions that were supposed to exist between the counter-revolutionaries and the rest of the people. For at the time of the campaign, hardly any evidence of a broadly-based counter-revolutionary movement existed.[9] In conducting the campaign, Mao intended to do nothing less than terrorizing his conquered multitude into what the Chinese called *shun min,* compliant subjects.

The campaign was a blood-curdling movement exceeding the scope of the reign of terror perpetrated by the Leninists in the Bolshevik Revolution or the Jacobins in the French Revolution. According to a 1954 report issued by Xu Zirong, Deputy Minister of the Department of Public Safety, by the time when the campaign winded down in 1953, 2,620,000 persons were arrested; of these 712,000 were executed.[10]

Concurrent with the Suppression of Counter-Revolutionaries Campaign was *the Land Reform Campaign.* It involved the rural population of the entire country excepting Xinjiang and Tibet, which, according to government statistics, consisted of 105,540,000 farming families in the early 1950s. The campaign first classified these families into "poor farm workers, poor farmers, middle farmers, rich farmers, landlords, and others" and forcefully transferred land from those who had it to those who did not. When the campaign concluded in 1953, seven hundred million *mu* (each *mu* was about one sixth of an acre) of land was redistributed to 300 million farmers, averaging two and half *mu* per farmer.

At the beginning of the campaign, when the Political Consultative Assembly was to frame a land reform law, some delegates suggested that the reform be carried out in a peaceful process under a government-administered program. Mao categorically rejected it and insisted that the landless farmers be organized to fight the landlords to get the land. To explain Mao's position, Liu Shaoqi—his top deputy at the time—stated, "Our Party...wants to fully raise the class consciousness of farmers, especially poor farmers who should complete the mission through their own struggle." He went on to say that in this way, "the great farming masses would stand up and organize themselves and closely follow the steps of the Communist Party and the People's Government and strengthen our political hold of the villages...."[11]

As a result, the landless farmers were organized and directed by the Communist cadres to battle the landed class; torture, beating, public trial and killings of landlords were deliberately promoted. The total number of people killed was difficult to tabulate; estimates ranged from 2 million to 4.5 million people.[12] Clearly, Mao initiated land reform not just for redistributing land but also for insuring the Communists' hold of the villages by sponsored rural violence.

In 1958 Mao launched *the Great Leap Forward Campaign.* China was then under Mao's rule for merely nine years, but he already harbored a fantasy of creating a communist society in the country, leaping over the socialist society that was not yet fully established. In the campaign he forced upon the country two programs: the People's Commune in rural areas and rapid industrialization in cities.

In the Communes, farmland was collectivized, production was done through teams of farmers, community mess halls were set up, and public nurseries were maintained. Mao set the goal of increasing grain production from 1.95 trillion kilograms in 1957 to 5.25 trillion kilograms in 1959, more than doubling the output in two years. With 700 million farming population packed into 26,578 communes, averaging 5,000 households each, Mao threw the whole countryside into a frenetic campaign of drumbeating, public harangues, and cadre coercion in a relentless drive to reach the production goal.

To advance industrialization, Mao took increase of steel production as index of progress. He wanted to raise it from 12,000,000 tons to 30,000,000 tons in five years beginning in 1958, with a still greater output to come later. His objective was to surpass the national steel output of two of the world's most industrialized nations, Britain in 15 years and the United States in 20 years. Without a rudimentary knowledge of metallurgy, Mao forced the whole nation to set up cone-shaped, backyard furnaces—totaling 600,000 of them—to forge steel. Without adequate ore supply, people grabbed door handles, kitchen pots, nails, any metal they could get their hands on and dumped them into the pitiful-looking furnaces that dotted the landscape. And as many as 90 million peasants were diverted from farm work to man the furnaces in a ferocious race with Britain and America for industrial production. The scene of entire China looked rather comic if it were not tragic.

The results of the Great Leap came down as an unmitigated disaster, of a magnitude never seen in Chinese history. The backyard furnaces devoured enormous resources but produced good-for-nothing piles of gray ingots left to rust on the ground. And agricultural production dropped sharply. By 1960, grain output had fallen by a quarter from the 1957 level, from 195 million tons to 143.5 million tons, and the economy as a whole, as of 1961, "declined by as much as 15 per cent from a peak in 1958."[13] Compounding the human-created fiasco, extensive droughts, floods, and locust plight struck many provinces, leading to a severe famine, with victims in astonishing numbers. The officially announced death toll was 14 million; estimates by Chinese and foreign scholars ranged from 20 to 40 million; and a most recent study on the subject by Frank Dikötter, which is based on an exhaustive research of provincial archival materials and an unpublished national report ordered by the former premier Zhao Ziyang, revealed a toll of "at least 45 million."[14] On the basis of all these estimates, it appears reasonable to accept 30 million as the number of people having perished because of the Great Leap. Such a gigantic catastrophe forced the Communist Party to stop the program in 1961. The government termed euphemistically the period from 1958 to 1961 as the Three Years of Great Natural Disaster. Liu Shaoqi was more forthright in claiming in 1962 that the catastrophe "was caused 30 percent by natural disaster and 70 percent by human error."[15] He was laying the blame squarely at Mao's feet, though never mentioning Mao's name.

Mao was, however, callously and persistently defending the Great Leap throughout the campaign. At its beginning, he did anticipate hardship the campaign would impose on the people and cautioned Party cadres to be prepared for rising death tolls. At a Party conference in 1958, he said cavalierly, without a slight concern for human life, "Death is a good event. Imagine, if Confucius still lived today…he would be more than two thousand years old. That is rather absurd." He told the cadres in another conference, in November 1959, that the campaign, together with other economic construction projects, "in my view, will cause the death of half of the Chinese. If not half of the people dead, at least one third or one tenth of them, 50 million deaths."[16]

Mao was intolerant of any criticism of the campaign. When Peng Dehuai and other top leaders identified in a conference in Lu Shan in 1959 the problems of the Great Leap, he charged them as forming an anti-party group and purged them all.

Mao did pay a price for the Great Leap fiasco. He resigned in 1959 as chairman of the government but kept his position as head of the Communist Party. This move, to paraphrase a Mao's military jargon, was a tactical retreat to prepare for a strategic offensive. He had no intention to give up power or his radical brand of socialism. He needed time to cook up ideas for a new campaign and to work out a scheme to carry it out.

In the early 1960s he sensed that the Chinese economy had recovered from the Great Leap and that many people were lulled into slowing down the pace of socialism. He chastised his comrades, "Nowadays some people are sold out to [non-socialist thoughts] when they are given three catties of pork and a few packs of cigarette [in their rations]. Only by launching a Socialist Education campaign can we prevent Revisionism [from occurring in China.]" Revisionism was a Mao-invented term to describe the retreat from Socialism by Soviet leaders since the late 1950s. Applying it to China, he used the term to refer to the Communists going to the capitalist road.

Starting *the Socialist Education Campaign* in 1962, Mao harangued the people to cleanse "politics, economy, organization, and ideology" (known also as the Four Cleanups Campaign). Nationwide rallies, persecution of "bad elements," mutual criticism sessions, and physical punishment of the alleged culprits were routinely conducted—under the direction of Mao's second man in command, Liu Shaoqi and his wife Wang Guangmei. The campaign tapered off by 1966, leaving people wondering what more campaigns were to come.

Yet by this time, the wave of campaigns initiated by Mao had so terrorized and exhausted the masses that they would do whatever they were ordered to, though millions of peasants and the uneducated workers could hardly comprehend what Mao's brand of socialism was, to say nothing of wholeheartedly embracing it. They were totally subdued and would rise to Mao's battle call for the next round of campaign with frenzied rallies, street demonstrations, and severe denunciation of the freshly identified targets for struggle.

Forging the Cadres as a Submissive Workforce

Since the establishment of the People's Republic of China in 1949, tens of millions of cadres staffed the governmental, party, military, social, and enterprise organizations. While relying on the cadres to conduct the campaigns of struggle to tame the masses, Mao turned around to make use of the campaigns to shape the cadres into a submissive workforce.[17] In each campaign of struggle he made sure they play a double role: an instrument to conduct the campaign and, incredible as it may seem, a target of the campaign.

Two pre-1949 antecedents of the campaign against the cadres must be noted in this connection, for they established the pattern of Mao's way to discipline the cadres. One was the anti-A B Corps campaign during the Jiangxi period. It was designed to root out from the rank and file of the Communist Party the suspected elements of a 1926-formed, short-lived Nationalist Anti-Bolshevik Corps. In October 1930, long after the group's extinction, Mao reported to the Communist underground headquarters in Shanghai, "The entire Party [branch in Jiangxi] is under the leadership of kulaks [rich farmers]...filled with the ABs....Without a thorough purge of the kulak leaders and of the ABs...there is no way the Party can survive." In December he reported again, "over 4,400 ABs have been uncovered in the Red Army" in just one month's time. A purge of cadres under the trumped-up charges of being the Nationalist spies ensued. Cadres were tortured to confess their "crime," and many of those who confessed were sent to the firing squad. By the following year when the campaign was completed, from 1,000 to more than 3,000 people were estimated to have been killed. The real purpose of the campaign, as Mao's opponents at the time charged, was to make Mao "the Party Emperor."[18]

Twelve years later, in 1942, the Chinese Communist Party commenced the Rectification Campaign in Yan'an. The campaign ostensibly sought to extirpate three ideological errors the cadres exhibited: "subjectivism, dogmatism, and empiricism." These slippery terms were defined by Mao through a series of writings and speeches, including "Reform in Learning, the Party and Literature," "Combat Liberalism," and "Improving the Party Work Style and Thought." These statements converted, in effect, the three ideological errors into political crimes. At the end of the campaign in 1943, as many as 10,000 cadres were killed, and the rest of the cadres were cowed into silent and obedient sinews of the Party. Mao's leadership position in the Party, first recognized in the Zunyi Conference in 1935, was now reaffirmed through this campaign. He became figuratively the Red Sun of the East from then until his death.[19]

In 1951 Mao initiated *the Three-Anti Campaign* to eradicate three political sins some cadres were accused of committing: "corruption," "waste," and "bureaucracism." In the next year, *the Five-Anti campaign*—against "bribery," "theft of state property," "tax evasion," "fraud on government contract," "stealing of state economic information"—followed suit. The two campaigns mobilized some 20,000 cadres and 6,000 workers—those supposedly with correct behavior and thinking—to criticize, intimidate, and attack a far larger number of cadres for having committed wrongful acts; they were sent to labor camps for reform; many were killed. The number of victims is difficult to ascertain; one estimate is that the "two campaigns took several hundred thousand more lives, the great majority by suicide...."[20]

In all subsequent campaigns, the cadres had to play continuously their double role, as campaign's enforcer and target. They were like a slab of metal coming out of the furnace, hammered again and again to thresh out the impurities, and shaped in the end into a fine-honed sword. With its handle in his hand, Mao could use it to drive his followers into furious action and to hack his targeted villains.

Two of Mao's designated successors had most aptly described how the repeatedly chastened cadres were supposed to behave. In his preface to the famed *Little Red Book* (*Quotations from Chairman Mao*), Lin Biao, the once Defense Minister and Mao's heir-apparent, wrote: "Study Chairman Mao's writings, follow his teachings, act according to his instructions, and serve as his good soldiers." At the end of the Cultural Revolution in 1976, Hua Guofeng—Mao's final chosen heir—issued what was known as the "Two-Whatever" directive to all Communist cadres: "Firmly support whatever policies adopted by Chairman Mao. Consistently follow whatever directives given by Chairman Mao."

Never Let the Intellectuals Kill People with Their Pens

Mao probably read more books on Chinese history than many historians, composed more evocative poems than any other Chinese political leader, and wrote out more philosophical treatises than any of his comrades. He was clearly qualified as an accomplished intellectual. Yet he maintained a complicated relationship with other Chinese intellectuals. For those scientists and engineers whose talents were valued for the development of the military know-how, he allowed them to pursue their professional activities without much interference.[21]

For all other intellectuals, especially those in the fields of philosophy, history, and social sciences, he displayed a very wary attitude. He would coerce those who deviated from his political thinking to total conformity. He would lash out mercilessly at those suspected of challenging him as the sole master of the state orthodoxy.

It may be of interest to note briefly how Mao dealt with three prominent scholars who incurred his political wrath before we proceed to discuss how he assaulted on the intelligentsia en mass.

Shortly following the founding of the Communist regime, Mao thought it necessary to chastise a world-renowned Chinese philosopher, Feng Youlan, for making intellectual errors in the past. Feng published *History of Chinese Philosophy* in 1934, a seminal work still in print today, and other widely acclaimed works on Chinese philosophy. Mao found two elements of Feng's works unacceptable: his espousal of Western approach to philosophical studies and his advocacy of rationalism in the Confucian thought. Both of these were inconsistent with the Marxist line of thinking. Mao gently lectured Feng in a letter dated October 13, 1949: "It is good for someone like yourself, who has committed errors in the past, to be prepared to correct them now, if this can indeed be carried out in practice. You do not need to be overly anxious about seeing results in haste."[22]

Four years later, in 1953, Mao was not so civil in his confrontation with Liang Shuming, an eminent scholar on Confucianism and an advocate for rural reform. A sympathizer of the Communist Party and Mao's personal acquaintance, Liang criticized the Communist Party at the meetings of the Political Consultative Assembly in September 1953 for misplacing emphasis on industrialization at the expense of rural reform. Taking Liang's criticism as a veiled attack on the Communist main policy line, Mao on September 17 vociferously condemned Liang at the Assembly with these accusations: "Liang Shuming is a thoroughly reactionary....To put it plainly, Chiang Kai-shek used the gun to kill [people]; Liang Shuming uses the pen to kill [people]."[23] The vehemence with which Mao attacked Liang took the whole assembly by surprise. A man of strong character, Liang vigorously defended himself in a protracted debate with Mao lasting intermittently for several days.

Mao soon let the Assembly know the reason for his attack on Liang. "In criticizing Liang Shuming it is not a matter of criticizing just one individual," he explained, "but of using this individual to expose the kind of reactionary thought he represents."[24] What were the reactionary thoughts embraced by Liang so enraged Mao? Though never so explicitly saying so, Mao detested the basic Confucian tenets permeating Liang's works, something he took as feudalistic, hence reactionary. More significantly, Mao repudiated Liang's reformist approach to agricultural development, which presented an unacceptable alternative to Mao's radical rural change through revolution and class struggle. Confucianism and reformism had to be nipped in the bud so as to arrest their harmful consequences.

On September 22, Liang came to admit his guilt: "Chairman Mao said I used the pen to kill people. At first, I couldn't take it at the meetings. But it became clear to me [now]. It referred to the harmful consequences of the reactionary ideas I have long circulated in the society."[25] So, Mao demonstrated through the Liang case that he held exclusively the pen to define what reactionary or revolutionary thoughts were supposed to be. Any one else attempting to hold that pen to advocate ideas different from Mao's thoughts committed the crime of ideological murder. He had to resolutely prevent that from happening.

Another four years later, Mao had an intellectual skirmish with a widely respected economist, Ma Yinchu. Ma, a leading theorist on population changes and president of Beijing University from 1951 to 1960, presented his "New Population Theory" at the First National People's Congress in 1957. He believed that the high fertility rate of the population and the low rate of capital formation in China would increase consumption and lower labor quality, hence outstripping the economic gains of the nation. He suggested that China adopt a policy of population control.

Mao rejected Ma's suggestion and reiterated human labor as the sole source of all economic value—a basic tenet of Marxism. Mao argued that the more Chinese there were, the more labor was available for increasing economic output. In the following three years, under Mao's personal direction, the Communist Party propaganda machine launched two rounds of attack on Ma's theory, ending in Ma's dismissal from the presidency of Beijing University and banishment from public life.[26]

Mao maintained his view on population and economic growth till the end of his life in spite of mounting evidence on the harmful effect of uncontrolled population growth on the economy. In 1979, following Mao's death, Chinese population growth had so accelerated that China had to adopt the drastic one-child-per-family policy. Reflecting on Mao's monumental error for criticizing Ma, one magazine article headlined: "An Erroneous Criticism of One Person Begot Additional Four Hundred Million [persons]."[27]

Mao's broad-front assault on the intellectuals started with *the One-Hundred Flower Campaign* that was launched in February 1957. In a speech at the Supreme Council of the State, he requested the intellectuals, particularly *dang wai* (non-Communists) personalities, to appraise the rule of the Communist Party and to identify any fault the

Party may have committed. His initial motivation was obscure, but he apparently assumed that the Party had made enough economic gains under his rule to stand any criticism.

To make his request truly appealing to "the intellectuals and the educated,"[28] Mao borrowed a term that was current in the One Hundred School Era (around Confucius times): "Let One Hundred Flowers Bloom and Let One Hundred Schools Contend." To underscore Mao's sincerity in solicitation of criticism, *The People's Daily* emphasized in an editorial dated May 1, 1957 that the Party should urge the critics to speak up openly and freely: It "must firmly uphold the principle, 'Never keep silent when you know something [wrong]; never skip anything when you speak up; never be penalized for what you speak about; never repeat the mistake [the Party has made, as] you pointed out.'"

From May 5 to June 3 the Party's United Front Department conducted more than a dozen open forums to encourage politicians, journalists, college faculty, and artists to utter their concerns. Following an initial hesitation, these people soon gave a piece of their mind, with a flood of criticism directed at the Communist Party and Mao himself. Speakers after speakers condemned the Party and Mao for practicing dictatorial rule and demanded to install a truly democratic government. They attacked Party members, especially the higher echelons, for enjoying privileges at the expense of the masses. They chastised the Party for its erroneous working style. Zhang Xiruo, a civic leader, said the Party "impetuously looks for short-term gains, despises the past, is obsessed with the future, and gloats over grandiose plans."[29]

The criticism, which rose in volume and stridency as time went on, alarmed many Communist leaders. But Mao looked at the matter differently. In April, at the early stage of the campaign, he told a close circle of his sycophants that "the intellectuals today still have their souls attached to the bourgeoisie."[30] That ominous statement was little known to the public then. He told his listeners: "let the intellectuals…change their mood from cautious to more open….One day punishment will come down on their heads…."[31]

Indeed, his intention to trap the intellectuals soon became apparent. On May 14, the Politburo at an enlarged meeting presided by Mao announced: "Our newspapers…should continuously and thoroughly report on the opinions of non-Communist personalities. Those of the Rightist and anti-Communist elements should especially be reported on in their original form without any alteration so that the masses can recognize their true faces."[32]

On the following day, May 15, Mao worked out a statement that was to be circulated within the Party in June. Titled "Things Are Now Changing," the statement accused certain elements within the Party of harboring "the thought of the bourgeoisie" and "Revisionism." By directing his ire at the Rightist elements *within* the Party, Mao threw these elements into the crowd of non-Communist critics, thus enlarging the scope of the attack. "Let them rant and rave for a while so that they could go to the extreme," the statement emphasized. And this was the way of "luring the enemies out so we can annihilate them." He estimated that the Rightists accounted for one to ten percent of non-Communist intellectuals.[33]

In early June, Mao started a full-court attack on the intellectuals within and without the Communist Party. In the following three months, the One Hundred Flower Campaign was transformed to *the Anti-Rightist Campaign*; it went rampant in criticism sessions throughout the nation. Based on Mao's estimate of Rightists at 10 percent of all intellectuals, the campaign had classified as many as 552,877 persons—the cream of Chinese intellectuals and artists—as the Rightists by 1958, when the campaign winded down.[34] Mao authoritatively characterized the nature of contradiction in the anti-Rightist Campaign with these words: It was "a contradiction between the proletariat and the bourgeoisie; between the Socialist Road and the Capitalist Road. Undoubtedly this is the principal contradiction of our society today." With a few strokes of his pen, Mao transformed what appeared to be non-antagonistic contradiction to antagonistic one. The intellectuals who criticized the Communist Party at Mao's earnest request became, thus, the enemy of the people. Chang and Halliday described how these more than half of a million intellectuals fared in the campaign:

> Most of those branded as "Rightists" were put through hellish, though largely non-violent, denunciation meetings. Their families became outcasts, their spouses were shunted to undesirable jobs,...To protect their children—and themselves—many people divorced their spouses when they were labeled as Rightists....After they were denounced, most Rightists, were deported to do hard labour in remote areas.[35]

While wreaking havoc on the nation's top intellectuals, Mao seemed to take pleasure in the way he handled the contradiction with his designated enemies. In 1957 in a talk with Zheng Zhenduo, a widely-known writer, Mao said he used *"yang mu"* or "open conspiracy"—a term he coined—as the stratagem to deal with the Rightists. "Some people say this is a plot in secrecy," Mao was quoted as saying. "We call it open conspiracy, because we told the enemy ahead of time [that they could talk openly]. Ox devils and snake demons would then come out of their lair so we can annihilate them. Poisoned weeds would burst out of the ground so we can nip them."[36]

It was not until 1981, five years following Mao's death, the Party admitted that the campaign was a grave mistake. It declared in a resolution, "As the Anti-Rightist Campaign was drastically expanded, many groups of intellectuals, patriotic personalities and cadres of the Party were erroneously classified as 'Rightist Elements,' with unfortunate consequences."[37]

Removing the Second Most Powerfuls

In all the campaigns described above, Mao targeted individuals or groups of people who maintained, by and large, no personal relations to him. In each case—the masses, the cadres, or the intellectuals—he was able to thoroughly subdue them to fulfill his specific wishes. Could he thoroughly subdue the recalcitrant top echelon of the Party as well? Some of whom were the founding members of the Party; some were ideologically more attuned with the Marxism and Leninism than he was; some were his closest, battle-toughened, conspiracy-minded comrades in arms; and some were his personally chosen heirs.

In a tour of military regions in August and September 1971, Mao confided to the field commanders that ten Communist leaders had been consecutively removed from the Party in the power struggle in the past five decades. These consisted of Chen Duxiu (a founder and the first leader of the Party), Qu Qubai (the Party's second leader), Li Lisan (a Soviet-trained Chinese Communist leader), Luo Zhanglong (a short-term Party leader), Wang Ming (the next Party leader), Zhang Guotao (a rival of Mao's during the Long March), Gao Gang (Party chief in Manchuria after the Second World War), Peng Dehuai (the Defense Minister), Liu Shaoqi (head of the government), and Lin Biao (Mao's designated successor). Mao was in serious rivalry with most of these leaders and was directly responsible for ejecting the last five (Zhang Guotao, Gao Gang, Peng Dehuai, Liu Shaoqi and Lin Biao) from power.[38]

Mao's way of removing Peng Dehuai, Liu Shaoqi, and Lin Biao deserves more attention, for it revealed in full how Mao defined, created, and manipulated contradictions to destroy the once second most powerful persons in the Communist hierarchy.

Second in Military Command: Peng Dehuai[39]

From 1927 to 1959, Peng Dehuai served continuously as one of Mao's top commanders. He fought the guerrilla war in the Jiangxi hills, went through the Long March, engaged the Japanese army during the Second World War, stood shoulder to shoulder with Mao in the Yan'an battle of 1947 and the ensuing civil war, and commanded the Chinese army in the Korean War in 1950-1953. In 1954 he was appointed defense minister, a deputy chairman of the Central Military Commission, and a Politburo member in the following year. He was second in command in the People's Liberation Army—second to Mao.

During the Great Leap Forward Campaign, he became seriously concerned about its failings. Under the Party's direction, he went on in 1958 an inspection tour of the provinces. In July 1959 as he was called to an enlarged conference of the Politburo in Lu Shan to assess the results of the Great Leap, he delivered a 10,000-word private letter to Mao on his findings. He disclosed that the steel output and agricultural production reported by provincial and local governments to the Party were overly inflated and that the Commune system had brought widespread food shortage in the villages. He also spoke openly at the conference about his misgivings of the Great Leap. Three other critics of the campaign—Huang Kecheng (chief of staff of the army), Zhang Wentian (deputy foreign minister), and Zhou Xiaozhou (Party chief in Hunan Province) expressed the same opinion.

Mao took Peng's presentations not a reality assessment of the Great Leap but a rejection of the basic line of economic policy Mao had been pursuing. More ominously, he condemned Peng and the other three critics as having formed a "Military Club" to engage in anti-Party activities. Making use of his agenda-setting authority at the conference, he set the tone for criticizing Peng and turned around mobilizing the Party's senior leaders, Liu Shaoqi, Zhou Enlai, and Zhu De, to join him in condemning Peng. These leaders, who had endorsed the Great Leap when it was initiated, were left with nothing but the job of defending it.

At a crucial meeting of the conference on July 23, 1959, Mao started the attack. At the outset, Mao admitted that the Great Leap had suffered some failures, such as spotty production decline and deliberate falsification of output in certain localities. He declared, "Comrades, the principal responsibility for [these problems]...is mine. I should be criticized." With his voice registering a sad note, he quoted a Confucian metaphor to indicate his plight. The metaphor stated "*shi zuo yong zhe, qi wu hou hu"*—a man committing serious mistakes would have no heir. So, he said chokingly, "I have no heir. One son was killed [in the Korean War], and the other has gone mad."

The audience went deadly silent.

Then Mao turned on the offensive. Facing Peng directly, he threatened, "If the People's Liberation Army goes with you, I will go to the hills to fight a guerrilla war."

Mao followed up with still something else at a Politburo's meeting on July 26. He said that he had criticized Peng during the Yan'an Rectification Campaign in 1942; hence, Peng had harbored a grudge against him since. Now Peng criticized Mao for the Great Leap's failure seventeen years later in revenge. He continued, "You cursed me for twenty days [here in Lu Shan], explicitly referring to my name and fussing to no end. What do you want?"

Peng suddenly rose up from his seat and roared, "You f... my mother for forty days in Yan'an [referring to Mao's criticism of him lasting forty days then]. I can't f... your mother even for twenty days [in Lu Shan]?"

The participants of the meeting, stunned speechless for a moment, went on one by one to chastise Peng for his outburst and use of profanities.

A few days later, a power play took place in an even more emotionally charged atmosphere. Several top Party leaders gathered at Mao's Lu Shan residence to unleash a barrage of attack on Peng. They included Mao, Liu Shaoqi, Zhou Enlai, Zhu De, and Lin Biao. Lin, who had been recuperating elsewhere from an illness, just arrived in Lu Shan at Mao's urgent summon. Sighting Lin as a counterweight to Peng in the military establishment, Mao elevated Lin in 1958 from a field marshal to a deputy chairman of the Communist Party and a member of the Standing Committee of the Politburo. As such, Lin enjoyed a higher standing and a stronger voice in the Communist power structure than Peng, who was a merely deputy chairman of the Central Military Commission and a regular Politburo member.

Lin soldierly defended Mao's Great Leap and criticized Peng for challenging Mao's leadership. Then, he raised an extraneous issue. "Comrade Peng Dehuai, you recently visited Eastern European countries," Lin said. "Now you came to Lu Shan to make a big fuss. Is there any connection? Khrushchev spoke so highly of you. Did you promise him anything?"

In 1959, China and the Soviet Union were in the beginning stage of political split, and Mao had condemned Khrushchev as following a

"Revisionist" policy. Any Chinese leader identified with Khrushchev was considered politically and ideologically treasonous.

Peng promptly fought back; he denied any connection with Khrushchev, whom he had met when leading a Chinese military delegation to visit the Soviet Union and Eastern Europe in April-June, 1959. He retorted, "I couldn't speak even one sentence in a foreign language. What did I talk with the bald-headed Khrushchev? You can ask the interpreter to find out." [40]

Soon afterwards, the Politburo, under Mao's behind-the-scene direction, sealed the fate of Peng and other critics of the Great Leap by passing "A Resolution on the Errors of the Peng Dehuai-led Anti-Party Group" and "A Resolution to Safeguard the Party's General Line and to Oppose the Rightist Opportunism." Peng and Huang Kecheng, Zhang Wentian, and Zhou Xiaozhou were immediately placed under surveillance,[41] and within the year, Peng was stripped of his positions as deputy chairman of the Central Military Commission and Defense Minister, with both positions handed to Lin Biao; and the other three critics were relieved of their positions as well.

Years later, in 1967, at the height of the Cultural Revolution, Peng was dragged out of a prison and displayed in a parade on the street. Severely beaten by the Red Guards, with his lung punctured and breastbone broken, he slouched forward in halting steps, with his arms held behind him by two Red Guards and his head limping downward— an imagery of a victim of sadism and humiliation caught in a widely circulated photograph. The second highest-ranking commander of the People's Liberation Army died years later a broken man.

In June 1981 the Communist Party recanted its condemnation of Peng Dehuai, Huang Kecheng, Zhang Wentian, and Zhou Xiaozhou, with its Central Committee passing a resolution to rehabilitate these people and to declare the accusation of them as the Rightists "completely erroneous." But that was long after both Peng and Mao were dead.

Second in Political Command: Liu Shaoqi

If Peng Dehuai was one of Mao's closest comrades-in-arms, Liu Shaoqi was one of Mao's most intimate political associates. The two men were born in the same province, (Hunan), attended the same school (the Hunan Provincial Normal School), organized together a leftist group (the Socialist Youth Corps) in their native place, and joined the Communist Party in the same year, 1921. Since then, like a soldier rising through the ranks to reach the top command position, Liu started out as a Leftist labor organizer and rose to the Party's regional chief and the army's political commissar and, finally, the second most important political leader of the Party, second to Mao, in 1943.

After the Party came to power in 1949, Mao and Liu collaborated smoothly, Mao as the ideological propagator and policy initiator, and Liu as the interpreter of Mao's conceptual statements and administrator of Mao's policies. In April 1959, with Mao's endorsement, Liu succeeded him as chairman of the government. Liu remained deferential to Mao, who retained the all-powerful positions of chairman of the Party and head of the Central Military Commission.

Like Mao, Liu believed that revolution was the only road to power. But he was not a perennial radical, and once the Communists controlled the government, he saw no need for adopting revolutionary methods—in the form of mass campaigns and violence—to force rapid industrialization and agricultural collectivization. Here was the seed of the evolving difference between him and Mao, for Mao remained a fanatic Leftist obsessed with achieving economic gains by war-like means. Still, when Peng Dehuai sparked a fiery confrontation with Mao in Lu Shan, Liu came to Mao's defense even though he shared Peng's misgivings about the Great Leap.

As he became head of the government in 1959, Liu engaged in an arduous task of recovery from the severe economic losses caused by the Great Leap. He was assisted by Deng Xiaoping, the Secretary General of the Party. The two men took steps to undo the Great Leap's major programs. In the countryside, they started replacing the Commune with a kind of contract system in agriculture, whereby farmers pledged to deliver to government a realistic amount of grains while being allowed flexibility in managing their farms. The backyard furnace program was abolished.

Mao took these developments not only as an unacceptable departure from his preferred ideological line in economic development but also, more seriously, as manifestations of a potential challenge by Liu to Mao's leadership position. In the next three years the discord between Mao and Liu rose in intensity as Liu and Deng achieved considerable economic progress and earned increasing respect both within and without the Party. Mao decided to attack Liu. He started with a seemingly routine and perfunctory appeal to his colleagues not to forget class struggle. Yet he was preparing a way for dividing the Party into two ideological camps, his camp being dedicated to socialism, and the other, headed by Liu, turning increasingly to capitalism and

Revisionism. The invectives he used to condemn the opponent camp gained poisoning intensity as time went on.

Then in 1966 Mao went back to Lin Biao again for political backing. Lin dispatched his most trusted 38th Army to Beijing; he secured through his subordinates the control of the Garrison Command and wrested control of the most important public media—*The People's Daily*, the Central Broadcasting Station, and the New China News Agency—from officials allied with Liu. Mao, on his part, toured the provinces to insure the regional military chiefs' continuing loyalty to him. Having fought decade-long battles under Mao's directions and inspirations, they had been his most reliable subordinates.

When the Cultural Revolution was launched, Mao instigated the Red Guards to attack Liu as "China's Khrushchev," "the Number One Capitalist Roader" within the government. From early 1967 on, Liu and his wife Wang Guangmei, both of whom had already been previously placed under house arrest, were repeatedly subject to "struggle" sessions and beating by the Red Guards in the Zhongnanhai—the compound in Beijing containing the central government's and Party's offices and the senior leaders' residences. Though such struggle secessions took place while Mao was away from Beijing, it was logical to assume that they were conducted with his approval, since Wang Dongxing, Director of the Regiment of the Central Security Guards (Unit 8341), a confidant of Mao's, was in charge of security of the compound.

Within the year Liu disappeared from public view. In October 1968, the Communist Party officially condemned the head of the People's Republic of China as "a traitor, hidden spy, and parasite of the labor movement." In 1969 Liu died from multiple illnesses in a detention center in Kaifeng, Henan Province, without having received any rudimentary medical care. His disheveled body was wrapped in a urine- and feces-soaked blanket and carried away with his bare legs exposed; it was cremated as non-identifiable person's remains.

In February 1980, three and half years after Mao's death, the Communist Party rehabilitated Liu, with a belated state funeral for Liu.

Second in Military and Political Command: Lin Biao

Like Peng Dehuai and Liu Shaoqi, Lin Biao was one of Mao's decades-old comrades and subordinates, stretching from the Jiangxi days in the 1920s all the way to the late 1960s. A master military strategist and brilliant commander, the Whampoa-educated Lin fought many battles against the warlords, the Japanese, and the Nationalists. Over these years, Lin steadily rose in political stature and, in 1969, became "China's most powerful soldier and second most powerful politician."[42]

Yet, precisely it was then that the contradiction between Mao and Lin began to appear. Unlike Peng Dehuai, who harbored no political ambition, Lin was repeatedly drawn into the fray of power struggles. As noted earlier, he was appointed in 1958 vice chairman of the Party and a member of the Standing Committee of the Politburo. Judging by the revelations at the Lu Shan conference of 1959, one can say that Lin gained such aura of authority because Mao had planned to use Lin to balance out the influence of Peng, who was popular in the military ranks.

Yet, Lin had developed no popular following, had no widespread respect within the top echelon of the Party or among the senior generals, and, above all, possessed no political acumen remotely matching Mao's. He was a brilliant general but a political simpleton. Since the late 1950s he had built up a symbiotic relationship with the Helmsman. Lin initiated a campaign for personality cult of Mao in the army, symbolized by *The Little Red Book* he compiled and prefaced. In the spring of 1966 when the Cultural Revolution started, Lin moved his 38th Army to Beijing to take over the garrison command as well as the Party's propaganda apparatus, as noted above. He provided Mao with physical security when the Helmsman was hatching a plot to dismantle the vast government and Party instrumentalities held firmly by Liu Shaoqi and Deng Xiaoping. And the People's Liberation Army stood behind the Red Guards, enabling them to go on a nationwide rampage unhindered.

Mao took steps to reward Lin for his vital services. In 1969 Mao called the Ninth Congress of the Communist Party into session to pronounce Lin as his "closest comrade-in-arms" and successor. He also allowed Lin to expand dramatically his hold of the army, with the top echelon of the Defense Ministry filled with Lin's choices, including Huang Yongsheng as Chief of Staff, Wu Faxian as Chief of Air Force, Li Zuopeng as Political Commissar of the Navy, and Qiu Huizuo as Chief of the General Logistics Department. In addition, Lin's son, Liguo, became Director of War Operations of the Air Force.

Rising so high and so fast in stature and power, Lin unwittingly let his political ambition surface in 1970, when he made an unexpected move at a Party conference in Lu Shan in August. He requested that the office of chairmanship of the government, which had stayed vacant since the downfall of Liu Shaoqi, be restored with Mao re-occupying it. Such a request was immediately perceived by conference participants, especially Mao, as a masked move for early transfer of power from Mao to Lin. Intolerant of any gesture hinting a challenge to his leadership position, Mao adamantly opposed the move and lashed out at Chen Boda (Mao's one-time secretary) for endorsing it. Lin took Mao's stance as recanting his decision on making Lin his successor and resented the bluff.

The dispute between Mao and Lin quickly came to a head in 1971. Mao decided to remove Lin from power but faced the formidable task of dismantling Lin's sweeping hold in the army. He made elaborate preparations and took his actions deliberately. In August and September 1971, he took an extensive tour of the nation's military regions to line up their commanders' support in an expected showdown with Lin. In this tour, he revealed in startlingly frank terms to the army commanders his intrigues against Lin then in progress:

> I used three methods to [deal with the Lin Biao clique]: *shuai shi zi, can sha zi,* and *wa qiang jiao,* ["throw rocks," "mix sand," and "puncture the wall at its base"]. Lashing out at Chen Boda [Lin Biao's principal supporter outside the army] is to throw rocks at them. A piece of densely compacted dirt has no air in it. Mix it with sand will allow air to circulate. We haven't inserted enough people into the Secretariat of the Central Military Commission [controlled by Lin]; we need to insert more. This is to mix sand. Reorganize the Beijing Military Region [also controlled by Lin] is to puncture the wall at its base.[43]

So, it was with the old-fashioned political infighting—attacking the opponent's underlings, spying on his activities, and sagging his power base—Mao battled Lin Biao.

Lin was plotting his moves, as well. While staying in Beidaihe, a coastal resort east of Beijing, he approved a plan devised by his son Liguo, known as the 571 Project, for a coup d'état. The plan called for a series of plots to assassinate Mao during the last days of his tour of the military regions: an air raid of Mao's train when he returned from Shanghai to Beijing following the tour, a bomb planted in a railroad bridge on Mao's return route, and other moves.

But Mao outwitted Lin by returning Beijing earlier than Lin had expected so as to avert the assassination attempt. On September 12, 1971, as Mao's train sped to Beijing unscathed, Lin knew his plots had failed; he and his wife Ye Qun and son Liguo hurriedly took a flight on September 13 to the Soviet Union on a Trident jet, but all died in a firestorm from a crash of the plane in Outer Mongolia the same day.[44]

Thus Mao's officially designated successor was burned to skeleton two years after the previous successor died from painful illnesses. Two years later still the Communist Party issued its verdict on Lin in the form of "A Report on the Counter-Revolutionary Crimes of the Lin Biao's Anti-Party Group," including a full account of the 571 Project.[45] The Party, however, never since exonerated Lin, as it did Peng and Liu.

Mao had battled all his most powerful rivals within the Chinese Communist Party to their ignominious death.

The Only Revolution of Its Kind

The Great Proletarian Cultural Revolution of 1966-1976 is a Mao Zedong designed, directed, and completed upheaval unique in the chronicle of revolutions of the world. It was a movement to dismantle a gigantic power structure by the very head of that structure. It threw nearly one billion people into a political arena of chaos and violence. It targeted the masses, the intellectuals, the cadres, and top political leaders of China in a decade-long campaign of struggle. It deliberately damaged the cultural heritage of a nation that has long been proud of its history.

What is presented below is not an account of what had transpired in this Chinese great scourge, for numerous works have been published on the subject.[46] Instead, the focus of attention is narrowed down to its two intertwining dimensions: a power struggle and a massive cultural rampage—more on the former than on the latter.

When sponsoring the Cultural Revolution to destroy the government and Party establishment, Mao attacked from the bottom up, using a strategy of deception. He began by commending a historical play written by Wu Han, Deputy Mayor of Beijing, "The Dismissal of Hai Rui from Office." The play described how an emperor of the Ming Dynasty removed an upright court official, Hai Rui, for having offended him. Mao considered it a case exemplifying a virtuous official who was challenging a corrupt emperor. Then, on second thought, he turned around to raise the issue that the author of the play, Wu Han, erred in praising feudalistic institutions and practices, thus giving the impression of an attempt to promote the traditional culture.

Mao did not, however, raise the issue by himself but through a then obscure person, Yao Wenyuan, a Shanghai journalist, whom Mao came to know via his wife Jiang Qing. In an essay criticizing the play, Yao submitted his "ninth draft" to Mao, who revised it three times before it was published in November 1965.[47] Once the essay was published, Mao blessed it with his endorsement, considering it a clear exposition of the survival of the traditional culture. He decided to wage a cultural revoltion to combat it. Mao's idea of cultural revolution caught the attention of Wu Han's superior, Mayor of Beijing Peng Zhen as well as other ranking officials of the Party, including Tao Zhu and Lu Dingyi—the two officials in charge of literary and propaganda matters. These officials took Mao's idea as an effort to initiate a literary debate or dialogue on what constituted the proper content of the Socialist culture and what elements of the traditional culture should be banned. They quickly embraced it, set up a Cultural Revolution Group at the Party center, and dispatched working teams to the provinces to promote the dialogue.

They misread Mao's intention, badly so, for Mao had changed his perception of the play. He suspected that it was a metaphorical device to criticize his dismissal of Peng Dehuai in 1959, the same year the play was written. And since Peng Zhen, Tao Zhu, and Lu Dingyi were all known to have been closely associated with Liu Shaoqi and Deng Xiaoping, he suspected further that these "people in power" were using the play to undermine his authority. He immediately formed a coterie of his faithful followers for action. These included, in addition to Yao Wenyuan, Mao's wife Jiang Qing, Zhang Chunqiao (chief of the Party's Shanghai branch), and Wang Hongwen (a worker-activist who eventually rocketed to the position of vice chairman of the Communist Party during the Cultural Revolution). They became known later as the Gang of Four.

Thus what appeared at first a matter of literary issue became a matter of power play. As Mao's Cultural Revolution was launched in the spring of 1966, Wu Han, Peng Zhen, Lu Dingyi, and Tao Zhu were all publicly condemned in street demonstrations and were removed from office, the first casualties of the Revolution. On August 18, 1966, a million of high school and college students, wearing Red Guard armbands, from all over the country gathered in the Tiananmen Square to meet with the Helmsman. Subsequently more of them gathered at this site several times, totaling 11 million.

The most violent, chaotic phase of the Cultural Revolution began. In all units of the government, the Party, schools, economic enterprises, factories, and professional associations, rival factions emerged; they verbally and physically attacked each other in a demonstration of zeal for supporting the Revolution. In 1967 the power struggle reached the greatest intensity when Liu Shaoqi and Deng Xiaoping were forced out of office. And those government and Party cadres who were denounced as supporters of the Liu-Deng policy line, numbered at tens of thousands, were sent to the 5-7 Cadre Schools—labor camps—for reform and redemption. The power structure of the government and the Party led by people considered by Mao as his opponents was thus decimated.

So much of this discussion has dealt with the power-struggle dimension of the Cultural Revolution. How was its cultural dimension manifested? Ironic as it may seem, Mao had no idea on how to abolish the old culture and build the new one. He never took the trouble to delimit the content of "the old thought, old culture, old habits, and old customs"—"The Four Olds"—that he asked the people to abandon; nor did he define "The Four News" that he wanted people to adopt. As a result, the Red Guards interpreted their mandate for destroying the old culture in any way they pleased. They ransacked temples, historical monuments, cemeteries, and ancestral halls all over the country; they broke ancient artworks into pieces; they burned books on the classics; they beat scholars and drove them to suicide. Their path of destruction ran crisscross from Manchuria to Tibet, from Xinjiang to Fujian, reducing the precious Chinese cultural heritage to ruins. The whole nation seemed to have gone mad.

The Cultural Revolution took a much heavier toll than any other mass campaign—or even war—that Mao was involved in. Ye Jianying, a principal political/military leader who survived Mao, stated at the Central Working Conference of the Party on December 13, 1978 that 100 million people were subject to "struggles" in the ten years of the Revolution; 20 million died; 800 billion Chinese dollars worth of asset was wasted.[48] Accounts by academic specialists show vastly different numbers. Roderick MacFarquhar and Michael Schoenhals, who studied the Cultural Revolution with care and intensity, estimated that in rural China alone some 36 million people were persecuted, of whom between 750,000 and 1.5 million were killed. Chang and Halliday indicated that more than 3 million people perished in violent death.[49]

Recalling five years later such an unprecedented catastrophe, the Chinese Communist Party was forced to give a verdict of the Cultural Revolution at a meeting of its Central Committee on June 27, 1981: "The 'Cultural Revolution,' which lasted from May 1966 to October 1976, was responsible for the most severe setback and the heaviest losses suffered by the Party, the state and the people since the founding of the People's Republic. It was initiated and led by Comrade Mao Zedong...."[50]

Reaching the Limit of the Art of the Possible

In handling the contradictions among the people, Mao made it a practice to dichotomize people into conflicting categories: revolutionaries v. counter-revolutionaries; proletariats v. bourgeoisie; Rightists v. Anti-Rightists; anti-Party group v. Party-faithfuls; and feudalists, capitalists, and Revisionists v. Mao's brand of Socialists. He instigated the conflicting groups to battle each other out, with him serving as the final arbiter of the contest.

Mao often backed up the campaigns of struggle with the barrel of the pen and the barrel of the gun. As seen in his criticism of Liang Shuming, he condemned the Confucian scholar as having used "the pen to kill people," i. e., writing out reactionary materials poisoning the mind of the proletariats. That could not be tolerated. In the People's Republic of China only Mao and his apostles could hold the barrel of the pen to propagate the progressive, revolutionary, proletarian thoughts and to kill the reactionary, counter-revolutionary and bourgeois "poison weeds." His various statements issued during the Cultural Revolution—from the *Da Zi Bao* (wall posters), to the editorials of the central media organs, to conference pronouncements—monopolized the mind of the people and rallied the frenzied millions for action.

Mao held firmly as well the barrel of the gun to ward off any potential challenge during the Cultural Revolution. As chairman of the Central Military Commission, he held the right of appointment of army commanders and had exclusive authority over troop movements. He maintained a strong hold of the military regions of the nation with frequent inspection tours.[51] Whenever he found it necessary to use the gun to meet a critical political threat, he would maneuver with patience and care to achieve his objective. He cultivated the political ambition of one field marshal, Lin Biao, to check on the unruliness of another field marshal, Peng Dehuai. He created the Red Guards as the Cultural Revolutionists, but when the Red Guards went out of control, he ordered the army to banish millions of them to the countryside, without mincing one word of appreciation for his youthful revolutionists' help in toppling his powerful rivals. And Mao also had Unit 8341 as his hidden gun to exert the ultimate control of his opponents.

To exercise his art of the possible, Mao was facilitated by a very fertile mind. He invented or borrowed from others such terms as the Three Antis, Five Antis, a Hundred Blooming Flowers, the Great Leap Forward, the Four Cleanups, and the Four Olds and the Four News; and gave each term an ideological and policy content. When these terms began to serve as battle cries of campaigns, all Communist cadres, high or low, could not find reason to oppose them. Who could object the movement to sweep clean the Nationalist remnants in the first days of the Communist regime? Who could argue that the Party should not combat the undesirable practices as identified in the Three-Anti and Five-Anti campaigns? Who could challenge the idea that the Party might be benefited from criticisms of non-Party personalities during the Hundred Flowers campaign? So it went with other campaigns. Mao was always able to use the right words to characterize the right campaigns that others could not but join and push forward.

Mao was an unparalleled strategist of deception. He invented the idea of "conspiracy openly played out" (*yang mu*) during the One Hundred Flowers campaign to fool the people with the most intelligent minds in China into revealing frankly their disgust with the Communist rule. He then put them to a hellish treatment lasting two whole decades for baring their mind. That he could fool these intelligent people because, one supposes, these people were sophisticated only in intellectual pursuits but totally naïve in terms of Mao's style of politics. Yet he played open-conspiracy a second time, in the 1966 initiated Cultural Revolution. He lured Liu Shaoqi, Deng Xiaoping, Peng Zhen, Tao Zhu, and Lu Dingyi to embracing a Cultural Revolution that later did their political undoing. These people were not politically uninitiated activists but veteran Communist leaders who had gone through the crucible of prolonged wars and had been trained in intrigues in the decades of underground life. Then, in his last power struggle, he played the open conspiracy tactics the third time to trigger Lin Biao to take a desperate action leading to his demise. He trapped both the intellectuals and the veteran Communist leaders into miserable predicament and did so without the slightest concern that he had been glaringly and persistently dishonest.

Mao's mastery of his theory of contradictions and skillful application of it allowed one man to dominate nearly one billion people with impunity, to devastate millions upon millions of people in order to enforce his brand of Socialism, and to secure his position as the supreme leader. And he retains to this day the homage of still millions upon millions of Communists. In the exercise of the art of the possible, he seemed to have reached its uttermost limit.

NOTES

[1] Alexander Hamilton, James Madison, and John Jay, *The Federalist* (New York: The New American Library, 1961), pp. 78-79.

[2] At a conference in 1956, Mao told his listeners, "There are people who are very optimistic, considering that once the Communist society is established, there won't be contradictions anymore. I, for one, don't believe it. Contradictions do exist." He went on to explain. This is so because "[people] have different beliefs and view things differently." Zhong Gong Zhong Yang Wen Xian Yan Jiu Shi (The Institute on Documentary Research of the Chinese Communist Party), ed., *Mao Zedong Zhuan [Biography of Mao Zedong 1949-1976]*, Vol. 1 (Beijing: Zhong Yang Wen Xian Chu Ban She, 2003), p. 527. In 1971, Mao repeated essentially the same point, substituting the word "struggle" for "contradiction": "Will there be no struggle when Communism is realized? I don't believe it. There still will be struggles in the Communist [society]. It is only that struggles occur between the new and the old and between the correct and the erroneous." Guo Li Zheng Zhi Da Xue, Guo Ji Guan Xi Yan Jiu Zhong Xin (National Chengchi University, Institute of International Relations), *Zhong Gong Ji Mi Wen Jian Hui Bian [A Collection of the Confidential Documents of the Chinese Communist Party]* (1978), p. 36.

[3] Mao Zedong, "On the Correct Handling of Contradictions among the People," in *Four Essays on Philosophy*, Beijing: Foreign Language Press,1968.Http://www.elext.or/Politics/MIM/wim/onhandling.html (The essay came first in the form of a speech before the Supreme State Conference on February 27, 1957). Mao described how the meaning of "the people" and "the enemy" could change under different circumstances with the following illustrations: "Take our own country for example. During the War of Resistance against Japan, all those classes, strata and social groups opposing Japanese aggression came within the category of the people, while the Japanese imperialists, the Chinese traitors and the pro-Japanese elements were all enemies of the people. During the War of Liberation, the U. S. imperialists and their running dogs—the bureaucrat-capitalists, the landlords and the Kuomintang reactionaries who represented these two classes—were the enemies of the people, while the other classes, strata and social groups, which opposed these enemies, all came within the category of the people. At the present stage, the period of building socialism, the classes, strata

and social groups which favour, support and work for the cause of socialist construction all come within the category of the people, while the social forces and groups which resist the socialist revolution and are hostile to or sabotage socialist construction are enemies of the people."

For an extensive exposition of Mao's theory of contradictions and his application of the theory to the anti-Rightist campaign, see Roderick MacFarquhar, *The Origins of the Cultural Revolution, 1. Contradictions among the People, 1956-1957*, New York: Columbia University Press, 1974.

[4] See Mao, "On the Correct Handling of Contradictions among the People."

[5] For details, see *Biography of Mao*, Vol. 1, p. 484.

[6] The principal works consulted for this section include Gordon A. Bennett, *Yundong: Mass Campaigns in Chinese Communist Leadership*, Berkeley, CA: Center for Chinese Studies, University of California, 1976; David E. Apter and Tony Saich, *Revolutionary Discourse in Mao's Republic*, Cambridge: Harvard University Press, 1994; Roderick MacFarquhar and Michael Schoenhals, *Mao's Last Revolution*, Cambridge: Harvard University Press, 2006; and Michael Robert Dutton, *Policing Chinese Politics: A History*. Durham: Duke University Press, 2005.

[7] These included the Great Sparrow Campaign (initiated in 1958), the Learning from Comrade Lei Feng Campaign (1963), and the derivatives of the Cultural Revolution: the Cleansing of the Class Rank Campaign (1967), the One Strike-Three Anti Campaign (initiated 1970), the Criticizing Lin, Criticizing Kong Campaign (1973), the Criticizing Deng and Repulsing the Right-Deviationist Campaign (1975).

[8] *Biography of Mao*, Vol. 1, p.199; and Yang Kuisong, "Reconsidering the Campaign to Suppress Counterrevolutionaries," *China Quarterly*, No. 193 (March 2008) : 108.

[9] Recently declassified Chinese government documents reveal that in 1950 eleven spies of foreign countries were convicted in trial in China and that in 1951 through 1954 a total of 230 secret agents from Taiwan were apprehended in the country. Xu Jingli, *Jie Mi: Zhongguo Wai Jiao Dang An [Declassified Chinese Diplomatic Archive]* (Beijing: Zhong Guo Dang An Chu Ban She, 2005), pp. 227-34 and 289-90. With their minuscule size, these convicted individuals were in no position to mount any large-scale anti-regime movement. See also Yang, "Reconsidering the Campaign to Suppress Counterrevolutionaries," 103.

[10] Ibid.,120; and http://zh.wikipedia.org/wiki/%E9%95%87%E5 %8F%8D%E8% BF%90%E5%8A%A8.

[11] Liu Shaoqi, "Report on the Land Reform Issues" at the Political Consultative Assembly, First Plenary Session, Second Meeting, in1950. http://zh.wikipedia.org/wiki/%E5%9C%9F%E5%9C%8B0%E6%94%B9%E9%9D%A9%E8%BF%90%E5%8A%A8".

[12] Li Su, "Yi Jiu Si Jiu Zhi Hou: Tu Gai He Yi Yao Sha Ren?" [Why People Were Killed in the Post-1949 Land Reform?] (December 2, 2007); and Pan Guangdan, Chuan Weitian, *Su Nan Tu Di Gai Ge Fang Wen Ji* [*Interviews on Land Reform in South Jiangsu*] (Beijing: San Lian Shu Dian, 1952), p.108, quoted in http://zh.wikipedia.org/zh-cn/%E5%9C%9F%E5%9C%B0%E6%94%B9%E9%9D%A9%E8%BF%90%E5%8A%A8; William Hinton, *Fanshen: A Documentary of Revolution in a Chinese Village.* New York : Monthly Review Press, [c1966].

[13] See Thomas P. Bernstein, "Mao Zedong and the Famine of 1959-1960: A Study in Willfulness," *The China Quarterly,* Issue 186 (June 2006): 435; and Nai-ruenn Chen and Walter Galenson, *The Chinese Economy under Communism* (Chicago: Aldine Pub. Co. [1969]), p. 216.

[14] For official estimates, see Peng Xizhe, "Demographic Consequences of the Great Leap Forward in China's Provinces," *Population and Development Review* 13, No. 4 (1987): 639-70. For field reports, see Yang Jisheng, *Mu Bei: Zhong Guo Liu Shi Nian Dai Da Ji Huang Ji Shi* [*Tomb Stone: A Factual Account of the Great Chinese Famine in the 1960s*], Hong Kong: Da Di Tu Shu You Xian Gong Si, 2009; and Frank Dikötter, *Mao's Great Famine: The History of China's Most Devastating Catastrophe, 1958-62* (London: Bloomsbury, 2010), pp. x and 324-325. For estimates by Chinese and foreign scholars, fourteen in all, see Matthew White, "Source List and Detailed Death Tolls for the Twentieth Century Hemoclysm... People's Republic of China, Mao Zedong's regime (1949-1975)." C:Documents and Settings\Owner\Desktop\20th C. Death Tolls.mht.

[15] Qi Maoji, *Mao Zedong he Peng Dehuai, Lin Biao de He Zuo yu Chong Tu 1954-1971* [*Cooperation and Conflict between Mao Zedong and Peng Dehuai and Lin Biao*] (Taipei: Xin Xin Wen Wen Hua Shi Ye Gu Fen Gong Si, 1997), p.158.

[16] Cited in http://zh.wikipedia.org/wiki/%E5%A4%A7%E8%B7%83%E8%BF%9B.

[17] See Kenneth Lieberthal and Michel Oksenberg, *Policy Making in China: Leaders, Structures, and Processes* (Princeton: Princeton University Press, c1988), pp. 408-09.

[18] Chang and Halliday, *Mao, The Unknown Story*, pp. 91-94.

[19] For a recent work on the Yan'an Rectification Campaign, see Gao Hua, *Hong Tai Yang Shi Zen Yang Sheng Qi de: Yan'an Zheng Feng Yun Dong de Lai Long Qu Mai* [*How Did the Red Sun Rise: The Whole Story of the Yan'an Rectification Campaign*], Hong Kong: Zhong Wen Da Xue Chu Ban She, 2000.

[20] Short, *Mao: A Life*, p. 437.

[21] See *Biography of Mao*, Vol. 1, pp. 639-41; and Chang and Halliday, *Mao: The Unknown Story*, p. 419.

[22] Michael Y. M. Kau and John K. Leung, eds., *The Writings of Mao Zedong, 1949-1976* (Armonk, NY: M. E. Sharpe, 1986), p. 18.

[23] Ibid., p. 397.

[24] Ibid., p. 403.

[25] "Liang Shuming Shou Mao Zedong Yan Li Pi Ping de Li Shi Gong An Zhen Xiang" [A Historical Case: the True Story of Liang Shuming Being Severely Criticized by Mao Zedong], http://sznews.com/culture/content/2008-09/25/content_ 3272124.htm.

[26] Feng Zejun and Wang Shuoxun, "Pi Cuo Yi Ren, Duo Sheng Si Yi—Ji Nian Ren Kou Xue Jia, Jiao Yu Jia Ma Yinchu Xian Sheng" [An Erroneous Criticism of One Person Begot Additional Four Hundred Million— In Memory of the Population Theorist and Educationist Mr. Ma Yinchu], *BL*, No. 504 (May 2004): 12-14.

[27] Ibid., p. 4.

[28] Chang and Halliday, *Mao: The Unknown Story*, p. 417.

[29] For criticisms voiced at the forums, see *Biography of Mao*, Vol. 1, pp. 685-92; and Chang and Halliday, *Mao: The Unknown Story*, pp. 417-18.

[30] *Biography of Mao*, Vol. 1, p. 666.

[31] Quoted in Chang and Halliday, *Mao: The Unknown Story*, p. 417.

[32] Quoted in *Biography of Mao Zedong*, Vol. 1, p. 691.

[33] Ibid., p. 691-92.

[34] Ibid., p. 712; and Qi, *Mao Zedong he Peng Dehuai*, p. 18.

[35] Chang and Halliday, *Mao: The Unknown Story*, p. 420.

[36] http://culture.people.com.cn/GB/40479/40480/3905491.html.

[37] *Biography of Mao*, Vol. 1, p. 712.

[38] For the text of Mao's talks, see *Confidential Documents of the Chinese Communist Party*, pp. 32-37. At this time, Mao had not yet removed Lin from power but was about to.

[39] Voluminous writings on the case of Peng Dehuai have been published, including several biographies on Peng. Three studies are relied on for this section: Qi, *Mao Zedong he Peng Dehuai*, pp. 71-109;

Sun Daluo, *Mao Zedong Quan Su Shi* [*A Chronicle of Mao Zedong's Power Play*] (Hong Kong: Xia Fei Er Chu Ban Gong Si, 2001), pp.139-64; and Jia Shinan, *Mao Zedong Ren Ji Jiao Wang Shi Lu, 1915-1976* [*A Factual Record of Mao Zedong's Social Life*] (Nanjing: Jiangsu Wen Yi Chu Ban She, 1989), pp. 171-78.

[40] For the emotional confrontation of Mao and Lin with Peng at the Lu Shan meetings, see ibid., pp. 257-58; and Xin Ziling, *Mao Zedong Quan Zhuan* [*The Complete Biography of Mao Zedong*], Vol. 6 (Taipei: Shu Hua Chu Ban Shi Ye Gong Si, 1993), pp. 82-112.

[41] Wang Dongxing, chief of Mao's bodyguards and head of a military organization known as Unit 8341(the Regiment of Central Security Guards), kept the accused under surveillance. Xin, *The Complete Biography of Mao*, pp. 83-84.

[42] Thomas W. Robinson *A Politico-Military Biography of Lin Piao*, with translations by Anna Sun Ford (Santa Monica, CA: The Rand Corporation, 1971), p. iii.

[43] *Confidential Documents of the Chinese Communist Party*, p. 35.

[44] Wang Dongxing, who was with Mao during the 1971 regional military tours, has written a book detailing the Lin Biao affair. Wang Dongxing, *Wang Dongxing Hui Yi*: *Mao Zedong yu Lin Biao Fan Ge Ming Ji Tuan de Dou Zheng* [*Wang Dongxing's Reminiscences: Mao Zedong's Struggle with the Lin Biao Counter-Revolutionary Group*], Beijing: Dang Dai Chu Ban She, 1997.

[45] Several studies on the Lin Biao affair raised various questions on the official report. Now, forty years after the event, we have to accept this report as a truthful account unless or until credible evidence challenging the veracity of the report surfaces. For these studies, see citation at http://zh.wikipedia.org/wiki/%E6%96%87%E5%8C%96% E5%A4% A7% E9%9D%A9%E5%91%BD#_ref-2.

Two facets of the Lin Biao affair, unknown at the time, came to light in later years. One involved the question as to why Mao in his tour of the military regions was so openly telling the commanders the steps he was taking to sack Lin. Such information was bound to be leaked to Lin, thus giving him the chance to make a preemptive strike at Mao. Indeed, Gu Tongzhou, Chief of Staff of Air Force in the Canton Military Region, a key figure in the Lin camp, did pass on Mao's talks during the tour to Lin around September 6, 1971. *www.tianshannet.com/culture/content/ 2008-03/04/content_2470980.htm*

A likely explanation lies in Mao's deliberate attempt to trick Lin into taking some untoward action—either an early start of the coup that Mao was able to foil or a desperate move like a forced flight. Only when

Lin did so could Mao be justified to declare Lin a counter-revolutionary criminal. Some observers in China termed Mao's talks in the tour as *qiao shan zhen hu*, to flush out the tiger by pounding the mountain—in other words, one more exercise of *yang mu*, a conspiracy openly played out.

The other aspect of the Lin affair concerned the critical role of the Regiment of Central Security Guards (Unit 8341) in the episode. Unit 8341 had deployed guards in residences of all top Communist leaders, including the Lin compound in Beidaihe. On September 13, 1971 Lin Liheng, Lin Biao's daughter, alerted Unit 8341 guards of Lin's escape plan moments before Lin's party fled in a car to the airport. She was suspecting that Ye Qun, her mother, coerced his father into flight. The guards tried to stop the Lin party from leaving their residence but failed. They chased the party to the airport, not in time to prevent it from taking off on a Trident jet; but the plane's wing was damaged as it hit a building. That was one of the reasons cited in the official report as the cause of the crash of the plane.

Unit 8341, an elite force of the Communist army whose origin could be traced to the Long March days, performed a double role in regard to all top Communist leaders, protecting and keeping a watch on them. Over the years, it was directed by either Wang Dongxing or his trusted subordinates, answerable to Mao. For a witness account by Lu Xuewen, a Unit 8341 officer in the Lin compound in Beidaihe, on Lin's flight, see "Kou Shu Li Shi: 1971 Nian 9 Yue 13 Ri: Wo Suo Qing Li de Lin Biao Chu Tao" [Oral History: My Personal Witness Account on Lin Biao's Flight on September 13, 1971" in news.china.com/zh_cn/history/all/11025 807/20050427/12275709.htm.

[46]Two standard works on the Cultural Revolution may be identified: Roderick MacFarquhar, *Origins of the Cultural Revolution*, Vol. One, *Contradictions among the People*; Vol. Two, *The Great Leap Forward, 1958-1960*; and Vol. Three, *The Coming of the Cataclysm, 1961-1966*, New York: Columbia University Press, 1974, 1983, 1997; and Yan Jiaqi and Gao Gao, *Turbulent Decade: A History of the Cultural Revolution*, translated from the Chinese and edited by D. W. Y. Kwok, Honolulu: University of Hawaii Press, c1996.

[47]MacFarquhar and Schoenhals, *Mao's Last Revolution*, p.17.

[48]Xin, *The Complete Biography of Mao*, Vol. 6, p. 378. Li Xiannian, a top Communist official responsible for economic planning, estimated in 1977 that the economic loss from the Cultural Revolution at 500 billion Chinese dollars, amounting to 80 percent of the country's total investment for thirty years. http://zh.wikipedia.org/wiki/% E6% 96%87%E5%8C%96%E5%A4% A7%E9%9D%A9%E5%91%BD.

[49] MacFarquhar and Schoenhals, *Mao's Last Revolution,* p. 262; and Chang and Halliday, *Mao: The Unknown Story*, p. 547.

[50] Cited in MacFarquhar and Schoenhals, *Mao's Last Revolution,* pp. 3, 483.

[51] One researcher provided detailed information on the regional tours Mao took during his rule of mainland China, 12 in all. Most of these tours included meetings with military commanders as well as top civilian administrators. Zhao Zhichao, *Mao Zedong Shi Er Ci Nan Xun* [*Mao Zedong's Twelve Tours of the South*], Beijing: Zhong Yang Wen Xian Chu Ban She, 2000. Since Mao started his tours from Beijing, which is located in north China, "Mao's tours of the south" is a figurative expression of all his tours, including a tour to the northeast—Manchuria.

PART FOUR

TOWARD A PROSPEROUS AND STRONG NATION

Chiang and Mao shared with all other Chinese leaders since the Self-strengthening Movement in the 1860s two long-term national goals: to create *fu guo qiang bing,* a prosperous nation and a strong army or, simply, a prosperous and strong nation. They fully embraced "prosperity" and "strength" as modern concepts derived from the industrial revolution experiences of Western nations. Hence, they set their sights on emulating these nations' achievements and sought to adopt their methods for building up their national prosperity and strength.

When Chiang and Mao endeavored to realize their national goals, they also confronted Western nations—and Japan—as foreign powers dominating China. They found their nation-building undertakings at times aided by some of these powers and frustrated by others. To proceed with their task, they had to engage far deeper and wider in foreign relations than had their predecessors.

In the next three chapters, Chiang and Mao's drive to achieve the two national goals will be analyzed by reference to their political interaction with foreign powers and their application of these powers' economic development experiences.

CHAPTER TEN

HANDLING FOREIGN FRIENDS AND FOES, I

In June 1900 swarms of Chinese Kung-fu fighters besieged for a month and a half foreign legations in Beijing. The Boxer Rebellion, as the incident has been known since, provoked a joint expedition against China by eight foreign powers: Austria-Hungary, Britain, France, Germany, Italy, Japan, Russia, and the United States. Their forces, 20,000 strong, stormed Beijing and suppressed the rebellion. To settle the incident, these powers imposed on the capitulated Qing Court the Beijing Protocol of September 7, 1901. The protocol allowed these powers, among other things, to station troops on Chinese soil and exacted an indemnity of 450 million taels of silver (one tael per Chinese); in addition, diplomatic corps of foreign nations would from then on act as a body superior to the Qing Court insofar as its conduct of foreign relations was concerned.[1] Talks of dismembering China as a nation were afoot—a development that recalled the division of Africa by European powers a decade and a half ago. Only a seemingly fortuitous pronouncement of the Open Door policy by the United States saved China from that tragic fate.

Though the danger of foreign conquest of the nation was averted, China had since been, as William C. Kirby has observed, subject to a progressively heavier influence from international politics.[2] Over different periods of time, China and foreign powers fought increasingly brutal wars against each other, formed close alliance at one time that was broken up by new armed conflicts, engaged in extensive economic cooperation that was followed by prolonged trade disruptions, and sealed their fate in ideological unity that fell later to a bitter contention over orthodoxy. It was in this state of affairs, in which China found foreign powers constantly switched their role as its friends and foes, that Chiang and Mao had to expend enormous energy to deal with them in order to protect their country's interests.

Chiang and Mao: Shared Traits

Chiang and Mao shared a number of traits in the conduct of foreign relations. They had scant diplomatic experience when assuming power. Chiang was first initiated to foreign affairs in his three-month visit with the Soviet Union in 1923, a nation that later turned out to be his decades-long arch foe. Soon following his return, he was continuously immersed in domestic battles and wars, and it was not until Japan seized Manchuria in 1931 that he was drawn to the power game of international politics.

Mao's first diplomatic encounter occurred in his meeting with a United States army's observation group in Yan'an in 1944. He later expressed willingness to visit America for improving relations with a nation that was destined to become his most entrenched enemy for nearly quarter of a century.[3] Like Chiang, he was for decades involved in internal wars, and it was not until 1949 that he performed his first diplomatic task by going to the Soviet Union to negotiate a security treaty.

When dealing with foreign powers, Chiang and Mao were acutely conscious of the fact that they headed a poor and divided country. China was the most populous nation on earth, but its people were among the most impoverished in the world for much of the twentieth century. In 1928 when Chiang assumed power, only the eastern one-third of the nation's territory was subject to his direct rule, with the rest—in the form of a grand arc ranging from Manchuria in the northeast, Mongolia in the north, Xinjiang in the northwest, then south to Tibet, and southeast to Yunnan—under the sway of warlords and/or foreign powers. In 1949 Mao secured the control of entire continental China, but not of Taiwan, which, with the aid of a foreign superpower, posed a potential threat to the country. These realities underscored the fact that when dealing with foreign powers, Chiang and Mao had to bargain from a position of weakness.

Yet when Chinese sovereignty and territorial integrity were being challenged, both bristled as strong nationalists in their defense. This is clearly seen in the cases of Manchuria, Taiwan, and Tibet. Chiang fought an eight-year war against Japan to regain Manchuria but was coerced to restore to the Soviet Union the imperialist privileges Russia had previously enjoyed in the area. In 1949 when Mao was in Moscow for treaty negotiation, he, not without rancor and insistence, forced Stalin to renounce these privileges.

In the case of Taiwan, the United States suggested in May 1950 to Chiang to place the island under United Nations trusteeship to avoid a Communist takeover.[4] Chiang adamantly rejected the suggestion, considering it a step toward taking Taiwan away from his country, which he had fought long and hard to recover. In spurning the suggestion, Chiang meant he would rather face the imminent danger of Communist invasion of the island than see China losing its title to Taiwan. Years later, the United States and other nations floated the "Two-China" idea in the United Nations so as to preserve Nationalist China's seat there. Chiang rejected it because he preferred the mainland and the island united under one government to a separation of the two territories under international aegis.[5] In taking such a stand, he willingly risked losing Nationalist China's seat, which, indeed, happened in 1971. Chiang's stance on the status of Taiwan won a rare praise from Mao, who considered Chiang a true patriot, putting the interest of the nation ahead of that of his regime. He said, "On this point we are in complete agreement."[6]

In regard to Tibet, Chiang took steps within the month he became the head of the Chinese government to reconnect with the isolated land after decades of revolution and war in China. In October 1928 he sent an official letter to this effect to the 13th Dalai Lama, Tibet's spiritual and political leader.[7] Subsequently he followed up with other measures to reestablish Chinese presence in Tibet, as will be discussed later in this chapter. If Chiang made an effort to maintain China's presence in Tibet, Mao took military action to back up China's claim to the territory. On October 28, 1950 he instructed the Chinese Ministry of Foreign Affairs to take a stand that "Chinese troops must reach all places in Tibet that should be reached, and that there is no room for say by any foreign country in this matter...."[8] The Communist army then battled into Tibet and occupied the entire territory.[9]

Finally, both Chiang and Mao were dedicated to building China as a major military power. They created and commanded the largest conventional army in the world and sought earnestly to acquire nuclear weapons. Mao launched a crash program in the late 1950s to develop the weapons and conducted an explosion of a nuclear device in 1964. From the late 1960s to the mid1970s Chiang conducted a clandestine program to develop nuclear weapons by making use of foreign technology for production of electric power and by attempting to cumulate U.S.-provided plutonium as weapon-grade explosive. Chiang's nuclear option, however, was closed as the United States repossessed the plutonium it had supplied to Taiwan and strongly advised against any attempt to revive the program.[10]

In general, Chiang and Mao commanded severely limited resources while playing high-stake games with China's constantly changing powerful friends and foes. Yet both emerged unexpectedly masterful diplomatic strategists at one time or another, and each persisted in his own way, through setbacks and triumphs, in the pursuit of China's national interests in a tumultuous world.

Chiang: Multiple-Power Diplomacy, 1931-1945

The Policy Guideline

Chiang's conduct of foreign relations falls into two time periods: one, from 1928 to 1945, and the other, from 1945 to 1975. In the first period, he became more actively involved in foreign relations from 1931 to 1945, which may be broadly designated as the war years since China was in intermittent military conflicts with Japan in Manchuria, Shanghai, Inner Mongolia, and north China, culminating in the Chinese-Japanese war of 1937-1945.

The Manchurian Incident of 1931 marked the beginning of Chiang's direct, intensive involvement in high diplomacy.[11] On September 20, two days after the occurrence of the Incident, Chiang urgently noted in his diaries, "I have [so far] very much neglected diplomacy because of my preoccupation with resolving domestic conflicts" (CKSD, 9/20/31). He pointed out that he was then confronted with five challenges on the home front: warlord Yan Xishan in Shanxi; the Communists in Jiangxi, a maverick Shi Yousan in Henan, the rebellious regime in Guangdong Province, and the wavering provincial authority in Hunan (CKSD, 8/16/31). If he were to take on the much more powerful Japan at that time, he would have been defeated by his foreign enemy and/or undermined by his domestic foes. For this reason, he set forth his overriding policy principle as "securing domestic unity before resisting foreign aggression." Still, he reminded himself he had to devote immediately more energy and time to the conduct of foreign relations. Two years later he crystallized his thoughts on how to deal with the four foreign powers that he regarded as exerting deep impact on China: Japan, Russia (the Soviet Union), Britain, and the United States.[12]

Japan is feuding with us but also fears us; we can deal with it by making compromises. Russia is an enemy that hates us; it intends not only to undermine our government but also to conquer our country. Britain and America want to make use of us to restrain Japan and Russia but do not have any territorial ambition [against us]. In general, we can treat Britain and America as friendly nations, Japan as a feuding nation, and Russia as the only enemy nation. To friendly nations, we act with good faith; to feuding nation, we offer favors; to enemy nation, we have to stand up to it with strength, for it won't change its stance (CKSD, 6/20/33).[13]

In the next twelve years Chiang steadily followed this simple policy guideline in handling China's relations with his targeted foreign powers.

In his initial years of diplomatic engagements, Chiang followed a rather flawed approach to the rapidly rising conflicts between China and Japan. "In regard to the Japanese invasion of our Three Northeastern Provinces [Manchuria]," he wrote immediately following the Incident, "I believe we should first refer it to the League of Nations and the signatory powers of the Pact of Renunciation of War [for solution] so that international justice may prevail" (CKSD, 9/21/31). But he did not commit to using any force to defend the territory. What he did was to expect foreign nations to solve a problem China could not solve by itself. Such was an unrealistic expectation in a world in which nations seldom, if ever, took altruistic action against the powerful nation for the benefit of the weak. Then, to think that justice would prevail over power politics—an idea deeply ingrained in Chiang's mind—was a faulty assumption. In the end, all the League did was nothing more than sending a commission for a perfunctory investigation of the incident.

Yet six years later, after the outbreak of the Chinese-Japanese war in July 1937, Chiang still held, at least initially, such unrealistic expectation and faulty assumption in dealing with the much more serious crisis. With Japan having dropped out of the League, he now pinned hope on the Nine-Power Treaty for the resolution of the conflict.[14] "The only way to resolve the Chinese-Japanese dispute," he reminded himself, "is to call the attention of the international community to it and to have foreign powers intervene in it" CKSD, 10/31/37). However, by mid-November, when the Japanese army had conquered Shanghai and was poised to attack China's capital, Nanjing, he recognized that the idea of relying on international intervention to save China from Japanese aggression was totally useless (CKSD, 11/19, 21/37).

Four years later—just a few days after Japan sneakily attacked Pearl Harbor—Chiang finally came to the conclusion, not without self-chastisement: "International relations are mainly governed by considerations of advantages and disadvantages. There never is a nation sacrificing its interests for the benefit of others. Any one regards this situation...as odd is nothing but an idiot" (CKSD, 12/11/41)! It took ten years, from 1931 to 1941, for Chiang to recognize the futility of conducting foreign policy based on moralism—a mental baggage never burdening any of his foreign friends or foes.

If Chiang had once placed a premium on moralism in his diplomatic activities, he turned a pure realist when engaging in actual bargaining with foreign powers. He immersed himself in a continual calculation of the interests, fears, expectations, strengths, and weaknesses of China as well as of his targeted foreign nations and put all these factors into play in order to achieve momentary or long-term gains.

Multi-nationalizing the Conflict with Japan

Beginning in 1931, Chiang saw Japan's increasing aggression against China would eventually lead to war. Convinced that he could not win the war because of Japanese superior military strength, he reasoned that the best policy was to multi-nationalize the war by drawing Britain, the United States, and the Soviet Union into it on China's side.

When Japan attacked Shanghai in January 1932, in consequence of the Manchuria Incident, he successfully sought British and American intervention for a ceasefire agreement between Chinese and Japanese forces in the city. In September 1934, after Japan had invaded Inner Mongolia from Manchuria, Chiang told himself to "watch carefully [for the possibility of a] British-Japanese rapprochement and a British-Russian conflict and to make the best use of [these developments]. We should still emphasize a balance of power [among these nations] while waiting for the opportunity of a major war [among them]. Without such a war it would be difficult to recover our losses by our own effort" (CKSD, 9/21/34).

While waiting for the major war, Chiang also negotiated with the Japanese, asking it to stop aggression against China. He did so because he perceived Japan as facing then two potential threats. One was from the Soviet Union, which had been looking for an opportunity to avenge its loss in the 1904-1905 War to Japan over the issue of controlling Manchuria. Japan's occupation of Manchuria twenty-six years later only heightened Soviet security concerns over its territories bordering

Manchuria. In 1933 Chiang saw "a Japanese-Russo war as inevitable" and alerted himself to "adapt that war to our need for time to prepare [for war against Japan]" (CKSD, 7/21/33).

Chiang let the Japanese government know through his personal emissaries that both China and Japan opposed the spread of communism to East Asia under the aegis of the Soviet Union. If Japan went to war with the Soviet Union, he implied that he would show sympathy to it. As a quid pro quo, he hoped that Japan would acknowledge Chinese sovereignty over Manchuria and evacuate its forces from other Chinese territories under its occupation (CKSD, 3/2/36).

Japan's other potential threat, Chiang shrewdly calculated, was from China—if it went under communism. Such a development, he intimated to the Japanese leaders, would bolster the appeal of the Japanese Communist Party in Japan, thus intensifying the Party's conflict with the ultra-nationalists in the country, with unsettling consequences. He asked Japan to leave China alone so that he could put down the Communist rebellion, thus forestalling a threat to Japan's internal stability.

The Japanese, however, were not easily persuaded. They indicated that they would not return to China any territory they had conquered. On the contrary, they asked Chiang to recognize Manzhouguo, the Japanese-sponsored puppet state in Manchuria, and to acknowledge Japan's special interest in north China (CKSD, 10/6/36). They tempted Chiang with an offer of their own: to form an anti-Communist front with China. Chiang rejected the offer, for he could not align with a country still occupying large chunks of Chinese land (CKSD, 3/2/36). The Chinese-Japanese negotiations went nowhere.

When the Chinese-Japanese war broke out in July 1937, Chiang decided to tip to the Soviet side in the triangular relations of China, Japan, and the Soviet Union in spite of the fact that he regarded that country as China's "only enemy." He wrote down why he came to this decision:

> Japan has asked us to forge a common front against Russia, to recognize the puppet Manzhouguo, and to acknowledge North China as its special sphere of influence. If we go ahead with signing a mutual nonaggression treaty with Russia first, we will shatter Japan's...unrealistic dreams, so that it would not make anymore demand [on us]. If we agree to its demand to forge an anti-Russia common front, then not only North China will fall to its hand, but also the whole country will become the second

puppet Manzhouguo. Now, if we form a United Front with Russia, we might antagonize Japan. In that case Japan could at most grab only North China...not able to conquer our entire country. Accepting the lesser of the two evils, I have made up my mind (CKSD, 7/31/37, Weekend Review).

Chiang's policy of uniting with the Soviet Union against Japan, however, did not prompt that country to join the war on China's side, but it did result in significant amount of Soviet military and financial assistance to China to prosecute the war, as to be discussed later.

On another diplomatic front, Chiang repeatedly asked the intervention of Britain and America to stop the war, but all to no avail (CKSD, 7/15, 17, 25/37). He immediately made a significant war move calculated to draw the two powers to the fray. He opened a battlefront in Shanghai in east China by throwing a massive army, eventually totaling 700,000 men, into the area to engage an un-provoking Japanese army there. On August 13, the day the battle started, he told himself that he had to "apply the [right] tactics to compensate for our shortage of weapons and to apply the [right] strategy to compensate for the inadequacy of our tactics. The point is to put the enemy on the defensive" (CKSD, 8/13/37).[15]

The right strategy meant in the short run to "draw the enemy deep into the area south of the Yellow River, thereby causing Britain and the Soviet Union enough anxiety so that they have to participate in the war" (CKSD, 9/29/37). The area south of the Yellow River was the British-invested area. The strategy's longer-term objective, historians and others have agreed, was to allow China to make the best use of the space and time factors to thwart Japan's conquest of the country. Since China was a large country, it could afford losing territories in a prolonged war. A prolonged war meant to draw the Japanese army from the east coast to China's interior in the west, where the rugged mountain ranges would provide almost insurmountable barriers to an advancing enemy increasingly burdened by a lengthening supply line.[16]

Though foreign powers did not intervene in the Chinese-Japanese war for several more years, Chiang continued to believe in the inevitability of a war between Britain, America, and the Soviet Union, on the one hand, and Japan, on the other (CKSD, 12/12/40). He pointed to especially the prospect of Japan's war with Britain and America:

> The enemy has just two ways out of its increasingly deepened domestic conflict [between the ultra-nationalists and

the rising Communists]. One is to gamble with a war against Britain and America in the hope of winning it by luck so as to avert domestic revolution. The other is to avoid provoking a war with Britain and America, to preserve its naval strength, and to suppress domestic revolution....In my view, it would definitely choose the former by risking a war. It would rather lose to foreign powers than to let the domestic revolution break out (CKSD, 12/18/40).

Based on this assessment, he predicted on November 4, 1941 that America would join the war against Japan within half of a year (CKSD, 11/4/41). As the Pearl Harbor Incident occurred on the following December 7, America and Britain finally joined China to fight Japan. With his multi-nationalizing the Chinese-Japanese conflict finally realized, Chiang was more than ever determined to fight the war to its end.

Seizing on Soviet Fear of Two-Front Wars

Chiang perceived the Soviet Union as a cunning, greedy, and dangerous country intent on persistent aggression on China. Even with such a perception, he felt he had to bargain with the country in the 1930s because China faced a greater and more urgent threat from Japan. In doing so, he seized on Soviet incessant fear of two-front wars: one with Japan on the east and the other with Germany on the west. As noted earlier, he viewed as early as in 1933 a Russian-Japanese war as inevitable (CKSD, 4/27/33). In 1936 he pondered how China would react if Japan attacked the Soviet Union first (CKSD, 2/29/36). In that case he believed that Japan would seek China's neutrality. If that happened, he would entertain such an idea in return for Japanese acknowledgment of Chinese sovereignty over Manchuria and renouncing its special privileges in north China (CKSD, 3/31/36).

On the other hand, Chiang learned in the early 1930s that the Soviet Union was keenly interested in negotiating a mutual nonaggression treaty with China. He fully understood that the Soviet gesture was intended to strengthen his resolve to deal with Japan so that the consequent rising tension between China and Japan would lessen the prospect of Japan's taking hostile action against the Soviet Union. In 1936 when Germany, Italy, and Japan signed the Anti-Comintern Pact, Soviet fear for a two-front war was intensified. Its need for a treaty with China became more urgent. When the Chinese-Japanese war broke out in

July 1937, the Soviet Union promptly offered military assistance to China on condition that the treaty be concluded (CKSD, 8/1/37). For reason already noted, Chiang agreed, and the treaty was signed in Nanjing on August 21.

The Soviet Union immediately started delivery of military supplies. Between September 1937 and June 1941, it provided China with 900 aircraft, 1,140 artillery sets, 82 tanks, close to 10,000 machine guns, 50,000 rifles, 2,000 trucks, 2 million hand grenades, 31,160 airborne bombs, 2 million shells, and 180 million bullets; by the end of 1941 it had granted China loans totaling US$250 million.[17] Soviet assistance, however, tapered off by the early 1940s as the Chinese-Japanese war settled into a stalemate, thus reducing the possibility of a Japanese attack on the Soviet Union.

The Soviet Union was frantically engaged in multi-front negotiations of its own. It signed a nonaggression treaty with Germany in August 1939 and a similar treaty with Japan in April 1941. It seemingly had assured of its security on all fronts while the Chinese-Japanese war was raging on.

Yet events changed rapidly. In September 1939, Germany attacked Poland and swept over much of Western Europe in the following year. In June 1941 Germany unleashed a blitzkrieg on the Soviet Union and forced the country to a harsh fight for four years. With its successful counter-offensives against the German army beginning in 1944, the Soviet Union experienced a dramatic shift in fortunes. Coming back from a near-perishing war, it, together with its allies, the United States and Britain, was poised in early 1945 to crush the German army, with a spare power to bear on Japan.

In February 1945, at the solicitation of the United States and Britain, the Soviet Union signed a secret agreement with them in Yalta in which it promised to attack Japan three months following the allied powers' expected victory over Germany. In return, the two Western powers pledged, among other things, to exert pressure on Chiang to yield to the Soviet demand for restoring all the privileges Russia had enjoyed in Manchuria prior to the 1904-1905 Russian-Japanese war (Russian control of the Changchun railroad system and use of two seaports, Lushun and Dalian) and, in addition, allowing Outer Mongolia—a territory the Soviet Union had sought to dominate—to become independent from China. The Soviet demand was in direct contravention of the Soviet declarations of 1919 and 1920 on the renunciation of these privileges.[18]

When learning of the Yalta Agreement, Chiang expressed "outrage and sadness to no end" (CKSD, 6/15/45). He was, as Jay Taylor observed, "compelled to concur in the decisions made without his knowledge." Not only that, "Roosevelt also agreed not to tell Chiang of the secret accord until twenty-five Soviet divisions had completed ... their move to the eastern frontier" bordering China. What was particularly galling to Chiang was, as Taylor continued to observe, "the way the Anglo-Saxons had assumed the right to give away Chinese sovereign rights."[19] In that sense, the Yalta Agreement was not different from the Munich Agreement of 1938, in which Britain assumed the right to give away Czechoslovakia's sovereign right to Sudetenland to Germany.

As it happened, Germany was defeated in May 1945, and the Soviet troops swept into Manchuria in August. Chiang was in a bind. While the United States and Britain exerted intense pressure on him to recognize the Yalta Agreement, the Soviets took direct action to force him to give in by military incursion into several cities in north Xinjiang and north China (CKSD, 7/28/45, 8/1/45, 8/31/45, Month-end Review; 9/6,10/45). Chiang reluctantly accepted the terms of the Yalta Agreement relating to China and signed a treaty with the Soviet Union in August 1945, conceding to it the privileges imperial Russia had enjoyed.

In his bargaining with the Soviet Union, Chiang tried to take advantage of the Soviet fear of two-front wars. He was, at best, half successful. He obtained considerable Soviet military and financial assistance in the early years of the Chinese-Japanese war, but lost out on the Yalta Agreement. Ironically, the Soviet Union did end up fighting two-front wars, but not simultaneously. Only after it defeated Germany did it mount an offensive against the Japanese army in Manchuria—at a time when Japan was already on the verge of surrender.

Bargaining with Britain: A Double Deal on India

During much of the 1930s, Chiang depended mainly on Britain to restrain Japanese expansionism in China but could not reciprocate with any meaningful favors to Britain. He thus lacked bargaining power when dealing with this potential ally. He acquired such power when the Pacific War occurred in 1941, and he used India as leverage. Considered the Jewel of the British Crown, India had by then fallen to be, in Winston Churchill's terms, Britain's "Soft Underbelly" in Asia. When the Japanese soldiers slashed through the Burmese jungles to appear on the doorstep of India in 1942, the British Empire was in danger of losing its largest territorial component, for the British, Indian, and Burmese troops the empire then commanded in the area were woefully inadequate to meet the Japanese challenge.[20]

Chiang took advantage of the situation by adopting a stratagem to shield and to poke the British Soft Underbelly simultaneously. In 1942 he boldly threw a large Expeditionary Army to Burma to thwart the Japanese advance to India and to ward off Japanese potential threat to Yunnan. But his military adventure suffered a serious setback as the Japanese army routed both Chinese and British forces in Burma. The British forces and some of the Chinese forces retreated to India while the bulk of Chinese troops was withdrawn to Yunnan. In 1943 the Chinese Army in India and the Chinese Expeditionary Army in Yunnan, with a combined force of more than 220,000 men, joined the British and American forces to launch the second Burma campaign; they won a series of decisive battles in the next two years, clearing out Japanese threat to India and Yunnan once and for all.

When the Chinese army came to the defense of India, Chiang also opened a diplomatic front. As the British authorities in India were then challenged by Mahatma Gandhi's non-cooperation movement and the Congress Party's demand for independence, Chiang was seriously concerned that the internal dissension in India would undercut the British capacity to prosecute the war. Yet he was basically in sympathy with "the national liberation of India" (CKSD, 12/5/41). Under such delicate circumstances, Chiang took the position of continuing collaboration with the British in the war while supporting India's aspiration for self-governance in the future (CKSD, 1/2/42).

In a February 1942 visit in India, Chiang reiterated his position in meetings with the British leaders as well as Gandhi and Nehru of the Congress Party. In a radio broadcast to India on February 21, he suggested that the British "grant the Indian people real political power without being first asked to." Later, he continued to uphold his position, to the consternation of the British leaders, particularly Churchill, who for a time threatened to discontinue British-Chinese joint military operations against Japan. Yet Chiang adhered to his position and went so far as to endorse the independence of India after the war (CKSD, 11/9/42; 12/31/43, Month-end Review).[21]

Taking a military action to protect the British Soft Underbelly and a political action to support India's right to self-governance, Chiang was able to secure British cooperation in several areas. First, he received British support at the Cairo Conference in 1943 of China's right to recover Manchuria and Taiwan from Japan. Second, he reached agreement with Britain—and the United States—to repeal the unequal treaties it imposed on China in Qing times, effective January 1943. Third, he obtained British help for opening a road linking India to China via Tibet for transporting American supplies to China that were first delivered to Indian ports. And fourth, he secured British acquiescence to China as a Big Power in the post-war world.

It must be noted that in addition to his double-tract approach to the British-Chinese relations, Chiang was able to achieve his diplomatic objectives in regard to Britain because of American intervention on China's behalf, as seen below.

Bargaining with America: Letting the Future Serve the Present

Prior to the Pearl Harbor Incident in 1941, Chiang's efforts to draw the United States into the Chinese-Japanese conflicts did not bear fruit. As China and the United States became allies following that Incident, Chiang laid out his objectives that he wished to accomplish with American support. These included the formation of a long-term China-United States alliance and Chinese recovery of its lost lands (CKSD, 11/9/42). But the problem for Chiang was that he had little to offer to the United States in return for its support. If he found in 1942 Britain's Soft Underbelly as a bargaining chip when contending with that country, he possessed nothing of the sort in regard to the United States.

Ironically, Chiang found his bargaining chip in China itself—a large and poor country at present and a potential world-class power in the future. Such a China was what the United States needed to meet the exigencies of the war with Japan at hand and to safeguard its interest in the Pacific in the future. Chiang was able to make effective use of this condition because of, in no small measure, an American president in the person of Franklin D. Roosevelt who, until the last year of his life, held very sympathetic and optimistic views on China. Roosevelt presented these views in his conversation with Churchill on July 16, 1943:

> Churchill thinks of China as one huge, indigestible mass and he will still talk in terms of trading concessions and so on. I have been telling Churchill that the Chinese are much cleverer than the Japanese, who are just imitators. Japan contrived to become a great power between 1880 and 1905. China is very much bigger than Japan and has given remarkable proof of her vitality and has made an astounding progress. But this progress should be accelerated so that she should become a great power.

Indeed, I believe she will become the greatest power in the world....The British must be shocked into taking notice of China. I want to put China in the sun even before she has the economic power.[22]

A month later, on August 30, Roosevelt contrasted his idea of accepting China as one of the Four Big Powers—along with the United States, Britain, and the Soviet Union—to Churchill's initial resistance of it:

> He [Churchill] finally accepted—and this for the first time—the idea of concerted action by the Four Powers. He kept on insisting that his difficulty was that China had no stable government and thus could not be treated on the same footing with the other three. I said to him, Chiang may die just as you or me, and still there will be a China. Split she may into North and South, and still it will be China. Split into Communist and Kuomintang, China will still be China. China, I said, with her 425 million is bound to become the strong Power in the Far East and she will be the necessary adjunct to the success of our great enterprise [of defeating Japan].[23]

It was such an American president that Chiang was working with to achieve his objectives. To proceed with the task, Chiang appointed T. V. Soong his Special Representative to the United States to engage in direct negotiation with American government. Serving in Washington from June 1940 to September 1943, Soong carried on his assignment with extraordinary zeal and established a cordial and intimate relationship with Roosevelt and American diplomatic and military high echelon. In three years, Chiang and Soong accomplished several important objectives, including an initial American economic loan of $100 million to China, establishment of an American military mission in Chongqing, American commitment of a military assistance package of $600 million, creation of the Flying Tigers program (American air pilot volunteers in China), a subsequent American approval of a $500 million loan to China, and American and British abolition of unequal treaties with China in January 1943.[24]

At the Cairo Conference in November 1943, Chiang achieved still more of his objectives. He noted:

Our political accomplishments are the greatest, military accomplishments the second, and economic accomplishments the next....The results go beyond our expectation....Britain and America have jointly announced the return of Manchuria, Taiwan, Penghu to us after we have lost them for fifty or twelve years....What an extraordinary event!" (CKSD, 11/28/43, Weekend Review)[25]

The wartime Chinese-American cooperative relations reached the apogee at the Cairo Conference. Soon afterwards, American government, from the War Department to the While House, expressed growing dissatisfaction with the Chinese army's battle performance as it suffered a string of losses in Henan, Hubei, Hunan, Guangxi, and Guizhou in 1944-1945. The Americans attributed the Chinese army's failures to the corruption of the Nationalist government, Chiang's incompetence as the Supreme Commander of the China War Theater, and his running dispute with the Chinese Communists. At the heart of the deteriorating Chinese-American relations was the Stilwell Affair.

Serving as Chief of Staff of the China War Theater under Chiang's command since 1942, the American general fell to serious disputes with Chiang over war strategy, the performance of Chinese commanders, the Nationalist-Communist relations, and a host of other issues. Hot in temper, acid in language, brash in mannerism, Joseph Stilwell went so far as to ask the American War Department and, eventually, Roosevelt to demand Chiang to appoint him, Stilwell, as commander of all Chinese forces, including the Communists. Roosevelt made precisely such a demand in July 1944 and reiterated it in the following September (CKSD, 7/7/44 and 9/19/44).

This dispute has been too extensively treated in Western literature to require any further detailed discussion.[26] The newly released Chiang's diaries, however, provide fresh insights into his personal feelings and his possible actions during the incident. He wrote down the fast-paced "unbearable pressures" the American government had exerted on him.[27] He regarded the American demand as "a crude demonstration of American imperialism;" he viewed the circumstances he was in "as the most dangerous in thirteen years" [since the Manchurian Incident of 1931] (CKSD, 7/16/44, 8/23, 26/44).

He faced an unprecedented dilemma. While his disastrous defeats in the battlefields allowed the enemy to reach a striking distance to China's wartime capital Chongqing, rejection of American demand could lead to a withdrawal of American military aid, only sharply intensifying the Japanese threat. Yet succumbing to the demand would render him nothing but an American "puppet" (CKSD, 8/29/44), with unfathomable political repurcussions.[28]

For a while, he contemplated to resign from all his "political and military positions" and let other Chinese leaders handle the crisis. He then wondered why the American president had not asked him to do just that. The reason, he soon realized, was that his resignation would very likely result in the disintegration of the Chinese army, but that "Roosevelt wants the Chinese army to continue to fight the war so that he does not have to send over at least one million soldiers to fight [Japan] in Asia" (CKSD, 8/29/44).

He made a further, critical observation: "America faces the necessity of depending on China to restrain Japan [during the war] and to restrain the Soviet Union in the future even after defeating Japan. America really cannot afford losing China" (CKSD, 8/31/44, Month-end Review). With these perceptions in mind, he gambled in rejecting Roosevelt's demand in October. Within the month, he received a reply from Roosevelt in which, Chiang noted, the American president "decided to recall Stilwell to the United States and to replace him with my [Chiang's] suggested choice, Wedemeyer, as Chief of Staff of the China War Theater" (CKSD, 10/19/44).

Chiang's decision on the Stilwell Affair epitomized his entire approach to the Chinese-American relations since the early 1930s. He made use of what might happen in the future to serve his purposes at present. Before the Pearl Harbor Incident he enticed America to come to China's side in the conflict with Japan by stressing that China's loss to Japan would damage American economic interest in China and intensify Japanese threat to American security in the Pacific Ocean. Following the Incident, he impressed the Americans with the argument that Chinese-American military alliance was indispensable to the eventual victory over Japan. Though he had since suffered a series of battle defeats, he continuously told the United States that with more American aid, he could fight better in the next battle, eventually winning the war. Thus, giving the United States a continual hope for a better fighting China, he perpetuated America's dependence on him.

Chiang's judgment that the United States needed China to restrain Japan and the Soviet Union was in line with a view long held by American historians. They believed that as the United States emerged as a Pacific power at the turn of the 20th century, it had persistently sought to shore up China as a countervailing power against any other nation threatening American security in the region.[29] Prior to 1945, Japan was that nation; after 1945, it was the Soviet Union. Thus it was America's expectation of what China was to become determined U.S. wartime or even postwar policy in the Far East.

The Domestic Dividends

To Chiang, the Chinese-Japanese war yielded unanticipated domestic dividends. By interfacing military actions with diplomatic maneuvers, he vastly expanded the territorial scope of his rule. Prior to the war, he exercised authority largely in the eastern one third of Chinese territory; after the start of the war, he vigorously pushed his army, together with his political apparatus, to the remaining two thirds of the territory.

This latter territory consisted of three belts of land. The first was the southwestern belt, composed of Sichuan, Guizhou, and Guangxi provinces. The second was the frontier belt, bordering on foreign nations, including Yunnan, Tibet, and Xinjiang. The third was an inner belt lying between China proper and Tibet and Xinjiang; it included Qinghai, Ningxia, Gansu, and Xikang provinces.[30]

The southwestern belt was the first going under Chiang's control, as his army, following the trade-space-for-time strategy, kept retreating toward this area in the early phase of the war. This belt, which was once lying on the fringe of the territory under his rule, became his wartime operation base.

On December 29, 1941, just three weeks after the start of the Pacific War, Chiang contemplated on "how to make use of the world war to resolve the problems of Xinjiang and Tibet," which were subject to the influence of the Soviet Union and Britain respectively (CKSD, 12/29/41). But, in reality, the first frontier land he took over was not Xinjiang and Tibet but Yunnan.

Bordering on Vietnam and Burma, Yunnan had since 1927 been tightly controlled by Governor Long Yun, a warlord who had pledged token allegiance to the Nationalist government in Nanjing. In 1941 as Japan was staging a massive force in Vietnam and posing an imminent threat to Yunnan, Chiang sent a substantial force from his Central Army to Yunnan to help Long ward off a possible Japanese invasion. The warlord governor could not resist Chiang's military move, though the Japanese offensive turned out to be directed at Burma. Chiang took great satisfaction in his move: "A major force of the Central Army has marched into Kunming [Yunnan's capital]. This is a very important step [to implement] our policy of securing domestic unity and resisting foreign threat. It is realized only after years' patient waiting" (CKSD, 11/30/41, Month-end Review). Later, as his Burma Expeditionary Army used Yunnan as its command center and supply base, his position in the province became unchallengeable. He removed Long Yun as governor in 1945.

Chiang's effort at absorbing Xinjiang involved complicated maneuvers. The province had been ruled since 1933 by Governor Sheng Shicai, a maverick warlord switching his political loyalty like a straw swinging with the wind. With his territory bordering on the Soviet Union, Sheng flirted with that country for collaboration, reportedly having joined the Soviet Communist Party in 1938. With the influx of Soviet military personnel and aid into his land, he kept Xinjiang as a semi-independent territory, effectively excluding the Nationalist government's authority.

In 1942, as the Soviet Union suffered stunning military setbacks at the hand of the German army, Sheng sought to return to the Nationalists' fold and expelled the Soviet personnel. Chiang had in the meantime deployed Hu Zongnan's army in western Gansu at the doorstep of Xinjiang. He then moved decisively against Sheng by placing his military and administrative personnel in Xinjiang. Losing Soviet backing and intimidated by the Hu army, Sheng left the province in 1944 when Chiang replaced him with Wu Zhongxin as governor. Chiang was elated: "This is the best news in months. With God's blessing, Xinjiang now belongs to us" (CKSD, 9/2/44).

Chiang's venture in Tibet was not as fruitful as in Xinjiang or Yunnan, though no less elaborate. In 1942 as the Japanese army swept over Burma and threatened not only Yunnan and India but Tibet as well, Chiang started planning political and military moves. One of his dominant concerns was how to ship to China the supplies America had first delivered to Indian ports. He proposed to build a road linking India to China via Tibet for such purpose.

Yet the authorities in Tibet opposed the road project because they did not wish to involve in the Chinese-Japanese war. They also attempted to demonstrate their semi-independent status by opening a Foreign Office Bureau in Lhasa (Tibet's capital), to the considerable consternation of Chiang's government. Ironically, Britain, the foreign power with preponderant influence in Tibet, persuaded Lhasa to agree to the road project, for it wished to strengthen the Nationalist army's fighting capacity against the Japanese. Lhasa agreed and participated in the construction of a pack-transport route, which was open in 1943.

Piqued by Lhasa's initial reluctance for the road project and by its independence pretensions, Chiang ordered in 1942 to mobilize Chinese forces on a broad stretch of land bordering on Tibet for possible military action. Such a move prompted Winston Churchill to protest to T. V. Soong at a meeting of the Pacific War Council on May 20, 1943 in Washington: "I hear Chinese troops are mobilized for action against Tibet and this provoked in that independent country a very great alarm." Learning of the British Prime Minister's expression that Tibet was an independent country, Chiang immediately ordered Soong to seek Roosevelt's support of China's claim to the territory.[31] Roosevelt did, and with further diplomatic exchanges on the issue, Britain issued a statement to affirm China's "suzerainty over Tibet."[32] The long-term consequence of the Chinese-British wartime diplomatic exchanges on Tibet is that Britain—or any other power—never again asserted that Tibet was an independent country.

As it became known later, Chiang's troop movement on the Tibet border in 1942 was part of his plan to assert his authority in the inner belt of lands, not really intended as a punitive move against Tibet. This belt, as noted earlier, consisted of Qinghai, Ningxia, Gansu, and Xikang provinces. From the 1920s to the 1940s the first three provinces were under the control of a number of military chieftains of one Muslim clan named Ma.[33] Xikang came under the reins of Liu Wenhui, a warlord squeezed out of Sichuan by other warlords. Chiang's mobilization order was designed to move the Ma and Liu forces toward Tibet and to fill in the vacated spaces with his Central Army. He was not entirely successful in these maneuvers, as the military chieftains understood his purpose and kept the bulk of their forces in their provinces. In the end, he made use of the resources at his disposal to provide the chieftains with military supplies and financial subsidies. With these supplies and subsidies came his administrative, military, and party personnel to the inner belt of land, whereby he gained an administrative and military presence that was not conceivable five or six years before.

Chiang's Diplomatic Achievements

By the end of the Second World War in 1945, Chiang had accomplished most of his diplomatic objectives he had set out twelve years ago. He recovered the Chinese territories he had lost to Japan in 1931 (Manchuria) and also the lands the Qing Dynasty lost in the 19th century (Taiwan and Penghu). He terminated the unequal treaties with foreign powers. He elevated China from a poor and intimidated nation in the prewar years to one of the Four Great Powers in the postwar era. He was then modest enough to concede that China was not deserving this status (CKSD, 9/1/45). The reality was that China did in 1945 possess one of the world's most powerful armies, ranking behind only that of the United States, Britain, and the Soviet Union. And, significantly, China had begun to reestablish national control of the vast stretches of Chinese territories that had since the beginning of the 20th century been regionalized by warlords and foreign powers.

To the Chinese, Chiang's accomplishments meant that he had stopped China's century-long political decline and permanently arrested the trend of peeling-off of Chinese lands by foreign powers, thus having eradicated "the national shames" universally felt by the Chinese people since the Opium War of 1839. These were monumental accomplishments of historical significance. His setback at Manchuria and Outer Mongolia at Stalin's hand pained him deeply, but he had never exercised direct rule over these territories in the first place, and with the combined weight of the United States, Britain, and the Soviet Union thrown at him, his Chinese compatriots could not fault him for succumbing to the pressure.

Many historians may point to other factors accounting for Chiang's successes: Japan's mistaken military adventure in the Pacific, America's victory at sea, the advent of the atomic bombs, and the receding power of the British Empire. These may all be relevant. What has not been fully recognized by the Chinese public as well as foreigner observers is Chiang's personal contribution to his successes. In 1933 he set out his policy guideline in dealing with the world's major powers. Short, simple, with remarkable clarity, the guideline was insightful of the prevailing international politics and almost prescient of what was to come in the next twelve years. Following them consistently till the end of the Second World War, he played the diplomatic games with surprising finesse and initiative to achieve his objectives.

Moreover, though a military leader, Chiang actually was more heavily engaged in diplomacy at wartime years than most people realized, as seen in three little-known pieces of evidence. First, his diary entries from 1930s on showed that he had been continuously and attentively conducting China's tangled foreign relations. He made detailed notes on his diplomatic maneuvers and, at times, devoted more attention to foreign policy than to domestic politics or even the conduct of warfare. Second, from 1940 to 1943, when he dispatched T. V. Soong to Washington to negotiate with Roosevelt to strengthen Chinese-American relations, he spent enormous amount of time on directing the negotiation. He and Soong exchanged a total of 441 telegrams in thirty-nine months, averaging two telegrams every five days.[34] His instructions were detailed and wide ranging, covering every facet of China's relations with foreign powers. And third, he arguably devoted more energy to the conduct of China's foreign relations than did his principal foreign policy aides, including such veteran diplomats as Guo Taiqi and Wang Chonghui who served as his foreign ministers, and Hu Shih, China's ambassador to America in the early 1940s. In his diaries he constantly belittled these individuals for their lack of competence, drive, and perspective in the conduct of China's foreign policy (CKSD, 11/30/41, 12/6/41, 12/8/41, and 12/29/41).

Indeed, Chiang became China's diplomat in chief in wartime years. From conception, initiation, to implementation of foreign policies he largely acted on his own. Bargaining from a position of weakness in a face-off with the world's greatest powers, he overcame his disadvantages in several ways. First, as a military leader immersed in war, he experienced naked power brutally applied in the battlefield for a far longer time than his principal foreign protagonists such as Roosevelt, Churchill, Stalin, or Stilwell. Not to be intimidated by any of them, he dared making demands on them and insisting on his views. Second, his effort at multi-nationalizing the Chinese-Japanese conflict prevented him from being defeated in a war he had previously regarded as unwinnable and allowed him to reap the benefits of victory other nations help him secure. Third, he adroitly applied one fundamental truth of international politics to his diplomatic undertakings. That is, power is relative; hence, no nation possesses absolute power. He identified the needs or weaknesses of his targeted nations—the mutual fears of Japan and the Soviet Union, the vulnerability of British India to Japanese invasion, and America's desire to build China into a countervailing power against Japan and the Soviet Union—and exploited all of them to his advantage.[35]

Three of his strategic decisions strikingly illustrate his diplomatic approaches. His option for aligning with "the lesser of the two evils"—the Soviet Union—against the greater one—Japan—in 1937 reflects a timely, realistic, and prudent choice beneficial to China. His dispatch of an Expeditionary Army to Burma for the defense of British India in 1942 dramatically demonstrated how one of the weakest nations of the world could safeguard the interest of one of the mightiest powers on earth. His bold rejection of Roosevelt's demand for appointing Stilwell as China's military commander in 1944 showed how his firm grasp of America's policy preference in the Pacific region allowed him to defy with impunity the nation on which he depended for survival.

With these decisive and profound actions, Chiang effectively refuted the conventional view that a weak nation has no diplomacy.

Chiang: Single-Power Dependency, 1945-1975

From Euphoria to Despondency

In a radio broadcast on August 15, 1945 Chiang spoke to the Chinese people in an ebullient mood. He declared China's victory at the war against Japan as "a final proof that justice has prevailed over arrogance of power." He magnanimously asked his countrymen to forgive Japan for its aggression, not to seek revenge against the fallen nation. Otherwise, he said, retribution of the victorious against the vanquished would likely lead to a vicious cycle of retaliations.[36]

He had many reasons to be ebullient. The nation he led had won, arguably, the longest and harshest foreign war it had ever fought. Speaking for the Han Chinese, he was in a position to claim that he had saved them from the third foreign conquest in their millennium-old history, the two previous ones being those by the Mongolians and the Manchus in the thirteenth and seventeenth century respectively. He commanded a vastly expanded and modernized army that gave him enough confidence to settle score quickly with the Chinese Communist Party, the only political force not yet amenable to his rule. But he opted for reconciliation with the Communists by inviting Mao on the previous day, August 14, to Chongqing for peace talks. This gesture evoked enormous gratitude from his countrymen who looked yearningly for reconstruction of their battered homeland, without having to go into a new civil war on the heel of an exhaustive international war.

Chiang's moment of euphoria lasted preciously short. The Chongqing talks produced an accord on October 10, to create a broadly based government and to integrate the Nationalist and Communist troops into a national army. Yet, the troops of the two sides already started racing to take over the Japanese-evacuated areas, with skirmishes along the way. Affirming America's interest in the emergence of a stable and strong China, President Harry Truman sent George Marshall to Chongqing to mediate the Nationalist-Communist conflict. Arriving in China in December 1945, Marshall worked out on the following January 10 a Nationalist-Communist ceasefire agreement. But by the summer of 1946 skirmishes had grown to full-dressed battles in many areas, particularly in Manchuria, and by the end of the year the nation verged on an irreversible all-out civil war. A dispirited Marshall left China in January 1947 to report to Truman for his failing mission.

In the ensuing three years, Chiang met a succession of gigantic battle losses, yielding the entire mainland to the Communists in December 1949. In these years, he was absorbed in the war with relatively little attention to foreign relations. In August 1949, the United States issued its *White Paper* on China in which it placed the responsibility for the Nationalists' defeat on the militarily incompetent and politically inept Chiang regime and absolved itself of any culpability for the fiasco.[37]

With the United States about to abandon his regime, Chiang tried to seek new international allies in a last-ditch effort to multi-nationalize his conflict with the Communists. He targeted two nations he thought most threatened by the victory of the Communists, the Philippines and South Korea. On July 10-12 he visited Manila and proposed to the Philippine President Elpidio Quirino to establish a Pacific anti-Communist alliance. He received a polite but cool response (CKSD, 7/11/49 and 8/6/49). A month later, on August 6-8, he went to Seoul, making a similar proposal to South Korean President Syngman Rhee, who gave the proposal a warm endorsement but made no commitment for its implementation.[38]

The early days of 1950 were harsh on Chiang in Taiwan. While the Communists actively prepared for an invasion of the island, the United States took a series of steps to disassociate from his regime. In his "hands off" statement issued on January 5, Truman indicated, "The United States will not pursue a course which will lead to involvement in the civil conflict in China."[39] On the next day, Britain announced its recognition of the newly established Communist government in Beijing, an action widely interpreted as a test move for America's own recognition that had been under consideration.[40] In a speech on January 12, U.S. Secretary of State Dean Acheson stated that the American "defense perimeter runs along the Aleutians to Japan and then goes to the Ryukyus…to the Philippine Islands." And he continued, "So far as the military security of other areas in the Pacific is concerned, it must be clear that no person can guarantee these areas against military attack."[41] The speech, which conspicuously left Taiwan and South Korea out of the American defense line, virtually invited Asian Communists to pick these two places for attack. As it happened, the Chinese Communists amassed in early 1950 the Third and Fourth Field Armies, totaling 820,000 troops, which, according to a CIA estimate, were likely to conquer Taiwan in the middle of the year, and the North Korean Communists actually launched their attack on South Korea in June 1950.[42] It was the gravest diplomatic blunder the U.S. made in the early years of the Cold War.

If the Stilwell Affair in 1944 marked as the nadir of Chiang's relations with the United States, the developments in early 1950 may be considered the nadir of his entire political career. He was in maximum danger of being vanquished by his Communist enemy while his once close ally was abandoning him. He was in a state of despondency.

Security at a Price

So it was an enormous relief to Chiang that the Korean War broke out on June 25, 1950, which resulted in a President Truman's announcement on June 27 that the United States would join the war on the side of South Korea and neutralize the Taiwan Strait by America's Seventh Fleet. Though unexpected by him, these dramatic events were the kind of change in international climate Chiang was looking for, perhaps something comparable to the Pearl Harbor Incident nine years ago that brought America to his side in the fight against Japan.

The Truman announcement, however, was not a total blessing to Chiang. It stated that Taiwan's international status was undetermined, which Chiang regarded as an unjustified repudiation of America's previous commitments to making Taiwan part of China. More irksome to him was Truman's order to neutralize the Taiwan Strait. Though the order protected Taiwan from the Chinese Communist invasion, it also prevented Taiwan from attacking the mainland. He registered in his diary his anger at the American president for treating the Republic of China (ROC) on Taiwan "as something less than a colony" (CKSD, 6/28, 29/50). Yet, for the security of the island, he had to swallow his pride by not challenging the order.

The Quemoy Crises

With their participation in the Korean War in 1950, the Chinese Communists had to delay their military moves against Taiwan. When the war ended in July 1953, Mao began to explore ways to take over the island, targeting first at the Nationalist-held offshore islands. Geographically part of the Chinese mainland, these islands were separated from Taiwan by a strait with a distance ranging from 100 to over 200 miles; they formed three groups, centering Quemoy (Jinmen), Matsu, and Dachen respectively. In 1954 and again in 1958, Mao ordered massive bombardment of these islands and directed their heaviest fire at

Quemoy, the largest of all these islands.[43] The resultant conflicts have since been known as the Quemoy crises. The first crisis lasted from September 3, 1954 to May 1, 1955; the second, from August 23 to October 6, 1958.[44]

To Chiang, the bombardments meant a test of his resolve to hold on to the islands that symbolically testified to his fervent hope for recovering the mainland. He met the challenge with counter-bombardment of the Communist coastal batteries and significant troop reinforcement of the islands. The crises, thus, represented a clash of will between Mao and Chiang: one wanted to seize Taiwan; the other, to retake the mainland. The crises also drew the United States and the Soviet Union into the conflicts. The United States first tried to press the Nationalists to withdraw from the islands and, failing that, came to their defense—which will be discussed below. The Soviet Union responded to the two crises in significantly different ways that resulted in momentous changes in the Sino-Soviet relations—which will be treated in the next chapter.

Chiang perceived the immediate cause of the 1954 crisis as Mao's attempt to prevent the United States from concluding a security treaty with Nationalist China (CKSD, 11/14/54, 11/30/54, Month-end Review).[45] Because the Korean War had heightened American sense of anti-Communism, the United States had painstakingly built in 1951-1953 an anti-Communist defense chain in the West Pacific through a series of security treaties with Japan, South Korea, the Philippines, Australia, and New Zealand, without including Taiwan. In 1953, Chiang proposed to conclude a security treaty with the United States to fill this conspicuous void in that defense chain. But U.S. Secretary of State John Foster Dulles was initially not disposed to the idea, for he considered Nationalist China still in a civil war without a defined territory to which the treaty would apply.[46] The negotiation for the treaty was held in abeyance.

But the 1954 Quemoy crisis led U.S. President Dwight Eisenhower and Dulles to believe that the Communist camp was launching, in the aftermath of the Korean War, a next wave of aggression in Asia. Demonstrating their determination to stop this wave of attack, they decided to resume negotiation with the Chinese Nationalists in October 1954 for a security treaty.[47] On December 2, 1954 the treaty was signed, with a secret supplement in which Nationalist China promised not to attack the mainland without American consent. The treaty limited its application to Taiwan and Penghu, excluding the offshore islands as the area under joint defense.

In the meantime, the crisis in 1954 became especially acute around the Dachen group of islands where Taiwan's air and naval support was tenuous because of geographic distance. Moreover, according to Chiang's estimate, the Communists maintained in the area a naval and air strength several times that of the defenders (CKSD, 5/18/54). On November 14, the Communists sank the Nationalist Taiping warship, a gift from the United States; and on the following January 11, they overwhelmed the Dachen islands with bombing by more than 100 planes and sank more ships (CKSD, 11/14/54, 1/11/55). On January 18, they occupied Yijiangshan, one island of the Dachen group, and killing the 1,000 defenders and their commander.

The United States urgently asked Chiang to withdraw the 14,000 troops from Dachen's main island and offered American naval protection for the withdrawal. In spite of the overwhelming odds against him, Chiang rejected the American offer, for he feared that if he withdrew from Dachen, the United States might next ask him to withdraw from Quemoy and Matsu. In his negotiation with the Eisenhower administration, he stuck to the position that he would withdraw from Dachen only if the U. S. guaranteed the defense of Quemoy and Matsu. A secret deal to this effect was struck in January 1955, followed by the Nationalist evacuation from Dachen in February (CKSD, 1/31/55; 2/5/55).[48] On January 29, 1955, Eisenhower obtained passage by U.S. Congress of the Formosa Resolution, which authorized the president to use American forces to repel Communist attack on the offshore islands if in his judgment the attack constituted a prelude to invasion of Taiwan.

The Nationalists' Dachen evacuation, however, did not lessen the intensity of the Communists' bombardment of Quemoy and Matsu. In fact, their artillery fire effectively cut off Quemoy from its supply base in Taiwan, making it likely for them to conquer the island with an amphibious attack. To avoid that prospect as well as the necessity for American direct participation in the conflict, Eisenhower indicated on March 16,1955 that a "use of tactical nuclear weapons" for the defense of Quemoy and Matsu was possible; in the same month Dulles said as much in a report to the U.S. National Security Council.[49] Such forceful statements by America's highest authorities apparently had enough an impact on the Communists that they soon reduced the intensity of the bombardments, with a complete stoppage on May 1, 1955.

When the Chinese Communists launched in 1958 the second Quemoy bombardment, the scale of attack was much greater than that of the first. They killed on the first day of attack, August 23, three deputy Nationalist commanders of the Quemoy defense command and wounded

Taiwan's defense minister, Yu Dawei. Chiang struck a stance of defiance. In fact, he had already in the 1954 crisis increased his troop strength to 55,000 on these islands, with the bulk of them deployed in Quemoy in deeply dug rock caverns with a network of truck-passable tunnels.

In his private reflections, Chiang even *welcomed* Communists' attack, for he thought it might provide him with an opportunity for counterattacking the mainland (CKSD, 1955, Major Events of the Year). Now in the 1958 crisis he even increased the Nationalist troop strength to 100,000, one-third of the total combat-effective force he commanded.[50] Not to be intimidated by the Communist barrage, he visited Quemoy on August 20, 1958, just three days before the Communists resumed bombardment. And he hoped, with a sense of urgency, that this attack would give him a last chance of counter-attack. He noted: "Quemoy is a sweet bait to lure the Communist bandits [to invade the island]. Now, after nine years of agony [since the loss of the mainland in 1949] and four years of perseverance [since the last bombardment in 1954], if we can't hook them this time, we wouldn't have another good chance. Must carefully plot out our strategy so that we can reach the goal of recovery of our country" (CKSD, 8/26/58). His understanding with the United States then was that he would not initiate a military offensive against the mainland without American consent but that he had a self-defense right to attack the mainland, without American consent, if the Communists invaded the offshore islands first.

Chiang's stance put the United States in a dilemma. Both President Eisenhower and Secretary of State Dulles considered the islands indefensible without involving American forces. While they did not wish to see the Nationalist troops on these islands annihilated by the Communists, they were not willing to commit American forces to defending these islands because such action would risk a direct military conflict with Communist China, with uncontrollable consequences. They initially decided not to provide the Nationalist troops on the offshore islands with military support and repeatedly exerted pressure on Chiang to evacuate from the islands. Western media also reported continuously during the height of the crises on how untenable the Nationalist defensive position on these islands was and pressed for a diplomatic solution to ease the Nationalists out of the islands.

Chiang would not yield, insisting that the defense of the offshore islands was vital to the security of Taiwan. "If Kinmen [Quemoy] were lost," he told Dulles, "the effect…on the morale on Taiwan would be so serious that the defense of Taiwan itself would crumble."[51] Such a fiasco would have far-reaching destabilizing consequences to entire East Asia.

The crisis at first put the Eisenhower administration in a quandary, and the Joint Chiefs of Staff of American Defense Department had some division of opinion on whether or not to help defend the islands.[52] But in the end, both Eisenhower and Dulles and their advisers were all convinced that the fall of the offshore islands to the Communist hands under the threat of the gun would be unacceptable. They believed that if the offshore islands were lost to the Communists, "this would have serious impact upon the authority and military capability of the anti-Communist, pro-U. S., government on Formosa. It would be exposed to subversive and/or military action which would eventually advocate union with Communist China and the elimination of U S positions on the island." These developments "would jeopardize the anti-Communist barrier consisting of...Japan... [South] Korea...the Philippines, Thailand and Vietnam."[53]

On September 4, with authorization of Eisenhower, Dulles declared, "We have recognized that the securing and protecting of Quemoy and Matsu have increasingly become related to the defense of Taiwan.... Military dispositions have been made by the United States so that a Presidential determination, if made, would be followed by action both timely and effective."[54] In other words, the U. S. was ready to invoke the Formosa Resolution to deal with the crisis.

The "military dispositions" of the United States meant preparation for the use of nuclear weapons. On September 2, 1958, ten days after the Communist resumed bombardment, General Nathan Twining, Chairman of U.S. Joint Chiefs of Staff, indicated that the United States "would strike at Communist air fields and shore batteries with small atomic weapons" if the president so decided. These weapons would include "7-10 kiloton airburst bombs."[55] Other American dispositions included shipping of twelve 8-inch nuclear-capable howitzers to Quemoy and equipping Taiwan's air force with Sidewinder missiles. These new weapons proved to be so powerful as to gradually tip the military balance in the offshore islands area in favor of the Nationalists. Seeing that they were not likely to conquer Quemoy and Matsu, the Communists suspended bombardment on October 6, 1958; they followed the suspension with bombardment on odd days and then gradually discontinued it. The second Quemoy crisis ended.

Chiang's handling of the Quemoy crises can be considered a diplomatic success. He used the "collapse" thesis to convince Eisenhower and Dulles to take substantial measures for the defense of the offshore islands. His tactics echoed the one he used to persuade Roosevelt to support China to fight Japan during the Second World War:

let what might happen in the future serve the purpose of the present. Now, in the Quemoy crises, he argued that the loss of the offshore islands would so seriously demoralize the Nationalist forces on Taiwan that the island's defense would crumble, leading to a Communist takeover. In turn, the loss of Taiwan would considerably weaken American military and political positions in the West Pacific—an unacceptable risk in the heyday of the Cold War. Chiang's argument convinced Eisenhower and Dulles enough that they concluded a mutual security treaty to protect Taiwan and secured a Formosa Resolution to safeguard Quemoy and Matsu.

Chiang paid prices for his gains. He lost the Dachen group of islands; he suffered military and civilian casualties in the thousands; and he lost naval ships and fighter planes. And in his negotiations with the United States over the crises, he conceded to several American demands: not to initiate any offensive action against the Communists without American consent; not to deploy the Nationalist forces and American supplies from Taiwan to the offshore islands without American approval; and not to use military means, but relying on political means, for the recovery of the mainland.[56]

The prices Chiang paid can be considered minor in proportion to his gains. For all his losses, he won the contest of will against Mao in the glare of worldwide publicity. He retained Quemoy and Matsu islands that his powerful enemy's hundreds of thousands of bombs and the unrelenting pressure of his diplomatic ally were not able to dislodge. Viewed from the perspective of the Cold War, his retention of these islands can be, in a sense, likened to the West's retention of West Berlin in terms of strategic and symbolic significance. The crises also produced for Chiang an unforeseen benefit. They could have driven a wedge in the relations between Nationalist China and the United States, but that did not happen. Instead, as will be discussed in the next chapter, they contributed to the split of Communist China and the Soviet Union.

Attempts to Recover the Mainland

Chiang never gave up—either before or after the Quemoy crises—his policy of recovering the mainland, despite objection by the United States, on which he depended for military protection. During the Korean War and the Vietnam War, he offered to the United States Nationalist troops to join in these wars in the hope that opportunities might arise allowing him to fight back to his homeland. Precisely for that reason, the United States rejected his offers.

Chiang also conducted a variety of small-scale raids against the mainland. Prior to the Quemoy crisis, he launched commando operations against the East China coast from Dachen.[57] In 1951, Chiang's remnant forces that fled to Burma in the final days of the civil war attacked Yunnan; in 1953, the Nationalist army launched from Taiwan an amphibious attack on Dongshan in Fujian/Guangdong border area. Still there were many other paramilitary actions against the mainland. John Garver has documented, in detail, the "U.S.-ROC Unconventional Warfare Exercises" and the "Nationalist Limited Offensive Operations" in the 1960s.[58] Chiang's sporadic offensive operations, however, all ended in failure as the Communists had sealed off the coastal areas with heavy forces and tight social control.

The United States took an ambiguous and changeable position on these military operations. During the Korean War it provided logistical support to the Nationalist military incursions from Dachen in order to divert attention of the Chinese Communists from that war. But its security treaty with Taiwan in 1954 restricted Chiang's option to attack the mainland, and it obtained commitment from Chiang in 1958 not to undertake any military actions against the mainland at all, as noted earlier.[59] Thus, it ceased support of the Nationalists' commando operations against the mainland.

These American restrictions aside, Chiang secretly established in 1961 a "National Glory Planning Office" (Guo Guang Ji Hua Shi), staffed with hundreds of elite officers, in a mountain cavern in northern Taiwan to formulate plans for offensive actions against the mainland— by relying on Taiwan's own resources.[60] It never went into the operation phase and was abolished in 1972 when President Richard Nixon began normalizing relations with Communist China, rendering Chiang's dream of returning to the mainland all the more remote.

Taiwan in the International Community

Chiang never viewed his government's stay in Taiwan as anything but temporary, nor did he consider the Chinese Communist government having any right to represent his country in the United Nations. From 1950 to 1970 he not only fought to retain his government's membership in the UN but also kept the Communist government out of it. He succeeded in achieving this twin objective principally because the United States exercised enough influence at the UN to postpone consideration of the issue of Chinese representation. However, during this period of time the United States felt increasing difficulty in supporting Chiang's position, as many new members of the world organization, particularly those from Africa, expressed sympathy for seating the Chinese Communist delegation.

In April 1961 one issue relating to the Chinese representation suddenly rose. As the Soviet Union and Communist China then experienced increasing political strains, the United States sought to achieve a "strategic advantage" by recognizing Outer Mongolia—the country geographically straddling the two Communist powers—with the intent to support its admission to the UN. Chiang strongly opposed the American move, for he had always regarded Outer Mongolia as a part of China but was forced by the United States through the Yalta Agreement of 1945 to grant that country its independence, which turned out to be nothing but a Soviet satellite. He subsequently renounced Outer Mongolia's independence and could not now tolerate the idea that Outer Mongolia and the Republic of China would be members of the same world organization—and on an equal footing. Moreover, he suspected that the United States was contemplating a proposal to seat both the Chinese Communist and Nationalist delegations in the UN. He immediately indicated that his government would veto Outer Mongolia's entrance to the world organization and wrote U.S. President John F. Kennedy that his government "cannot possibly accept the so-called 'two-Chinas' or any other arrangement that would affect the character of the Republic of China's representation in the United Nations."[61]

In the fall of 1961 Mauritania, an African country, applied for admission to the UN, which complicated the issue of Chinese representation. In a display of power politics, the Soviet Union indicated it would tie the admission of Mauritania to the UN to that of Outer Mongolia and would veto the former if the latter was denied. In the judgment of the Kennedy Administration, if Nationalist China vetoed the admission of Outer Mongolia, it would so antagonize the African bloc of nations that they would mobilize votes for the support of the admission of Communist China. Hence, it repeatedly appealed Chiang not to veto Outer Mongolia's admission.

Chiang steadfastly rejected American appeal, causing an intensive consultation between Washington and Taipei in September through much of October. By the middle of October, a formula was found to resolve the crisis. Chiang pledged not to veto Outer Mongolia's admission while the United States publicly reaffirmed its strong support of the Nationalist representation in the UN and President Kennedy privately assured Chiang for using American veto to stop admission of Communist China, if necessary.[62] As a result, the UN Security Council voted on October 25 for the admission of Outer Mongolia, with the United States abstaining and Nationalist China not voting. The council voted separately for the admission of Mauritania.

In the aftermath of the Quemoy crises, Chiang's actions in the case of admission of Outer Mongolia to the UN may be regarded as another victory in his diplomatic engagements with the United States. He paid a small price to achieve a relatively large gain. His forfeiture of his right to veto Outer Mongolia was of little significance to him, for whatever he did in this case, that country remained independent of China and would likely join the UN in the future, if not in 1961. On the other hand, he obtained a commitment from the American administration to safeguard his delegation's position in the world organization—a matter of significance to Nationalist China's international standing.

Chiang's victory, however, was of limited duration, lasting no more than a decade. With Nixon's drive toward normalization of relations with Communist China beginning in 1971, Chiang lost his only staunch supporter in the UN as well as in the international community at large. On October 25, 1971 the UN General Assembly voted to replace Nationalist China's delegation with Communist China's. Chiang's loss at the UN was largely his own making. In the previous three years, the United States had been in consultation with Nationalist China and other nations for a compromise on the issue of Chinese representation. Declassified Department of State documents in 1969-1971 revealed that while the American government foresaw the inevitability of Chinese Communists' admission to the UN, it endeavored to preserve the Nationalist representation with various forms of dual Chinese representation.[63] However, Chiang would not accept any of them, for he regarded any such arrangement as forcing him to give up his cherished goal of recovering the mainland.[64] Chiang would rather accept defeat at the UN than seeing his delegation sitting together with the Communists'.

Simultaneous with its loss of seat in the UN in 1971, Nationalist China saw a large number of nations severing diplomatic relations with it. In 1970, 66 nations recognized Nationalist China; in 1971, 55 did; in 1972, 42. In contrast, 47 nations recognized Communist China in 1970, 65 in 1971, and 86 in 1972.[65] In the next few years, nations maintaining diplomatic relations with Nationalist China further dwindled, to an insignificant 30 or less, without one single large power among them.

Chiang's loss at the UN and in diplomatic relations would not have happened had the United States not sought reconciliation with Communist China. During his visit in Beijing in 1972, Nixon conceded to Beijing's demands on normalizing relations between Beijing and

Washington: America's severance of diplomatic relations with Nationalist China, repudiation of its mutual security treaty with Taiwan, and withdrawal of American forces from the island.

Nixon made all these concessions, Chiang realized bitterly, not because Nationalist China had not remained a faithful ally of the United States but because of Nixon's desire to promote his recalculated American interests in Asia and to improve his re-election prospect. But, as John Holdridge, a ranking official of U.S. National Security Council involved in Nixon's approach to Communist China, said bluntly, Chiang had "nowhere else to go" but to accept the fait accompli.[66]

Yet this does not mean Nationalist China could not take minor measures to improve its international status. Beginning in the 1960s it launched a variety of informal or flexible diplomatic programs, endeavoring to maintain and even expand relations with foreign countries. These programs included maintaining unofficial representations in countries having established diplomatic relations with Beijing, economic assistance to friendly nations, participation in non-governmental international organizations, cultural exchange projects, and even military training for foreign countries.[67]

It should be noted that these programs were not administered by Chiang. Believing that they would in no way affect the overall power relations with Communist China, the United States, and the Soviet Union, he let his son, Chiang Ching-kuo, administer them. He had since 1969 groomed Ching-kuo steadily to be his successor when the younger Chiang was appointed vice premier, who took increasing responsibilities for the country's domestic and foreign policies.[68]

The Unexercised Soviet Option[69]

In October 1968 Victor Louis, a Soviet correspondent of *London Evening News,* visited Taiwan and met with the then Nationalist Defense Minister Chiang Ching-kuo. Reputedly with a KGB connection, Louis proffered an incredible idea of Soviet Union-Taiwan joint attack on Communist China.[69] The Louis Affair was widely reported by the public media at the time and has been analyzed by researchers since, but it was not until 2009 when the final segment of the Chiang Kai-shek diaries was released at Stanford University's Hoover Institution that the details of the Soviet-Taiwan contacts became known to the public.[70]

Upon receiving reports on the Louis visit, Chiang made a careful and realistic appraisal of the position of Nationalist China, stating, among other things, that "our air force is not strong enough to assure our successful landing operations [of our forces on the mainland]...nor capable of destroying the Communist intermediate-range missiles and nuclear bases." He also expressed concern that "until we securely occupy key sites on the mainland, we could not free ourselves from the control of American naval and air forces." Nevertheless, he considered that "now is the best time to overthrow Mao's [government]—an opportunity that should not be missed "(CKSD, 10/26/68, Week-end Review). In numerous of his diary entries from 1968 to 1972, he recorded how he pondered the Soviet offer and set the parameters for negotiation.

His liaison with Louis was Wei Jingmeng, a former director of the Nationalist government's information office. The Louis-Wei rendezvous took place in Taipei, Vienna, and other unidentified places. The Soviets also made extensive contacts with Taiwan's personnel elsewhere, spanning several continents. Among them were meetings between Wang Shuming (head of Nationalist China's military mission to the United Nations and former chief of staff of the Nationalist army) and the Soviets in New York; between Nationalist ambassador to Japan, Peng Mengji, Nationalist ambassador to Mexico, Chen Zhiping, Nationalist ambassador to Brazil and their respective Soviet counterparts; between Taiwan's reporter Song Fengsi and the Soviets in West Berlin; and between another Taiwan's reporter and the Soviets in Tokyo (CKSD, 1/9/69, 1/24/69, 3/4/69, 9/21/69, and 10/3/69).[71] Some of these contacts continued well into 1972, while others appear to be one-time liaisons. Chiang channeled the information he gathered from all these contacts to Wei and instructed him to exchange concrete proposals with Louis.

In April 1969, Louis presented the first set of terms on Soviet-Taiwan cooperation to Wei, most of which concerned preliminary matters. One of these terms, however, was of some importance. It was a Soviet request that Taiwan not to receive assistance (in the contemplated joint attack on Communist China) from any other foreign country. Chiang considered it a Soviet ploy to drive a wedge in his relations with the United States (CKSD, 4/14/69). The Nationalist government had by this time informed the United States of the on-going negotiations, and American Ambassador to Taiwan, Walter McConaughy, had expressed "neither opposition to nor endorsement of" the negotiations (CKSD, 4/23/69).

In the spring of 1969, Soviet relations with Communist China sharply deteriorated, resulting in military clashes on Zhenbao Island (Damansky) on the Chinese-Soviet border river, the Ussuri. Talks of a Soviet preemptive strike on the Chinese nuclear facilities were afoot while hundreds of thousands of Soviet troops were being deployed along the Chinese-Soviet frontier. Louis kept in constant touch with Wei, urgently pushing for military cooperation between Soviet and Nationalist armies.

On the basis of Wei's report, Chiang found that "the Soviet Union is so eager in seeking our government's [cooperation] that it is willing to lend its military bases to us, and it intends to invade Xinjiang, thereby solving its problem [with the Chinese Communists there]" (CKSD, 5/25/69). He also learned that the Soviet Union offered to supply Nationalist China with weapons, willing to "ship them to Taiwan...but [some of them] could be delivered to the vicinity of our landing sites [if we launch an attack on the mainland]" (CKSD, 6/16/69).

By early September, when rumors about a possible Soviet preemptive strike on Chinese nuclear facilities went a new round in the public media, Chiang commented, "In seeking our cooperation, the Soviet Union is now setting the destruction of Chinese Communists' nuclear facilities as its top priority. To overthrow the Mao regime becomes its secondary objective" (CKSD, 9/6/69). At this time, Chiang became concerned that his extensive contacts with the Soviets might "prompt the Chinese Communists to use their short-range or intermediate-range atomic weapons to strike us." On the other hand, he pondered whether such a strike might give the Soviets an excuse to attack China, thus deterring the Chinese Communists from attacking Taiwan (CKSD, 9/23/69). He expressed increasing alarm that the Chinese Communists had conducted an underground nuclear test in Xinjiang on September 22 and an air-drop nuclear test—the ninth—on September 29 (CKSD, 9/23/69 Weekend Review; and 9/29/69).

Chiang decided to set forth his terms for serious negotiation with the Soviets. He insisted on maintaining "complete independence in Chinese [Taiwan's] foreign policy, not subject to any restriction" and preserving Chinese territorial integrity and administrative independence without foreign interference. He was willing to let the Soviet Union participate in economic development of Xinjiang; he would refrain from concluding anti-Soviet alliance with other country. All these terms were predicated on his successful recovery of the mainland (CKSD, September 1969, Month-end Review). Chiang also contemplated at this time on how to work with the Soviets to destroy the Chinese Communist nuclear weapons in localities most threatening to Taiwan—south of the Yangzi River (CKSD, 10/1/69).

Yet the Soviet Union suddenly lost interest in the negotiation. Louis failed to show up for a scheduled meeting with Wei in Italy in early October. During the rest of 1969, Chiang's diaries made no further reference to Taiwan's contact with the Soviets. Not until the next April did he return to the subject, pointing out that the Soviet attitude had been "changeable and unpredictable" (CKSD, 4/4/70). For the next two years, until April 21, 1972, Chiang's diaries showed that Taiwan remained in contact with the Soviets, but the liaison became increasingly sporadic, and nothing of substance came out of it.

Looking at all of Chiang's diary entries relevant to the Louis episode, one may identify two reasons why Chiang did not exercise the Soviet option. The first is that the Soviets began in the fall of 1969 to ease tensions with the Chinese Communists. In September, Soviet Premier Alexei Kosygin met with Zhou Enlai in Beijing to initiate talks on the settlement of the two nations' disputed borders. Chiang believed that this event was part of the reason for Louis' failure to meet with Wei on the scheduled appointment (CKSD, October 1969, Month-end Review). The border talks went on intermittently until December 18, 1970 when a treaty was concluded. The treaty lessened the prospect of war between the Soviet Union and Communist China, thus making the Soviet approach to Taiwan for military cooperation less urgent.

The border settlement, however, did not fundamentally alter the hostile relations of the two Communist powers. Hence, the Soviets continued to engage in talks with Taiwan through Louis and Wei, who had resumed contact (CKSD, 11/7/70; 12/5/70; 10/25/71). Ambassadorial talks between the two sides also took place in Mexico and Tokyo from 1970 to 1972 (CKSD, 4/4/70, Week-end Review; 11/16/70, 11/17/71; 3/30/72; 4/21/72). These lingering Soviet-Taiwan contacts did not result in any cooperative arrangement between the two sides—for a second reason: Chiang's resistant frame of mind. Chiang had long shown a strong distrust of the Russians. He characterized the Russians as "cunning" and reminded himself to guard against their "fraudulent" activities (CKSD, Plan for the week following 5/10/69). No doubt he had in mind that Russia had acquired through chicanery and outright aggression pieces of Chinese land since mid-Qing times. And he often lamented that the Soviet Union had gained unjustified advantages over China through the Yalta Agreement of 1945.

That was why he warned Wei to be vigilant when dealing with Louis and why he refused to supply to the Russians a list of weapons he might need from them. And he was especially concerned about the risk of a joint military adventure with the Soviets, citing a well-known Chinese historical episode as a warning to himself. In that episode, General Wu Sangui of the Ming Dynasty appealed to the Manchu army for help to put down a rebellion threatening the dynasty. The invited

Manchu army did suppress the rebellion but went on to topple the Ming Dynasty as well (CKSD, 7/15/69).

With this risk in mind, Chiang nevertheless continued the talks with the Soviets because he wanted to explore any possibility that might help him realize a goal he regarded as important as his life: recovery of the lost Chinese mainland. "Anyone helping me recover the mainland is my friend," he once wrote when weighing the Soviet option. "Otherwise, he is my enemy" (CKSD, 1/29/70).

But late into the negotiations, he encountered a Soviet condition he could not accept. "The Soviets have taken the United States as an enemy," he wrote in June 1970. "And they have told us that the only condition for their cooperation is that we must act against the United States." He branded the condition "unthinkable," for he regarded acceptance of it as a betrayal of the United States (CKSD, 6/20/70, Week-end Review). In realpolitik terms, he could not trade the support of the United States, a decades-old ally, for an uncertain cooperation with the Soviet Union, a nation that had historically proven to be inimical to Chinese interests.

A year later, as he became seriously ill in June 1971, Chiang struggled to jot down his thoughts about the Soviet offer for military cooperation: "The Soviet Union is luring me to oppose the United States for the sake of fighting the Chinese Communists. I must never be tempted by it" (CKSD, 6/22/71).

Chiang made up his mind not to exercise the Soviet option.

Declining Diplomatic Efficacy

From the second half of 1970 to his death in April 1975, Chiang was in sharply declining health, hence not actively involved in Taiwan's foreign policies. He realized he had lost irreversibly his diplomatic efficacy. In his first period of international engagements, from 1931 to 1945, he possessed enough bold initiatives, farsighted judgments, hard-driving bargaining tactics to achieve the kind of gains his compatriots, including the Chinese Communists, admired and his followers had not anticipated.

In his second period of international engagements, from 1945 to 1975, Chiang registered no diplomatic achievements comparable to what he had done in the first. His successes in the management of the Quemoy crises did not arrest the long-term diplomatic decline of Nationalist China, and his handling of the Outer Mongolia case can be considered, at best, only a short-term gain. On the other hand, he suffered many diplomatic setbacks: he was denied the right to counterattack the mainland, he was not permitted to develop nuclear weapons, he was expelled from the United Nations, he was in his last years of life sequestered on an island without one major power on his side, and his once "close friend," Nixon, began normalizing relations with his bitterest foe. Why did Chiang suffer such diplomatic losses so precipitously and irreversibly?

Upon reflection, one may say that Chiang did not—as his critics have said he did—lose his diplomatic competence. His handling of the two Quemoy crises and the case of admission of Outer Mongolia to the United Nations indicates he had the same diplomatic skills as what he demonstrated during the Second World War. Bargaining with powerful allies from a position of weakness, he was able to secure major gains at relatively small costs. When dealing with the case of potential Soviet-Nationalist military cooperation against the Chinese mainland, he had a penetrating analysis and objective assessment of the complicated relations of China, Taiwan, the Soviet Union, and the United States. He timely grasped information on the development of the Chinese Communist nuclear weaponry. His instructions to the Nationalist diplomats on how to negotiate with their Soviet counterparts were reasoned and appropriate. All these cases show he was as a tough and effective bargainer on the diplomatic front as before.

Yet what accounted for his diplomatic losses? Many causes may be identified, but two are most conspicuous. The first has to do with a fundamental realignment of world politics in post-Second World War years. In Chiang's first period of diplomacy, as he faced several foreign powers—his four targeted nations mentioned earlier (Japan, the Soviet Union, Britain, and the United States) and, at least, Germany—he had chances to manipulate one power against another in an interactive diplomatic game to the advantage of China. In his second period, as Chiang became militarily dependent on the United States in a bipolarized world, he was deprived of opportunities for multiple-power diplomatic engagements. When Victor Louis put the Soviet card tantalizingly on the table, Chiang did not risk playing it to the end for fear of antagonizing the power that assured the survival of his regime.

The second factor accounting for his diplomatic defeats is clearly the loss of the mainland to the Communists. With that loss, he was forfeited of a bargaining chip on the diplomatic table: a large landmass, with enormous inactivated human and economic resources. A once poor, weak, and divided China, if properly harnessed as it was in the 1930s and early 1940s, could allow him to win concessions and benefits from foreign friends and foes alike. In his Taiwan days, as he presided an island whose territorial size was mere three-tenths of a percent of what he used to govern, he lost much of his bargaining power in the diplomatic engagements with other nations. If diplomatic game has a gambling quality in it, Chiang did not win the game in the last years of his life because he had lost most of his capital to the Chinese Communists, whereas the other players—the United States and Russia—had plenty of it.

NOTES

[1] Hsu, *The Rise of Modern China*, pp. 495-96.

[2] William C. Kirby, "The Internationalization of China: Foreign Relations at Home and Abroad in the Republican Era," in Frederic Wakeman, Jr. and Richard Louis Edmonds, eds., *Reappraising Republican China* (Oxford: Oxford University Press, 2000), pp. 179-204.

[3] Tao Wenzhao, Yang Kuisong, and Wang Jianlang, *Kang Ri Zhan Zheng Shi Qi Zhong Guo Dui Wai Guan Xi* [*China's Foreign Relations during the War of Resistance against Japan*] (Beijing: Zhong Gong Dang Shi Chu Ban She, 1995), pp. 436-53; Jiang Jiannong and Wang Hongbin, *Mao Zedong Wai Jiao Sheng Ya di Yi Mu* [*The First Chapter of Mao Zedong's Diplomatic Life*], Changchun, China: Jilin Ren Min Chu Ban She, 1999; and Chen Jian, *Mao's China and the Cold War* (Chapel Hill: The University of North Carolina Press, 2001), pp. 41-43.

[4] See Taylor, *The Generalissimo*, pp. 403, 433-34.

[5] Gao Lang, *Zhong Hua Min Guo Wai Jiao Guan Xi zhi Yan Bian, 1950-1972* [*Evolution of Republic of China's Diplomatic Relations, 1950-1972*] (Taipei: Wu Nan Tu Shu Chu Ban You Xian Gong Si,1993), p. 32; and Taylor, *The Generalissimo*, p. 512.

[6] Quoted in Li, *The Private Life of Chairman Mao*, p. xx.

[7] For Chiang's letter, see Second Historical Archives of China, Nanjing, *Guo Min Zheng Fu Dang An* [*Archive of the National Government*], Microfilm 16J2803, Item #389.

[8] *Mao Zedong on Diplomacy*, p. 112.

[9] Chiang and Mao's policies toward Tibet may well be interpreted as manifestation of Han chauvinism, but they demonstrated the two leaders' strong resolution to safeguard China's territorial rights.

[10] Public media and academic literature on Taiwan's secret nuclear program, known as the Hsin Chu Program, is very extensive. The following articles are the most revealing: David Albright and Corey Gay, "Taiwan: Nuclear Nightmare Averted," *Bulletin of the Atomic Scientists*, Vol. 54, Issue 1 (Jan/Feb 1998): 54-60; William Burr, ed., "New Archival Evidence on Taiwanese 'Nuclear Intentions,'1966-1976," *National Security Archive Electronic Briefing Book*, No. 18, October 13, 1999. http://www.gwu. edu/~nsarchiv/ NSAEBB/NSAEBB20/; and Ta-you Wu, "A Footnote to the History of Our Country's 'Nuclear Energy' Policies." http://www.fas.org/nuke/ guide/Taiwan/ nuke/index.html.

[11] In the late 1920s China experienced two minor international conflicts. One related to the clash of Chiang's forces with the Japanese army in Jinan, Shandong during the Northern Expedition in 1928. The other concerned the Soviet attack on Manchuria in 1929 in retaliation of Chinese takeover of the then Soviet-controlled railroad system. In both cases, Chiang's diplomatic involvement was minimal. See Lu Weiming, *Jiang Jieshi de Wai Jiao Mi Wen* [*Secret Information on Chiang Kai-shek's Diplomacy*] (Changchun: Jilin Ren Min Chu Ban She, 1999), pp. 32-43; Hong Junpei, *Guo Min Zheng Fu Wai Jiao Shi* [*The Diplomatic History of the Government of the Republic of China*] (Taipei: Wen Hai Chu Ban She, [1968]), pp. 165-94.

[12] These four powers were among the eight that put down the Boxer Rebellion. The other four—Austria-Hungary, France, Germany, and Italy—exercised little influence on Chiang's China except Germany. In the 1930s Germany provided military advisers to train Chiang's army, sold a significant quantity of arms to China, and its ambassador to China mediated the Chinese-Japanese war in late 1937. But German impact on China was of limited duration, practically ceased in late 1941 with the advent of the Pacific War. See William C. Kirby, *Germany and Republican China*, Stanford: Stanford University Press, 1984; and Ma Zhendu and Qi Rugao, *Jiang Jieshi yu Xitele: Min Guo Shi Qi de Zhong De Guan Xi* [*Chiang Kai-shek and Hitler: Chinese-German Relations during the Republican China Period*], Taipei: Dong Da Tu Shu Gong Si, [1998].

It is of interest to note that in his study on wartime China, Hans J. Van de Ven identified the same four foreign powers as did Chiang that exerted strong influence on China's foreign relations. Van de Ven, *War and Nationalism in China,* p. 14.

[13] Later, in December 1941, Chiang enumerated his foreign policy objectives as: British recognition of Tibet and Jiulong (Kowloon) as Chinese territory; Soviet recognition of Xinjiang and Outer Mongolia as Chinese territory; recognition by all foreign powers of Manchuria as Chinese territory; and abolition by foreign powers of their consular extraterritorial jurisdiction in China and unequal treaties with China (CKSD, 12/20/41). At the Cairo Conference in 1943, he added Taiwan and Penghu (Pescadores) as the lost territories to be recovered.

[14] In 1922, the United States, Belgium, Britain, China, France, Italy, Japan, the Netherlands, and Portugal concluded a treaty in Washington to pledge respect for the sovereignty and territorial integrity of China.

[15]While battling Japan in Shanghai, Chiang did not forsake diplomatic resolution of the conflict. He thought if he could stop the war while restoring Chinese sovereignty in Japan-occupied areas through negotiation, it would be so much better for the country. In October he accepted German Ambassador to China Oskar P. Trautmann's mediation of the war. See Wang Jianlang, *Kang Zhan Chu Qi de Yuan Dong Guo Ji Guan Xi* [*Far Eastern International Relations in Early Anti-Japanese War*] (Taipei: Dong Da Tu Shu Gong Si, [1996]), pp. 143, 144, and 215. Later, in 1938 and 1940, he gave tacit consent to Chinese-Japanese peace talks in Hong Kong largely under private auspices. See Yang Tianshi, *Zhao Xun Zhen Shi de Jiang Jieshi: Jiang Jieshi Ri Ji Jie Du* [*A Search for the Real Chiang Kai-shek: An Exposition of the Chiang Kai-shek Diary*] (Hong Kong: San Lian Shu Dian You Xian Gong Si, 2008), pp. 253-96. All these peace attempts failed because Japan would not agree to Chiang's insistence on restoration of Chinese sovereignty in Japan-occupied areas.

[16]Ma Zhendu, "Zhong Guo de Kang Ri Zhan Lue" [Chinese War Strategies against Japan] in Yang Tianshi and Zhan Yunhu, eds., *Zhan Lue yu Li Ci Zhan Yi* [*Strategies and Military Campaigns*] (Beijing: She Hui Ke Xue Wen Xian Chu Ban She, 2009), pp. 76-77, 162-63; Van de Ven, *War and Nationalism in China,* pp. 196-99; Hsi-sheng Ch'i, *Nationalist China at War: Military Defeats and Political Collapse, 1937- 45* (Ann Arbor: University of Michigan Press, c1982), pp. 41-42; and Jonathan Fenby, *Chiang Kai-shek, China's Generalissimo and the Nation He Lost* (New York: Carroll & Graf Publishers, 2004), pp. 296- 97.

[17]Maochun Yu, *The Dragon's War: Allied Operations and the Fate of China, 1937-1947* (Annapolis, MD: Naval Institute Press, 2006), p. 13; and Zhang Baijia, "China's Experience in Seeking Foreign Military Aid and Cooperation for Resisting Japanese Aggression," unpublished conference paper, January 2004, p. 6.

[18]Liu Jiecheng, *Mao Zedong he Sidalin* [*Mao Zedong and Stalin*] (Beijing: Zhong Gong Zhong Yang Dang Xiao Chu Ban She, 1993), p. 381.

[19]Taylor, *The Generalissimo*, pp. 301-03.

[20] See Nicholas Tarling, *Britain, Southeast Asia and the Onset of the Pacific War,* Cambridge: Cambridge University Press, 1996; and Alan K. Lathrop, "The Employment of Chinese Nationalist Troops in the First Burma Campaign," *Journal of Southeast Asia Studies,* 12, No. 2 (September 1981): 409-10.

[21] Chiang's moves on India were also influenced by the consideration that the fall of the country to Japan would completely block China off from accessing American military supplies, which were delivered via India. Yu, *The Dragon's War*, pp. 7-8.

[22] Roosevelt told of his talks with Churchill to T. V. Soong, who recorded them. "Conversation between Roosevelt and T. V. Soong, Special Representative of Chiang Kai-shek in Washington, on July 16, 1943." The T. V. Soong Collection, Hoover Institution Archive, Stanford University, Box 62, File 11.

[23] Ibid.

[24] See Paul H. Tai, "Talents v. Weakness: A Documentary Research on T. V. Soong in Washington in 1943," in Wu Jingping, ed., *Song Ziwen yu Zhan Shi Zhong Guo, 1937-1945* [*T. V. Soong and Wartime China, 1937-1945*] (Shanghai: Fudan Da Xue Chu Ban She, 2008), p. 33.

[25] Chiang identified several other important issues at the Cairo Conference but was pragmatic enough not to demand a resolution of them in terms of China's preferences. On the issue of China's lost territories, for example, he suggested Liuqiu (Ryukyu) to be placed under international trusteeship instead to be returned to China, for he had detected that America had such intention (CKSD, 11/23, 24/43). As for Hong Kong, Korea, and Tibet, he agreed to let them be "unresolved issues temporarily" (CKSD, 11/15/43). Earlier, in Washington, Roosevelt had the idea of asking Britain to return Hong Kong to China after the war but to retain its economic interest through the establishment of the area as a free port. See "Conversations between President Roosevelt and T. V. Soong on March 31, 1943 and August 30, 1943," T. V. Soong Collection, Hoover Institution Archive, Stanford University, Box 62, File 11. The idea was not discussed at the Cairo Conference.

With respect to the issue of Japanese reparation, Chiang believed that it "should be up to Britain and America to raise the issue first. We should by all means avoid initiating it. This is so not only because we want Britain and America to have a free hand on it but also because we would like to win their respect for our fighting the world war without any selfish motivation" (CKSD, 11/17/43).

[26] Until very recently, American academic, journalistic, and governmental reporting on the Stilwell affair has been heavily tilted to Stilwell's perspective on his wide-ranging disputes with Chiang. See particularly Theodore H. White, ed., *The Stilwell Papers*. New York: W. Sloane Associates [1948]; and Barbara W. Tuchman, *Stilwell and the American Experience in China, 1911-45*. New York: Macmillan [1971].

Lately several works presented a different perspective. In a chapter on "Stilwell Revisited" of his 2007-published book, Van de Ven refuted what he called the Stilwell-White paradigm with a meticulous research on the differences between the Chinese leader and the American general, see Van de Ven, *War and Nationalism in China*, pp. 19-63. Similarly, in his 2009-published book, Taylor devoted one hundred pages to an exposition of the clashes of the two personalities over strategy, personal behavior, and cultural disposition. Taylor, *The Generalissimo*, pp. 194-295. Both Van de Ven and Taylor laid blame for the disputes more on Stilwell than on Chiang. Maochun Yu of the U.S. Naval Academy held a comparable view in his presentation at Session 9, "Foreign Military Aid and Assistance," Conference on the Military History of the Sino-Japanese War of 1937-1945, January 7-10, 2004, sponsored by the Asia Center, Harvard University.

[27]These pressures included, among other things, the following actions by the American government: promoting Stilwell to a full general from lieutenant general, authorizing Stilwell to assume exclusive authority for allocating American war supplies to China, tying a $500 million foreign aid program to Stilwell's appointment as commander of all Chinese forces, hinting at evacuation of American businessmen from Chongqing, contemplating to support a move of replacing Chiang with Sun Fo (Sun Yat-sen's son, often at odds with Chiang) as the Chinese political leader, threatening to discontinue Chinese-American cooperation in the war against Japan, and suspending half of the 14th Air Force from air operations. See Paul H. Tai, "Chiang Kai-shek's Wartime Diplomacy: Bargaining Strategies and Internal Dynamics," Conference on Political Change and Leadership of Nationalist China, 1911-1949, November 1-2, 2008, Beijing, China, p. 93.

[28]In Chiang's view, letting an American general be supreme commander of Chinese forces was tantamount to making China an American colony, in contravention of the nation's long struggle for independence. One can only understand Chiang's reluctance to concede to Roosevelt's demand when looking at the British-Indian wartime relations. British Lord Louis Mountbatten served during World War II as supreme commander of all forces in India, a colony then struggling for independence. Chiang would learn later of a comparable case of crude demonstration of imperialism during the Cold War when Soviet Marshal Konstantin Rokossovsky was made Defense Minister of Poland, 1952-1957.

[29]Reflecting this view were the remarks of Bill Donovan, Director of U.S. Office of Strategic Services during the Second World

War: "China is by far the largest and most important area outside of the Western Hemisphere in which the United States has the predominant interest. The interest is political, military and economic, as the United States wishes to aid in the creation and maintenance of a strong, unified and friendly China. China is, however, surrounded by powers whose interests are not necessarily the same as those of the United States. The most important of these are Russia on the north and west, the British, Dutch and French colonial empires on the south, the Japanese on the east." Quoted in Maochun Yu, *OSS in China: Prelude to Cold War* (New Haven: Yale University Press, c1996), p. 209.

[30] Hsiao-ting Lin has done several path-breaking studies on the Nationalists' penetration of the frontier belt and inner belt of Chinese lands during the Chinese-Japanese war. Much of the discussion in this part of the present book is inspired by his works, particularly the following: *Tibet and Nationalist China's Frontier, Intrigues and Ethnopolitics, 1928-49*, Vancouver, Canada: UBC Press, 2006; "War or Stratagem? Reassessing China's Military Advance towards Tibet, 1942-1943," *The China Quarterly* (2006): 446-62; "From Rimland to Heartland: Nationalist China's Geopolitics and Ethnopolitics in Central Asia, 1937-1952," *The International History Review*, Vol. 30, No. 1 (March 2008): 52-75.

[31] For the Chinese-British-American exchanges on the Tibet issue in Washington, see the T. V. Soong Collection, Hoover Institution Archive, Stanford University, Box 64, File 1 and Box 39, File 1.

[32] See Lin, "From Rimland to Heartland," pp. 57-61; and Lin, "War or Stratagem?" p. 461.

[33] Qinghai was ruled by Ma Bufang as governor; Ningxia, by Ma Hongkui as governor; and Gansu, under the domination of Ma Hongbin and Ma Buqing, as governor and military commander respectively.

[34] Soong maintained during his three-year tenure in Washington a record on the telegrams, in verbatim, between him and Chiang. See Chiang-Soong Telegrams, June 1940-September 1943, in the T.V. Soong Collection, Hoover Institution Archive, Stanford University.

[35] Agreed John Garver, "There should be no doubt that Chiang Kai-shek was a hard and effective bargainer on China's behalf." John W. Garver, "China's Wartime Diplomacy," in James C. Hsiung and Steven I. Levine, eds., *China's Bitter Victory: The War with Japan,1937-1945* (Armonk, N.Y.: M. E. Sharpe, c1992), p. 28.

[36] *Chronology of Chiang Kai-shek*, p. 313.

[37] United States, Department of State, *United States Relations with China* (Washington: Government Printing Office, 1949), p. xvi.

[38] *Chronology of Chiang Kai-shek,* pp. 385, 387.

[39] U, S., *Department of State Bulletin,* January 16, 1950, p. 79.

[40] Tang Tsou, *America's Failure in China, 1941-50* (Chicago: University of Chicago Press, 1963), pp. 513-20.

[41] United States, *Department of State Bulletin,* January 23, 1950, p. 115.

[42] Chinese Communist troop strength was based on estimate of U.S., Central Intelligence Agency, "Prospects for an Early Successful Chinese Communist Attack on Taiwan," July 26, 1950, IM-312, D/FE. Cited in Taylor, *The Generalissimo,* p. 430.

[43] The aggregate area of the three groups of islands is about 200 square kilometers, of which Quemoy possesses 150.

[44] The massive and intensified bombardments on the offshore islands were rarely seen in the history of modern warfare. In 44 day's shelling during the 1958 crisis, the Communists fired a total of 474,910 rounds of shell on the offshore islands, with 1,472 falling on Quemoy per square kilometer. Wang Shuming, Chief of Staff of the Nationalist Army, "823 Tai Hai Zhan Yi Zuo Zhan Jian Tao Zong Jiang Ping" [Final Commentary and Assessment of the August 23 Battle in the Taiwan Sea], Republic of China, Ministry of National Defense, *Guo Jun Zhan Shi Cong Shu* [*Collections on the National Army's War History*], Vol. 4, Appendix 2 (Taipei, Taiwan), pp. 367-68. The shelling in the 1954 crisis was substantial but not as heavy as that in the 1958 crisis—with more than 70,000 rounds of shell falling on the main island of Quemoy alone.

[45] Both American intelligence community and Western academic community shared the view that Mao intended to use the bombardments of the offshore islands to prevent the conclusion of the ROC-U.S. defense treaty. See "Special National Intelligence Estimate, Washington, 4 September 1954: The Situation with Respect to Certain Islands off the Coast of Mainland China," *FRUS, 1952-1954,* Vol. 14, Part 1, pp. 563-69; Thomas E. Stolper, *China, Taiwan, and the Offshore Islands: Together with an Implication for Outer Mongolia and Sino-Soviet Relations* (Armonk, NY: M.E. Sharpe, c1985) pp. 26, 36-39; and Gordon H. Chang and He Di, "The Absence of War in the U.S.-China Confrontation over Quemoy and Matsu in 1954-1955: Contingency, Luck, Deterrence?" *The American Historical Review,* Vol. 98, Issue 5 (December 1993): 1508-09.

[46] Nationalist China's ambassador to the U.S. Wellington Koo's conversation with Dulles on March 19, 1953, *FRUS, 1952-1954,* Vol. 14, Part 1, p. 158.

[47] "Memorandum of Conference [of Dulles] with the President, The White House, October 18, 1954," and Memorandum of Conversation, by the Assistant Secretary of State for International Organization Affairs (Key) [Washington,] October 18, 1954," *FRUS, 1952-1954*, Vol. 14, Part 1, pp. 770-75.

[48] See also "[Dulles'] Memorandum of a Conversation, The White House, January 19, 1955," *FRUS, 1955-1957*, Vol. 2, pp. 42-43; and Stolper, *China, Taiwan, and the Offshore Islands*, pp. 69-70.

[49] Dwight D. Eisenhower, *The White House Years* (Garden City, N.Y.: Doubleday, 1963-65), Vol. 1, p. 477, and Vol. 2, pp. 691-92; "Memorandum of a Conversation between the President and the Secretary of States, Washington, March 6, 1955," *FRUS, 1955-1957*, Vol. 2, pp. 336-37.

[50] Taylor, *The Generalissimo*, p. 494; and Steve Tsang, "Chiang Kai-shek and the Kuomintang's Policy to Reconquer the Chinese Mainland, 1949-1958," in Steve Tsang, ed., *In the Shadow of China: Political Developments in Taiwan since 1949* (Honolulu: University of Hawaii Press, 1993), p. 57.

[51] "Memorandum of Conversation [between Chiang and Dulles], Taipei, October 21, 1958," *FRUS, 1958-60*, Vol. 19, p. 419.

[52] See the debates and split views on American defense of the offshore islands within the U.S. Joint Chiefs of Staff in "Memorandum by the Chairman of the Joint Chiefs of Staff (Radford) to the Secretary of Defense (Wilson), 11 September 1954," *FRUS, 1952-1954*, Vol. 14, Part 1, pp. 598-604.

For a time, Dulles sought to resolve the crisis through the intervention of the United Nations and persuaded New Zealand to make a proposal for the UN's Security Council to issue an order of ceasefire in the offshore islands area. The Security Council did not fully consider the proposal because both Chiang and Mao opposed it. See Chang Su-ya, "An Li Hui Ting Huo An: Mei Guo Ying Fu Di Yi Ci Tai Hai Wei Ji Ce Lue Zhi Yi" [The Issue of United Nations Security Council's Ceasefire Order: One of the American Tactics to Cope with the First Crisis of the Taiwan Sea], Academia Sinica, Institute of Modern History, *Compendium*, Vol. 22, Part 2 (June 1993): 63-106.

[53] "Memorandum Prepared by the Secretary of State Dulles, September 4, 1958," *FRUS, 1958-1960*, Vol. 19, pp. 131-34. See also Eisenhower, *The White House Years*, Vol. 1, pp. 474, 495; and Vol. 2, p. 691.

[54] "White House Press Release: Statement by the Secretary of State, September 4, 1958," *FRUS, 1958-1960*, Vol. 19, p. 135.

[55]"Memorandum of Conversation, September 2, 1958," *FRUS, 1958-1960*, Vol. 19, pp. 118 and 120. Recent declassified U.S. government documents revealed in detail other types of nuclear weapons to be used in the crises and the locations where they were readied for operation. See Hans M. Kristensen, "Nukes in the Taiwan Crisis (May 13, 2008)." *www.fas.org/blog/ssp/2008/.../nukes-in-the-taiwan-crisis.php.*

[56]See Dulles' statement on Chiang's concessions, *FRUS, 1955-1957*, Vol. 2, p. 277; and also Chiang-Dulles "Joint Communiqué, Taipei, October 23, 1958," *FRUS, 1958-1960*, Vol. 19, p. 444.

[57]Hu Zongnan Shang Jiang Nian Pu Bian Zuan Wei Yuan Hui, ed., *Hu Shang Jiang Zongnan Nian Pu* [*The Chronology of General Hu Zongnan*] (Taipei: Wen Hai Chu Ban She, [1978?]), pp. 278-94.

[58]John W. Garver, *The Sino-American Alliance: Nationalist China and American Cold War Strategy in Asia* (Armonk, N.Y.: M.E. Sharpe, c1997), pp. 76-77, 99-109.

[59] See Note 56, above.

[60]Lin Bowen, *1949: Shi Po Tian Jing de Yi Nian* [*1949: An Earth-shaking Year*] (Taipei: Shi Bao Wen Hua Chu Ban She, 2009), pp. 209-11.

[61]Quoted in "Telegram from the Department of State to the Embassy in the Republic of China, Washington, April 5, 1961" *FRUS, 1961-1963*, Vol. 22, p. 46.

[62] See "Telegram from the Department of State to the Embassy of the Republic of China, Washington, October 16, [1961]," ibid. p. 160; and CKSD, 10/20/61.

[63]See "Response to National Security Study Memorandum 107, Washington, Undated," U.S. National Archives, RG 59, S/S Files: Lot 80D 212, National Security Files, NSSM 107, Secret.

American diplomats detected in 1969 that the Soviet Union, because of the then intensified Sino-Soviet conflict, preferred to keep Communist China out of the UN for a while. In their "private statements," Soviet diplomats at the UN expressed a mild support of the idea of dual representation. See "Telegram from the [U.S.] Department of the State to the [U.S.] Mission to the United Nations, Washington, May 19, 1969," U.S. National Archives, RG 59, Central Files 1967-69, UN 6 CHICOM. Secret.

[64]See "Telegram from the [U.S.] Mission to the United Nations to the [U.S.] Department of State, New York, October 27, 1970," U.S. National Archives, Nixon Presidential Materials, NSC Files, Box 299, Agency Files, USUN, Vol. V. Secret; and "Telegram from the [U.S.]

Embassy in the Republic of China to the [U.S.] Department of States, Taipei, February 1, 1971," U.S. National Archives, RG 59, Central Files 1970-73, UN 6 CHICOM. Secret. During the Nationalist-U. S. negotiations over the issue of dual representation, Chiang at one time was considering acceptance of the idea of dual representation on condition that Nationalist China's delegation retain seat in the United Nations Security Council with the veto power. He knew full well such an arrangement would not be acceptable to Communist China. Thus, his endorsement of the idea of dual representation was meaningless, nothing more than a ploy.

[65] Gao, *China's Diplomatic Relations*, p. 53.

[66] *FRUS, 1969-1976*, Vol.17, p. 858.

[67] David W. Chang and Hung-chao Tai, "The Informal Diplomacy of the Republic of China, with a Case Study of ROC's Relations with Singapore," *American Journal of Chinese Studies*, Vol. 3, No. 2 (October 1996): 148-76.

[68] Wang Wenlong, "Chiang Ching-kuo Yuan Zhang Yu Zhong Hua Min Guo Wai Jiao" [Premier Chiang Ching-kuo and Diplomacy of the Republic of China], *BL*, No. 548 (January 2008): 22-28; and Taylor, *The Generalissimo's Son,* pp. 292ff.

[69] For a fuller treatment of this subject than what is presented below, see Paul H. Tai, "The Russian Option," *Hoover Digest*, No. 3 (Summer 2010): 182-90.

[70] For a sample of academic works on this subject, see John W. Garver, "Taiwan's Russian Option: Image and Reality," *Asian Survey*, Vol. 18, No. 7 (July 1978): 751-66; Michael B. Share, *Where Empires Collided: Russian and Soviet Relations with Hong Kong, Taiwan, and Macao* (Hong Kong: Chinese University Press, c2007), pp. 203-30; Czeslaw Tubilewicz, "Taiwan and the Soviet Union during the Cold War," *Communist and Post-Communist Studies,* Vol. 38, Issue 4 (December 2005): 457-73; Shaohua Hu, "Russia and Cross Strait Relations," http://www.soas.ac.uk/taiwanstudies/eats/eats2008/file43181. pdf; and Shin Kawashima, "Soviet-Taiwanese Relations during the Early Cold War," http://www.wilsoncenter.org/index.cfm?topic_id=1462& fuseaction=topics. item&news_id=538730.

[71] The dates cited here refer to the dates of Chiang's diary entries, not those of contact between Taiwan's and Soviet personnel.

CHAPTER ELEVEN

HANDLING FOREIGN FRIENDS AND FOES, II

As noted before, Chiang Kai-shek and Mao Zedong shared a number of traits in their conduct of foreign relations. Yet they differed sharply in their perspectives on world politics and in the execution of specific foreign policies. In the previous chapter, we have examined Chiang's diplomatic experiences from 1931 to 1975. In this chapter we shall treat Mao's diplomatic engagements from late 1949 to 1976, ending with an assessment of the two Chinese leaders' effort at building up China as a Big Power.

Mao: One, Two, and Three Grand Strategy

Henry A. Kissinger once characterized the respective roles of Mao Zedong and Zhou Enlai in Chinese foreign policymaking in these terms: "Mao was the boss, although he left day-to-day administration and tactics to his Prime Minister [Zhou]...." As the boss, Mao acted as "the philosopher...the grand strategist" rather than the manager of foreign policy.[1] This is an apt observation. In dealing with international politics, Mao characteristically adopted a global perspective and had the knack of digitizing his concepts. Over the years he introduced the concepts of "lean to one side," "two camps" and "three worlds."

Mao's concepts are derived from his theory of contradiction. He reduces nations to two categories, friends and enemies. Friendly nations have compatible conflicts (non-antagonistic contradictions), which would not jeopardize their peaceful and cooperative relations. Yet compatible conflicts may change under certain circumstances to incompatible ones (antagonistic contradictions), which cause friendly nations to become enemies. Enemy nations have incompatible conflicts that may lead to disruption of relations or war. But these conflicts may change over time into compatible ones, converting enemies to friends. In short, nations always have transformable contradictions; friendly nations may become enemies, and vice versa. Mao cited China's changing relations with Japan, Britain, the United States, the Soviet Union, Germany, and Italy in the 1930s and 1940s to illustrate his point.[2]

In dealing with foreign nations, "our tactics" Mao declared, "are guided by one and the same principle: to make use of contradictions [among nations], win over the many, oppose the few and crush our enemies one by one."[3] Or, to use the Chinese Communist jargon, let the United Front principle operate in foreign policy: Unite with friends and secondary enemies to oppose the primary enemy.[4]

Lean to One Side

The first friendly nation Mao wanted China to be united with was the Soviet Union, to which he paid a visit two months following the establishment of the People's Republic. In his initial meeting with the Soviet leader Joseph Stalin in Moscow on December 16, 1949, Mao said, "For all these years, I have long been under attack. I really want to tell you how much I have suffered."[5] Like a child long left in the cold begging his mother's sympathy, Mao was beseeching Stalin to conclude a defense treaty to safeguard his newly founded regime, to provide economic aid to reconstruct his war-torn country, and to render military assistance to the Chinese Communist army in an expected invasion of Taiwan to finish the civil war.

Stalin was not a person easily conferring on other countries benefits without receiving reciprocal advantages. So Mao did not come to Moscow empty handed. What he brought to the Soviet Union was his unqualified allegiance to the leading Communist nation in contention with the United States in the emerging Cold War. In June 1949, half a year before his meeting with Stalin, Mao already declared, "we must lean to one side"—that of the Soviet Union. He emphasized that "all Chinese without exception must lean either to the side of imperialism or to the side of socialism....We oppose the Chiang Kai-shek reactionaries who lean to the side of imperialism, and we also oppose the illusions about a third road."[6]

What Mao pledged to Stalin was not merely his unequivocal loyalty to the Soviet Union. He also presented to the Soviet leader his freshly conquered China, a country considered the second most powerful nation in the Communist camp. The prospective alliance of the two Communist giants was of enormous appeal to Stalin.

The Moscow Treaty of 1950.—With what appeared to him these two impressive gifts to Stalin, Mao held talks with the Soviet leader with unexpected difficulties. The crux of the problem concerned the Chinese-Soviet Treaty of Friendship Stalin concluded with Chiang in 1945. Mao thought a replacement of that treaty with a new one between the two Communist powers only natural, since the final defeat of the Nationalist regime was within sight, hence all the treaties it concluded losing effect. Stalin preferred not to change the 1945 treaty, for that treaty restored to the Soviet Union the privileges Russia had enjoyed in Manchuria, including the control of the railroad system there and the use of two seaports, Lushun and Dalian.

Mao wanted Stalin to abolish these privileges because they were of an imperialistic legacy the Nationalist regime was forced to embrace. Now the Chinese Communist Party, a fraternal partner of the Soviet Communist Party, had come to power; its regime had to be treated differently than the Nationalist.

Stalin was not willing to give up these privileges, insisting that he had won them through war with Japan. He would not do something, as the Chinese saying goes, like a tiger spitting out the meat already in its mouth. He gave Mao a trumped-up pretext: The replacement of the 1945 treaty would be a violation of the Yalta Agreement, which would give the United States and Britain an excuse to demand other changes of the Yalta Agreement, such as abrogating its provisions on Soviet acquisition of Sakhalin and Kuril Islands previously owned by Japan.

As for Mao's request for economic aid, Stalin took a conciliatory attitude, easily agreeing to provide China with a US$300 million loan. However, he dodged Mao's request for assistance in the attack on Taiwan by claiming that the form of assistance had to be carefully studied so that it would not give the United States a reason for military intervention.[7]

Incensed by Stalin's position on the treaty, Mao told his staff members that the issue concerned Chinese sovereignty. "On the question of sovereignty," he said with passion, "we cannot make concessions. We will fight for even one iota of our right; we will secure even one inch of our land."[8] Stalin, in a display of concealed arrogance, put Mao in his villa as an honored guest and treated him with warm hospitality but froze the talk on the treaty.

On December 21, as Mao saw Stalin in a party celebrating the latter's 70th birthday, the Soviet leader did not touch on the issue of the treaty. Three days later, as Stalin held the second meeting with Mao, he talked on the expansion of international Communist movements but again said not one word on the treaty. Further piqued by Stalin's ignorance of him, Mao burst out later to a Soviet liaison officer, Ivan Kovalev, that he was not coming to Moscow merely for celebrating Stalin's birthday and that he was sick and tired of doing nothing at the villa excepting "eating, going to the bathroom, and sleeping." He told his staff members in no uncertain terms that if Stalin wanted to keep the old treaty with Chiang, they should pack up and go home.[9]

Mao's emotional outburst seemed to have prompted Stalin to change his mind, who informed Mao of his willingness to negotiate a new treaty. Mao immediately asked, in a telegram of January 2, 1950, Zhou Enlai to come to Moscow from Beijing for the actual negotiation, the details of which he did not want to be occupied with. On January 22, Mao and Stalin and Zhou began a new round of talks, but the process was not smooth sailing.[10] Though agreeing to forfeit the Soviet privileges in Manchuria, Stalin exacted two concessions from Mao and Zhou, which were included in secret, supplementary agreements. One was that the Soviet Union would retain its privileges in Manchuria for three years after the conclusion of the treaty; the other was that China would not permit any third countries to engage in economic and financial activities in its areas bordering the Soviet Union—in effect, Manchuria and Xinjiang. The Sino-Soviet Treaty of Friendship, Alliance and Mutual Assistance was finally signed in Moscow on February 14, and Mao and Zhou returned to Beijing three days later. Recalling years later his talks with Stalin, Mao said his adamant position on the Manchuria question forced Stalin to change his mind on the treaty issue. "After all, the meat in the tiger's mouth can be taken out."[11]

Stalin changed his mind on the treaty question not without cool calculations.[12] He was not concerned about Mao's emotional outburst over the stalled negotiation. He was more concerned about the possibility that Mao might pursue a Titoist neutralist line of foreign policy, by being independent from both Moscow and Washington, if Mao's demand on Manchuria was not satisfied. It was only a little more than a year ago that the Communist leader of Yugoslavia Josef Tito shocked Stalin by refusing to accept Soviet dictates on international affairs. Now as the Cold War was raging on, Stalin critically needed to keep in the Soviet camp a Communist nation with an expected preponderant influence in East Asia. Thus, to give back China the Soviet privileges in Manchuria was by far less costly to the Soviet Union than to force Mao to become another Tito. Still another factor influencing Stalin's decision concerned Outer Mongolia. It used to be nominally a Chinese territory but declared independence after the Second World War in consequence of the Yalta Agreement. It had since fallen into the Soviet sphere of influence. Mao did not demand Outer Mongolia be returned to China, thus proving to be pleasing to Stalin.

By agreeing to Mao's demand, Stalin would keep Mao as a dependent partner in the continuing contest with the United States. Mao thought he was benefited from his deal with Stalin too. He said in April 1950, "the recently signed Sino-Soviet treaty and agreements would ensure for us a reliable ally" and would allow China to proceed with the urgent task of national reconstruction. More importantly, "If the imperialists prepare to attack us we shall have someone to help us."[13]

The Korean War.—If the Moscow treaty of February 1950 was Mao's first application of his "Lean-to-one-side" policy,[14] China's participation in the Korean War ten months later was the second time that this policy was followed. In June 1950 the army of North Korea under the command of Kim Il-sung crossed the 38th parallel on the Korean Peninsula and started the Korean War. A Communist with a strong nationalist sentiment, Kim had long dreamed of being the leader of an independent nation on the peninsula. Totally dissatisfied with the division of his country into two halves under the Soviet-American agreement in 1945, he was determined to unify the country by force.

Kim solicited Stalin's support for his venture in a visit of Moscow in March 1949; but the Soviet leader, unwilling to run the risk of precipitating a war with the United States, rebuffed Kim's request. Stalin firmly held his position until January 30, 1950, when he cabled Kim of his decision to support Kim's attack on South Korea.[15] The reasons for Stalin's momentous change of mind have long been a matter of great historical interest—even to the early 21st century. U. S. Secretary of State Dean Acheson's speech on January 12, 1950, in which he excluded South Korea and Taiwan from American defense perimeter, was accepted by some as a significant factor. With American forces already withdrawn from South Korea, the speech could be construed as an open invitation to North Korea to attack. Then another reason related to Stalin's suspicion of revival of militarism in Japan, a country holding deep grudges against the Soviet Union. A united Korea under Kim's leadership could serve as a bulwark against the threat from the Soviet Union's eastern neighbor.

Recently a Chinese specialist on the Sino-Soviet relations, relying on declassified Soviet government documents, pointed out a further reason for Stalin's changed position. Shen Zhihua believed that Russia's perennial search for warm seaports prompted Stalin's support of Kim's war move. Shen observed that the Moscow treaty Stalin concluded with Mao resulted in Soviet loss of use of two warm seaports, Lushun and Dalian. In the southern Korean peninsula, Inchon and Pusan might be alternative warm seaports available to the Soviet Union if Kim conquered the south with Soviet assistance.[16]

Two other related developments that occurred at this time merit attention. One was that when Stalin cabled Kim of his endorsement of the latter's war move on January 30, the Soviet leader did not give Mao, who was still in Moscow, any inkling of his decision. He only asked Kim to obtain Mao's consent to the war move at a later time. The other was that Stalin had told Mao during the Moscow treaty talks that the two Communist leaders would share in the responsibility for directing the international Communist movement, with Stalin covering the European area and Mao, East Asia.

Then, why did not Stalin tell Mao directly his endorsement of Kim's war move? Stalin or Kim was not known to have given any public explanation.

Subsequent events provided a clue to this enigma. As indicated earlier, Stalin had sidetracked Mao's request for military assistance to the Chinese Communists' expected attack on Taiwan; in fact, this was the second time he had spurned the Chinese Communists' request.[17] Thus, Stalin would find it awkward to tell Mao that he was willing to help with Kim's military adventures, but not Mao's. This explanation only begs another question: why did Stalin ask Kim to obtain Mao's consent to the war move? The answer seemed to be that Stalin wanted *to force* Mao's hand on the war, which the Soviet and Korean leaders already agreed to launch. If Mao refused to support Kim, Stalin calculated, he would lose his leadership position in the Communist movement in East Asia. If Mao supported Kim, the burden of sustaining the war would fall on China and North Korea. As he revealed later, Stalin would not join the war because of his fear of a military conflict with the United States, and he could not rule out an American military involvement in the Korean Peninsula no matter what Dean Acheson had said. He even refused to provide air support to the Chinese Communist army after it joined the war.

Stalin's maneuvers had one simple objective: let Kim and Mao battle the United States without risking a war for himself. If the Communists won the war, he earned the credit for supporting Kim; if they lost, he spared his country from war.

In May 1950, a month prior to his invasion of South Korea, Kim came to Beijing to request Mao's endorsement. Kim's request surprised and angered Mao, for he could not understand why Stalin and Kim made so momentous a decision without consulting him first. He was placed in an acute dilemma. For several reasons he opposed the invasion. First of all, though Acheson had excluded Korea from American defense perimeter, Mao, like Stalin, thought it militarily prudent NOT to rule out American intervention as a possibility. If that happened and if China was forced to be involved in the war, he was seriously concerned with the severe disparity of national power between the United States and China—a crucial determinant of outcome of war. According to China's estimate at this time, America produced 88 million tons of steel in 1950, with industrial and agricultural production valued at US$280 billion; China produced only 600,000 tons of steel, with its industrial and agricultural output valued at US$10 billion.[18] In terms of firepower, according to Zhou Enlai's calculation, one U.S. army was equipped with 1,000 artillery pieces and 500 tanks. In contrast, one Chinese army in Manchuria had no more than 190 artillery pieces, without a tank force to speak of.[19] Then, the United States possessed the all-powerful atomic bombs. Under such circumstances, Mao questioned whether China should risk an unwinnable war with the United States for the benefit of North Korea.

Secondly, after just going through a nearly four-year, yet-unfinished, civil war following an eight-year war with Japan, China as a nation was economically in shambles, physically decimated, and psychologically exhausted. It needed desperately a respite for national reconstruction.

Finally, Mao was in active preparation for invasion of Taiwan around the time of Kim's visit with him, amassing forces in Fujian Province across the Taiwan Strait for the attack. On May 17, Su Yu, the Chinese Communist Commander in Chief of the Taiwan campaign, requested to increase the first attack force from four to six corps, which was approved by Mao.[20] In fact, imminent military action by the Communists against Taiwan was widely expected by the Nationalist and American authorities as well. Since China could ill-afford a two-front war, one on the Korean peninsula and the other in the Taiwan Strait, Mao could not see why North Korea's military action against South Korea should take precedence over China's action against Taiwan

Yet Mao found it hard to oppose North Korea's venture. To do so would pit him squarely against Stalin and Kim and potentially cause a split between China and two of its most important Communist neighbors. It would be tantamount to a repudiation of the "lean-to-the-one-side" policy he had reaffirmed in Moscow. It would undercut his supposed leadership position in the East Asia Communist international front.

Mao and his colleagues reluctantly decided to endorse Kim's move and suspended their preparations for invading Taiwan but made no commitment to participate in the war. In July Mao authorized to deploy five armies on the bank of the Yalu River in Manchuria bordering North Korea. Chinese forces, he and his colleagues further decided, would not intervene in the war unless American and South Korean forces marched across the 38th Parallel.[21]

On October 4, as American and South Korean forces had approached the 38th parallel, Mao and 21 of his most senior political and military colleagues held in Beijing an emergency meeting of the enlarged Politburo to debate on whether to send Chinese forces across the Yalu River. An overwhelming majority of the participants opposed the move—for the same reasons that Mao had earlier.[22] And Lin Biao, the war hero who won decisive battles against the Nationalist forces in Manchuria two years ago, refused to be considered as the commander of Chinese forces in Korea if the meeting decided to intervene. He pleaded he was ill.

However, Mao now insisted on joining the war. Foremost on his mind was the security of the nation, particularly Manchuria. Though record on his talk at the meeting is not available, Mao did reveal on other occasions his thoughts on the subject. In a cable dated October 13, 1950 to Zhou Enlai, Mao stated his position: "If we do not send [over] our troops and let the enemy press forward to the banks of the Yalu River, the arrogance of the domestic and international reactionaries will be inflated, causing disadvantages to all concerned, first of all to northeast China, with the entire northeast border-guard forces pinned down and the electrical power of southern Manchuria brought under enemy control."[23] On October 23, 1951, Mao explained to the Chinese Political Consultative Conference: If American forces did not threaten the border of Manchuria by crossing the 38th parallel, it was not likely that Chinese forces would enter the Korean War.[24] On September 12, 1953, following the armistice of the Korean War, he recalled, "If we did not fight back to the 38th Parallel... all the people in Shenyang, Anshan, Fuxun, [Manchuria's industrialized belt] could not be at ease for production."[25]

In short, the security of Manchuria was one important factor prompting Mao to join the war. Chinese and Western analysts studying the origin of the war agreed.[26] Among these, Chen Jian emphasized two other factors influencing Mao's position: his attempt to assert Chinese leadership in the east Asian Communist movement and his desire to strengthened his regime's domestic control of China by playing up the foreign threat.[27]

Still, Mao's reasons for joining the war rested merely on his personal conviction, not necessarily more persuasive than the reasons against the war held by his senior colleagues. He pondered long and hard on how to change his colleagues' view. He could not fall to sleep one night even with three dosages of sleeping pills. In the end, he held a private meeting with Peng Dehuai, the second most senior military leader, next to Zhu De, and successfully obtained the general's endorsement.

On October 5, at the final meeting of the Politburo, Peng declared, "It's necessary to send forces to help [North] Korea. If we mess up in the battle, it's just like having delayed the victory of our war of liberation [against the Nationalists] for a few years. If American army is [allowed] to stage at the banks of the Yalu River and in Taiwan, it could launch an aggressive war [against us] anytime it can find an excuse."[28] Peng's statement carried sufficient weight to swing the Politburo members to Mao's side. In the meantime, Mao demonstrated his resolve on the war by letting his newly married son, Anying, join the war. "Sending my son to the Korean War," he told his wife Jiang Qing and his personal staff later, "reflects my most firm action to support [North] Korea and to oppose American aggression."[29] On October 19, 1950 the Chinese People's Volunteers Army, with Peng as Commander in Chief, marched across the Yalu into Korea.

In the ensuing three years, the war on the Korean peninsula became seesaw battles between the Chinese and North Korean forces, on one side, and the American and South Korean forces, together with minor military contingents of other nations under the aegis of the United Nations, on the other. A total of more than 2.3 million Chinese foot soldiers were thrown to the battlefield during the war, braving the overwhelming firepower of American artillery pieces, tanks, and airplanes.[30] By the end of the first year of the battle, both sides knew this war of attrition would leave neither side a winner. Formal ceasefire negotiations started on July 10, 1951 but were bogged down because both sides frequently sought momentary advantages in the battlefield. The two sides also disputed over the disposition of war prisoners and other peripheral issues relating to the Chinese-American relations. On June 27, 1953 a ceasefire agreement was reached, with the forces of North and South Korea still divided largely around the 38th Parallel.

The Chinese Communists considered the draw in the battlefield an event of enormous significance. It demonstrated that an ill-equipped army from a very poor country could stand up to the might of the most modernized and most powerful army of the world. It enhanced China's prestige in the world community beyond the country's expectations. It vindicated Mao's long-held conviction that human will, not weapons, decided the outcome of war. It cautioned America against future invasion of China.[31]

Yet, these gains were achieved at horrendous costs. The Chinese Volunteer Army suffered enormous casualties, with 152,000 dead, 383,000 wounded, 450,000 hospitalized, 21,300 captured, and 4,000 missing in action. Compared to American casualties, the Chinese suffered 3.4 times as many as the Americans in deaths, 2.5 times in wounded soldiers, and 5 times in missing persons. China spent Renminbi 6.2 billion in the war, with battlefield expenditure accounting for 32 percent of the national budget. It delayed immeasurably Chinese planned investment in economic reconstruction.[32]

One of the Chinese casualties was Mao's son, Anying. In the battlefield for a little more than a month, he was killed on November 25, 1950 in an American air raid. As reported in the press, when Peng Dehuai expressed regret in a meeting with Mao on Anying's death, Mao said dispassionately, "Don't mention it. Just because Anying was my son didn't mean he could not be sacrificed for the common task of the Chinese and Korean people."[33] Privately, his reaction was much more painful and sorrowful.[34]

China's loss at the Korean War was not limited to war casualties and delayed economic reconstruction. One more serious setback was the loss of the opportunity to conquer Taiwan. Years later Mao accused the Soviet leader of making "a very serious mistake…a 100 percent mistake" in endorsing Kim's war move.[35] He believed if Stalin had not done it, China could have successfully invaded Taiwan first and could then turn around to help North Korea conquer the South later.

The reality is that the Soviet leader did not make a serious mistake in the Korean War as Mao had accused. Stalin schemed to have the Soviet Union's two neighboring nations fight a brutal proxy war that sagged America's power and will, without itself suffering ill consequences. A serious mistake was, in fact, made by Mao. Sticking to his self-imposed lean-to-the-one-side policy, he paid the heavy price of war without creating a united Korea under Kim, and he forever missed the chance of acquiring Taiwan. Like Chiang who lost a diplomatic game to Stalin over Manchuria in the 1940s, Mao suffered a diplomatic defeat at Stalin's hand over Korea in the 1950s.

Bombardments of Quemoy.—In the analysis of the Quemoy crises of 1954 and 1958 in the last chapter, attention was drawn to Chiang's perspective and his diplomatic interactions with the American leaders. In the discussion of these crises here, the focus is placed on Mao's perspective and his diplomatic transaction with the Soviet leaders.

In the military chronicles of the world it would be difficult to find conflicts comparable to Mao's bombardments of the Chinese offshore islands. His shelling of the few Nationalist-held islets was massive and intensive,[36] yet he did not plan to conquer them. Then why did he initiate this kind of conflict—a conflict that nearly engulfed China in a new war with the United States one year following the end of the Korean War?

With respect to the crisis in 1954, Mao's dominant concern—just as Chiang believed—was to prevent America from concluding a security treaty with Nationalist China. From Mao's point of view, such a treaty would transform the nature of the Communist-Nationalist military conflicts from civil war to international war. It would make it extremely hazardous for the Chinese Communist army to invade Taiwan; it would in effect create two separate states across the Taiwan Strait—"two Chinas" or "one China and one Taiwan." On July 7, 1954, Mao said before an enlarged meeting of the Politburo: "In our relations with the United States a very important problem is Taiwan—a long-term problem. We must destroy the possibility of America's conclusion of a treaty with Taiwan."[37]

Mao also wanted to probe American posture on the defense of the offshore islands and of Taiwan if no security treaty was concluded. He always emphasized that the bombardment of the islands was part of a move to take over Taiwan, even though he never categorically stated that the bombardment was actually a prelude to an invasion of the offshore islands or Taiwan.[38] Another factor contributing to Mao's initiation of the 1954 crisis has to do with the Nationalists' commando activities launched from the Dachen islands against the Chinese coastal areas. When he found out that he commanded military superiority over the Nationalist defenders in these islands, he ordered bombardment *and* amphibious attack to capture Yijiangshan and forced the Nationalists to evacuate from Dachen in 1955.

As for Mao's motivation in initiating the 1958 crisis, Chiang again attributed it to the Communists' attempt to test his—and also American—resolve of defending the offshore islands and, in turn, Taiwan. Others, primarily mainland Chinese researchers, identified a number of additional factors influencing Mao's action. They believed that Mao initiated the crisis to synchronize with the anti-American movement in Lebanon and Jordan then in progress, to repudiate the peaceful coexistence policy pursued by the Soviet Union, and to demonstrate his determination to pursue his Taiwan policy independently, without involving Soviet assistance.[39]

The last point deserves elaboration, for it reflected the emergence of contentious relations between China and the Soviet Union with profound international repercussions. In November 1957 Mao was attending a conference in Moscow to celebrate the 40th anniversary of the founding of the Soviet Union. Speaking with confidence and buoyancy, he declared in his customary colorful language: "The east wind prevails over the west wind."[40] He was referring to the accelerating growth of the communist camp under the Soviet leadership, now with delegations over sixty communist parties gathered in Moscow to celebrate the event. He was further referring to the successful launching of the world's first space satellite, the Sputnik, by the Soviet Union, thus beating the United States in the race for technological supremacy in outer space. He continued to adhere to his lean-to-one-side foreign policy by supporting unquestionably Soviet leadership in world politics.

Yet within eight months, Mao's attitude toward the Soviet Union drastically changed. In a long conversation with Soviet Ambassador to China Pavel Yudin on July 22, 1958, Mao suddenly vented his anger at several Soviet leaders on their attitude toward China. He criticized them in so caustic language and with so much vehemence that had to be shocking to the ambassador. Mao said:

> You [Russians], especially Stalin, have all along distrusted the Chinese, regarding them as a second Tito, a backward nation.... I think some Russians despise the Chinese. At the most critical junctures Stalin would not allow us to make revolution.... Besides, we are dissatisfied with [Anastas] Mikoyan [Soviet Vice Premier who secretly visited Chinese Communist leaders in Xibanpo in China during the last phase of the civil war in January 1949]. He used to put on superior airs, regarding us as his sons....
>
> To celebrate the 40th anniversary of the October Revolution [in 1957] was our common cause. I remarked then that the relationship among so-called fraternal parties was nominal, in fact it was a father-and-son, or cat-and-mouse relationship. I talked about this to [Nikita] Khrushchev and other [Soviet] comrades....They admitted it.[41]

Mao went on with a tirade against other Soviet abuses in the Chinese-Soviet relations.

Mao's characterization of Soviet-Chinese relationship as that of father and son carried bitter connotations. In Chinese eyes, such a relationship signified not only international servitude—as seen in historical times when enfeebled Chinese imperial courts were subjugated by foreign kingdoms—but also a violation of deeply ingrained Chinese social ethics. It was a national humiliation no patriotic Chinese could countenance.

Mao's outburst at Yudin was triggered by something that happened the previous year. Apparently because the first Quemoy crisis of 1954 made him deeply conscious of superior American naval and air power, Mao requested the Soviet Union to assist China to develop nuclear weapons and to provide it with nuclear submarines. In a secret agreement with China on October 15, 1957, Khrushchev, the then Soviet leader, authorized to supply technology necessary for developing nuclear weapons to China. As for the request for submarines, Khrushchev proposed that, instead of furnishing China with such warships, the Soviet Union would establish a joint submarine fleet with China and, in addition, would create a long-wave radio station in China for communication with the submarines when operating overseas. Yudin presented Khrushchev's proposal to Mao the day before their conversation.

Mao was deeply suspicious of Khrushchev's proposal as a Soviet attempt to re-impose on Chinese territory foreign military bases of imperialist vintage, something China had struggled for more than a century to get rid of. He told Yudin he was against Khrushchev's proposal and he had decided to "withdraw our request for nuclear submarines." "Or else," he said with passion, "we would rather hand over to you all our coastline." He continued, "You may call me a nationalist, the emergence of a second Tito.... I can well answer that you have extended Russian nationalism to Chinese coast."[42]

Eager to revive his proposal, Khrushchev went to Beijing for meetings with Mao on July 31-August 3, 1958, hoping to explain away Mao's suspicions. Apparently showing his snub at the Soviet leader, Mao held one of the meetings in no other place than the side of his swimming pool, with himself wrapped in a robe. Seemingly unmindful of the treatment, Khrushchev told Mao that all he wanted was to have a "joint consultation" with him for the creation of the fleet. Mao cut him short, saying, "What do you mean by joint consultation? Do we have any sovereignty or not? Don't you wish to take over all of our coastal areas?"[43] He turned down Khrushchev's proposal, sending the Soviet leader home empty-handed.

Mao's anger at Khrushchev and other Soviet leaders apparently affected his handling of the Quemoy crisis in 1958. During Khrushchev's entire stay in Beijing, Mao never said one word to him about his decision to resume bombardment of Quemoy that was just three weeks away.

When asked later why he did not do so, Mao said that it was a Chinese internal matter, having nothing to do with the Soviet Union.

Yet Mao ignored the fact that during the first Quemoy crisis, in 1954, he did consult with Khrushchev, who actually endorsed Mao's move against the offshore islands and that in 1957 Khrushchev promised to assist China to develop nuclear weapons to boost its military power. Even in the early phase of the 1958 crisis, Khrushchev reiterated his support of China's claim to the offshore islands in a letter, dated September 7, 1958, to President Eisenhower. He told the president that "The situation...of the Taiwan Straits seriously disturbs the Soviet Government" and warned that the Soviet Union would defend the Chinese People's Republic if it was attacked.[44] Subsequently, because of his nationalistic sensitivity over the nuclear submarine issue, Mao impetuously fell out with Khrushchev.

As Khrushchev learned of Mao's position on the 1958 Quemoy crisis, he readily consented to it. He treated the crisis as a part of China's continuing civil war, not a matter involving his country. He even told Eisenhower, in another letter, dated October 12, 1959, that "The so-called Taiwan question is one of relations between Chinese and Chinese, a purely internal affair of China." He advised America not to intervene in it.[45] As the 1958 crisis progressed, he saw a rising risk of a nuclear conflict between America and China, which, in turn, might endanger Soviet security if he continued to render nuclear assistance to China. He cancelled such assistance in 1959, sowing a seed for the Sino-Soviet split.[46]

In handling the Quemoy crises, Mao appeared to have let his whims and feelings dictate his decision. He ordered General Ye Fei to launch massive bombardment of Quemoy but left the General guessing as to why the bombardment was not followed by an amphibious attack. In the 1958 Quemoy crisis, Mao ordered Defense Minister Peng Dehuai on July 17 to resume shelling Quemoy "without consulting other top leaders in Beijing." Then on July 27, when the bombardment was ready to began, he put the action on hold at the last minute.[47] When he saw the bombardment, which did not start until August 23, fail to achieve result, he resorted to shelling on alternative days and then sending out bombs with propaganda materials—like "a child play," as Chiang had scorned. All these actions indicated that Mao played brinksmanship in a dangerous game, not following a carefully thought-out strategy. In the end, he lost the game. He failed to stop America from concluding a security treaty with Nationalist China; he could not conquer Quemoy; he was deprived of full Soviet nuclear assistance; he saw a once close ally soon turned a hostile nation.

Viewed in retrospect, Mao committed a serious diplomatic blunder on Korea by supporting Kim's invasion of South Korea before he could invade Taiwan, and his idiosyncratic way of handling the Quemoy crises must be considered a major strategic error. In the former case, he followed his lean-to-one-side line too closely—by slavishly accepting Stalin's dictate. In the latter, he deviated from that line haphazardly—by letting his nationalistic oversensitivity jeopardize his relation with Khrushchev.

From Two Camps to the Triple Worlds

Mao's lean-to-one-side policy line reflected, of course, the existence of the two camps—the Communist and the anti-Communist—into which the Cold-War world was divided. When the second Quemoy crisis occurred in 1958, the two ideological camps had been consolidated into military blocs as well. The Warsaw Pact Organization of 1955, the Sino-Soviet alliance, and the Soviet-North Korea alliance were arrayed against the North Atlantic Treaty Organization of 1949, the Southeast Asian Treaty Organization of 1954, and American bilateral security treaties with Asian and Pacific nations. Such a global military confrontation, together with the regional wars the two sides fought, heightened the sense of universal insecurity and compelled the concerned nations to take measures to protect their vital national interests.

All out for Nuclear Weapons.—Under these prevailing world conditions, Mao urgently sought to develop nuclear weapons. It will be recalled that he made the famous statement in 1946, "the atomic bomb is a paper tiger." He repeated it nine years later, in 1955, "We have a population of 600 million, and a territory 9.6 million square kilometers. That little bit of atomic weaponry that the United States has cannot annihilate the Chinese people."[48]

On the surface of these statements, it would appear that Mao was contented with having a powerful army minus nuclear weapons. Yet during the 1954 Quemoy crisis he was forced to recognize that his army was like a toothless tiger when facing the danger of nuclear attack from America, as Eisenhower and Dulles so threatened in order to end the crisis. That threat, more than any other factor, prompted Mao to go nuclear.[49] On January 15, 1955, Mao decided at an enlarged meeting of the Central Secretariat to proceed with the nuclear program. Three years later, in 1958, the Central Military Commission adopted "the Guidelines for Developing Nuclear Weapons" to implement the 1955 decision.[50]

Mao was not thwarted by Khrushchev's cancellation of nuclear assistance to China. He believed that the nuclear technology and equipment already delivered by the Soviets would provide an adequate foundation for his country to launch its own program.[51] He spoke confidently, "Let us work on atom bombs and nuclear bombs. Ten years, I think, should be quite enough."[52] He knew China was severely short of scientific manpower and knowhow, and the country began experiencing at this time the economic disruption of the Great Leap Forward. But Mao and his colleagues avowed to go all out for the bomb. Marshal Chen Yi, the then foreign minister, declared emphatically that the Chinese would sell their pants to get it.[53] Varying from Chen's metaphor, Mao was reported to have said that China would make the bomb if two Chinese had to share one pair of pants.

Under General Nie Yongzhen's direction, the program employed thousands of scientists and engineers, provided them with maximum budgetary support, and shielded them from disruptions of political campaigns. They worked at full speed for several years till October 16, 1964, when China exploded its first nuclear device in Lop Nur in Xinjiang. From that time on, Mao pushed relentlessly the program forward by creating a credible inventory of nuclear bombs and ballistic missiles by the time of his death in 1976.

China's entrance to the nuclear club had profound consequences. Its nuclear weaponry was small and unsophisticated as compared with that of the United States and the Soviet Union. But it served as a meaningful deterrent to foreign attack on China. It showed China as the only non-industrialized country in the 20th century having mastered the nuclear technology. It thereby advanced the country to a powerful bargaining position in international councils. It contributed eventually to a realignment of the world's greatest powers in the early 1970s.

The Sino-Soviet Split.—The Sino-Soviet split, one of the most momentous events of the 20th century, has been too extensively analyzed to require further inquiry on these pages.[54] What follows is a study of Mao's role in the evolution of this epochal event.

The split can be traced to Khrushchev's speech denouncing Stalin at the 20th Congress of the Soviet Communist Party in 1956. As Mao perceived it, the speech revealed not just Khrushchev's criticism of Stalin's personality cult as it was so widely reported. More importantly, it represented the new Soviet leader's radical departure from the fundamental tenet of Communism as enunciated by Marx and Lenin.

That tenet meant that Communism had to be achieved by revolutions—by revolutions alone—both within a given country as well as in the world at large. Now what the new Soviet leader advocated was that a peaceful transition to Communism was possible. Moreover, the policy of "peaceful coexistence" championed by Khrushchev meant tolerance of capitalism in non-Socialist countries and even acceptance of capitalist tendencies in Socialist countries. Such a patent revision of Communism had to be resolutely repudiated.

With the full backing of his colleagues, Mao took charge, beginning in the late 1950s, of a series of public debate with the Soviet leadership on Communist ideology, culminating in 1963 when *The Chinese Communist Party's Proposal Concerning the General Line of the International Communist Movement* and an *Open Letter of the Communist Party of the Soviet Union* were respectively released in Beijing and Moscow.

The ideological fissure between the two Communist nations gradually degenerated to conflicts threatening the security of the two nations. While Mao's handling of the Quemoy crisis of 1958 appeared to set the first fuse of conflict, Khrushchev's unilateral cancellation of Soviet program for nuclear assistance to China in 1959 and, later, recall of nearly all Soviet technical experts from China only exacerbated tension between Beijing and Moscow. Added to these contentious issues was Khrushchev's taking a sympathetic stand toward India when it fought in 1962 a border war with China, which was supposedly still a Soviet ally. In the latter part of 1960s minor clashes began to occur on the Sino-Soviet borders. In 1968 Leonid Brezhnev, the then Soviet leader, ordered Soviet troops to invade Czechoslovakia to put down the unrest against the Communist regime there. He stated that the Soviet Union, as the leading nation of the Communist camp, had the right to use force to protect a foreign Communist regime under threat. Known as the Brezhnev Doctrine, the Soviet leader's statement alarmed Mao enough to think of a possible Soviet invasion of China to punish the recalcitrant Chinese leadership.

Brezhnev and other Soviet leaders had their reasons to be wary about Mao's foreign policies. They were concerned that the militancy Mao displayed in the Quemoy crisis of 1958 risked an American nuclear attack. They believed that Mao verged on irrational adventures that they had to stay clear of. They were especially astonished when recalling Mao's remarks in 1957: "Once [a world] war breaks out, atomic and hydrogen bombs will start dropping." In such a case, Mao empasized, "half of the world population is wiped out and half left, imperialism will be wiped off the earth, but the whole world will be socialized."[55] They regarded Mao as close to being a lunatic when making these callous remarks at a time when he had yet acquired the nuclear weapons. Now as he had begun piling up these weapons since the mid1960s, they thought Soviet-Sino relations had entered a most dangerous phase.

In March 1969 the Chinese and Soviet forces clashed in the up-to-then most serious border dispute over Zhenbao (Damansky) Island in the Ussuri River to the northeast of Manchuria. In August a clash also occurred on the Chinese-Soviet border over Xinjiang. Chinese and Western analysts attributed the Zhenbao Island clash to Chinese provocations, as China was then entering a most violent phase of the Cultural Revolution. They believed that Mao intended to use the clash to galvanize domestic support for his regime. Indeed, Mao immediately mounted a frenetic nationwide anti-Soviet campaign, alerting the people of a major military confrontation to come.[56]

In this intensified war atmosphere, the Soviet Union seriously contemplated a surgical air strike at China's fledgling nuclear facilities. Media speculation about such possibility went rampant, and the Soviets even sent an official to U.S. Department of State to probe American reactions.[57] Parallel to this move, the Soviets deployed tens of divisions of troops along its borders with China, seemingly poised for a ground assault at a moment's notice. And, as noted in the previous chapter, the Soviets were eagerly courting the Nationalists on Taiwan for a joint military operation against mainland China.

Mao's reactions to these Soviet moves were prompt and sweeping. He made it known that any Soviet air attack on the Chinese nuclear facilities would be regarded as a total war, requiring a full Chinese response. His government issued a statement aimed squarely at the Soviet leadership: "Should a handful of war maniacs dare to raid China's strategic sites, that will be war,…and the 700 million Chinese people will rise up in resistance and use revolutionary war to eliminate the war of aggression."[58] To prepare for a ground war with the Soviet Union, Mao transported tens of divisions of forces to the Chinese frontiers as well.[59] The two sides suddenly staged on their borders the largest troop concentration of anywhere in the world since the Second World War. In the meantime, Mao coined a nine-word statement to energize the Chinese for war preparations: "Sheng Wa Dong, Guang Ji Liang, Bu Zheng Ba." He whipped up a national frenzy for a campaign of *"Dig Deep Tunnels, Store Food Everywhere, Not Seeking Hegemony"* as a way to cope with the Soviet threat. And he warned the Soviets that he would use his long-practiced "people's war" strategy to entrap the

Soviet forces if they should invade his country, from which they could not easily extract themselves.

The measures taken by Mao appeared to have dissuaded the Soviet leadership from rushing to an air attack or a land war against China. An air attack could not assure a complete wipeout of China's nuclear arsenal, leaving enough of a chance of Chinese nuclear counterstrike. And a land war might engulf both nations in a battle of attrition to the advantage of neither side but benefiting the United States as an uninvolved party. American intelligence community subscribed to this view.[60]

One additional major factor restraining the Soviets from engaging the Chinese militarily relates to Nixon's initiative for détente with China at this time. They saw a moderation of their policy toward China as a prudent step to head off any kind of Chinese-American alliance against the Soviet Union.

As a result, the Soviets took steps to deescalate the border tensions, beginning with a visit by Soviet Premier Alexei Kosygin in Beijing for a talk with Zhou Enlai in September 1969. The talk led to negotiations for settlement of the disputed Sino-Soviet borders, and an agreement was reached a year later. Both sides gradually pulled back from the brink of war, but the Sino-Soviet relations remained tense and volatile.

The Rising Triple Worlds.—While the Sino-Soviet disputes underscored the emergence within the Communist camp two power centers, Mao also came forward with the concept of Three Worlds as guidance to China's foreign policy in the changed international relations. The concept, which evolved over a period of time, proposed that the two superpowers, the United States and the Soviet Union, constituted the First world; "Europe, Japan, Australia, and Canada," the Second; and Asia (minus Japan), Africa, and Latin America, the Third.[61] Mao regarded China's relations with the First World as antagonistic. He took the Soviet Union as an ideological rival and a security risk; he engaged the U.S. in diplomatic talks in Warsaw while unleashing virulent propaganda attack on America as a hegemonic, imperialist power. He courted friendship with some of the nations of the Second World while leaving the rest alone.

With respect to the Third World, Mao considered it a sort of virgin land of world politics, being relatively neglected by the two superpowers. Here, he attempted to assert a leadership role for China on several fronts. First, while claiming China itself as a Third World nation, Mao provided economic assistance to it as a fraternal gesture. One study indicated that from 1953 to 1975 China aided 58 Third World countries with US$4,945 million.[62] Mao's foreign aid adventures placed an onerous burden on the Chinese people, for China was itself one of the poorest countries in the world. As many as 38 countries receiving Chinese aid had a higher per capita income than did China.[63]

Second, treating Vietnam as a Third World country, Mao was heavily involved in the Vietnam War. "Between June 1965 and March 1969...[a total of] more than 320,000 Chinese troops entered Vietnam," with a peak strength at 170,000. In addition, between 1968 and 1975 China provided North Vietnam with a profusion of guns, tanks, aircrafts, and ammunition.[64] China's heavy involvement in the war reflected, in no small measure, Mao's determination to compete with the Soviets for the friendship of North Vietnam and, in addition, to weaken American position in Asia. Yet Mao would have a bitter taste in his mouth if he could have foreseen that his assistance to North Vietnam earned only the enmity of that country, so much so that Mao's successors had to wage a war in 1979 to "teach Vietnam a lesson."

Third, he propagated his brand of Communism in certain areas of the Third World susceptible to violent changes. His strategy of rural revolution that had helped the Communists gain power in Cuba and Vietnam in a by-gone age still claimed faithful followers in pockets of territory in India, Nepal, and Peru long after his death.[65]

Finally, Mao attempted to assert Chinese leadership in conferences of the Third World countries, such as the Bandung conference in Indonesia in 1955 and the First Conference of Solidarity of the Peoples of Asia, Africa, and Latin America (the Tricontinental Conference) in Cuba in 1966. Dedicated to the promotion of causes of poor countries, these conferences exerted no substantial impact on world politics, and Mao's uncompromising stand on excluding Soviet participation in these gatherings practically led to their discontinuation afterwards.

Mao's attempt to lead the Third World was largely ineffective, for this part of the world was too large, diversified, and impoverished for him to satisfy its needs. All he could do was to build a strong political relationship with a few countries, such as Pakistan, through substantial economic and military assistance.[66] He could also construct a large transportation project, like the 1,060-mile railway between Tanzania and Zambia, to impress the Third World with China's capacity for large-scale project assistance. But no comparable project was replicated elsewhere during Mao's time.[67] And his rural insurrection strategy appealed mainly to fringe groups in a few countries, without an impact on their mainstream politics.

Sino-American Détente and the Strategic Triangle

Not the least concerned with what happened to China's role in the Third World, Mao had always placed a far greater weight on China's strategic relationship with the First World, for the two superpowers could exert a critical impact on the security—indeed, survival—of his regime.[68]

Foremost on his mind was to avert ruinous wars with the Soviet Union; beyond that, he also intended to engage both superpowers in such a way that he might hoist China to the pedestal of a world triumvirate, in which China was accepted as the third player. This task was extraordinarily difficult. China was by far weaker than the United States and the Soviet Union, not really in a same class of power. Besides, as Mao and his colleagues often suspected, both of these powers had enough grievances against China that they might form an unholy alliance to contain it. Under the circumstances, Mao did one thing he seldom did late in his life—deferring to his senior colleague' opinion before he was to make, probably, the most momentous foreign policy decision in China's relations with the Soviet Union and the United States.

The Four Old Marshals' Report.—In February 1969, just days before the Zhenbao Island incident, Mao asked Vice Premier Chen Yi, a Marshal of the People's Liberation Army, to chair a panel with three other Marshals, Ye Jianying, Xu Xiangqian, and Nie Rongzhen, to assess the prevailing tense international situations and to recommend appropriate response to them. In July, the Four Old Marshals, as they were so known, submitted to him a report on "the Initial Evaluation of the War Situations," in which, as paraphrased by a ranking Chinese military specialist, they expressed the belief that "there were more contradictions between China and the Soviet Union than between China and the United States, and more contradictions between the United States and the Soviet Union than China and the Soviet Union." They suggested seeking reconciliation with the United States by resuming the stalled bilateral ambassadorial talks in Warsaw.[69]

The report, as summarized by another top Chinese official, further stated:

> The Soviet Revisionists take China as the principal enemy. They pose a greater threat to Chinese security than do the American Imperialists....
>
> [Since] China and America both regard the Soviet Revisionists as enemy, the Soviet Revisionists dare not fight wars on two fronts simultaneously. The American Imperialists deliberately show aloofness toward the Sino-Soviet conflicts, not taking a stand, not getting involved. In reality, they are...sitting on the top of mountain to watch two tigers fight. They are letting China and the Soviet Revisionists weaken each other so that they could penetrate and take over East Europe, even hitting directly at the Soviet Revisionists' home base.[70]

Mao could not agree more. As early as 1964 he urged his colleagues to pay close attention to not just the threat of the east (the United States) but also the threat from the north. He came to accept the possibility of a Soviet attack on China and raised the issue of preparing for a defensive war.[71] He concurred with the Four Old Marshals' judgment that the Soviet Union, or the United States, or China could afford a two-front war.[72]

He also accepted the view that China had more contradictions with the Soviet Union than with the United States. The threat of Soviet application of the Brezhnev Doctrine to China, the Chinese-Russian border clashes in 1969, the possibility of Soviet preemptive strike on Chinese nuclear facilities, and the heavy concentration of Soviet troops on Chinese frontiers—all these developments spoke of no possibility of reconciliation between the two nations. The United States had fought China directly in the Korean War and indirectly in the Vietnam War; and both nations had many other unsettled issues, particularly in regard to Taiwan. Yet, he believed that the draw in the Korean War and the stalemate in the Vietnam War spelled a strong probability that the United States would shun any new military venture against China.

Mao's calculations led decisively to one conclusion, as suggested by the Four Old Marshals. "Between the two hegemonic powers, we must seek out one"—the United States.[73] He had to get the help of the less threatening enemy to confront the more dangerous one. In doing so, he repudiated the "lean-to-the-Soviet-side" policy and veered toward leaning to the American side.

The Battle of Mind between Mao and Nixon.—Mao deliberated on this matter with extraordinary care. Shrewd as he was, Mao felt he had to strike a cool—or even hostile—stance toward the United States so that he would not appear too eager to embrace his enemy, thus giving the latter a bargaining advantage. Under his directions, China continued from 1969 on its propaganda campaign against the United States and vociferously condemned American aggression against Indochina and Taiwan. The campaign went far into the early 1970s, when Henry Kissinger, already actively seeking conciliation with China, found in his guest room full of anti-American materials during one of his Beijing visits.

Mao authorized the resumption of the ambassadorial talks in Warsaw, which led to nowhere because the diplomats of the two sides could not find a common ground for rapprochement. Mao knew, as pointed out by the Four Old Marshals, the United States could stand to gain from observing China and the Soviet Union fighting each other out. He realized he had to offer to the United States some substantial advantage to induce its cooperation with China against the Soviet Union.

Weighing all factors at play in the triangular relations, Mao found a right inducement and advanced it to Richard Nixon, his equally calculating and shrewd antagonist. Elected U. S. president in 1968 with a promise to end the Vietnam War, Nixon pursued a two-prong strategy to achieve his objective: escalating the war against North Vietnam and seeking China's intercession in the war. For the latter purpose, he signaled to China his intention of reconciliation with Beijing by discontinuing American Seventh Fleet's patrol of the Taiwan Strait and relaxing American trade and travel embargo against China. In addition, he channeled through Romania and Pakistan his desire for high-level talks between Washington and Beijing. Mao fully understood Nixon's desire to settle the Vietnam War through diplomatic means and decided to help him—and that was the right inducement he had in mind.

In a conversation with Zhou Enlai on July 9, 1971, Mao revealed his calculations. Pointing to the two principal problems then confronting China and the United States—Taiwan and Vietnam—Mao told Zhou, "We are not in a hurry on the Taiwan issue because there is no fighting there....*But the Indochina [Vietnam] issue is more important as there is a war in Vietnam and people are being killed there. We should not invite Nixon to come just for our own interests [in Taiwan].*"[74]

Mao decided to help Nixon on the Vietnam front in two ways. First, he endorsed the U.S. proposal for setting up a coalition government in South Vietnam to govern the country so as to ease American forces out of the area. In August 1971, Mao sent a message, through Zhou Enlai, to Pham Van Dong, North Vietnamese prime minister, during the talks in Paris for a peaceful settlement of the Vietnam conflict:

> It is all right to found a government [in South Vietnam] that unites the left, the middle, and the right. [But] first you should ask the United States to withdraw all its troops....You might [then] discuss the establishment of a united government directly with Nguyen Van Thieu [South Vietnamese president]....If talk fails, you might fight again.[75]

Mao took a second measure—which was much more substantial than his endorsement of the coalition government idea—to help Nixon end the war. He cut down China's military aid to North Vietnam, on which Hanoi had heavily depended to carry on the war. As Li Danhui has observed, while endorsing the coalition government idea in the Paris talks, "China shifted its material support for Vietnam from military to economic aid....China...began a gradual withdrawal of [its] support troops. Between February 1969 and July 1970, China repatriated more than 320,000 Chinese troops from Vietnam, where they had engaged in road-building, air defense, defense engineering, and railway maintenance."[76]

Such decisive action, taken behind headlines, was Mao's strongest signal to Nixon that the American president's rapprochement with China had produced concrete benefits to America in Vietnam. In February 1972 Nixon visited China and, following an extensive talk with Mao, sealed the rapprochement by signing the Shanghai Communiqué.

In reaching out to China, Nixon might have appeared overly solicitous and conciliatory toward Mao, especially so in television images, but he was a tough bargainer, fully comprehending what Mao wanted and well prepared for advancing his own agenda. On his way to China, he jotted down on a legal yellow pad his thoughts on the expected power play in Beijing in so shrewd and naked expressions that would make Machiavelli smile with admiration in his grave:

> "1. What is he [Mao] like inside?
>   Strong, Decisive, Spartan, Earnest
> 2. Is he strong so that I must respect him or weak so that I can attack him?
> 3. Does he have determination & shrewdness?
> 4. Is American Culture strong or weak?"

Nixon decided on his approach:

"Treat him (as Emperor)
1. Don't quarrell [sic].
2. Don't praise him (too much).
3. Praise the people—art, ancient.
4. Praise [Mao's] poems.
5. Love of country."

With Mao thus sized up, Nixon laid down the agenda of the Beijing talks fully reflective of the two men's wishes.

"What they want:
1. Build up their world credentials.
2. Taiwan.
3. Get U. S. out of Asia.
What we want:
1. Indochina (?)
2. Communists—to restrain Chicom [Chinese Communist] expansion in Asia.
3. In Future—Reduce threat of a confrontation by Chinese Super Power.
What we both want:
1. Reduce danger of confrontation and conflict.
2. A more stable Asia.
3. A restraint on USSR."[77]

Stripped to the fundamentals, the agenda consisted of Mao's wish to settle the Taiwan issue, Nixon's wish to settle the Vietnam issue, and the two men's wish to restrain the Soviet Union.

An Extraordinary Document from Shanghai.—With the agenda of the Beijing talks thus set, Nixon, Kissinger, Mao, and Zhou—the two national teams with symmetrically balanced powerful minds—produced a Shanghai Communiqué that must be considered an extraordinary document in the chronicles of world diplomacy.[78] In its substance, the document recorded more of what the two sides disagreed than what they agreed (857 v. 597 words), said something they did not mean, meant something they did not say, accomplished substantially what they had set out to accomplish.

Following its prefatory provisions, the document devoted more than half of its space to an elaboration on the "essential differences between China and the United States" in ideologies, social systems, and foreign policies toward Indochina, Korea, Japan, India, Pakistan, and Taiwan.

Then the two sides issued several declarations saying that they did not intend to do the very things they were actually doing. The Chinese side declared that China never intended to become "a superpower." This is patently untrue. One does not have to delve into the lengthy volume of *Mao, The Unknown Story* by Jung Chang and Jon Halliday to be convinced of Mao's ambition of seeking precisely such a status for China. Reading Mao's own work, *Mao Zedong on Diplomacy*, one could not escape the conclusion that Mao was seized with such ambition, obsessively so, since he became the head of the People's Republic of China in 1949.

Both sides declared that "neither should seek hegemony in the Asia-Pacific region" and "neither is prepared to negotiate on behalf of any third party or to enter into agreements or understandings with the other directed at other states." This declaration is as disingenuous as a Chinese folklore saying, "With 300 taels of silver laid on the spot, you say it's nothing of value there" (*ci ti wu yin san bai liang*). The United States and China have fought each other directly in a harsh war in Korea and indirectly in a long war in Vietnam. If they did not attempt to dominate the Asia-Pacific region, why did they fight these enormously costly wars in others' lands? And contrary to what they said, the two nations were clearly "prepared to negotiate on behalf of" third parties, Taiwan and Vietnam. Finally, they declared that they did not "collude with [one] another against other countries." In reality, one of the major purposes of the Beijing talks was precisely for the United States and China to collude against the Soviet Union. If not for that purpose, Nixon and Mao probably would not have met in the first place. Thus, the United States and China in the glare of worldwide publicity formed an unholy alliance against the Soviet Union without ever mentioning the latter's name, not one word of it throughout the text of the Shanghai Communiqué.

The Strategic Triangle Formed.—Through the Beijing talks, Mao obtained most of what he had wanted. He firmly grasped the fundamental realities in Far Eastern international politics: the most serious threat to China came from the Soviet Union and that the most pressing problem to America was the Vietnam War. He made use of America's Vietnam problem to reduce the Soviet threat to China. His changed stance on Vietnam had prompted Nixon to come to Beijing. He knew that a mere presence of a sitting American president in his capital was a factor weighty enough to dissuade the Soviet Union from taking any rash military action against China. Moreover, he saw the Shanghai Communiqué, which promised of normalization of relations between China and the United States and wide-ranging bilateral collaboration, has put China on an equal footing in international relations with the United States. And the two nations' pledge to consult each other on world affairs in the future, including their relations with the Soviet Union, helped bring about the strategic triangle—an interactive game of three powerful players: the U. S., China, and the Soviet Union.

Mao also obtained substantial concessions from the United States on its relations with Taiwan. America's pledge to accept Taiwan as part of China, to withdraw American military forces from the island, and, implicitly, to sever diplomatic relations with Nationalist China—all these concessions allowed Mao to fancy the possibility of China's eventual acquisition of Taiwan by diplomatic means.

Nixon realized his objectives at the Beijing talks as well.[79] In regard to Vietnam, he did not receive any overt concessions from Mao. But Mao's endorsement of the idea of a coalition government in South Vietnam and, more significantly, his withdrawal of China's sizeable support troops from Vietnam must be regarded as Mao's most decisive actions to help America ease out of Vietnam. Though taken prior to the Nixon-Mao meeting, these actions can be considered an integral part of the Beijing talks, for they constituted the unspoken pre-conditions of the talks. That America failed subsequently to ease itself out of Vietnam peacefully in 1975 does not mean that Nixon had committed a diplomatic fiasco in Beijing. It means only that diplomatic agreement cannot override battlefield outcome.

To the United States, the Shanghai Communiqué marked the beginning of a dramatic change in the world's power constellation in favor of the United States. The Sino-Soviet alliance of the 1950s gave the Soviet Union a two-to-one advantage against the United States. With China now throwing its weight to its side, the United States enjoyed from the 1970s on a two-to-one advantage against the Soviet Union. Thus, the United States could engage the Soviet Union in a full-throttled competition in economics, technology, and disarmament and in the contest over the Middle East and East Europe. That competition and contest, along with the Soviet internal drive for reform as represented by Mikhail Gorbachev's perestroika and glasnost movement, brought down the Soviet Union in 1991.

To Nixon personally, his Beijing trip allowed him to return to Washington triumphantly as a statesman initiating a new era of international politics and as the new spokesman of Republican and

Democratic parties' China policy. And, as expected, the trip helped him win a landslide victory in the 1972 presidential election.

In the eyes of Chiang's Nationalist China on Taiwan, the Shanghai Communiqué reflected a totally unjustified American betrayal. Nixon broke decades-old US-Nationalist China alliance without the latter having committed a single wrongful act against the United States. Yet, the Taiwan Relations Act in 1979 enacted by U. S. Congress and America's continual sale of arms to Taiwan mean that American commitment to Taiwan's security remains substantial. Taiwan is still out of Beijing's reach today. As in the case of Vietnam, diplomacy has its limits. America's handling of the Taiwan issue meant that what Mao failed to conquer in the battlefield could not be obtained at the conference table.

Chiang and Mao: Building up China as a Big Power

Both Chiang Kai-shek and Mao Zedong were perceived as militarists, but both were so heavily and extensively involved in China's foreign relations that they became, during their respective periods of rule, China's chief diplomats. They handled foreign powers with skills, committed mistakes, and made great gains.

As pointed out on the beginning page of the previous chapter, Chiang and Mao expended enormous energy in their dealing with China's changeable foreign friends and foes. How did they fare?

In his first period of diplomacy, from the 1930s to the mid-1940s, Chiang appeared to have significantly altered China's relations with most of its friends and foes to his country's advantage. During the Chinese-Japanese war years, he devised and executed varying strategies suitable to China's engagement with Japan, the Soviet Union, Britain, and the United States. At the war's end, he, along with his wartime allies, was able to reduce Japan from a fiercely threatening foe to an insular neighbor incapable of encroaching upon China again. He transformed the once most dominant imperialist power in China, Britain, to the country's new friend. He made the United States, considered the imperialist power least hostile to China, a potential supporter of his country's expected post-war reconstruction enterprise. Only in the case of the Soviet Union, all Chiang's diplomatic efforts failed to make what he regarded as China's "only enemy" a friend.

In his second period of diplomacy, from 1945 to 1975, Chiang found that the country he headed was trapped in a single-power dependency status, shorn of capacity to interact effectively with foreign powers. He retained the United States as the only friend of Nationalist China while facing Communist China as a powerful, implacable foe.

In comparing Chiang's two periods of diplomatic performance, it cannot be overemphasized that his achievements in the first period were of profound significance, far outweighing his gains and setbacks in the second. To China as whole, he had by 1945 substantially eradicated warlordism and imperialism and built one of the largest conventional armies in the world, with a military strength ranking behind only that of the United States, the Soviet Union, and Britain. In addition, he restored—for the first time in the 20th century—the central government's authority in two-thirds of the nation's territories, particularly in Yunnan and Xinjiang. These were monumental achievements in the 100 years of Chinese history since the mid19th century, with consequences extending to the future. That he soon lost control of mainland China to Mao does not diminish his contribution to the re-creation of China as a continental power.

If Chiang had a far superior performance in his first period of diplomacy than in his second, Mao's performance was immeasurably more successful in his second period of diplomacy, 1958-1976, than in his first, 1949-1958. In the first period, he converted the enemy of Chiang's China—the Soviet Union—to a close ally of his China. But, under the pressure of this ally, he joined the Korean War in violation of China's national interests: at enormous human and economic costs, he ended up not creating a united Korea under Communism but depriving himself of the chance of acquiring Taiwan. His miscalculated bombing ventures in Quemoy cost him, arguably, the possibility of acquiring these islands through diplomacy and contributed to a dangerous rupture of relations with the Soviet Union.

In the second period, Mao launched a crash program to obtain nuclear weapons, which added a significant dimension of power to his conventional army, already the world's largest. In doing so, he altered the strategic balance with foreign military powers to China's benefit. During the Sino-Soviet split, he took resolute measures to challenge the ideological position of a superpower and to defy its military threat. In words and deeds he intervened deeply in the Vietnam War, thus confronting the world's other superpower. When it became obvious that he urgently needed America's help to cope with the Soviet threat, he switched ally as foe, and enemy as partner. In the process, he maneuvered to form a triumvirate with his switched foe and partner, thereby exerting a worldwide impact in his times—and beyond.

Both Chiang and Mao had elevated the status of China in the world constellation of power. By 1945 Chiang had raised it to the world's fourth biggest power; by the mid1970s Mao had advanced it further to the third biggest. They had reached one of their long-term goals, making China a strong nation.

NOTES

[1] Kissinger's Memorandum for the President, "Meeting with Mao Tse-Tung," 15 February 1972, p. 1, Folder 2, Box 847, National Security Council Files, cited in Yafeng Xia, *Negotiating with the Enemy: U.S.-China Talks during the Cold War, 1949-1972* (Bloomington: Indiana University Press, 2006), p. 191.

[2] *Mao on Diplomacy*, p. 3.

[3] Ibid.

[4] For detailed description of Mao's application of the United Front principle to foreign relations, see Yin Qingyao, *Zhong Gong de Tong Zhan Wai Jiao* [*Communist China's United Front Diplomacy*], Taipei: You Shi Wen Hua Shi Ye Gong Si [1985]; and Lyman P. Van Slyke, *Enemies and Friends: The United Front in Chinese Communist History*, Stanford: Stanford University Press, 1967.

[5] Di Yansheng, *Li Shi de Zhen Qing: Mao Zedong Liang Fang Mosike, 1949-1957* [*Reality as Revealed in History: Mao Zedong's Two Moscow Visits, 1949-1957*] (Beijing: Xin Hua Chu Ban She, 2004), p. 129.

[6] *Mao on Diplomacy*, p. 73.

[7] *Biography of Mao*, Vol. 1, p. 35.

[8] Di, *Mao's Two Moscow Visits*, p. 183.

[9] *Biography of Mao*, Vol. 1, pp. 39-41.

[10] For a vivid description of Mao's feelings toward Stalin during his Moscow visit in 1949-1950, see Di, *Mao's Two Moscow Visits*, pp. 180-83.

[11] *Biography of Mao*, Vol. 1, p. 52.

[12] For Stalin's calculations, see Yuan Nansheng, *Sidalin, Mao Zedong yu Jiang Jieshi* [*Stalin, Mao Zedong, and Chiang Kai-shek*] (Changsha, China: Hunan Ren Min Chu Ban She, 2005), pp. 464-72; and Shen Zhihua, *Mao Zedong, Sidalin yu Chaoxian Zhan Zheng* [*Mao Zedong, Stalin, and the Korean War*] ([Guangzhou]: Guangdong Ren Min Chu Ban She, 2003), pp. 317-19.

[13] *Mao on Diplomacy*, p. 103.

[14] See *Biography of Mao*, Vol. 1, p. 56.

[15] Yuan, *Stalin, Mao, and Chiang*, p. 514.

[16] Shen, *Mao, Stalin, and the Korean War*, pp. 176-77.

[17] In June 1949, in the final days of the Chinese civil war, Liu Shaoqi, the then Mao's most senior colleague, made a secret visit in

Moscow and requested Soviet naval and air support of the contemplated Chinese Communist attack on Taiwan. He was rebuffed. Ibid., pp. 112ff.

[18] *Biography of Mao*, Vol. 1, p. 113.

[19] Yuan, *Stalin, Mao, and Chiang*, p. 521.

[20] Simei Qing, *From Allies to Enemies: Visions of Modernity, Identity, and U.S.-China Diplomacy, 1945-1960* (Cambridge: Harvard University Press, 2007), p. 153.

[21] *Biography of Mao*, Vol. 1, pp. 108-09.

[22] Ibid., p. 118.

[23] *Mao on Diplomacy*, p. 111. Mao made the same point in his letter to Stalin, dated October 14, 1950: "if the U.S. troops advance up to the border of China, then Korea will become a dark spot for us…and the Northeast [China] will be faced with constant menace." James G. Hershberg, ed., *The Cold War in Asia, Cold War International History Project Bulletin*, Winter 1995/1996, Woodrow Wilson International Scholars, Washington, D. C., p. 118.

[24] Li, *Mao and America*, p. 380.

[25] *Biography of Mao*, Vol. 1, p. 188.

[26] See, for instance, Shen, *Mao, Stalin, and the Korean War*; Chen Jian, *China's Road to the Korean War: The Making of the Sino-American Confrontation*, New York: Columbia University Press, 1994; Allen S. Whiting, *China Crosses the Yalu: The Decision to Enter the Korean War*, New York, Macmillan, 1960; and Bruce Cumings, *The Origins of the Korean War*, Princeton: Princeton University Press, c1981.

[27] Chen, *China's Road to the Korean War*, pp. 5ff.

[28] *Biography of Mao*, Vol. 1, p. 119.

[29] Cited in Di, *Mao's Two Moscow Visits*, p. 363.

[30] Li, *A History of the Modern Chinese Army*, pp.110-11.

[31] For Mao's assessment of the impact of the Korean War, see his report to the State Council of the government on September 12, 1953 in *Biography of Mao*, Vol. 1, pp. 186-90.

[32] Li, *A History of the Modern Chinese Army*, p.111; and Shen, *Mao, Stalin, and the Korean War*, pp. 358-59.

[33] Di, *Mao's Two Moscow Visits*, p. 399.

[34] When Jiang Qing and Mao's personal staff first learned about the news of Anying's death, they took days to prepare for breaking the news to Mao. Upon hearing it, Mao was shocked speechless, his bean-sized tears streaming down his face. Ibid., pp. 389-94.

[35] Yuan, *Stalin, Mao, and Chiang*, p. 517.

[36] For the scale of Communist bombardments of Quemoy, see the report of General Wang Shuming, Chief of Staff of the Nationalist army, as cited in previous chapter.

[37] *Biography of Mao*, Vol. 1, p. 584.

[38] In the opinion of Li Zhisui, Mao "did not even want to take over Quemoy and Matsu." Li accompanied Mao, as his personal physician, to an enlarged meeting of the Politburo at Beidaihe in August 1958, where Mao issued the order to shell Quemoy and Matsu. He quoted Mao as saying: "Quemoy and Matsu are our link to Taiwan....If we take them over, we lose our link....The islands are two batons that keep Khrushchev and Eisenhower dancing, scurrying this way and that." Li, *The Private Life of Chairman Mao*, p. 270. Li's characterization of Mao's position on Quemoy and Matsu was in reference to the 1958 crisis. It is reasonable to assume that Mao held the same position in the 1954 crisis.

For American intelligence community's analysis of Mao's intention, see "Probable Development in the Taiwan Strait Area," Special National Intelligence Estimate 100-9-58, dated 26 August 1958, in US National Intelligence Council, *Tracking the Dragon: National Intelligence Estimates on China during the Era of Mao, 1948-1976* (Pittsburgh: Superintendent of Documents, Government Printing Office, [2004]), p. 166.

[39] Chen, *Mao's China and the Cold War*, pp. 175-76; Shen Zhihua, "Shi Lun Zhong Su Tong Meng Po Lie de Nei Zai Yuan Yin" [A Preliminary Explanation of the Internal Causes of the Sino-Soviet Split]. Http://www.shenzhihua.net/zsgx/000167.htm; Zhang Baijia "The Changing International Scene and Chinese Policies toward the United States, 1954-1970," in Robert S. Ross and Jiang Changbin, eds., *Re-examining the Cold War: U.S.-China Diplomacy, 1954-1973* (Cambridge, MA: Harvard University Asia Center: Distributed by Harvard University Press, 2010), p. 57; Gong Li, "Tension across the Taiwan Strait in the 1950s, Chinese Strategy and Tactics," in Ross and Jiang, *Re-examining the Cold War*, pp. 156-57.

[40] *Mao on Diplomacy*, p. 226-27.

[41] Ibid., p. 251. Mao's characterization of the Soviet-Chinese relationship as that of father and son was not from a momentary emotional remark but represented his deeply held opinion. He elaborated on this point a year later at the Central Working Conference of the Communist Party in November-December 1959. See Li Jie, *Mao Zedong yu Xin Zhong Guo de Nei Zheng Wai Jiao* [Mao Zedong and the

Domestic Administration and Diplomacy of New China] (Beijing: Zhong Guo Qing Nian Chu Ban She, 2003), pp. 121-22.

[42] *Mao on Diplomacy*, p. 254.

[43] Quoted in Zhang Shude, *Mi Yue de Jie Shu: Mao Zedong yu Heluxiaofu Jue Lie Qian Hou* [*Honeymoon Is Over: Events Surrounding the Breakup of Mao Zedong and Khrushchev*] (Beijing: Zhong Guo Qing Nian Chu Ban She, 1999), p. 188.

[44] For Khrushchev's letter to Eisenhower, see *FRUS, 1958-1960*, Vol. 19, pp. 145-53.

[45] "Letter from Chairman Khrushchev to President Eisenhower, Moscow, October 12, 1959," *FRUS, 1958-1960*, Vol. 19, pp. 606-09.

[46] See Shen, "The Internal Causes of the Sino-Soviet Split;" Garver, *The Sino-American Alliance*, p. 142; and Taylor, *The Generalissimo*, p. 502.

[47] See Chen, *Mao's China and the Cold War*, pp. 175-78.

[48] Kau and Leung, *The Writings of Mao Zedong*, Vol. 1, p. 516.

[49] John Wilson Lewis and Xue Litai, *China Builds the Bomb* (Stanford: Stanford University Press, c1988), pp. 38-40; and Li, *A History of the Modern Chinese Army*, pp. 148-49.

[50] Wang Shouzhu and Li Baohua, *Mao Zedong de Mei Li* [*Mao Zedong's Charisma*] (Beijing: Zhong Yang Wen Xian Chu Ban She, 2003), pp. 387-88; Lewis and Xue, *China Builds the Bomb*, p. 70; and Li, *Mao and New China*, p. 203.

[51] According to Lewis and Xue, the Soviet Union had delivered 60 percent of its promised nuclear-industrial equipment and raw materials to China by the time when the Soviet nuclear assistance program was cancelled. *China Builds the Bomb*, p. 72. For a detailed analysis by two former Soviet nuclear specialists on the Soviet nuclear assistance to China, see Evgeny A. Negin and Yuri N. Smirnov, "Did the USSR Share Atomic Secrets with China?" Parallel History Project. http://www.php.isn.ethz.Ch/ collections/coll_china_wapa/negin_smirnov _engl.cfm?navinfo= 16034.

[52] Lewis and Xue, *China Builds the Bomb*, p. 71.

[53] Li, *A History of the Modern Chinese Army*, p. 170.

[54] See Thomas W. Robinson, *The Sino-Soviet Border Dispute: Background, Development, and the March 1969 Clashes*. Santa Monica, CA: Rand, 1970; Odd Arne Westad, ed., *Brothers in Arms: The Rise and Fall of the Sino-Soviet Alliance, 1945-1963*. Stanford: Stanford University Press, 1998; Lorenz M. Luthi, *The Sino-Soviet Split: Cold War in the Communist World*. Princeton: Princeton University Press, c2008; Yang Kuisong, "The Sino-Soviet Border Clash of 1969: From

Zhenbao Island to Sino-American Rapprochement," *Cold War History* 1/1 (2000): 21-52; Lyle J. Goldstein, "Return to Zhenbao Island: Who Started Shooting and Why It Matters," *The China Quarterly* 168 (2001): 985-97; Shen Zhihua and Li Danhui, *Zhan Hou Zhong Su Guan Xi Ruo Gan Wen Ti Yan Jiu: Lai Zi Zhong E Shuang Fang de Dang An Wen Xian* [*A Study of Certain Post-War Problems in the Sino-Soviet Relations: Archival Materials from China and Russia*]. Beijing: Ren Min Chu Ban She, 2006; Shen, "The Internal Causes of the Sino-Soviet Split."

[55] *Mao on Diplomacy*, p. 230.

[56] Goldstein, "Return to Zhenbao Island," pp. 994-95; and William Burr, ed., "The Sino-Soviet Border Conflict, 1969: U.S. Reactions and Diplomatic Maneuvers," *A National Security Archive Electronic Briefing Book*, Document 4, "Communist China: Peking Inflates Soviet War Threat," 3 June 1969, Secret. http://www.gwu.edu/~nsarchiv/ NSAEBB/ NSAEBB49/index2.html

[57] The Soviet officer was Boris Davydov. See Burr, "The Sino-Soviet Border Conflict."

[58] Cited in Lewis and Xue, *China Builds the Bomb*, p. 216.

[59] U.S. intelligence sources estimated that as of June 1969, the Soviets had 30 divisions of ground forces on the Chinese borders against nine Chinese divisions on the front line, 50 divisions behind. US National Intelligence Estimate 11/13/69, "The USSR and China, 12 August 1969," US National Intelligence Council, *Tracking the Dragon*, p. 548. Both sides rapidly built up their force levels. From 1968 to 1976, Soviet "Far East" forces rose from 22 to 43 divisions; from 1969 to 1976 total Chinese forces on the Sino-Soviet border increased from 47 to 78 divisions. For details on the deployment of forces of the two sides, see Thomas Robinson, "China Confronts the Soviet Union: Warfare and Diplomacy on China's Inner Asian Frontiers," in Roderick MacFarquhar and John K. Fairbank, eds., *The Cambridge History of China,* Volume 15, *The People's Republic,* Part 2: *Revolutions within the Chinese Revolution 1966-1982* (Cambridge: Cambridge University Press, 1991), p. 299.

[60] See US National Intelligence Estimate 11/13/69, "The USSR and China, 12 August 1969," U.S., National Intelligence Council, *Tracking the Dragon*, pp. 550-51.

[61] For Mao's articulation of the concept of the Three Worlds over the years, see his talks on the subject in *Mao on Diplomacy*, pp. 46, 223, 387, and 454-55.

[62] John F. Copper, *China's Foreign Aid: An Instrument of Peking's Foreign Policy* (Lexington, MA: Lexington Books, c1976),

pp. 2, 23. See also Yin Qingyao, *Communist China's United Front Diplomacy*, pp. 130-31.

[63]Copper, *China's Foreign Aid*, p. 3.

[64]Li Danhui, "Vietnam and the Chinese Policy toward the United States," in William C. Kirby, Robert S. Ross, and Gong Li, eds., *Normalization of U.S.-China Relations: An International History* (Cambridge: Harvard University Press, 2005), pp. 185 and 325; see also Li, *A History of the Modern Chinese Army*, pp. 218-19.

[65]In India, the origin of the Maoist rebellion can be traced to the Naxalite movement in 1967 in the State of West Bengal. As late as November 2009, Maoists rebels claimed a "presence in 20 states" and dedicated to rural insurrection. Jim Yardley, "Maoist Rebels Widen Deadly Reach across India," *The New York Times*, November 1, 2009, pp. A1 and A16; see also Rita Khanna, "War against the Maoists: But Who Are They and What Do They Want," *Radical Notes Journal*, November 19, 2009.http://robertlindsay.wordpress.com/2009/11/23/who-are-the-maoists-and-what-do-they-want-by-rita-khanna/

In Nepal, the Communist Party of Nepal (Maoist) gave up a decade-long rural rebellion against the government in 2006 by agreeing to participate in the peaceful political process. In 2008 its leader, Pushpa Kamal Dahal, became prime minister of a coalition government following the party's victory in a parliamentary election. But the party soon left the coalition government because of political feuds. Then, in August 2011, the Maoist party returned to power when Baburam Bhattarai, one of its senior leaders, was elected the new prime minister by the parliament. *The New York Times,* August 29, 2011, p. A7.

In Peru, the Shining Path (*Sendero Luminoso*) is a Maoist group operating in the hills since the 1980s. It remains a rebel group in the country today. Kathryn Gregory, "Shining Path, Tupac Amaru (Peru, Leftists)," August 27, 2007, US Council on Foreign Relations. http://www.cfr.org/publication/9276/

[66]See Samina Yasmin, *Chinese Economic and Military Aid to Pakistan 1969-1979*, Canberra: Department of International Studies, Australian National University, 1987.

[67]See Jamie Monson, *Africa's Freedom Railway: How a Chinese Development Project Changed Lives and Livelihoods in Tanzania*, Bloomington: Indiana University Press, c2009.

[68]Cf. Robert G. Sutter, "Strategic and Economic Imperatives and China's Third World Policy," in Lillian Craig Harris and Robert L. Worden, eds., *China and the Third World: Champion or Challenger?* (Dover, Mass.: Auburn House Publishing. Co., c1986), p. 32.

[69] Wang Zhongchun, "The Soviet Factor in Sino-American Normalization, 1969-1979," in Kirby, *Normalization of U.S.-China Relations*, p. 150. Holding the rank of colonel, Wang was a professor at the Chinese National Defense University in Beijing.

[70] Xiong, *My Career in Intelligence and Diplomacy*, p.173.

[71] Li, *Mao and New China*, p. 25; and Wang, "The Soviet Factor," p. 149.

[72] Ibid., p. 153.

[73] Li, *Mao and New China*, p. 23.

[74] Quoted in Xia, *Negotiating with the Enemy*, p. 170. Italics added. See also Gong Li, "Chinese Decision Making and the Thawing of U. S.-China Relations," in Ross and Jiang, *Re-examining the Cold War*, pp. 349-50.

[75] Quoted in Li Danhui, "Vietnam and the Chinese Policy toward the United States," pp. 201-02.

[76] Ibid., pp. 182-83.

[77] Nixon's notes, 16 February 1972, Folder 1, Box 7, White House Special Files. Quoted in Xia, *Negotiating with the Enemy*, pp. 190, 192.

[78] For the full text of the Shanghai Communiqué, see Paul H. Tai, ed., *United States, China, and Taiwan: Bridges for a New Millennium* (Carbondale, IL: Public Policy Institute, Southern Illinois University, 1999), pp. 251-57.

[79] In a review of what he had accomplished in the Beijing talks insofar as "a restraint of the USSR" was concerned, Nixon expressed satisfaction. He said he had to take the "China initiative…now, at a time when the Chinese leaders needed us. We needed them…too. Now…the Soviet Union could no longer take Sino-U.S. hostility for granted in its policy calculations." "Memorandum for the President's File by John Holdridge of the National Security Council Staff, Washington, March 23, 1972," *FRUS, 1969-1976*, Vol. 17, p. 858.

Speaking of "policy calculations," Mao was not shy in playing immediately the triangular game in China's favor. In a talk with Kissinger in 1973, Mao said bluntly: "We were at odds before, but now our relationship is called 'friendship'….As long as we share common objectives, we shall do no harm to you; so you should not do any harm to us. Let us fight together against one animal" (referring to the Soviet Union). He then proposed a so-called one-line strategy against the Soviet hegemony: "The United States, Japan, China, Pakistan, Iran, Turkey, and Europe should form an alliance along a line, that is, along a [north] parallel on the globe." Quoted in Wang, "The Soviet Factor," p. 160.

CHAPTER TWELVE

SEEKING NATIONAL WEALTH

If Chiang Kai-shek and Mao Zedong were not much experienced in the conduct of diplomacy upon their assumption of power, they were far less so in the management of the economy. Yet they regarded the task of creating a "Prosperous Nation" (*Fu Guo*) as a sacred mission dating back to the Self-strengthening Movement of the 1860s and earnestly sought wealth for their impoverished country. Since every other Chinese leader had from then on had failed to accomplish it, how did they proceed with the task?

To answer this question, we shall delve into the two Chinese leaders' concepts of economic growth, approaches to policymaking, and record of performance; we will conclude with an appraisal of their overall differences in the way they sought wealth.

Concepts of Economic Growth

Chiang's Scanty Writings

Chiang poured out from his barrel of the pen millions upon millions words, most of which were on political and military affairs. He seldom addressed himself to the subject of economy, and when he did, he articulated poorly and elaborated very little. His ideas derived from two sources. One is Chinese history, in which he identified one strand of economic thinking that evolved from the ancient time. In a treatise on "Chinese Economic Theory," he first cited the ideas of Guan Zhong (725-645 BC), a political philosopher and administrator predating Confucius' times, as the most significant. Guan advocated active state intervention in the economy, as Chiang explained,

> Kuan [Guan] endeavored to solve the question of prices from the standpoint of the relations between agriculture and commerce. He argued that gold is useful to the people only in business transactions, whereas grain is a necessity of life. The more gold

there is, the lower prices will be, and vice versa. Similarly, the more expensive grain is, the cheaper other commodities will be, and vice versa. Kuan maintained that the government must stabilize the price of gold and grain before it could stabilize prices in general, and that to do this…supplies of gold and grain must be controlled by the government….If [the general] prices rise, the supply of gold should be reduced. If grain becomes costly, the supplies in government granaries should be sold at reduced prices. Such a policy would facilitate the free circulation of all goods.[1]

Chiang also accepted similar ideas of other Chinese statesmen in the past, notably Wang Anshi (1021-1086), a prime minister of the Song Dynasty, which all involved state control of money and food supplies.[2] In a way, they envisaged a role of the government not fundamentally different from that of the United States government today: the management of money supplies by the Federal Reserve System and the management of food supplies by the Agriculture Department. Chiang's cherished ideas of China's past, however, are far too simplistic—perhaps even atavistic—for modern economy, which is characterized by organizational complexity, functional specialization, and significant reduction of the weight of agriculture in the national economy—something Chiang might not have fully aware of.

A second source of Chiang's economic ideas was Sun Yat-sen's writings. In his *Three Principles of the People*, Sun outlined his economic theory in "The principle of the people's livelihood."[3] Sun proposed, among other things, two key programs for economic growth. The first was a land reform program in two parts: to replace the traditional tenancy-centered land tenure system with a "land-to-the-tiller" system in rural areas and to tax the appreciation of land value for the benefit of the public in urban areas. The second program was for industrial development through investment mainly by public capital and a limited involvement by private capital.

Sun also authored another work, *The International Development of China* (published in 1921), which addressed to specifically the country's industrialization program.[4] Inviting advanced countries in Europe and America to participate in the program, he laid out in the book detailed plans for manufactures, railroads, motor roads, and seaports projects. He envisioned a combination of Western countries' capital and technology with Chinese labor in these projects to the benefit of both sides.

Chiang endorsed Sun's ideas in his public statements, incorporated them in the Nationalist Party's platforms, and supplemented them with a treatise of his own, relating to "the People's Livelihood."[5] Other than these writings, he wrote little on the subject.

Mao's Abundant Ideas

Like Chiang, Mao was limited in knowledge on the fundamentals of economics. In a party conference in 1961 he admitted, "We have more experience with fighting wars and struggling against the landlords but lack experience with directing economic reconstruction. I have told [Edgar] Snow that I am no good in handling economic reconstruction, just don't have the experience." Nevertheless, he still envisaged that he could lead China to complete the job of basic reconstruction in twenty years—shorter than the twenty-eight years the Communist Party took to acquire power by eight years.[6]

In his more formal writings, he appeared rather modest in baring his knowledge on economic matters. In his *Selected Works,* covering the period from 1926 to 1949, he devoted 12 out of a total of 159 selections to agriculture, manufacturing, and finance. Similarly in the officially compiled *Biography of Mao Zedong* (*Mao Zedong Zhuan*), only nine out of a total of 43 chapters touched on these matters. But in his public announcements, speeches, talks and directives, he was overflowing with economic ideas.[7] From all these works, he revealed several strands of his economic thinking:[8]

- Marxism and Leninism: class struggle as impetus for progression of history, labor as the source of value, communal ownership of property, and egalitarianism as incentive for production.
- Centralized, planned economy; emphasis on development of heavy industries.
- New Democracy economics: land reform, reorganization of industrial structure to be dominated by public capital, and temporary operation of private enterprises.
- Rural communism through three stages: land reform, collective farming, and Commune.
- Chinese traditional work ethics: thrift, intensive labor, and hardship endurance.
- The idea of self-reliance.

The first two of these strands were derived from the Soviet experiences. The third was Mao's prescription for the transition from a pre-Socialist economy to the Socialist one in China. The fourth was Mao's invention, which contradicts Marxism's dictum that Communism can be achieved only in highly developed capitalist economy. The fifth came from Mao's reading of Chinese history. The massive Chinese peasantry, he believed, were able to expand agricultural areas to a continental scale, produced enough food to sustain tens of millions of people's life, with surplus labor to construct such mammoth projects as the Great Canal, imperial post roads, and the Great Wall, because they possessed the traditional work ethics.[9] And the last one was distilled from the Chinese Communist Party's experiences from the late 1920s to the mid1940s when the party had to survive economically by relying on resources indigenous to the isolated areas under its control.[10]

When coming to power, Mao was convinced that his economic thinking, when translated into policies, would enable his country to shed its millennia-old poverty and attain a kind of prosperity matching or even surpassing that of the most advanced Western countries. In order to reach that goal in the shortest time possible, he vigorously persuaded his colleagues to accept his ideas and harangued, with extraordinary zeal, his countrymen to follow his leadership to accelerate agricultural and industrial production.

Approaches to Policymaking

Chiang: Let Technocrats Take Charge

Knowing his limitations, Chiang did not attempt to translate his economic concept into reality. Instead, he entrusted men of expertise to formulate and implement policies. During his rule on the mainland, he employed several groups of economic, financial, and scientific talents for industrial development. First among these were T. V. Soong and H. H. Kung, who were with Chiang during the Northern Expedition all the way to the end of Chiang's mainland rule. Soong and Kung were trained in economics and science respectively at Harvard and Yale universities; they served as, alternatively, national bank president, finance minister, and premier. They brought out several major reforms: the establishment of a uniform national tax system and abolition of the regional commodity tax, the creation of a national currency known as *fa bi* (legal tender) in place of provincial currencies, the reduction of smuggling, the acquisition of international loan to support monetary and financial reform, the takeover of Chinese Customs Service from foreign control, and the creation of four national banks (the Central Bank, the Bank of China, the Bank of Communication, and the Bank of Agriculture). Soong, in addition, created a China Reconstruction Finance Corporation for the development of light industries through private capital from Chinese and foreign sources. He also established a bond system to harness banking resources of Shanghai to finance government budget shortfalls.[11]

Soong and Kung's prolonged conduct of economic and financial policies with practically unbridled authority brought out frequent charges of corruption against them. These charges, which are dealt with elsewhere in this book, should not negate the two men's contribution to the creation of a sound economic and financial system that enabled the government to function effectively in turbulent times.

In the 1930s Chiang established successively a number of high-level government agencies in charge of economic planning and industrial development, each of which was staffed with a variety of experts. In 1928 the Reconstruction Commission was established, with Zhang Jingjiang—a Shanghai financier and one-time Chiang's political confidant—as its head. In 1931 the National Economic Council came into being, which, with the assistance of League of Nations specialists, prepared national economic plans. And in 1932 the National Resources Commission (named the National Defense Planning Commission initially) was created, which was by far a more endurable and influential agency than its short-lived predecessors.

The National Resources Commission was headed by Weng Wenhao as Secretary General and Qian Changzhao as Deputy Secretary-General. Weng, with a doctorate degree in physics and geology from Louvain University in Belgium, and Qian, a British-trained economist, appointed dozens of high-powered specialists in science, technology, and economics as staff members. The Commission was engaged in several tasks: to develop plans for industrialization and transportation projects, to supervise publicly-owned manufacturing and mining enterprises, and to conduct national geological survey of raw materials. The Commission was placed under the supervision of the Central Military Commission in 1935 directly answerable to Chiang; it was transferred in 1946 to the Executive Yuan (the cabinet) following the Second World War; it moved to Taiwan in 1949 and ceased to operate in 1952, when its functions were taken over by the Council on U.S. Aid and Industrial Development.

The Commission, whose technical and managerial staff grew phenomenally to 33,000, with field branches in many parts of the country, became the single most important government agency managing the country's industrial development projects.[12] Many of its personnel continued to exercise influence on mainland China and Taiwan after it ceased to function. A number of scientists made significant contribution to the advanced defense and space projects on the mainland.[13] And as to be seen below, several of Taiwan's senior economic officials, including Yin Zhongrong, Li Kwoh-ting, Sun Yunxuan, and Zhang Zikai, were on the staff of the Commission.

Chiang also enlisted two groups of foreign experts for assistance to China's development effort. One group consisted of financial specialists, who "totaled about 65, including about 35 League [of Nations] experts from several European countries and 17 American members...." And the second group included military advisers of "more than 175, mainly Germans but including Americans, Frenchmen, and Italians."[14] The German advisers assisted Chiang, as widely known, in the training of his Central Army and in formulating strategies to battle the Chinese Communists in the Jiangxi period and the Japanese in the early stage of the Chinese-Japanese war. But they also helped China develop its military industry, with the Chinese-German trade heavily tilted in this direction.[15]

In Taiwan, Chiang followed essentially the same approach as before: let experts formulate and implement policies. And when it became obvious in the mid1950s that the United States would not support his military adventure against China, he embraced the idea of making Taiwan an example of economic progress—what he called the model province of *The Three Principles of the People*—as a means of political offensive against the Communists on the mainland.

With the assistance of his premiers and others, Chiang assembled a large entourage of technocrats to staff government agencies for rapid agricultural and industrial advancement on the island. These included:

Three key Economic Architects—

Yan Jiagan: Graduate from St. John's University in Shanghai majoring in chemistry; Economics Minister, Governor of Taiwan, Finance Minister, Premier, and Vice President; President (post-Chiang Kai-shek period), consistently involved in Taiwan's economic policymaking for nearly thirty years.

Yin Zhongrong: Graduate from Nanyang University (later, Jiao Tong University) in Shanghai, majoring in electrical engineering; Director of Central Trust of China, Deputy Director of Council on U.S.

Aid, Economics Minister, Chairman of Bank of Taiwan; a forceful and innovative policymaker with extraordinary zeal; the most influential official in Taiwan's industrialization drive until his death in 1963; dubbed "Father of Taiwan's Industrial Development."

Li Kwoh-ting: Research in Physics, Cambridge University; President, Taiwan Ship Manufacturing Company, Secretary-General of Council on U.S. Aid, Economics Minister, Finance Minister; played the same role as Yin for more than two decades after Yin's death; promoted science and technology programs essential to Taiwan's technology-intensive enterprises; known worldwide for his identification with the Taiwan Economic Miracle.

Senior Ministers—

Yu Hongjun: Graduate from St. John's University in Shanghai majoring in literature; President of the Central Bank, Finance Minster, Governor of Taiwan, Premier.

Sun Yunxuan: Graduate from an industrial college in Harbin; Chief Engineer of Taiwan Power Company, Communication Minister, Economics Minister, Premier (post-Chiang Kai-shek period).

Yu Guohua: Graduate from Harvard University, majoring in economics, Director of Central Trust of China, Chairman of Bank of China, Finance Minister, Premier (in post-Chiang Kai-shek period).

Zhang Zikai: Master's Degree from New York University, research in London School of Political Science and Economics; President of China Petroleum Corporation, Vice Finance Minister, Economics Minister; Chairman of Bank of Taiwan.

Xu Baiyuan: Research in economics and finance at Northern Illinois University, USA; Chairman of Bank of Taiwan, Finance Minister, President of the Central Bank; Chairman of Taiwan Foreign Trade Commission.

Yang Jizheng: Master's Degree from an engineering university in Germany; Director of Ordnance Administration, Chairman of Taiwan Sugar Company, Economics Minister.

Tao Shengyang: Research in Germany; Secretary-General, Council on International Cooperation and Development; Economics Minister.

Zhang Jizheng: Doctorate Degree from Cornell University; Deputy Economics Minister, Communication Minister, Secretary-General of Council on International Cooperation and Development, Finance Minister (post-Chiang Kai-shek period).

Zhang Guangshi; Graduate from Qinghua University in Beijing, majoring in chemistry; Engineer of China Petroleum Company, Deputy Economics Minister, Economics Minister (in post-Chiang Kai-shek period).

Joint Commission on Rural Reconstruction (JCRR)—

Jiang Menglin: Doctorate Degree from Columbia University; President of Beijing University, Director of JCRR.
Shen Zonghan: Doctorate Degree in Agronomy from Cornell University; Commissioner of JCRR, Director of JCRR.
Jiang Yanshi, Doctorate Degree in Agriculture from the University of Minnesota, USA; Secretary-General of JCRR, Deputy Director of National Science Council, Education Minister.
Xie Shenzhong: Doctorate Degree in Agricultural Economics from University of Minnesota, USA; Chief of Agriculture Section of JCRR, Secretary-General of JCRR.
Lee Teng-hui: Doctorate Degree in Agricultural Economics from Cornell University, Specialist of JCRR, Governor of Taiwan, Vice-president and President of the Republic of China (the last three posts in post-Chiang Kai-shek period).

Chinese-American Professorial Advisors—

Liu Dazhong: Professor of Economics, Cornell University
Jiang Shuojie: Professor of Economics, Cornell University
John Fei: Professor of Economics, Yale and Cornell Universities
Anthony Koo: Professor of Economics, Michigan State University
Gregory C. Chow: Professor of Economics, Princeton University

All these technocrats possessed similar professional backgrounds, impeccable expertise in areas most appropriate to Taiwan's transition from rural to industrial economy, and dedication to public service.[16] Chiang allowed them to deliberate, debate, formulate, and implement policies with maximum discretion and kept his role as an endorser and reviewer of the policies they adopted. In most cases, he played this role with two premiers as intermediaries. One was Chen Cheng, one of Chiang's most trusted generals who turned a civilian administrator upon the retreat of the Nationalist government to Taiwan in December 1949. Chen served successively as Governor of Taiwan, Premier, and Vice President of the Republic of China. Another was Yan

Jiagan, who served on exactly the same posts as Chen did, over different periods of time. As Wang Zuorong, a long-term senior staff member of the Executive Yuan, noted:

> Both President Chiang Kai-shek and Vice President and Premier Chen Cheng...fully trusted the officials in charge of finance and economic matters and granted them full powers. They [Chiang and Chen] never openly expressed their preferences, nor even gave out their opinions or directives in private. With a full grasp of the financial and economic situation, they listened to their subordinates' discussion, debate, recommendations, and made decisions in the end.[17]

For instance, when the Executive Yuan in 1959 was engaged in an intensive deliberation on a proposal for "Nineteen-Point Financial and Economic Reform," the most critical policy measure for Taiwan's industrial development, three key officials—Yan Jiagan, Yin Zhongrong, and Li Kwoh-ting—took it directly to Chiang. "Yan explained point by point of the proposal; Chiang approved it point by point."[18]

On several occasions, Chiang actively sought out counsels from Chinese-American professorial advisors, who became members of the Academia Sinica (the highest research institution of the Republic of China), and treated them with considerable courtesy. In the late 1960s, he invited them several times to Li Shan, a scenic resort in central Taiwan, for weekend retreats and picnic (CKSD, 7/12,13/67; 8/7, 23/69). On one occasion, he and four professors—Liu Dazhong, Jiang Shuojie, Anthony Koo, and John Fei—crouched around a table to listen to their 11 proposals for Taiwan's economic reform, which he regarded as very essential and timely. He noted in his diary: "I learned now why in the matter of economic and financial reforms only experts can achieve 'maximal result with minimal effort'" (CKSD, 7/12/67).

Chiang also endorsed the appointment of Professor Liu Dazhong in 1968 as Chair of a Fiscal Policy Reform Commission to revise Taiwan's tax structure in order to provide maximal fiscal support of industrialization and foreign trade. When Liu encountered serious resistance to his proposed tax code at the Legislative Yuan, even driven to tears, Chiang took the matter into his hand, admonished the legislators for non-cooperation and secured passage of the legislation. On June 29, 1970, barely recovering from a serious illness that nearly took his life, Chiang held a party in Liu's honor for his accomplishment on the fiscal reform (CKSD, 6/29/70).

Taiwan's technocrats adopted two elaborate sets of policies for the island's economic transformation. The first consisted of three land reform programs in 1949-1953: the reduction of tenant farmers' rent from the customary 50 percent of their harvest to 37.5 percent (in 1949), the sale of publicly-owned farmland to the current cultivators (in 1951), and the land-to-the-tiller program (in 1953). The programs received Chiang's strong endorsement, for he regarded his failure to carry out land reform on the mainland as one reason for his defeat by the Communists. Since the programs significantly benefited the farmers, Chiang was convinced they would blunt Communists' appeal to Taiwan's farming population, who constituted the majority of the people when the programs were implemented. A special feature of the land-to-the-tiller program was a unique and innovative compensation formula. Landlords received payment with 70 percent in crop-based bonds and 30 percent in stocks of four government corporations: Paper and Pulp, Cement, Industrial and Mining, and Agriculture and Forestry.

Taiwan's land reform was carried out under the direction of Premier Chen Cheng, with experts of the Joint Commission on Rural Reconstruction taking complementary measures to insure increase of agricultural output in the post-reform times. These included improvement of farming methods, supply of fertilizers and other inputs, expansion of irrigation, re-plotting of farmland, and farm mechanization.[19]

A second set of policies concerned a phased process of industrialization, foreign trade, and foreign investment. In broad terms these policies included the adoption of an import substitution program to shore up local light industries (in 1950-1962). When local firms took hold, the program was replaced by export expansion measures (1962-1980). The measures involved subsidies to exporters with loans and tariff reductions. More significantly, an Export Process Zone was created in the seaport of Kaohsiung in 1966, a world's first, where manufacturers were given concessions on land acquisition for factory construction and tariff exemption on imported materials for manufactured goods destined for export. In 1971 two more zones—in Nantze and Taichung—were added. To encourage foreign investment, several measures were adopted in the 1960s, including tax holidays for foreign investors, streamlining government regulations, assistance in land acquisition, and infrastructure construction. Multinational corporations from America, Japan, and Europe have since arrived in the island in increasing numbers.[20]

With these two sets of policies implemented, Taiwan's economy underwent two fundamental changes: an increasing integration with the global economy and a transition from labor-intensive industry (such as textiles) to capital-intensive industry (such as petrochemical manufactures) as the dominant component of the economy, with technology-intensive industry (such as consumer electronics) emerging on the scene.

Two other features in Taiwan's economic transformation should be noted. One related to the policy of promoting private industry. This policy was in direct contravention of Sun Yat-sen's idea of restraining private capital in his developmental plan for China, which was accepted as one of the ideological principles of the Nationalist Party. But Taiwan's technocrats strongly and persistently advocated this policy, received Chiang's approval, and put it into effect. This was first demonstrated in the land-to-the-tiller program in 1953, which involved the sale of public corporations to former landlords. As time went on, the private sector in Taiwan's manufacturing industry grew phenomenally from 44 percent in 1953 to 80 percent in 1976, as the public sector decreased correspondingly from 56 percent to 20 percent in the same period.[21]

The second feature was the implementation of a population stabilization policy—a policy also in conflict with Sun's position. The founder of the Nationalist Party believed that one way to avoid imperialistic powers' domination of China was for the Chinese to multiply their numbers. Yin Zhongrong and Li Kwoh-ting argued for a reduction of the fertility rate as a way to alleviate the population burden on economic growth. They were able to overcome the resistance of the Nationalist Party's ideologues and convinced Chiang of the necessity of the policy. The government created a family stabilization program in the early 1960s and achieved good results in the 1970s.[22] It will be recalled that on the issue of population policy, Mao for ideological reason repudiated economist Ma Yinchu's idea of fertility reduction, which resulted in unbridled population growth, necessitating the adoption of radical countermeasures by Mao's successors to control the undesirable consequences. In contrast, Chiang abandoned ideological principle in favor of technocrats' recommendation for a population stabilization program that facilitated economic growth.

Mao: "Let Politics Take Command"[23]

Though admitting his inexperience in managing the economy, Mao evinced supreme confidence in his ability to acquire sufficient knowledge in short order to perform the task. And, since he had a notorious bias against experts and specialists, he would not put the

Chinese Socialist economy in their hands and insisted on letting politics take command. That is, his ideology-based ideas had to dictate the formulation of policies, which, in turn, had to be carried out by cadres experienced in the Communist revolution. Believing that economic development should not be left to take its own course, he mandated the cadres to organize and direct the masses for accelerated economic development.

At a party conference on economic development in 1958, he enjoined his senior colleagues in no uncertain terms, "Don't be afraid of professors." What he meant was that specialists with cumulative knowledge like professors did not necessarily know what was good for the national economy. He said further that many initiators of new ideas and new schools of thoughts were not accomplished scholars. On the contrary, they were young and inexperienced individuals. He named Confucius, Jesus, Sakyamuni, Sun Yat-sen, and Marx as examples.[24]

On another occasion, when addressing the subject of industrialization, he disdainfully declared, "I didn't know about industry, but I don't think it's something so advanced that it is beyond reach. I have talked with several comrades in charge of industry. At first I could not understand it. But after studying it for a few years, I do. It's not such a big deal."[25] Thus laying a claim to leadership in economic management, he justified it further by pronouncing that, as a rule, experts were led by non-experts.[26]

Without the slightest hesitation, Mao took on the job of providing guidance to China's entire developmental process. Through several documents, he gave out his policy directives, including "The Transition Period," "Agricultural Cooperatives," "On Ten Great Relations," "The High Tide of Rural Socialism in the Countryside," and statements on the People's Commune and the Great Leap Forward movement, and, most importantly, the "General Line of Socialist Reconstruction."[27] Mao's directives, it should be noted, were issued prior to the early 1960s, without any new ones since. This is because, with the disastrous failure of the Great Leap in 1958-1961, he had since been preoccupied with defending his failing economic policies and with launching the Cultural Revolution to safeguard his leadership position.

The economic directives he issued included the following:

• Enforcement of New Democracy economics in 1949-1952: land reform campaign for compulsory, non-compensatory transfer of farmland from the landlords to the landless peasants; farms to be organized into cooperatives; confiscation of bureaucratic, monopolistic, comprador, and foreign industrial capital; preservation of private industrial capital of patriotic and progressive owners.

- Transition from Socialized economy to the Great Leap Forward Movement in 1952-1960: Initiating centralized planning process; nationalizing landownership in rural and urban areas; organizing farms into advanced form of cooperatives; introducing the Communes and nationwide campaign for increasing steel output; setting "high targets" to trigger the release of the people's production energy like the explosive force of a nuclear bomb;[28] preference given to heavy industry over light industry and to industrial development in coastal area over that in interior areas.[29]

- By way of an editorial of *The People's Daily* on January 1, 1958, Mao coined four words as the motto of China's developmental programs: *duo, kuai, hao, sheng*. These words, meaning "greater quantity, higher speed, better quality, lower cost" in industrial and agricultural production, constituted the General Line of Socialist Reconstruction (*she hui zhu yi zong lu xian*). Sanctified as an ideological principle, the General Line became the litmus test of political loyalty and competence of the cadres.

- Emphasis on self-reliance: Mao declared in a January 1945 speech, "We advocate regeneration through our own efforts…on the creative power of the army and the people" for economic production.[30] Self-reliance remained one of Mao's basic policy directives during much of his reign. It deemphasized foreign assistance to China (excepting Soviet economic assistance during the first decade of the People's Republic), foreign trade, and foreign investment as a major means of generating national wealth.

Mao entrusted the enforcement of his policy directives to a number of senior Communist cadres, among whom eight assumed most responsibilities in Mao's time.

Three Key Cadres—

Chen Yun: Probably not a high-school graduate; branch secretary of the Chinese Communist Party in various regions and political commissar in the guerrilla army; participant of the Long March; Director of the party's Organization Department beginning in 1937; in charge of the party's finance in Yan'an beginning in 1944 and Manchuria, later. In the People's Republic government: Director of the Finance and Economic Commission of the State Council, Commerce

Minister, and Director of the National Basic Reconstruction Commission; relieved of all of his government positions in the late 1960s during the Cultural Revolution; resumed his position as Director of the Finance and Economic Commission in post-Mao government.

Li Xiannian: Educational background unknown, but not a college graduate; branch secretary of the Communist Party in various regions and political commissar and commander of the guerrilla army; participant of the Long March. In the People's Republic government: Vice Premier and concurrently Finance Minister in 1954-1975; Deputy Director of the National Planning Commission beginning in 1962. In post-Mao times, Chairman of the People's Republic of China, 1983-1988.

Bo Yibo: Educational background unknown, but not a college graduate; branch secretary of the Communist Party in various regions and political Commissar and, briefly, commander of a guerrilla unit; participant of the Long March. In the People's Republic government: Vice Premier, Finance Minister, Deputy Director of the Finance and Economic Commission, Deputy Director and then Director of the National Planning Commission. In post-Mao government, resumed post as a top-ranking economic official; died in 2007—the longest-serving Communist senior leader.

Other Senior Cadres—

Li Fuchun: Educational background unknown, but not a college graduate; participant of the Northern Expedition; branch secretary of the Communist Party in various regions and political commissar in the guerrilla army; participant of the Long March. In the People's Republic government: Deputy Director of the Finance and Economic Commission, Heavy Industry Minister, and Director of the National Planning Commission.

Yu Qiuli: Probably not a high school graduate; commander and political commissar of the guerrilla army. In the People's Republic government: Petroleum Industry Minister and Director of the National Basic Reconstruction Commission and Vice Premier. In post-Mao government, member of the Finance and Economic Commission of the State Council.

Yao Yilin: Studied chemistry in Qinghua and Nankai universities without matriculation; journalist and propagandist of the Communist Party; manager of finance in a number of guerrilla bases. In the People's Republic government: Vice Premier, Deputy Trade Minister and

Commerce Minister. In post-Mao government: Secretary-General of the Finance and Economic Commission of the State Council and Director of the National Planning Commission.

Song Ping: Studied agriculture in Beijing University and other universities without matriculation; conducted educational, journalistic, and propaganda activities for the Communist Party. In the People's Republic government: Deputy Labor Minister, Deputy Director of the National Planning Commission. In post-Mao government, Director of the National Planning Commission.

Gu Mu: Educational background unknown; political commissar of the guerrilla army and branch secretary of the Communist Party. In the People's Republic government: Deputy Director and Director of the National Basic Reconstruction Commission, Deputy Director of the National Planning Commission. In post-Mao government, helped with the creation of four Special Economic Zones: Shenzhen, Zhuhai, Xiamen, and Shantou.

All these high-echelon cadres accepted Mao's economic thinking as an article of faith, followed nearly all of his directives without question, and proposed not any policies of their own. Some did express reservations about the Great Leap Forward programs but did not question their validity even when their disastrous results already became an established fact.[31] Only Chen Yun expressed criticism of the programs—and did so in oblique and subtle terms.

Record of Performance

Chiang: The Nanjing Decade and the Taiwan Miracle

Chiang's economic performance can be evaluated by reference to what he achieved in two periods, from 1928 to 1937 and from 1950 to 1975. In the years from 1937 to 1949, China's economy was severely devastated by the Chinese-Japanese war and the ensuing civil war; they were excluded, therefore, from consideration.

In the first period, known as the Nanjing Decade, Chiang did not pay much attention to agriculture, resulting in little increase of crop output or the expansion of cultivated acreage. In the industrial area, it was an entirely different story. In the period from 1928 to 1936, industrial output grew at an impressive annual rate of 8.4 percent. The total output doubled from the base year of 1927 at 100 percent to 203.6 percent in 1936 by reference to the net value index or 83.2 percent by reference to the gross value index.[32] A broad front industrial expansion—in electric power generation, railroad and motor road construction, coal and textile production, oil import, and shipping tonnage—took place in many parts of the nation.[33] In addition, the government maintained monetary stability, with the Chinese currency *fa bi* kept at an exchange rate of one Chinese dollar to US$0.30; and the foreign exchange reserve grew steadily, to US$379 million on June 30, 1937, just days before the Chinese-Japanese war started.[34]

Chiang's government, it should be noted, faced extraordinary difficulties in the Nanjing Decade. Japanese aggression in Manchuria, north China, and Shanghai; civil wars in central China; rebellion in the south and southwest; flood in the Yangzi River; a persistent 25 percent budget shortfall, and a worldwide depression—all these conditions tightly gripped China. Given these adversities, Chiang's economic achievements in the Nanjing Period were nothing short of spectacular. Most observers and academicians have so recognized. In a report to his government in 1937, American Ambassador to China Nelson T. Johnson noted that the Nationalist government was "pushing its economic reconstruction on all fronts...," and the economy was headed strongly upward.[35] Concluding his exhaustive studies on the Chinese economy, Arthur N. Young believed, "All things considered, the National Government in its first decade had made a good record in many fields of activity;" China's prospect for prosperity looked promising; and he attributed China's progressive record to Chiang's leadership and political skill.[36] Franz Michael, a noted China scholar, observed that Chiang's government achieved in its first decade "great progress in many fields..., [including] economic development." Thomas G. Rawski, an experienced economist, made a similar observation.[37] Lloyd E. Eastman, one respected academic nemesis of Chiang's, conceded, "It is a signal fact that industry grew at an impressive rate during the Nanking Decade." China's economic growth, he continued, was even faster than that of the then rapidly advancing German economy, to say nothing of the American and French economies, which had negative growth rates.[38] A minority of scholars held the view that the Chinese economy experienced no growth in the Nanjing Decade.[39]

If Chiang achieved success in the Nanjing Decade, his record on the economic growth in Taiwan stood as even more impressive. The following statistical composite provides the evidence.[40] The average economic growth rates were 8.2 percent in the 1950s, 9.1 percent in the 1960s, and 10 percent in the 1970s; from 1952 to 1980, the rate averaged at 9 percent. In 1952-1975, the value of Gross National Product rose 9 folds, from US$1,681 million to US$15,659 million, and per capita income rose 5 folds, from US$197 to US$979; in the same period, foreign investment rose from US$1,067,000 to US$118,175,000—a phenomenal 111-time increase. In 1953-1975, foreign trade rose from US$320 million to US$11,261 million—a 35-time increase. From the 1950s to the mid1970s, Taiwan's currency value was stable, with the exchange rate ranging from US$1.00 to Taiwan $40.00 to US$1.00 to Taiwan $38.00. In 1971 the island began to have a foreign exchange reserve of US$440 million, which rose to US$1,070 million in 1975. In addition, Taiwan's household income distribution became increasingly equitable: in 1952 the total income of the topmost 20 percent income households was 15 times the total income of the lowest 20 percent income households; in 1964, the ratio declined to 5.3 times; in 1980, 4.2 times.

As a result, the Taiwan Miracle became a world-recognized reality, and the island joined South Korea, Hong Kong, and Singapore as the Four Little Dragons—the fastest growing economies in the world in the 1960s through the 1980s.[41]

Mao: Great Progress and Great Setbacks

In the book on *Ten Great Years,* the Chinese State Statistical Bureau published data on the dramatic economic and cultural accomplishments of the People's Republic in its first decade of existence.[42] The progress of the Chinese economy, of course, must be understood with the extremely low the national output in 1949 brought about by the wars in preceding twelve years. Nevertheless, the country did maintain consistently high growth rates, especially compared with other similarly situated developing countries. Many Western analysts agreed.

Alexander Eckstein, a specialist on the Chinese economy, presented a representative view: "China's economic performance appears much more impressive than that of India and a good many other developing countries." This was so not only because China maintained high rates of growth but also because the country's growth was accompanied by significant reduction of income inequalities. Using 1952 as the base year, Eckstein showed China's industrial output increased one and half times, a gain of 156 percent by 1958, and farm output registered a 23 percent rise in the same period.[43] A. Doak Barnett, a specialist on Communist China, concurred. He cited that China's Gross National Product nearly tripled in ten years, from US$54 billion in 1949 to US$153 billion in 1958 (at 1977 prices), and per capita income more than doubled in the same period, from US$100 to US$234.[44]

The Communist regime's rapid economic growth in its first-decade, however, was followed by significant setbacks and fluctuations in the next decade and beyond. In terms of Gross National Product, as Barnett indicated, it declined precipitously from US$153 billion in 1958 to US$141 billion in 1960; it declined further to US$112 billion in 1961, an astonishing 27 percent drop since 1958; it did not return to the 1958 level until 1964, when it registered at US$157 billion; it rose in the next two years, reaching US$196 billion in 1966; it declined, again, to US$189 billion in 1968; it rose to US$210 billion in 1969.[45] Data gathered by other researchers indicate similar fluctuations in these years.[46]

A reading of all these data reveals one clear phenomenon: whenever Mao heavily intervened in the economy through his "politics-take-command" approach, economic disasters occurred. His first major intrusion in the economy was, of course, the Great Leap of 1958-1961. The GNP data of 1959 through 1961 showed the adverse consequences. In the post-Great Leap years, as Mao retreated to the second line, Liu Shaoqi, Zhou Enlai, Chen Yun and others took painstaking measures to resuscitate to life the economy he had wrecked. But then the second period of decline occurred from 1966 to 1969 in consequence of the most violent phase of the Cultural Revolution. In the following years it was incumbent upon Zhou Enlai, Chen Yun, and Li Xiannian to repair the damaged economy again.

After Mao's death, Chen Yun came forward, together with others, to criticize Mao's economic development approach as over-emphasizing "greater quantity, higher speed, and lower cost" at the expense of "better quality" and deliberately disregarding economic "rules and institutions."[47] Another Chen Yun (an academician, not Mao's political colleague, who examined China's economic record before and after Mao's death) rendered an overall judgment on Mao's decades-long involvement in the Chinese economy as his "negative legacy."[48]

To sum up the contrasting economic performance of Chiang and Mao in the 1950s through the 1970s, Chu-yuan Cheng, an economist who has studied the economy of Taiwan and China for over three decades, came to these statistical data. From 1952 to 1980, the period roughly approximating Chiang and Mao's rule in Taiwan and China, Taiwan's per capita income rose from US$50 (1952 exchange rate) to US$2,280, whereas China's per capita income increased from US$47

(1952 exchange rate) to US$256. Thus, in 1980 Taiwan's per capita income was nearly nine times China's. In the same period, Taiwan's Gross National Product grew at an annual rate of 9 percent, as compared with China's 5.6 percent. Hence, Taiwan's growth rate was 60 percent higher than China's.[49]

Appraisal of Differences

Two Principles Relevant to Economic Growth

Two basic principles appear intimately relevant to economic growth. One of these is that a growing national economy will experience a shift of weight among the three sectors of the economy. These are the primary (agriculture), the secondary (manufacturing), and the tertiary (service) sectors. In a stagnant economy the primary sector assumes the dominant position; in a growing economy the secondary sector will gradually become dominant, and in a highly developed economy the tertiary sector will be the most dominant. Thus, a wealth-seeking nation must adopt policies conducive to a shift of weight from the primary sector toward the secondary and then the tertiary. This is an immutable principle according to the experiences of all nations that have attained wealth.

A second principle is the idea of comparative advantage. It proposes that the growth of an economy depends on not only producers' efforts to increase production but also the exchange of specific types of goods the producers having the advantage to produce. If a producer enjoys the advantage of a low-wage labor force and another producer enjoys the advantage of high technology, the two producers should respectively produce, for example, textile goods and computers and exchange the two types of goods to the benefit of both producers. A contrary and un-economic way of production is for a producer to produce all types of goods without considering the specific advantage the producer enjoys and to refrain from exchange of goods with another producer. The comparative advantage principle, which a number of Western eminent economists from David Ricardo to Eli Heckscher and Bertil Ohlin and to Paul Samuelson have elaborated on, is a shorthand statement that trade is the path to wealth.[50] It is clearly and consistently validated by the experiences of established Western industrialized nations as well as the fast growing newly industrialized economies such as the Four Little Dragons.

Reading through Chiang and Mao's writings on economic development, one would seriously doubt that either of them had a full comprehension of these two principles—something college students would learn in an introductory course on modern economics. The difference between the two leaders is that Chiang let experts knowledgeable of these principles and other aspects of modern economics run the economy; Mao did not.[51]

Chiang: The Modern Way

During his mainland rule, Chiang allowed T. V. Soong, H. H. Kung, and Weng Wenhao and other experts to expand the manufacturing industry and to promote internal and external trade. In his Taiwan days, Chiang let Yan Jiagan, Yin Zhongrong, Li Kwoh-ting and a host of technocrats set—practically all by themselves—a well-defined course of development. They first introduced land reform to increase income of the farming community, which raised its demand for consumer goods produced by light industries. In addition, they insured the transfer of rural capital to industrial ventures through the land-to-the-tiller program, whereby the landlords became industrialists.

While the primary sector of Taiwan's economy grew, the technocrats took further steps to induce even greater growth in the secondary sector, including import substitution and export promotion programs. Simultaneously, they initiated measures for phased integration of Taiwan's economy into the world economy through expansion of foreign trade and investment, thereby mating Taiwan's low-cost labor force with foreign capital and technology. All these activities also helped stimulate the growth of such service businesses as banking, insurance, accounting, advertising, traveling, and so on.

All the measures the technocrats adopted, which were reflective of the two principles of national economic growth, seamlessly transformed Taiwan from a poverty-stricken island in the 1950s to a booming Newly Industrialized Economy in the mid1970s—precisely coinciding Chiang's reigning years in Taiwan.

Mao: The Antiquated Way

In the development experience of mainland China, Mao displayed an egomaniac tendency in policymaking. He thought he could master the complex process of industrialization "after studying for a few years." But, with his knowledge in economic matters actually rooted in his guerrilla war experiences and his perception of traditional Chinese work ethics, he likened the task of managing the Socialist economy to fighting battles. He stressed sacrifice, discipline, and exertion as the requisite conditions for his soldiering peasantry and workers to win the battles for increasing production.[52] In a way, he was running the Chinese economy of the 1950s through the 1960s as if he were still conducting warfare in the 1920s through the 1940s.

Mao's economic vision was limited to the increase of production in the primary sector (agricultural crops) and in the secondary sector (manufacturing goods, symbolized by steel), without even an awareness of the tertiary sector, to say nothing of adopting policies to facilitate the shift of weight of the three sectors.[53] He asked the Chinese to rely on their own human and physical resources to achieve national wealth, never evincing in his voluminous economic statements a slight interest in foreign trade and foreign investment. He did not appear to know that to ask the Chinese to produce every type of agricultural and industrial goods all by themselves was the most inefficient way of attaining national wealth.

Mao showed extreme impetuosity in attempting to bring about a wealthy China. He could harbor the fantasy of seeing the Chinese economy, one of the world's poorest, beat the British and American economies, two of the world's richest, in industrial production in fifteen to twenty years. He resorted to heavy political intervention in the hope of realizing his impossible dream. He coerced his policy implementers to blindly follow his economic dictates; he reveled in his ability to whip up passion of the lower-echelon cadres to mobilize the peasants and workers for economic action. "How wonderful our Chinese people and our cadres are," Mao once declared exuberantly in the aftermath of the Great Leap Forward campaign. "Twenty million people: we call and they come; we dismiss and they go." And he asked not without a sense of smugness, "Which party can manage this except the [Chinese] Communist Party?"[54]

Mao's political intervention in economic policy also manifested in his insistence on ideological purity. He rigidly adhered to the Marxist labor-as-the-sole-source-of-value theory by enforcing a let-population-grow policy. He rashly transformed the Chinese rural economy into the highest form of Communism by creating a Commune system well before the Marxist-prescribed conditions for such transformation had appeared.

If Mao's policies were fundamentally flawed, his senior cadres (and other cadres) in charge of economic development were boxed in by these policies. Chen Yun, Li Xiannian, and Bo Yipo possessed the same background as Mao's. They were long-time party secretaries, political commissars, guerrilla commanders, and Long Marchers. They never studied in a university, never possessed knowledge of modern economics, and were never permitted in Mao's times to learn about the contemporary developmental trends overseas. They were as likely to bring prosperity to China as their counterparts of Taiwan—Yan Jiagan, Yin Zhongrong, and Li Kwoh-ting—to score victories in guerrilla wars.[55]

It is appropriate in this connection to put into perspective the results of Taiwan and China's implementation of the two principles of national economic growth. In terms of sectoral shift of the economy, data on Taiwan show that in 1953 the primary sector accounted for 35 percent of the economy, the secondary sector, 21 percent, and the tertiary sector, 44 percent; the sectoral distribution in 1975 was 13, 46, and 41 percent.[56] Relevant data on China show that in 1952, the primary sector accounted for 48 percent of the economy, the secondary sector, 28 percent; and the tertiary sector, 24 percent;[57] in 1977 the sectoral distribution was 33, 39, and 28 percent.[58]

To compare Taiwan and China's experiences in implementing the comparative advantage principle, we take the weight of foreign trade in the national economy as the indicator. In Taiwan foreign trade has been since the adoption of the trade expansion program in the mid1960s the major engine of economic growth. In 1975 foreign trade accounted for as much as 72 percent of the gross national product, and in the following year, Taiwan's foreign trade volume for the first time exceeded that of China, even though the size of Taiwan's economy was a fraction of China's.[59] For China, foreign trade never played a major role in economic development during Mao's times. In his study of this subject, Gene Hsiao wrote, "The annual volume of [Chinese foreign] trade from 1950 to 1974 averaged no more than 4 percent of the gross national product."[60]

Path to Prosperity

In terms of their experiences with economic development, Chiang's successes precisely corrected Mao's deficiencies. Mao was never willing to learn from Chiang's experiences, but his successors, Deng Xiaoping—the paramount Chinese leader from 1978 to 1997—and his associates were, enthusiastically so. For when they were initiating in 1978 the reform of opening up the Chinese economy to the world, they were deeply impressed by the economic successes of the Four Little Dragons, of which Taiwan figured prominently.[61]

Fundamentally, they learned one crucial lesson from Chiang: let the technocrats—instead of revolutionary cadres—take charge of the economy. The change at the very top of the Communist Party leadership is most striking. When the party elected in 2002 the nine members of the Standing Committee of the Politburo (the party's fourth generation of leadership), none of whom was an ideologist or a revolutionary. They were all college-educated engineers: Hu Jintao, the party chairman and head of the government, majored in hydraulic engineering; Wu Bangguo, head of the parliament, electrical engineering; Wen Jiabao, the premier, geological engineering; Jia Qinglin, mechanical engineering; Zeng Qinghong, automation engineering; Huang Ju, electrical engineering; Wu Guanzheng, engineering mechanics; Li Changchun, industrial engineering; and Luo Gan, metallurgical engineering.[62] The political lineup has since changed, but the fact that expertise is the prerequisite of political leadership has not.[63] Compared with Taiwan's technocratic leaders, as seen earlier, the current top Chinese leaders are more technologically oriented and more attuned to industrial management.[64]

Mao's successors have also embraced Chiang's developmental policies, including measures facilitating a gradual sectoral shift in the domestic economy and a full application of comparative advantage principle to a country's foreign economic relations. They have replaced the Communes with Self-Responsible farms to improve the agricultural sector; they have adopted economic and financial reforms to enhance the manufacturing and service sectors; and they have abandoned the self-reliance policy in favor of foreign trade and foreign investment, mating China's low-cost labor with the capital and technology of the multinational corporations. What should be particularly noted is that the Special Economic Zones—the central piece of the Communist economic reform program—they created precisely coincide with the Export Processing Zones of Taiwan in terms of operating principles.[65]

In essence, Chiang established a sure path to acquire nation wealth; Mao's successors have followed it.

NOTES

[1] Chiang Kai-shek, "Chinese Economic Theory," an appendix to *China's Destiny*, p. 254.

[2] Ibid., pp. 255ff.

[3] Sun Yat-sen, *San Min Zhu Yi* [*Three Principles of the People*] (Taipei: Zhong Yang Wen Wu Gong Ying She, 1985), pp. 215-306.

[4] New edition, Taipei: China Cultural Service, 1953.

[5] Chiang, "Min Sheng Zhu yi Yu Le Liang Pian Bu Shu" [Two Essays on Education and Recreation, Supplement to the Principle of the People's Livelihood] in Sun, *Three Principles of the People*, Appendix, pp. 315-23; Ye Shichang and Ding Hsiaozhi, "Nanjing Guomin Zhengfu Shiqi Jiang Jieshi di Jingji Sixiang [Chiang Kai-shek's Economic Thoughts during the National Government Period in Nanjing], *Guizhou Shehui Kexue*, Vol. 206, No. 8 (August 2011), pp. 38-41.

[6] Gu Longsheng, ed., *Mao Zedong Jing Ji Nian Pu* [*Chronicle of Mao Zedong's Economic Writings*] (Beijing: Zhong Gong Zhong Yang Tang Xiao Chu Ban She, 1993), p. 535.

[7] *Chronicle of Mao Zedong's Economic Writings* devotes 660 pages to Mao's statements on economics. Similarly, in *Mao Zedong Jing Ji Si Xiang Da Ci Dian* [*Encyclopedia of Mao Zedong Economic Thoughts*], edited by Gu Longsheng, Qiao Dongguang, and Zhang Shengbin (Shenyang: Liaoning Ren Min Chu Ban She, 1993), 744 pages cover the subject.

[8] See also Jack Gray, "Mao in Perspective," *The China Quarterly*, September 2006, pp. 659-79; and Mark Selden, "Jack Gray, Mao Zedong and the Political Economy of Chinese Development," *The China Quarterly*, September 2006, pp. 680-85.

[9] Mao often gave a romantic interpretation of Chinese traditional work ethics. See, for instance, his oft-recited essay, "How Yu Kung Removed the Mountain," in *SW*, IV, pp. 316-18. In this essay, Mao praised the hero in a Chinese parable, the Foolish Old Man (Yu Kung), for his perseverance and diligence in removing a mountain that blocked his way.

[10] Mao wrote during this time several essays calling all his comrades to rely on ingenuity, hard work, and fighting spirit to produce sufficient food and other necessities in their prolonged battle for survival: "We Must Attend to Economic Work," *SW*, I, pp. 129-37; "Our Economic Policy," *SW*, I, pp. 141-46; "Economic and Financial

Problems during the Anti-Japanese War," *SW*, IV, pp. 105-10; "We Must Learn to Do Economic Work," *SW*, IV, pp. 228-35; and "Production Is Also Possible in the Guerrilla Zones," *SW*, IV, pp. 236-40.

[11] For these reforms, see Arthur N. Young, *China and the Helping Hand, 1937-1945*, Cambridge, MA: Harvard University Press, 1963; and Coble, *The Shanghai Capitalists*.

[12] See Xue Yi, *Guo Min Zheng Fu Zi Yuan Wei Yuan Hui Yan Jiu* [*A Study on the National Resources Commission of the National Government*], Beijing: She Hui Ke Xue Wen Xian Chu Ban She, 2005; and Zheng Youkui, Cheng Linsun, and Zhang Chuanhong, *Jiu Zhong Guo de Zi Yuan Wei Yuan Hui (1932-1949): Shi Shi yu Ping Jia* [*The National Resources Commission of the Old China (1932-1949): Historical Facts and An Appraisal*], Shanghai: She Hui Ke Xue Yuan Chu Ban She, 1991.

[13] At an October 1999 ceremony commemorating China's scientific achievements in the previous fifty years, Qian Xueshen, considered father of China's rocketry science program, said that a total of twenty-eight elite Chinese scientists had made the most vital contribution to the nation's nuclear and space projects. Among these, six were former associates of the National Resources Commission: Qian Ji, Yao Tongbin, Yu Min, Yang Jiachi, Wang Daheng, and Wang Xiji. Wang Huanruo, "Zhong Gong 'Huo Jian Fei Dan Zhi Fu' Qian Xueshen Gan Nian San Wei Zhe Ren" [Appreciation and Reminiscences of Three Wise Men by Qian Xuesen, Father of [Chinese] Missile [Program]," *BL*, No. 457 (June 2000): 60-65.

[14] Arthur N. Young, *China's Nation-Building Effort, 1927-1937* (Stanford: Stanford University, Hoover Institution Press, 1971), pp. 336-37.

[15] See Kirby, *Germany and Republican China*, Chapter Seven, "Germany and the Chinese Modernization, 1935-1937;" and Ma, *Chiang and Hitler*, pp. 91-97.

[16] Wang Zuorong, a veteran staff member of the Executive Yuan involved in Taiwan's industrial development from the 1950s to the 1970s, has characterized many of these technocrats in the following terms: "[They] have two distinctions. First, [they] were all in the 40s in age…graduated from prominent Chinese universities, studied in Europe or America or Chinese church-founded universities, were nurtured…in the Chinese Confucian culture and Western culture and education, and possessed strong brainpower and working competence….Second, [they] had impeccable personal integrity, lived a frugal life, clearly separated their public and private affairs, and showed a strong sense of loyalty to

the nation and dedication to the people....For any given assignment, large or small, they would do their outmost to carry it out." Wang Zuorong, "Li Kwoh-ting Xian Sheng Zai Taiwan Jing Ji Fa Zhan Zhong de Ding Wei" [The Definitive Role of Mr. Li Kwoh-ting in the Economic Development of Taiwan], *BL,* No. 470 (July 2001): 46-47.

[17]Ibid., p. 38.

[18]Sun Zhen, "Zhe Ren Qi Wei: Wo Suo Ren Shi de Li Kwoh-ting Xian Sheng" [The Passing of a Wise Man: The Li Kwoh-ting I Knew], *BL,* No. 471 (August 2001): 45. For a summary of the Nineteen-Point Financial and Economic Reform, see Shirley W. Y. Kuo, Gustav Ranis, and John C. H. Fei, *The Taiwan Success Story: Rapid Growth with Improved Distribution in the Republic of China, 1952-1979* (Boulder, Colo.: Westview Press, 1981), p. 74.

[19]Chen Cheng, *Land Reform in Taiwan,* Taipei, Taiwan, 1961; and Tsung-han Shen, *The Sino-American Joint Commission on Rural Reconstruction: Twenty Years of Cooperation and Reconstruction,* Ithaca: Cornell University Press, 1970. Hung-chao Tai has authored a book with a comprehensive treatment of land reform programs of Taiwan along with seven other developing countries: *Land Reform and Politics: A Comparative Analysis,* Berkeley: University of California Press, 1974.

[20]Taiwan's industrial policies were intimately told by Li Kwoh-ting in his two books: *Economic Transformation of Taiwan, ROC*, London: Shepheard-Walwyn, 1988; and *The Evolution of Policy behind Taiwan's Development Success*, New Haven, CT: Yale University Press, 1988.

[21]Ibid. p. 106.

[22]Taiwan's fertility rate declined to 2 percent in 1971 and 1 percent later. Li, *The Policy behind Taiwan's Development Success*, pp. 77, 79; Ye Wanan, "Guo Jia Xian Dai Hua de Dao Hang Zhe—Jin Dao Li Zi Zheng Kwoh-ting Xian Sheng" [A Pioneer of National Modernization—in Memory of Senior Presidential Counselor Mr. Li Kwoh-ting], *BL,* No. 470 (July 2001): 53-54; and Ralph W. Huenemann, "Family Planning in Taiwan: The Conflict between Ideologues and Technocrats," *Modern China,* Vol. 16, No. 2 (April 1990):173-89.

[23]So declared Mao in 1959. Gu, *Chronicle of Mao Zedong's Economic Writings,* p. 487. This statement meant, as Alexander Eckstein neatly put it, "substituting ideology and organization for technical inputs." Alexander Eckstein, *China's Economic Development: The Interplay of Scarcity and Ideology* (Ann Arbor: University of Michigan Press, c1975)**,** p. 18.

[24]*Biography of Mao,* Vol. 1, p. 797.

[25] Ibid., p. 817.

[26] Ibid., p. 818.

[27] These documents were summarized and analyzed in *Biography of Mao*, Vol. 1. In his 1956 speech "On Ten Great Relations," Mao discussed ten sets of relations that were central to China's development effort: The relations between (1) heavy industry, light industry, and agriculture, (2) industries in coastal areas and interior areas, (3) economic reconstruction and defense reconstruction, (4) public enterprises and individual producers, (5) national and local governments, (6) Han people and the minorities, (7) Communist Party and other parties, (8) revolutionary and counter-revolutionary movements, (9) the right and the wrong (policies), and (10) China and foreign countries. Ibid., p. 484.

[28] A paraphrase of Mao's statement in 1958, ibid., p. 781.

[29] *Biography of Mao*, Vol. 1, p. 484.

[30] Mao, "We Must Learn to Do Economic Work," SW, IV, p. 230. Some in China have claimed that after it came to power, the Communist government had to follow the principle of self-reliance because of the trade embargo of Western nations. However, Mao had always insisted that this principle had its intrinsic value. Li Lanqing, a Chinese vice premier in charge of international trade and investment in the late 1980s and early 1990s, took a different view. He considered "self-imposed seclusion" and "close-doorism" in Mao's times as a policy retarding economic growth. Li Lanqing, *Breaking Through: The Birth of China's Opening-up Policy*, translated by Ling Yuan and Zhang Siying (New York: Oxford University Press, 2009), pp. 12-27. See also A. Doak Barnett, *China's Economy in Global Perspective* (Washington, D.C.: Brookings Institution, c1981), pp. 122-32.

[31] Bo Yibo, one of the three key economic ministers in Mao's time, admitted in 1991 that he obediently followed Mao's decision to set "high targets" for production during the Great Leap movement because "I was dizzy with excitement." At the Lu Shan conference in July 1959, he said, he shared Peng Dehuai's view that the Great Leap was a disaster. But he confessed, "I completely lost my nerve" to speak up in support of Peng. Instead, he joined others to criticize Peng—something he felt he had done against his conscience. Bo Yibo, *Ruo Gan Zhong Da Jue Ce yu Shi Jian de Hui Gu*: [*Reminiscences of Certain Important Policies and Events*], Vol. 1 (Beijing: Zhong Gong Zhong Yang Dang Xiao Chu Ban She, 1991), pp. 698, 869.

[32] John K. Chang, *Industrial Development of Pre-Communist China: 1912-1949* (Chicago: Aldine Pub. Co. [1969]), pp. 60-61, 103. Cited in Young, *China's Nation-Building Effort,* pp. 309-11.

[33] Young, ibid., pp. 396-99. Young, in this book and the accompanying volume, *China and the Helping Hand*, provided numerous statistical tables on the Nanjing Decade.

[34] Young, *China and the Helping Hand*, pp. 6-7.

[35] Cited in ibid., p.10.

[36] Ibid., p. 11; and Young, *China's Nation-Building Effort,* pp. 424-25.

[37] Franz Michael, "The Role of Law in Traditional, Nationalist, and Communist China," *The China Quarterly,* 9 (January-March 1962): 124-28, cited in Taylor, *The Generalissimo,* p. 121; and Thomas G. Rawski, *Economic Growth in Prewar China* (Berkeley: University of California Press, c1989), pp. xxi-xxii, 344-45; and Nai-ruenn Chen and Walter Galenson, *The Chinese Economy under Communism*, pp. 16-17.

[38] Lloyd E. Eastman et al., *The Nationalist Era in China, 1927-1949* (New York: Cambridge University Press, 1991), p. 40.

[39] See, for example, Douglass S. Pauuw, "The Kuomintang and Economic Stagnation, 1928-1937," in Albert Feuerwerker, ed., *Modern China* (Englewood Cliffs, NJ: Prentice-Hall, 1964), pp. 126-35; and Tien, *Government and Politics in Kuomintang China,* pp. 177-82.

[40] Chu-yuan Cheng, *Taiwan Jing Yan yu Zhong Guo Chong Jian* [*The Taiwan Experience and China's Reconstruction*] (Taipei: Lian Jing Chu Ban Shi Ye Gong Si, [1989]), pp. 16-17; Li, *The Policy behind Taiwan's Development Success,* pp. 160, 161, 178; Taiwan, Council for Economic Planning and Development, *Taiwan Statistical Data Book, 2006,* p. 17; Kuo, *The Taiwan Success Story,* p. 45; Thomas B. Gold, *State and Society in the Taiwan Miracle* (Armonk, N.Y.: M. E. Sharpe, c1986), p. 4; and Yuan-li Wu and Hung-chao Tai, "Economic Performance in Five East Asian Countries: A Comparative Analysis," in Hung-chao Tai, ed., *Confucianism and Economic Development: An Oriental Alternative* (Washington, DC: The Washington Institute Press, 1989), p. 49.

[41] For comparative rates of economic growth of the Four Little Dragons, see ibid., pp. 39-43; and Gold, *State and Society in the Taiwan Miracle,* p. 7.

[42] Beijing: Foreign Languages Press, 1960.

[43] Eckstein, *China's Economic Development,* pp. 40, 47-48.

[44] Barnett, *China's Economy in Global Perspective,* p. 17, 18. Chen and Galenson also concurred; they showed the variance in the

industrial growth rates between China and India in a comparable seven-year period in the 1950s. China's growth rate was 198 percent against India's 51 percent. Chen and Galenson, *The Chinese Economy*, pp. 56, 57, 89. See also Chu-yuan Cheng, *China's Economic Development: Growth and Structural Change* (Boulder, Colo.: Westview Press, 1982), pp. 300, 306, and 320; and Nai-ruenn Chen, ed., *Chinese Economic Statistics in the Maoist Era, 1949-1965* (New Brunswick: Aldine Transaction [2009]), p. 141.

[45] Barnett, *China's Economy in Global Perspective*, p.18.

[46] Eckstein provided information corroborating Barnett's observations, though the two persons' statistical data are not entirely consistent because their data were derived from different sources. In terms of GNP index, Eckstein indicated that with the index standing at 100 percent in 1952, it rose continuously to 167 percent in 1959; it declined to 142 percent in 1963; it rose to 182 in 1966 and dropped to 171 percent in the following year. The decline periods reflected the adverse consequences of the Great Leap and the initial phase of the Cultural Revolution. Eckstein, *China's Economic Development*, p. 40. Comparable data from other economists were cited in ibid.

[47] Gu, *Encyclopedia of Mao Zedong Economic Thoughts*, p. 619. In a collection of his statements on China's developmental strategy, Chen Yun frequently expressed reservations about Mao's "high targets" tactics, over-centralization of policymaking, over-collectivization of farms, and over-restraining market forces. But he always subordinated his remarks to his praise of Mao's "General Line of Socialist Reconstruction." See Nicholas R. Lardy and Kenneth Lieberthal, eds., *Chen Yun's Strategy for China's Development: A Non-Maoist Alternative*, Armonk, NY: M. E. Sharpe, 1983.

[48] Chen Yun, *Transition and Development in China: Towards Shared Growth* (Burlington, VT: Ashgate, c2009), p. 57.

[49] Cheng, *The Taiwan Experience*, pp. 27, 30-31. Cf. Li, *Economic Transformation of Taiwan*, p. 364.

[50] Hung-chao Tai, *Xian Dai Guo Ji Zheng Zhi Jing Ji Xue: Fu Qiang Xin Lun* [*Modern Political Economy: A New Discourse on Wealth and Power*] (Taipei: San Min Shu Ju, 1995), pp. 73-74.

[51] As Alan P. L. Liu put it, "Mao...relied predominantly on charismatic appeal to mobilize mainland China, whereas Chiang relied on modern professionals to modernize Taiwan." In a detailed analysis of the policymakers of economic development in Taiwan and mainland China, Liu selected tens of them from each side for a comparison of their political and educational background. See Alan P. L. Liu, *Phoenix and*

the Lame Lion: Modernization in Taiwan and Mainland China,1950-1980 (Stanford: Hoover Institution Press, Stanford University, c1987), pp. 46-75.

[52] See Mao's statement to this effect in 1958 in *Biography of Mao,* Vol. 1, pp. 762-63.

[53] In fact, official publications on Chinese economic statistics prior to the death of Mao do not even show there was a tertiary (service) sector. See, for example, China, State Statistical Bureau, *Statistical Yearbook of China 1986* (Hong Kong: Economic Information and Agency, 1987), p. 24.

[54] Quoted in Chang and Halliday, *Mao, The Unknown Story,* p. 472.

[55] Interestingly, Ezra Vogel, a prominent specialist on East Asian affairs, regarded Chen Yun and Li Kwoh-ting as contemporaneous chief economic architects of China and Taiwan respectively; he considered them as having followed essentially the same policies. These included transfer of funds "from agriculture to industry" and attracting "foreign capital." It should be noted that Chen followed these policies *after Mao's death, not before.* See Ezra Vogel's "Forward" to Lutao Sophia Kang Wang, *K. T. Li and the Taiwan Experience,* Taipei: National Tsing Hua University Press, 2006.

[56] Li, *The Policy behind Taiwan's Development Success,* p. 161. For a detailed analysis of the sectoral shift in Taiwan's economy, see Simon Kuznets, "Growth and Structural Shifts," in Walter Galenson, ed., *Economic Growth and Structural Change in Taiwan: The Postwar Experience of the Republic of China* (Ithaca, NJ: Cornell University Press, 1979), pp. 15-131, especially, pp. 54-58.

[57] Cheng, *China's Economic Development,* p. 414.

[58] Ramon H. Myers, *The Chinese Economy, Past and Present* (Belmont, CA: Wadsworth, c1980), p. 19.

[59] Based on data from *Taiwan Statistical Data Book, 2006,* pp.17-18; and Angus Maddison, *Chinese Economic Performance in the Long Run* (Paris: OECD, 1998), p. 174.

[60] Gene T. Hsiao, *The Foreign Trade of China: Policy, Law, and Practice* (Berkeley: University of California Press, 1977), p. 10. Cf. Barnett, *China's Economy in Global Perspective,* p. 149.

[61] As Li Xiannian, one of the key economic ministers under Mao as well as Deng Xiaoping, commented in 1978, "South Korea, Singapore, Hong Kong, and Taiwan are such small countries and regions but their imports and exports are much larger than ours. Can't we surpass them?" (See Li, *Breaking Through,* p. 358). Similarly, Yu Qiuli, a former

Politburo member and vice premier, acknowledged in 1979 that Taiwan had made rapid economic progress, with its people's living standard several times higher than that of the people on the mainland (See Cheng, *The Taiwan Experience*, p. 457). Both Li and Yu urged to study the Taiwan experiences. Since the late 1970s mainland policymakers paid special attention to Taiwan's developmental experiences and created a number of research institutes with a focus on the political and economic changes on the island. (See ibid., pp.457-58). The government also systematically collected trade and investment information on foreign countries and Taiwan, through Chinese embassies and consulates and other channels, for purpose of research and study (See Li, *Breaking Through*, p. 386).

[62] For a background analysis of some members of the fourth-generation leadership before they were actually elected in 2002, see David M. Finkelstein and Maryanne Kivlehan, eds., *China's Leadership in the Twenty-first Century: The Rise of the Fourth Generation*, Armonk, N.Y.: M.E. Sharpe, 2003.

The four generations of Chinese Communist leadership are respectively represented by Mao Zedong, Deng Xiaoping, Jiang Zemin, and Hu Jintao.

[63] Of the nine members of the Standing committee of the Politburo for the 2007-2012 term, five were from the 2002-2007 term: Hu Jintao, Wu Bangguo, Wen Jiabao, Jia Qinglin, and Li Changchun; and four were new members: Xi Jinping (chemical engineering in college; doctorate in political thought), Li Keqiang (doctorate in economics), He Guoqiang (chemical engineering), and Zhou Yongkang (chemical engineering and geophysics). Xinhua News, October 22, 2007. In the 2012-2017 term, the number of members of the committee is reduced to seven. Xi Jinping and Li Keqiang retain their membership; the other five are newly elected: Zhang Dejiang, (studied economics in college) Yu Zhengsheng (studied missile engineering in college), Liu Yunshan (graduate from the Central Academy of the Communist Party), Wang Qishan (graduate from college, majoring in history), and Zhang Gaoli (graduate from college, majoring in economics).

[64] Taiwan's technocrats consist of more economic and financial experts than engineers, as compared to their counterparts on the Chinese mainland. A case in point, illustrating how the mainland's top political leaders used their technical expertise in formulating economic policies, is that former Prime Minister Wen Jaibao, who studied rare earth elements in graduate school, took a personal hand in shaping policies on the management and export of these elements—materials critical to today's

high-tech industries worldwide. *The New York Times*, August 25, 2011, p. B1.

[65]Li Lanqing, one key post-Mao economic minister, has described in detail the evolution of the Special Economic Zones in Shenzhen, Zhuhai, Xiamen, Shantou, and 14 other coastal areas in his *Breaking Through,* pp. 73-195.

CHAPTER THIRTEEN

CONCLUSION: FROM ENEMIES TO COMRADES

Chiang and Mao contended for power for nearly a half of a century. From the 1920s through the 1940s they waged intermittent gigantic battles against each other on the Chinese mainland; in the 1950s, they exchanged heavy bombardments along the Chinese offshore islands that drew the United States into the conflict, with potentially a nuclear response. In the mid1970s when they died, they bitterly regretted for failing to realize their last wishes. Chiang could not recover the mainland he had lost; Mao could not set foot on Taiwan he avowed to liberate. They remained enemies to the end of their lives.

Now, four decades later, how do we make sense of their deep-seated enmity? How do we appraise their long rule of China? Were they "the truly great heroes" as Mao had rated them to be in his epic poem, "Snow"? This chapter attempts to answer these questions by way of an analysis of their quality of leadership and their achievements and failures. Such an analysis has led to something unexpected: Though they were life-long enemies, Chiang and Mao can be viewed as comrades after their death, for during their tenure of office they had together established the preconditions of an emerging superpower.

Quality of Leadership

Leadership Characteristics

Chiang: Rectitude, Compromise, and Reticence.—If a great crisis can reveal a national leader's fundamental attitude toward politics, the Xi'an Incident of 1936 is certainly a telling case about Chiang's basic approach to politics. At first, he voiced a strong determination to pursue the policy he firmly believed in, i. e., defeating the Chinese Communists before fighting the Japanese. Anyone reading his diary entries and the wills he wrote at the time could not but be convinced that he was prepared to die for that policy rather than to accept his captors' demand to reverse it.

Yet, in the end, he did accept the rebels' demand to reverse that policy. He did so, as described in Chapter Four, because he came to realize that to die for that policy would engulf China in a full-scale civil war and encourage Japan to invade the country, and that to save his life while changing that policy would allow China to stand united against Japan. The interest of the nation, he concluded, weighed more heavily than keeping his personal honor by not succumbing to the rebels' demand. But he did not give out then to the public his reasoning for the policy reversal. He took the position that since he believed he had made the right decision, he did not have to explain it—even if his silence might be construed as weakness of leadership.

The Xi'an Incident reveals a set of Chiang's leadership characteristics: rectitude on policy, compromise by necessity, and silent self-assurance. In dealing with other critical issues, he consistently showed some or all of these characteristics. For instance, when embarking on the Northern Expedition in 1926, he commanded an army of no more than 85,000 soldiers against several warlords with a combined force of no less than one million men. He could have been defeated by any one of them, with his political future finished. Yet he resolutely marched northward from Canton, disregarding the objection of his then powerful Soviet advisers. In the next two years, he swept clean the warlords' armies that stood in his way.

However, he did not defeat all warlords nor absorbed completely the soldiers of the defeated warlords into his Central Army. He offered many of them, including Feng Yuxiang, Yan Xishan, Zhang Xueliang, and Li Zongren, high positions in his government, permitted them to retain command of their troops, and subsidized them with fat personal allowance and logistical supplies. His purpose was to enlist their support of his effort to consolidate his control of the country. He never told his countrymen why he did not make a clean break with his erstwhile enemies.

When the Chinese-Japanese war broke out in 1937, Chiang faced greater odds than what he had during the Northern Expedition. The Japanese army was incomparably superior to the warlord forces in terms of weaponry, fighting élan, and unity of command. In addition, Britain and France imposed in later years practically an embargo on China by cutting off the country's supply routes from Burma and Vietnam, while the United States sold such war materials as scrap metals and oil to Japan. Under such dire circumstances, he avowed to fight Japan to the bitter end—and he did.

However, he did not oppose the mediation of the conflict by the German Ambassador to China, Oskar P. Trautmann, in late 1937. Then in 1938 and again in 1940, he consented to secret talks with Japan—largely under private auspices in Hong Kong—for the termination of the war. He agreed to hold all these peace talks because he was convinced that China could not win the war under the prevailing circumstances. These talks failed because he insisted on restoring Chinese sovereignty in all Japanese-occupied areas—a condition unacceptable to Japan. He did not tell the people about these peaceful attempts apparently because he thought their revelation would demoralize the Chinese to carry on the fight even though his terms of settlement were honorable.

Following the Pearl Harbor Incident in 1941, he formed a military alliance with the United States and Britain against Japan. In 1944, Chinese-American relations fell to a severe crisis when the Stilwell affair occurred. Chiang was forced to make a stark choice: either giving up his military command to Stilwell so as to retain the American assistance critically needed to carry on the war or facing the possibility of losing such assistance as well as the war. He stood his ground and forced President Roosevelt to recall Stilwell. He made ample notes in his diaries on his painful deliberation over the affair but said hardly a word about it in public.

In the mid1950s, when the Communists relentlessly bombarded Quemoy and other offshore islands, Chiang took a highly risky position by repeatedly rejecting American demand for withdrawal of his forces from these indefensible islands. In the end, he was able to retain the islands but paid a price. He forfeited what he regarded as his sovereign right to recover the mainland by military means but said little about the forfeiture.

All the events noted above show that when facing a crisis threatening his political future, his life, or his nation's interests, Chiang almost invariably insisted on solving the crises his way. When he was unable to do so, he would compromise; and when he could not explain away the inconsistency between his resolute and compromising stands, he chose to be silent, convinced that he was doing the right thing. He won admiration from many of his supporters and even some of his adversaries for his rectitude; he earned sympathy from his close associates for his compromises; he suffered from his reticence, as he was perceived to have failed in the policies he pursued.

Mao: Context, Flexibility, and Persuasion.—If the Xi'an Incident symptomatically reveals Chiang's leadership characteristics, the Yan'an battle of March 1947 highlights Mao Zedong's way of handling politics. Mao commanded only 27,000 troops against a Nationalist force five times their size. He was facing a prospect of losing all of his troops as well as the Communist headquarters city. Such a disaster would severely demoralize the vast Communist troops deployed elsewhere in a civil war that began to shape up.

His decision to abandon Yan'an in order to save his troops surprised his comrades and his enemies. But his argument for abandonment was powerful and irrefutable. "If we save our men but lose the city," he told his senior colleagues, "we can recover it [later]. If we try to save the city by losing our men, we will lose both." He led his troops away, melting them into the surrounding hills, like mercury dumped to the ground. In the ensuing battle, his men used their familiar guerrilla tactics to rout several major units of the Nationalist army in hot pursuit and, indeed, reclaimed Yan'an in the following year.

This episode illustrates that in handling a crisis, Mao had due consideration of the total context in which the crisis occurred. For him, the total context was the emerging civil war, whose outcome was to be decided upon by whether the Nationalist or the Communist army controlled more area of the country. That was why he had rushed the bulk of his army to east and north China to contest the Nationalist control there. In May 1947 while he was fighting in the Yan'an area, the Communists forces in Shandong, 400 miles to the east, scored a decisive victory against the Nationalist 74th Reorganized Division, killing its commander Zhang Lingfu. The Communists thus gained a strong foothold in the area.

The Yan'an retreat also shows Mao's flexibility in dealing with a crisis, as expressed by his famous dictum on fighting a battle: "When we can win, fight; when we can't, run." When he ran away from Yan'an, he anticipated the Nationalist army to pursue his troops, whom he instructed to take advantage of the hilly topography to disperse and then concentrate, to attack and then retreat, and to attack again. He created a battle plan like a plate of spaghetti that confused his enemies enough to defeat them.

In all the battles he fought, Mao was never worried about losing face when dodging a fight, nor was he elated by the "prestige" of winning a prized territory. He seldom instructed his troops to defend at all costs any major city they occupied. His stance on battle engagement is in sharp contrast to Chiang's. Whenever fighting a powerful enemy at a key city, Chiang always ordered his commanders to *si shou*—to defend to the last person. He did that in the battles of Shanghai, Nanjing, Wuhan, Changsha, Hengyang, Luoyang, and Guilin during the Chinese-

Japanese war; and Changchun, Shenyang, Beijing, Xuzhou, Shanghai, and Chengdu during the civil war. In each case, he lost the *si-shou* city, with heavy casualties.

The Yan'an episode also reveals another of Mao's leadership characteristics. He endeavored to convince his comrades of the validity of his policies through discussion or debate. Prior to his retreat from Yan'an, many of his comrades seriously opposed the idea of cut-and-run without a fight. They pointed out that during the Chinese-Japanese war, they did not yield Yan'an to the hostile Nationalist army under Hu Zongnan, which was vastly superior in number and weapons. Why should they do it now? Mao patiently persuaded them to accept his views—and instructed them on how to handle the expected post-retreat battle.

In many other crises, Mao manifested some or all of these leadership characteristics: handling crisis from the perspective of the total context, flexibility in tactics, and persuasion. His decision to participate in the Korean War in 1950 was based on several considerations, one of which was to affirm his leadership position in the Communist international front in the Far East—an objective of overriding importance. Trying to convince his disagreeing senior colleagues on his war move, he held prolonged talks with them, summoned Peng Dehuai to back him up, and delivered the coup de grace by offering to send his newly married son, Anying, to the battlefield.

In the One Hundred Flowers campaign of 1957, he urged Chinese intellectuals to comment unreservedly on the Communist Party's performance and guaranteed against retribution for whatever they had to say. Yet when a torrent of scathing criticisms flooded the media, he responded to the challenge with moves characterized by guerrilla war tactics: subterfuges, deceptions, and ambushes. He explained to his critics—as well as his campaign followers—that he invited the intellectuals to criticize the party because he intended to lure the hidden "devils and demons" out of their holes. He claimed, not without a sense of smugness, that his violation of his non-retribution guarantee was an act of "open conspiracy" (*yang mu*)—a deliberate, open move to search out and punish those who opposed his party's leadership role in China. He rounded up no less than a half of a million "Rightist" intellectuals and subjected them to hellish treatment. That he was flagrantly dishonest, devious, faithless, and cruel toward the critics, Mao could not care less. In mounting the campaign, he never forgot that his top objective was to strengthen, not to weaken, the Communists' monopoly of power; his victims did.

Mao's handling of China's evolving relations with the Soviet Union and the United States reveals in full his leadership characteristics. In the 1950s he adopted a "lean-to-one-side" policy to emphasize Beijing's subservience to the Soviet Union while battling the United States in a harsh war in Asia. Yet deep in his mind, he already had an overriding objective of playing a leading role in the Communist international front, which surfaced and became abundantly clear in the early 1960s when the Sino-Soviet split occurred. It was then Mao claimed he alone possessed the ideological orthodoxy of the Communist world, denigrating the Soviet leaders as "the Revisionists."

By the late 1960s when the Sino-Soviet split was transformed from an ideological dispute to a military confrontation, Mao, with extraordinary alacrity, maneuvered to reach a Beijing-Washington rapprochement. On the pretense of ideological dispute, he broke with a Socialist ally; for the sake of safety of his nation, he embraced a capitalist adversary. In the 1970s when a dynamic balance of Washington, Moscow, and Beijing emerged on the scene, he saw his China finally emerged as the globe's third most influential power. A man steeped in Chinese history, he must have been amused by a certain resemblance of 20th century's strategic triangle to China's contending Three Kingdoms 18 centuries earlier.

Mao never failed to explain the stands he took on the major issues dividing the three powers. He argued with Stalin in 1949-1950 in the Kremlin on the need for a Sino-Soviet security treaty; he authorized Chinese diplomats to participate in the decades-long ambassadorial talks with the United States; he engaged in extensive ideological debates with the Soviet leaders in the early 1960s; he commissioned the Four Old Marshals in 1969 to write a report to lend support to his initiation of a Beijing-Washington détente; and he held lively conversations in his study in Zhongnanhai with Nixon in 1972 to set the tone for the Shanghai Communiqué.

Leadership Style

Chiang: Moralizing Leadership.—Heavily influenced by the traditional Chinese political culture, Chiang adopted a leadership style that reflected his status as head of the Chinese familial nation (*guo jia*). Like emperors of the past, he regarded the Chinese as having come from a common ancestry, who formed a gigantic extended family. He thus played a double role. As head of the nation, he enforced laws and policies; as head of the extended family, he socialized with the Chinese.

Toward the more prominent members of the extended family, he took extraordinary care to honor them at their birthdays or funerals. He established pseudo familial relations with his friends, associates, comrades, and even adversaries by addressing them as brothers, sisters, uncles, or aunts. And he formed sworn brotherhood with his close friends and colleagues.

By maintaining this kind of intertwined political and social relations with his compatriots, he hoped to create a strong emotional bond with them. He reinforced his position as head of the familial nation by enjoining his compatriots to follow a Confucianism-based moral code. This code consists of several precepts, of which he paid special attention to loyalty, faithfulness, and righteousness. To him, loyalty meant a total allegiance to one's nation; faithfulness referred to keeping one's promise or carrying out one's orders; and righteousness connoted mutual commitment or justice.

Chiang vigorously applied these and other Confucian virtues to his personal conduct. This is seen in his rigid adherence to a regimen for self-improvement, developed in the late1910s. From then to his last years in life, he rarely failed to follow his daily routine: rising early, practicing meditation, evaluating his behavior in accordance with his self-designed mottos, and reading books. And from the late 1920s on, he added Christian prayers as well.

Since becoming the national leader in 1928, Chiang probably was the only Chinese political personality to place a high premium on moralized leadership. Senior Nationalist leaders such as Wang Jingwei and Hu Hanmin; prominent warlord-turned politicians such as Feng Yuxiang, Yan Xishan, and Li Zongren; and Communist leaders such as Mao Zedong and Zhou Enlai—none of them was known for stressing upright behavior as the basis of governance. For this reason, Chiang earned the respect from those of his countrymen who adhered to the traditional notion of inseparability of the political and moral orders. To the common folks, particularly the illiterate rural residents—excepting the Communist-mobilized peasantry—Chiang was looked upon as the rightful ruler bordered on an exemplary emperor of the past age. In their private conversations, they referred to him as *Lao Chiang*, the Old Chiang, with the connotation that, as if, "he can do no wrong." Thus, obedience was automatically assured.

Yet moralizing politics created problems for Chiang. At times, he violated the moral code he urged others to follow. One does not have to fault him for his questionable personal conduct in the early years of his life, particularly during his sojourns in Shanghai, for many national leaders, Chinese or foreign, could act indiscreetly in their younger days. But since his coming to power, Chiang impaired himself as an upright national leader in a number of situations. He offered felicitations to Du Yuesheng and Huang Jinrong, reputedly underworld figures in Shanghai, on social occasions for the services they rendered to him in his early career. He reneged on his promise to free General Zhang Xueliang after a ten-year custody following the Xi'an Incident. And he failed to uphold the principle of equal justice by condoning the corruptive practices of some of his relatives and high-echelon subordinates while punishing others severely for the same type of offense.

A more serious problem was that many of Chiang's subordinates simply ignored his moral exhortations. Numerous of his field commanders defected to his enemies; a good number of his civilian administrators and army officers were seriously derelict in their duties, and some were notoriously corrupt. Their behavior deeply pained him. He lectured, harangued, and chastised them in the hope of honing them into corps of officials and officers of desirable conduct, but often to no avail. Tenacious as he was, Chiang often took his subordinates' jobs in his hand.

In military matters, he could take time to deal with such mundane affairs as the supplies of his soldiers, including undershirts, socks, toilet paper, and soap (CKSD, 11/8/33, 10/20/50). During his Taiwan days, he took up the matter of training and operation of frogmen (CKSD,10/16/54, 9/21/70, 2/5/71).[1] In civil affairs, he concerned himself with the adoption of *The Three-Word Classic* (*San Zi Jing*, a summation of Confucian moral precepts) as a school textbook; appointment of college presidents; change of street names in Beijing, erection of public restrooms, and children's proper sitting posture on public transportation. In Taiwan, he banned nightclubs and dance halls (CKSD, 10/16, 27/34, 1/4/35, 6/20/36, 12/23, 28/43, 10/30/50, 4/24/69).

Chiang was fond of issuing hand-written "Personal Directives" (*shou ling*) to his subordinates. A recent study on this subject revealed that his staff accumulated more than 120 boxes of directives in the period from 1936 to 1948.[2] Many of these directives related to matters noted above; many more dealt with battle orders. In the latter category, Chiang often bypassed the chain of command to reach down to the level of regiment commanders or even lower.

Chiang's excessive involvement in his subordinates' jobs may well stem from his personal habit, but he frequently justified his practice on the ground that his civilian and military officers failed to meet his moral standards. In any case, it reduced his effectiveness as the national leader, as he was left with less time to manage the more important policy matters. In addition, it made him exhausted, anguished, even depressed (see, for example, CKSD, 5/31/44, 11/15/44, 6/10-15/45, 10/12/45, 11/23/48). One gets the feeling that in politics, Chiang belabored in the middle of things, not rising above them.

Mao: Romanticizing Leadership.—Mao adopted an entirely different leadership style. For the lack of a better term, it may be characterized as a romantic one. He had no regimen for self-improvement and no code of conduct to follow. Dictated by his whims or calculations, he at times initiated far-reaching policies without consulting his colleagues. He worked at night and slept during day. He sometimes held crucial meetings with his senior colleagues in his bedroom; he debated with Khrushchev by his swimming pool; and he conversed with Nixon in his book shelf-lined reception room. He drew inspiration from tricks of bandits for his guerrilla war tactics. He delved into Chinese history when conducting the Hundred Flowers campaign and the Cultural Revolution. He energized millions of his cadres and soldiers with captivating poems.

Mao may be labeled a congenital iconoclast (or a man born with "a rebellious bone," as some Chinese would say). He could not subject himself to the authority of any other person. As a teenager he threatened to commit suicide to evade his father's disciplinary action. As a young revolutionary in the Jiangxi days, he stuck to his "minority of one" position in challenging the policy line of the Moscow-trained, Stalin-backed Chinese Bolsheviks. In the mid-1930s, as his way of revolution was vindicated by wars and the Long March, he ascended to the apex of Communist power where he remained until his death. As time went on, he arrogated more and more authority to himself and permitted fewer and fewer of his comrades to share power with him. He drove Chiang to Taiwan; he battled the United States to a draw in Korea; he disputed the Soviet leadership in the Communist world, and engaged Stalin's successors in military confrontation.

With exceptions for his involvement in the Korean War and the Quemoy crises, which will be discussed later, Mao had not lost, by the time he died, to his adversaries in the debates, battles, wars, and diplomatic wrangles he engaged with them. He approached being "The Never Defeated Oriental Man."[3]

Mao's style of leadership is characterized by other traits. He saw his job as leading the Chinese through a perennial revolution. Driving the entire society for radical changes, he persuaded and, more often, coerced the masses to participate in the political campaigns he sponsored. He accepted violence as the most effective means to insure political change.

In politics, Mao gave top priority to power over any other matter of concern, to be restrained the least by moral considerations. He rarely lamented that his subordinates fell below certain standards of conduct. He knew that those who were incompetent or politically incorrect would fall by the wayside through wars or political campaigns. He truly enjoyed politics, for he never perceived it to be anything but a complex set of contradictions, which he knew, better than anyone else, how to "handle correctly." In politics, Mao was on top of things, never falling in the middle of them.

Achievements and Failures

Chiang Kai-shek and Mao Zedong have been revered in China as great leaders by millions of people and vilified as arch villains by millions of others. Opinions about them in foreign countries have been similarly divided and have frequently changed. For decades, Chiang has been castigated by most Western scholars as an incompetent and corrupt dictator.[4] Lloyd E. Eastman summed up the criticism of the Nationalist leader in his *Seeds of Destruction: Nationalist China in War and Revolution, 1937-1949* (1984). On the other hand, Chiang was honored on *Time*'s cover ten times from 1927 to 1955 and has lately received an unexpected, overall favorable assessment of his career from an influential work, Jay Taylor's *The Generalissimo, Chiang Kai-shek and the Struggle for Modern China* (2009). Even more unexpectedly, scholars on the Chinese mainland have since the beginning decade of the 21st century started a reappraisal of Chiang's political life and unmistakably emphasized his meritorious services to China.[5]

In his 1938-published *Red Star over China*, Edgar Snow brought Mao to the Western audience as a refreshing, vigorous, dedicated Chinese revolutionary leader. More than a decade later, Mao was perceived in the West as Stalin's stooge. And in 1971 he became an overnight sensation in America when Nixon sought reconciliation with China. In the ping pong diplomacy that took place then, a visiting American table tennis player, seized with the excitement of his trip, exclaimed in Beijing that Mao was like a present-day Jesus! In the same year, Karl W. Deutsch, one of the most eminent political scientists in Western academia, and his associates reported that in their statistical analysis of the 62 most influential social science breakthroughs in the world from 1900 to 1965, Mao was ranked as one of the top three contributors.[6] A man never schooled in college was deemed by his presumed colleagues as one of the world's premier social scientists.

Recently Mao's sterling reputation has seriously eroded with the publication of two widely read books. Li Zhisui's *The Private Life of Chairman Mao* (1994) reveals in extraordinary detail Mao's unsavory life style and, more importantly, his capricious, dictatorial way of policymaking. In *Mao, The Unknown Story* (2005), Jung Chang and Jon Halliday made a sweeping criticism of Mao, challenging the merits of practically all of his doctrines, actions, and policies.

Against this kind of popular and academic perception of the two Chinese leaders, it is difficult to assure fairness and objectivity in appraising their achievements and failures. What is emphasized in this author's effort at such appraisal is to maintain the comparative perspective that has been used throughout this book. Chiang and Mao will be contrasted to each other and, where appropriate, to leaders in Chinese historical times and in foreign countries.

Achievements

Chiang: Known and Unknown Deeds.—Chiang's successes in the Northern Expedition of 1926-1928 and in the Chinese-Japanese war of 1937-1945 are indisputably his greatest achievements. The Expedition represents the beginning of a transformation of China from a disunited to united country. China's victory in the Chinese-Japanese war stopped the country's century-long decline and elevated China to the status of a big power. Aside from these successes, however, are certain of Chiang's meritorious deeds that have gone unrecognized, underrated, or unexplained.

In 1918, at age of 31, he served as a junior officer in the Chen Jiongming army in Guangdong Province, commanding a few hundred men. In 1926, he rocketed to the position of Commander-in-Chief of the National Revolutionary Army, with his forces growing from 85,000 to 264,000 men within the year. In 1928, his army swelled to one million men as he, at 41, became Chairman of the Nanjing government. In ten years' time he rose from an unknown quantity to the leader of a nation that ranked first in population and third in territory in the world.

Chiang's rapid rise in power has established a record difficult to match by other military leaders in China and elsewhere, in historical or contemporary times. Searching in the Chinese dynastic chronicles, one can identify two great generals with comparable achievements. One is Huo Qubing (140-117 BC) of the Western Han Dynasty, whose statue stands for public homage in Jiuquan in northwest China today, as described in Chapter Two. As a teenager, Huo joined his uncle, Grand Marshal of Rapid Cavalry Wei Qing's expedition force against Xiongnu, a vast kingdom in today's Outer Mongolia. He regularly drove deep into enemy territory with his fast-running horses and scored spectacular victories. Incredibly, in 121 BC when he was barely 20, Huo was also appointed a Grand Marshal of Rapid Cavalry by the deeply-impressed Emperor Wu. He was twice awarded by the emperor with fiefdoms, totaling more than 10,000 households. He died in the battlefield in 117 BC when he was 24.[7]

Another great general was Li Shimin (599-649) of the Tang Dynasty. As a young man, he joined the forces of his father Li Yuan, a Governor General in north China during the last years of the Sui Dynasty (581-618), to topple that dynasty and to found the Tang. Like Huo, he fought battles with bravery and speedy movement; moreover, he scored victories with ruses and cunning tactics. After his father ascended to the throne in 618, he went on to battle the remnant Sui generals to unify the country, quite similar to Chiang's battle with the warlords more than a thousand years later. His military prowess was such that his father, Li Yuan, felt compelled to yield the crown to him in 626, when he was 27.[8]

In Western nations, few generals widely known to the Chinese matched Chiang's relatively young age when reaching the pinnacle of their military careers. Dwight D. Eisenhower became Supreme Commander of the Allied Forces in Europe and North Africa in 1942, at 52. George Marshall was 59 in 1939 when appointed Chief of Staff of the U.S. Army. Bernard Montgomery gained fame in his North Africa campaign when he became commander of the British Eighth Army in 1942, at 55. All these generals were at least ten years older than Chiang when attaining the height of their military positions. Only George Washington was at a comparable age to Chiang when he was appointed Commander-in-Chief of the Continental Army in 1775, at 43.

While these comparisons of Chiang's career achievements with those of other military personalities have not been noted in previously published works on Chiang, one factor accounting for the rapid rise in his military career has not been adequately analyzed either. This refers to his strategic talents. "The essence of a commander," Chiang observed, "is his strategic vision, not his bravery." As noted before, from 1914 to 1931 he worked out no less than 33 battle plans that enabled him to score many victories. Among these, one clearly demonstrated his unusual strategic vision. In 1917, prior to his enlistment in any army, he submitted to Sun Yat-sen "A Plan for Fighting the Northern Army."

What is most remarkable about this document is that when the Northern Expedition was carried out a decade later, it followed exactly the plan in every detail: assessment of strength and weakness of the northern army; assemblage of a southern army from units in Guangdong, Guangxi, Yunnan, and Hunan; charting battle routes from Canton northward to Wuhan, eastward to Nanjing and Shanghai, and northward to Beijing; and, most importantly, adoption of the principle of *"Yuan Jiao Jin Gong"* (Negotiate with the Enemy Afar, and Attack the Enemy Close by—a stratagem practiced in the Chinese War States Period, 475-221 BC).

Chiang's strategic talents came to light in the Chinese-Japanese war as well. He initiated the Shanghai Battle in August 1937 to implement his twin war strategy: "Trade Space for Time" and multi-nationalization of the conflict. It was this strategy that saved China from being conquered by Japan. But most books on Chiang failed to emphasize the long-term consequences of his strategic foresight.

To highlight Chiang's strategic talents as a factor contributing to his military successes does not, of course, mean that he was invincible. Far from it. His military competence can be questioned on two grounds. During the Chinese-Japanese war he suffered reverses one after another throughout the eight-year conflict, giving away the eastern one-third of the nation's land to his enemy. And, in the final days of the war, as the Nationalist army continued to lose ground to the Japanese, many American diplomats, officers, and journalists in China voiced strong criticism of Chiang's conduct of the war.

Clearly this criticism has merit. But Chiang's military setbacks have to be assessed in the context of the prevailing conflicts in the world in the 1930s and the 1940s. In 1937 when China was invaded by Japan, Britain and France faced a prospect of war with Germany. When the European war broke out two years later, Britain and France, which were among the world's mightiest naval and land powers, soon succumbed to the blitzkrieg of Germany—a nation that had been for a decade and a half under British and French occupation. Britain beat an ignominious retreat at Dunkirk, and France, more ignominiously, totally capitulated. It is only reasonable to suggest that an assessment of Chiang's military conduct in the Chinese-Japanese war be balanced against British and French leaders' conduct in the European war.

Chiang's military competence can be questioned on another ground. In the Chinese civil war in the late 1940s he lost nearly all major battles to the Communists. Many factors can be offered to explain his defeats. But from a strict military point of view, Chiang had long fought positional warfare against the warlords and the Japanese. Confronting Mao's guerrilla warfare in the late 1920s as a complete novelty, he could neither devise an effective strategy against that warfare nor adopt himself guerrilla tactics to fight the Communists. To put it simply, the setting of the Nationalist-Communist war was not determined by Chiang but by Mao, who proved to be a superior strategist.

Returning to the subject of Chiang's achievements in the Chinese-Japanese war, we may note that the moves he took to consolidate Chinese territories have not received public attention.[9] As discussed in "The Domestic Dividends" in Chapter Ten, he gained control of three vast belts of Chinese territories through an artful mixture of military and diplomatic ventures. These territories included the southwestern belt of Sichuan, Guizhou, and Guangxi; the frontier belt of Yunnan and Xinjiang; and the inner belt of Qinghai, Ningxia, Gansu, and Xikang. Since the beginning of the 20th century, the Chinese central authority had been largely absent from these provinces. By the end of the war, Chiang had re-established the national government's preeminent military and administrative presence there. In addition, he had brought Manchuria and Taiwan to China's fold. Altogether these territories accounted for two-thirds of the total area of China.

Beyond what he had achieved in the Chinese-Japanese war, Chiang can be credited for initiating certain positive political and economic developments. He was often criticized for practicing a one-party authoritarian rule, but he did set the foundation for democratic development in Taiwan. When he retreated to the island in 1949, he had every reason to create a military government to cope with the imminent threat of Communist invasion. Instead, he upheld in Taiwan the constitutional government structure that he had introduced two years previously on the mainland. More significantly, he started in 1950 a local self-rule on the island at the provincial and local levels. Legislative assemblies and administrative heads of province, county, city, township, and village government—except governor—have all been regularly elected since. When opposition parties emerged in 1986, a large corps of democratic-oriented politicians came into being, exercising increasingly dominant influence at local and provincial levels as well as in the national government. In 2000 the dissident-formed Democratic Progressive Party (DPP) defeated the Nationalist Party in the national election and gained power.[10] Several DPP leaders, including Chen Shui-bian and Lu Hsiu-lien, respectively president and vice president of the government in 2000-2008, were once Nationalist Party members contesting in elections, as widely reported in 2007. The DPP leaders as well as many other politicians undeniably benefited from the local self-rule Chiang had introduced.

Chiang's final achievement relates to his economic performance in Nanjing and in Taiwan. In the Nanjing Period, China under Chiang's stewardship achieved an impressive industrial growth rate of 8.4 percent. In Taiwan, Chiang maintained an even higher growth rate, at 9 percent. He shepherded the island to economic takeoff in the mid1960s and made it a Newly Industrialized Country in the mid1970s.

For several reasons, this author regards Chiang's economic performance in Nanjing and Taiwan as the most striking of all of his achievements. Though he was much less experienced in managing the economy than conducting military and political affairs, he brought about an economic miracle not once, but twice. He achieved the stellar results because he knew how to lead men of competence to accomplish a goal he could not attain himself. That reflects his political craftsmanship in the highest order. And, it should be especially noted that whereas his achievements in the Northern Expedition and the Chinese-Japanese war pertain to his effort to redress the problems of *the past*, his developmental programs in Taiwan, which are duplicated in mainland China today to good effect, set the foundation of prosperity for his nation *in the future*.

Mao: Personalization of Power.—In 1950, at the call of one person, more than one million Chinese soldiers successively marched to Korea to battle the world's mightiest power. A decade and half later, millions of Red Guards worshiped this man with hysterical songs and slogans. In these years and beyond, hundreds of millions of Chinese, young and old, men and women, amassed in city streets and village grounds to pledge unswerving support for this man's preferred policies. Nowhere in the world could one find so many people were so thoroughly subjugated by one man as the Chinese under Mao from 1949 to 1976. In terms of personalization of power, Mao's achievement is so stupendous that no other political leaders, in China or elsewhere, in the past or today, are likely to match.

Such personalization of power was considerably aided by a system of thoughts he developed over the years. As analyzed in Chapter Five, the components of his thoughts—from the theory of contradictions to the theory "On Practice," to rural communism, to guerrilla warfare, and to the New Democracy—are logically consistent, basically his own creation, and fully applicable to Chinese realities of his time. It assured his ascendancy to power and his triumph over his rivals; it created an ideological appeal in some parts of the Third World to this day.

It may be noted in this connection that Chiang did not appear to have reached Mao's intellectual height. Chiang wrote out a large number of essays, pronouncements, and books, but altogether they failed to form a system of thoughts rivaling Mao's. Yet, conscious of his intellectual limitations, Chiang solicited others' advice to make up for his deficiency. He diligently recruited advisers of various talents and solicited their opinions with an eagerness comparable to that of some of the most illustrious Chinese emperors, such as Emperor Wu of the Han Dynasty, Taizong of the Tang Dynasty, and Kangxi of the Qing Dynasty. While heading the Whampoa Military Academy in the mid1920s, he regularly consulted the Soviet advisers. In the 1930s he employed on his staff "Eight Great Secretaries," who were first-rate scholars; he enlisted German marshals and generals to help him battle the Chinese Communists and, for a short while, the Japanese; he retained the Australian journalist William Donald as his personal aide; and he requested American government to appoint high-level counselors to him, such as Laughlin Currie, Owen Lattimore, Arthur N. Young, Joseph Stilwell, and Albert Wedemeyer. In Taiwan, he meshed the personnel of the American Military Assistance Advisory Group with his entire defense establishment; and he even secretly employed former German and Japanese military personnel to train his army.[11] And he gave Taiwan's technocrats a free hand to frame the island's economic and financial policies and courted Chinese-American professors to lecture him on economic reforms. What he tried to do was to make others' wisdom his.

In contrast, Mao acted in precisely the opposite way. With confidence in his intelligence sweeping across all fields of public concern—from literature to philosophy, from science to economics, from military strategy to the arts—he became the Supreme Leader of the land and acted as, not necessarily with a sense of self-indulgence, the Great Teacher of the People. Throughout his political life he employed no advisers, his secretaries not rising above the status of scribblers. By monopolizing the political truths, he made his wisdom others'. Herein lies the source of his achievements as well as failures.

Mao's personalization of power also results from his military successes. In the Jiangxi years, his tens of thousands soldiers could break out from the repeated sieges of a Nationalist army at least ten times their size. A decade later, he could command in Yan'an and elsewhere an army rising to three-quarters of a million soldiers, who, in Mao's graphic expressions, ate only millets and fought with nothing but rifles. Then in three short years, from 1947 to 1949, they could thoroughly decimate four and half million superiorly-equipped Nationalist soldiers. How Mao was able to win this civil war against such odds in such a short time is so stunning an event that many people are still groping for an answer today. Mao's military performance in Jiangxi and Yan'an must be viewed as miraculous as Chiang's economic performance in Nanjing and Taiwan. A man never trained in any military academy but learning his tricks in the bombed hills and ravaged rivers became one of the world's foremost strategists. That was a claim Mao could rightfully make.

Mao's military exploits sustained his bold, masterful diplomatic maneuvering in his last years of life to transform China as a nation leaning to the side of the Soviet Union to one leaning to the side of the United States. When he closed his eyes for the last time, he must have felt satisfied that his China, still one of the poorest nations in the world, ended up a major player in the power games of the strategic triangle. He successfully put into practice a foreign policy stratagem that Chinese leaders had been only talking about since the 1860s: "*Yi Yi Zhi Yi*" (Play one foreign power against another).

Mao's final achievement is his success in building up the Communist Party as a vital instrument of governance. From the party's First National Congress in 1921 to the Tenth National Congress in 1973, Mao, more than any other person, shaped the character and structure of the party. In these 52 years, the party members grew astronomically from 53 to 28 million. He infused them with his doctrines, established communication channels with them, disciplined them with rectification campaigns, and mobilized them to carry out his policies. He made the party a gargantuan organ of strength, endurance, and resilience.

One can discern these characteristics of the party by seeing what happens to it today. With its membership continuing to grow, to over 87 million as of 2014, the party survived the death of Mao in 1976, the Tiananmen Square Incident in 1989, and the collapse of the world communist movement in 1991. As the world's largest Communist party in, decidedly, non-Communist times, it has now shifted its mission from conducting revolution to making money. Cadres inured to political actions became as if overnight entrepreneurs skilled in manufacturing and commerce. Without them, China's red-hot economic growth in the last three decades could not have taken place.

Failures

Chiang: The Makeup of a Gargantuan Loss.—On December 10, 1949, within earshot of machine gunfire, Chiang, with a small entourage of his closest aides, threaded through a path behind the Central Military Academy's Chengdu campus to board a waiting plane. He left mainland China for the last time on a flight to Taiwan. On the following March 1, when he resumed the office of the presidency he had vacated a year earlier, he avowed to recover the mainland he had just lost. He kept that wish alive until his death a quarter of a century later. However, history registered that his loss was final, complete, and irrevocable. And the stake was extremely high, something no less than the right to rule the most populous nation in the world.

What accounts for Chiang's incomparable loss? More than any other person, Chiang himself pondered this question from the last days of the civil war to the last years of his life. In March 1949, he enumerated in his diaries quite a few reasons for the impending disaster. Among these the more important ones were: Diplomatic mishaps; military defeats; the Nationalists' factional split and organizational disarray; economic and financial collapses; political chaos resulting from the introduction of constitutional rule during the war; Chiang's haughty mannerism; and lack of an effective propaganda program (CKSD, Month-end Review, March 31, 1949).[12]

Twenty-one years later, Chiang agonized in his sickbed for a lengthy review, again, of the reasons for his loss of the mainland (CKSD, 6/1-7/70). He specifically focused on foreign interference in the civil war. He blamed the Soviet Union for aiding the Chinese Communists to gain control of Manchuria. He criticized the United States for its faulty mediation effort, which, he claimed, contributed to the shift of military balance in favor of the Communists.

Chiang did not appear to place enough emphasis on embezzlement by high civilian officials and ranking military officers as a factor accounting for his loss. But the problem was very serious, which can be illustrated by two cases. In 1945, Chiang discovered that H. H. Kung, his brother-in-law who served over the years as financial minister, premier, and Governor of the Central Bank, had illegally traded on American-dollar based bonds and pocketed a profit of more than US$11,500,000. Upon Kung's admission of guilt, Chiang merely asked him to resign as head of the Central Bank, meting out no other punishment (CKSD, 7/12-14, 18, 25/45).[13] In 1949 Kung's son, Lingkan, was involved in massive hoarding of commodities and illegal foreign trade operations in Shanghai in flagrant violation of the monetary reform regulations the government had just proclaimed (see CKSD, 8/1, 14, 16, 21/47; 10/9/48; 11/4, 5, 12/48). Yet, with Chiang's permission, his wife, Soong May-ling, personally shielded Lingkan, her nephew, from criminal liability. The case, which understandably caused quite a public outrage, dealt a severe blow to the monetary reform then underway and imposed irreparable damage to Chiang's reputation as an impartial leader.

In May 1944, General Tang Enbo, commander of a force of 300,000 troops in defense of western Henan Province against the Japanese army, incredibly lost the battle without much of a fight. In a diagnosis of the causes of the fiasco, Chiang unequivocally pointed out, "Tang could not put his mind to military affairs because he was taken up with smuggling and grafts" (CKSD, 5/4/44).[14] Yet instead of punishing Tang for his misdeeds, Chiang continued to give Tang important assignments—as commander of forces in defense of Guizhou in the following year and of Shanghai in 1949.

Chiang never explained why he tolerated these high-profile cases of corruption. From reading his diaries and other sources of information, one sees that Chiang, who consistently led a frugal life, had frequently made it known that he would not countenance corruption; he ordered severe punishment—often, the death penalty—on the guilty parties reported to him. Yet his disciplinary acts occurred haphazardly, and the punished individuals were invariably of low ranks.[15] He also claimed he lacked time to deal with corruption because he was occupied with more pressing business. What he did not realize was that his tolerance of corruption by others could be metamorphosed, as it indeed was, to his being a corrupt leader and his government a corrupt regime. Such an image, made indelible in the mind of the people during the civil war, contrasted sharply to the public perception of the Mao-led Communist Party, which had not been known for any major case of embezzlement and grafts. The contrast caused many people to abandon their support of the Nationalists.

Of all of his failings noted above, none appeared to be fatal to Chiang's rule on the mainland, with one exception. Diplomatic setbacks, factional disputes, introduction of constitutional rule in chaotic times, economic and financial difficulties, haughty mannerism, and ineffective propaganda—all these conditions happened in varying degrees on the mainland since the Communist takeover. They have not undermined the Communist order. Even corruption might not be considered a decisive factor ruining the Nationalist rule. In today's China, corruption is by far more serious and widespread a problem than it was in Chiang's China. The Chinese National Audit Office reported in 2009 that government officials' fraudulent use of public funds for the first 11 months of the year totaled a staggering US$35 billion![16] And the corruption cases

Conclusion: From Enemies to Comrades

exposed by Xi Jinping since he took over power in 2013 are so gigantic in scale and so pervasive in the Communist regime that truly alarmed the Chinese public and astounded the whole world. Still, this political disease has not adversely affected the endurance or vigor of the regime.

Military defeats, it must be emphasized, were the single most important factor accountable for the demise of the Chiang regime on mainland China. He allowed many warlords to retain their troops virtually free from central control and never created a national force unified in purpose and loyalty, as Mao had in the case of the Red Army. As extensively analyzed in Chapters Three and Eight, he pitted positional warfare against Mao's guerrilla warfare with patent ineffectiveness, and he failed glaringly to recognize the deep and extensive penetration of his army by the Communist massive spy network. These were the primary causes of his continuous battle defeats, driving him to Taiwan.

Mao: Infallibility and Disasters.—Over the decades, Mao scored a string of victories over his rivals in both the Nationalist and Communist parties; he expounded on his ideological propositions with force and tenacity to assure a mass following; he trudged in treacherous diplomatic waters to win a place in the triangular power games; and he shaped the Communist Party to an instrument of governance entirely to his liking. He did not have to take pride in these phenomenal triumphs, for he considered them only consequences natural to his political leadership.

His triumphs, together with the absence of voices within the Communist power hierarchy to restrain his excesses, spoiled him into believing he was an infallible and omnipotent leader. That he was in reality not such a leader constitutes the single important cause of the many disasters he had caused.

The Korean War represents Mao's first blunder in diplomacy and last major misadventure in war. He endorsed Kim Il-sung's military adventure for foreign nations' interests, not China's. These included North Korea's ambition to rule the entire Korean peninsula and Stalin's twin objectives—Soviet access to the warm seaports on the peninsula and sacking American military strength in the emerging Cold War. By participating in the war, Mao delayed China's effort to repair its economy ravaged by 12 years' international and civil wars and lost the opportunity to bring Taiwan under his rule. And he paid a horrendous cost, with 535,000 of his soldiers dead or wounded in the battlefield. He was never again to commit a mistake of this magnitude. This disaster was entirely of Mao's own making. It was he who pledged unquestioned allegiance to Stalin by initiating the lean-to-the-Soviet-side foreign policy. It was he who insisted on Chinese participation in the war at a crucial Politburo meeting in October 1950.

Compared with the Korean War, Mao's bombardments of Quemoy and other offshore islands in 1954 and 1958 were not as costly in terms of casualties. Still they created adverse consequences. The bombardments failed to realize Mao's objective of preventing the United States from forming a military alliance with Nationalist China. Instead, they goaded America to conclude a mutual security treaty to defend the island and to enact the Formosa Resolution to protect the offshore islands. To this day, these islands, like Taiwan, are off military limits to the Communist forces. The bombardments also contributed to the Sino-Soviet split in which China's failed attempt to obtain full Soviet nuclear assistance figured as a prominent issue.

Mao's decisions on the bombardments were, again, largely his own. In the 1958 bombardments specifically, he even did not consult any of his senior comrades when ordering the attack, and he kept Ye Fei, the field commander in charge of the bombardments, totally in the dark as to his purpose of the massive bombing. In the end, he let the bombardments taper off with, first, bombing on alternative days, then bombing with propaganda shells, and, finally, complete stoppage. He let his idiosyncrasies dictate his highly risky military adventures.

Compared with his military adventures, Mao's misguided Great Leap Forward campaign produced a far greater catastrophe. With fanatical impetuosity, with a pupil's knowledge about economics, and with a relentless pressure on the populace, Mao wanted to convert a backward rural economy to a most industrialized one in 15 to 20 years. The failed adventure resulted in not only a sharp decline in agricultural and industrial output but also a human cost of unbelievable proportions. The conservatively estimated death toll of 30 million people is larger by far than the number of people killed in any rural rebellion in Chinese history, the Holocaust initiated by Hitler, the massacre by the infamous Pol Pot regime of Cambodia, or even the eight-year Chinese-Japanese war.

Such a government-sponsored campaign causing such a great number of civilian deaths is unprecedented in human history. Any leader in any nation creating this kind of catastrophe must feel severe pang in his conscience and must be removed from power. But Mao dodged all his responsibility and could say so callously, as if he would not mind, that the Great Leap, together with other economic projects he favored, "will cause…at least…50 million deaths." In the 15 years following the

Great Leap, he remained the indomitable Chinese leader, while his critics toiled in labor camps or were persecuted to death.

In the cultural field, Mao had more than a share of atrocious misadventures. In the service for politics he consistently disregarded moral principles. In the Hundred Flower campaign and the Cultural Revolution, he drilled into the consciousness of millions upon millions of his countrymen that dishonesty could be preferred over honesty and deception over sincerity in the execution of public policy. Such a negative educational campaign contributed to a spectacular moral decline in post-Mao China. Beijing continues to deny the occurrence of the Tiananmen Square massacre despite widely circulated audio and visual record, and the Communists falsely claim credit for winning the war against Japan in spite of indisputable evidence to the contrary.[17] Today, "many scholars and Chinese complain," *The New York Times* reported, that "dishonest practices permeate society, including students who cheat on college entrance exams, scholars who promote fake or unoriginal research."[18] And it is all too familiar to note that business people rampantly pirate foreign intellectual properties and fraudulently manufacture toxic goods injurious to the health of consumers in China and elsewhere in the world.

Mao showed his ultimate disregard for morality with his contempt of human life. In the Suppression of the Counter-Revolution campaign of 1950-1953, he could set *a death quota* on the counter-revolutionaries, requiring 700,000 people to be executed, as they actually were. In his contention with foreign powers, he could say that he would not mind that a half of the globe's population would perish in a nuclear war, because the other half would build a more brilliant Socialist world.

The Mao-led Cultural Revolution inflicted irreparable damage to Chinese cultural heritage. Historical monuments and temples were defaced or destroyed, artifacts ransacked, and intellectual works burned—on a scale so massive that is beyond imagination or tabulation. Qin Shihuang's cultural rampage more than two millennia ago earned him eternal condemnation by his countrymen. But he killed only some 460 scholars and burned books of an unknown quantity. Compared with what Mao destroyed in the Cultural Revolution, Qin Shihuang's assault on Chinese culture was a child play.

An Overall Assessment

Both Chiang and Mao had superlative achievements, which were significantly marred by their failures. How do we render an overall judgment on them? Insofar as Mao is concerned, the Chinese Communist Party declared in a resolution of 1981:

> Comrade Mao Zedong...made gross mistakes during the "cultural revolution," but, if we judge his activities as a whole, his contributions to the Chinese revolution far outweigh his mistakes. His merits are primary and his errors secondary. He rendered indelible meritorious service in founding and building up our Party and the Chinese People's Liberation Army, in founding the People's Republic of China....[19]

The resolution elaborated on Mao's specific contributions, which, incidentally, coincided with some of Mao's achievements as described on the previous pages of this book. The resolution also identified Mao's specific errors, which were similar to the disasters as discussed on these pages as well. However, the party did not offer any explanation as to why it regarded Mao's "meritorious service" outweighing his "gross mistakes." Can any of Mao's contributions make up for the death of 30 million people in the Great Leap or the ten years' scourge of the Cultural Revolution? This resolution failed to render a balanced and impartial judgment on Mao.

This resolution, in a way, reveals unwittingly the Communist Party's true position on Mao: *his meritorious service benefited the Communist Party, the People's Liberation Army, the People's Republic, and Mao himself.* It left something unsaid: *his disastrous policies victimized millions upon millions of ordinary people and his arbitrarily targeted comrades.*

With respect to Chiang, the Nationalist Party did not adopt a resolution to assess his merits and mistakes. How does one assign weight to Chiang's achievements versus his failures remains an open question. Yet it appears that *Chiang's achievements in the Northern Expedition and the Chinese-Japanese war benefited the nation and the people. His failures harmed his party, his army, and himself, but he did not victimize the people in any way remotely approaching the scale of devastation that Mao wreaked on the Chinese.* His defeat at the hands of the Communists reduced the Nationalist Party and the Nationalist army to regional entities, never capable of challenging the continental power that his rival regime has become. And Chiang took the defeat especially hard personally; he regarded it a shame scorching his soul that he had to redress at all cost. When he realized in the last years of his life the impossibility of recovering the mainland, he languished in agony and disappointment, dying a man of eternal regret.

Given the two Chinese leaders' triumphs and defeats, two more questions, of historical significance, can be raised. How would they measure up to the greatest Chinese emperors in the past? In his poem, "Snow," Mao implicitly ranked himself above Qin Shihuang, Emperor Wu of the Han, Emperor Taizong of the Tang, and Genghis Khan of the Yuan. Were Mao and Chiang "the truly great heroes" of 20th century China? Perhaps the time elapsed since their death is not long enough for definitive answers. In this author's opinion, however, Chiang and Mao were the only two leaders with sufficient political skills and military talents to best cope with the exigencies of their times. Both of them rose, through a process of elimination, above their contemporaries in the Nationalist and Communist power structures respectively. Both accomplished great deeds that none of other Chinese leaders was likely to emulate. Despite their enormous failures, they could not be substituted as Chinese leaders in their times by others but only by each other.

Comrades for an Emerging Superpower

The Common Goals

In 1925 when the dying Sun Yat-sen asked, in a testament, his *tong zhi* (comrades) to complete the revolution he had initiated, he was addressing to Chiang and Mao, among others. For they were both then officials of the Nationalist Party that Sun had founded and they shared the common goals the party's revolution was supposed to realize. Hence, they were *tong zhi*. Their common goals were to affirm republicanism and to eradicate warlordism and imperialism as the immediate objectives and to build a prosperous and strong China in the long run.

Two years later, however, Chiang and Mao parted company with each other. Chiang purged the Communists from the Nationalist Party, and Mao went to the Jiangxi hills to start his rural revolution to topple the Chiang regime. Comrades became enemies. In the next half of a century they fought battles against each other and governed their parts of China in different ways. After they departed from the scene, they turned out to be comrades again—if viewed posthumously. That is, they were in reality collaborators in the process of realizing their common goals—in the sequence of time. They took complementary measures successively to eradicate warlordism and imperialism; they laid down together the foundation for China to emerge as an economic and military superpower in the 21st century.

What Chiang achieved in the Northern Expedition in 1926-1928 signifies the beginning of the end of warlordism. Within the decade, Wu Peifu, Sun Chuanfang, Zhang Xueliang, Feng Yuxiang, Yan Xishan, Li Zongren, and Chen Jitang had either bowed out of politics or pledged allegiance to Chiang. After the outbreak of the Chinese-Japanese war, while the power of most of the remaining military chieftains sharply attenuated, Long Yun of Yunnan and Sheng Shicai of Xinjiang surrendered their territories to Chiang's rule.

By the end of the war, military fiefdoms impregnable to the Nationalists' administrative and financial control had virtually disappeared. Thus, Chiang completed the mission of eradicating warlordism and dramatically expanded his territorial domain. But his territorial gains only benefited the Communists, for he saved them from battling the warlords piecemeal when they won the civil war. "For the most part," Robert E. Bedeski has observed, "the Communist victory was a matter of defeating a single government and its army rather than overcoming a series of entrenched regional militarists."[20]

After establishing the People's Republic, Mao continued Chiang's drive for territorial consolidation when he took over Tibet in 1950. Mao then began to push China's power to the full limits of the nation's boundaries. He deployed forces in the remotest corners of Chinese land, from the Ussuri River in the northeast to the Himalayan mountains in the southwest, from the Tian Shan villages in the northwest to islands in South China Sea. In most of these places he also set up administrative and party apparatus tightly controlled by the central authorities in Beijing.

For the first time in almost a century, China had re-established its exclusive control of its territorial domain. This was a development that Chiang and Mao together made possible. Chiang contributed in its first stage, beginning in 1926, and Mao in the second stage, beginning 24 years later in 1950.

Chiang's victory in the Chinese-Japanese war enabled him to realize another goal of the Sun revolution. He persuaded China's allies, the United States and Britain —later, other foreign powers—to renounce their imperialist privileges in China by abolishing the unequal treaties. He ended once and for all foreign concessions in Chinese port cities, foreign consuls' extraterritorial jurisdiction in Chinese lands, and foreign privileges in economic undertakings in China. When Mao took over China, he went beyond reaffirming the termination of unequal treaties;

he unilaterally abolished any other treaties he deemed violating Chinese sovereignty. In addition, his intervention in the Korean War and involvement in the Vietnam War, his defiance of the Soviet Union and the United States in world politics, and his contribution to the emergence of the Washington-Moscow-Beijing strategic triangle fostered a strong sense of nationalism among the Chinese. His military and diplomatic ventures abroad allowed the Chinese to enjoy *psychological equality* with foreigners, as Chiang's termination of the unequal treaties allowed China to enjoy *legal equality* with foreign nations.

Chiang's victory in the Chinese-Japanese war also earned China the status of Big Power—a Permanent Member of the Security Council of the United Nations, wielding the veto power. However, Chiang's China was too weak and war-torn, as he had pointed out, to deserve such a status. Indeed, in the 25 years in which Chiang's representatives were seated at the Security Council, from 1946 to 1971, they hardly exerted any influence on the issues before the Council. Elsewhere in the world, when conferences of foreign ministers of big powers were held to deliberate on the emerging Cold War problems, Chiang's representatives were not even invited.

The seating of Mao's representatives at the United Nations in 1971 symbolized recognition by the international community of China as a truly big power. It was the only non-industrialized nation that possessed nuclear weapons in the 20th century; it maintained the world's largest conventional army; and it exerted a preponderant influence in the Pacific Rim ranging from Korea to Indochina. President Nixon's trip to Beijing in the following year reaffirmed the significance of these transformative phenomena. Chiang made China a big power in name; Mao made China a big power in reality.

The Nationalist-Communist Symbiosis

Though by no means intentional, Chiang's fighting the Chinese-Japanese war contributed to the transfer of power from him to Mao. As James C. Hsiung has observed:

> By the time the war was over...China had lost some four million soldiers and an additional eighteen million civilians.... Total wartime property losses were estimated to run in excess of U.S.$100 billion.
> On the other hand...the Communists' Red Army had swelled to 1.3 million soldiers, supplemented by a militia of 2.2 million

and supported by a population of 100 million....The CCP [Chinese Communist Party] itself boasted a membership of 1.2 million.[21]

Chiang's war against Japan, concurred John W. Garver, "allowed his Communist rivals to expand their infrastructure, creating the basis for their subsequent victory over the Nationalists in the civil war."[22]

The Nationalist-Communist symbiotic relations can be seen from another perspective—institutional continuity. As William C. Kirby has noted, the Nationalist "Party-State was an essential, if unacknowledged, foundation of the Communist Party-State, which inherited concepts, institutions, and policies that had been central to Chinese political life in the decades before the People's Republic of China (PRC) was founded."[23] This institutional continuity manifested itself in several ways. First, both the Nationalists and the Communists maintained the same political structure, based on the Leninist model. Second, this structure was heavily dominated by the military. And third, the Nationalist army—with its defeats and defections during the civil war—filled the People's Liberation Army with millions of its soldiers and an inordinate amount of weapons.

Mainland-Island Economic Linkage

That Chiang and Mao became comrades posthumously can be viewed from a final perspective. As analyzed in the end section of the previous chapter, Mao's successors have marched on the path to prosperity that Chiang had first charted. That path is marked by two features: the technocrats being in full charge of economic development and a complete set of policies to implement the principles of sectoral transformation and comparative advantage.

While the transformation of mainland's political leadership and economic policies has made the economies of the mainland and Taiwan increasingly alike, a phenomenal growth of trade and investment across the Taiwan Strait cemented the two economies. In 1979, when the two sides resumed trading, cross-Strait export and import value registered at a mere US$78 million; in 2002 it reached US$ 40 billion—an astonishing 513-fold rise! In the latter year, value of export from Taiwan to the mainland accounted for as much as 30 percent of Taiwan's total export value; and value of mainland's import from Taiwan accounted for 13 percent of mainland's total import value.[24] Taiwan's investment on the mainland also rose rapidly, from US$466 million (in actually delivered amount) in 1991 to US$3,970 million in 2002, an 8.5-fold increase. As of 2003, with its cumulative investment on the mainland at US$37 billion, Taiwan ranked as the mainland's fourth largest external investor.[25]

Mainland's investment in Taiwan was insignificant because of restrictions imposed by Taiwan's government. But expansion in mutual investment and trade is expected to accelerate in consequence of recently-concluded agreements. In November 2008, the mainland and Taiwan agreed to establish direct services in air- and sea-transportation and postal services; and in June 2010 the two sides concluded the Economic Cooperation Framework Agreement to promote free trade. Mainland China and Taiwan are thus economically intertwined even though they remain politically divided.

Setting the Foundation of an Emerging Superpower

At the inception of the 21st century, China has emerged as the world's second largest economy (after that of the United States), the largest exporting country, the largest energy-consuming nation, and the largest foreign exchange reserve holder, the largest internet community, and the largest car market.[26] By any measurement except for per capita income, China is the world's newest economic superpower.

China has been regarded for some time as a rapidly-growing military power. With decades' rising military budget, China possesses the world's largest conventional army undergoing rapid modernization. And in the field of nuclear force, China ranks third in the world, after the United States and Russia. It has a whole phalanx of weapons, including inter-continental ballistic missiles with multiple independently targetable reentry vehicles (MIRV), intermediate-range ballistic missiles, short-range ballistic missiles, and submarine-launched ballistic missiles.[27]

When Chiang and Mao died in the mid1970s, China had not possessed the traits of a super-economy, and its nuclear force was still in the infant stage of development. But Chiang and Mao were only the first generation leaders who exercised authority over the entire Chinese Republic.[28] It was during their long tenure of service that they established several requisite preconditions for China to become a superpower.

First, they restored China as a united nation, not one divided into regions dominated by strong military men and foreign powers. A divided nation can never become a major power of the world, let alone a superpower.[29]

Second, they created a mammoth military force consisting of conventional and nuclear arms that is capable of preventing foreign invasion or foreign domination of Chinese territories, which China had suffered for a whole century beginning in 1839. An intimidated nation cannot be qualified as a superpower.

Third, they contributed to the creation of a market of continental proportions with massive flow of goods, services, labor, capital, and technology. Mao helped establish a national infrastructure to sustain the market; Chiang inspired the market to operate at maximal efficiency with his developmental experiences. A nation without such a market cannot give rise to a super-economy.

And fourth, they fostered a sense of confidence among the people in themselves—something the Chinese had missed for more than a century's time. United in purpose, the Chinese are striving to realize the common goal of *Fu Guo Qiang Bing* (prosperous nation and strong army) that Chinese leaders had first set in the 1860s.

Together Chiang and Mao have set the foundation for China to become a superpower.

NOTES

[1] While teaching at the University of Detroit Mercy, I came to know a student who was a retired frogman from Taiwan. He described how he and his comrades swam round trip at night from the Nationalist outpost Little Quemoy to the Communists-held Xiamen two miles away. Conducting intelligence and subversive activities, some of them did not carry firearms in order to avoid detection; they defended themselves with daggers and their two hands. Trained in martial arts, a frogman could use the edge of his hand to deliver a deathblow at the neck of an opponent. This student demonstrated to me one skill he had mastered. He folded a piece of notepaper to half and asked his classmate to hold the two ends of a bamboo chopstick horizontally. Breathing deep, he struck in a flash at the center of the chopstick with the paper, felling it to the ground in two evenly cut pieces.

[2] Chang Jui-te, "Chiang Kai-shek's Coordination by Personal Directives," in Stephen R. MacKinnon, Diana Lary, and Ezra F. Vogel, eds., *China at War: Regions of China, 1937-1945* (Stanford: Stanford University Press, 2007), pp. 65-87.

[3] Jin Yong, widely known as the literarily-talented, history-minded Chinese Kung-Fu novelist, has created a fictional character dubbed "Dong Fang Bu Bai" (The Never Defeated Oriental Man). Millions of his readers, in China and overseas, accepted this figure as a caricature of Mao.

[4] Hans Van de Ven has observed the dramatic changes of Western journalists and scholars' appraisal of Chiang's leadership during the Chinese-Japanese war, 1937-1945—from highly positive to totally negative. The turning point related to the Stilwell affair late in the war. Then, recently Western scholars changed their appraisal again, being favorable to Chiang. See Van de Ven, *War and Nationalism in China*, pp. 1-8. Noticing this pattern of changing perception of Chiang, Paul H. Tai and Tai-chun Kuo provided an extensive treatment of this subject, identifying the major criticisms as well as reappraisals of Chiang by Western and Chinese writers in "Chiang Kai-shek Revisited," *American Journal of Chinese Studies*, Vol. 17 (April 2010): 81-84.

[5] This is clearly seen in most of the papers presented at the two conferences held by the Chinese academic community on the mainland: The first one, Conference on "Political Change and Leadership of Nationalist China, 1911-1949," was sponsored by the Institute of Modern

History of the Chinese Academy of Social Sciences and the Hoover Institution of Stanford University in Beijing, November 2008; the second, "Thy Symposium of Re-research and Revaluation on the Republic of China Leadership," was sponsored by the History Department, Fudan University and the Hoover Institution of Stanford University in Shanghai, September 9-11, 2011.

    Yang Tianshi of the Institute of Modern History of the Chinese Academy of Social Sciences in Beijing, in an effort at reappraisal of Chiang's career, published two path-breaking volumes on the Nationalist leader: *Jiang Shi Mi Dang yu Jiang Jieshi Zhen Xiang* [*Secret Archive on Chiang and the True Story of Chiang Kai-shek*]; and *Zhao Xun Zhen Shi de Jiang Jieshi: Jiang Jieshi Ri Ji Jie Du* [*A Search for the Real Chiang Kai-shek: An Exposition of the Chiang Kai-shek Diaries*] (cited before). Yang Kuisong, a historian at Beijing University, has made a dispassionate and lucid analysis of the political life of Mao and Chiang in a speech: "Mao Zedong yu Jiang Jieshi de Bi Jiao Yan Jiu" [A Comparative Study of Mao Zedong and Chiang Kai-shek], http://www.yangkuisong.net/xsyj/000069.htm. Other scholarly appraisals on Chiang can be seen in the following publications: Zhuang Chuanwei and Zhang Yongchun, *Mao Zedong yu Jiang Jieshi* [*Mao Zedong and Chiang Kai-shek*], Changchun, China: Changchun Chu Ban She, 1993; Chen Fuzhong, "Da Lu Xue Zhe Dui Guo Min Dang Kang Zhan Gong Ji di Song Yang"[Commendation by Mainland China's Scholars of the Accomplishments of the Nationalist Party during the War of Resistance] *Zhuanji Wenxue* [*Biographic Literature*, a periodical published in Taiwan], No. 492 (May 2003): 125-30; Hui Xin, "Bai Nian Min Guo Ji Huai Jiang Jieshi Xian Sheng" [Commemoration of Mr. Chiang Kai-shek on the 100th Year of the Republic of China], *China News Digest, WWW.CND.Org,* April 2010; Wu Zhengrong, "Xiao Yi Mao Zedong yu Jiang Jieshi" [A Brief Commentary on Mao Zedong and Chiang Kaishek],http://www.peacehall.com/news/gb/pubvp/2006/09/200609282 1 b 40. shtml; Sun Wenguang, "Wo Men Ying Gai Dao Nian Jiang Jieshi" [We Should Commemorate Chiang Kai-shek], http://www. peacehall. com/ news/gbpubvp/2008/04/ 200804062259. shtml; "Jiang Jieshi Bu Wei Ren Zhi de Qi Da Gong Xian" [Chiang Kai-shek's Seven Unknown Major Contributions], http://www.peacehall.com/news/gb/ pubvp/2007/12/20071 2111311. shtml.

    [6]The other two top contributors were Max Weber and Mahatma Gandhi. Deutsch once served on the faculty of Harvard and European universities and as president of the American Political Science Association. His associates in the study were University of Michigan

Biophysicist John Platt and University of Frankfurt Political Scientist Dieter Senghass. Their findings appeared in *Science*, as cited in *Time*, March 29, 1971.

[7]Sima Qian, *Shi Ji* [*The Records of History*], Vol. 111, "Wei Jiang Jun Biao Qi Lie Zhuan" [Biography of Marshal of Rapid Cavalry Wei.]

[8]Liu Xiang, ed., *Jiu Tang Shu* [*History of the Tang Dynasty, The Old Version*],Vol. 2, "Ban Ji" [Biographies of Emperors], No. 2; Ouyang Xiu and Song Qi, eds., *Xin Tang Shu* [*History of the Tang Dynasty, The New Version*], Vol. 2, "Ban Ji" [Biographies of Emperors], No. 2.

[9]To his knowledge, this author was the first writer to analyze on this subject, in a paper titled "Chiang Kai-shek's Wartime Diplomacy: Bargaining Strategies and Internal Dynamics" (see p. 247, note 27).

[10]For a full description of the transition of Taiwan's political system from a one-party authoritarian regime to a plural-party competitive polity, see Linda Chao and Ramon H. Myers, *The First Chinese Democracy: Political Life in the Republic of China on Taiwan*, Baltimore and London: The Johns Hopkins University Press, 1998.

[11]For the Japanese and German military advisers Chiang hired while in Taiwan, see respectively Nojima Tsuyoshi, *Zui Hou di Di Guo Jun Ren, Chiang Kai-shek yu Bai Tuan* [*The Last Imperial Warriors, Chiang Kai-shek and the Bai Corps*], Taipei: Lian Jing Chu Ban Gong Si, 2015; and Wang Yuqi, "Chiang Wei-kuo Jiang Jun yu 'Ming De Xiao Zhu'" [General Chiang Wei-kuo and 'Ming De Group'], *BL*, No. 460 (September 2000): 65-69. For a full documentation on Chiang's Chinese and foreign advisers, see Wen Hao, ed., *Jiang Jieshi de Zhi Nang Gao Can* [*Chiang Kai-shek's Confidants and High Counselors*], Beijing: Zhong Guo Wen Shi Chu Ban She, 2004; and Fang Ke, ed., *Jiang Jieshi he Ta de Gao Ji Mu Liao* [*Chiang Kai-shek and His High-Rank Staffers*], Zhengzhou, China: Henan Ren Min Chu Ban She, 2000.

[12]Yang Tianshi has commented on Chiang's self-diagnosis of failures in Yang Tianshi, "Jiang Jieshi 'Fan Xing Shi San Tiao: Shan Zi Du Da Wei Da Bing'" [Chiang Kai-shek's Thirteen Points of Self-Reflection: Arrogance as the Major Fault], http://www.chinareview news.com/doc/ 1011/3/4/6/101134602.html?coluid=0&kindid=0&docid= 101134602&mda te=1113103320.

[13]For a full exposition of this case, see Yang Tianshi, "Jiang Jieshi Cha Chu H.H. Kung Deng Ren de Mei Jin Gong Zhai Wu Bi An" [Chiang Kai-shek's Investigation of the Case of Embezzlement by H.H. Kung and Others], *BL*, No. 552 (May 2008): 4-16.

[14]Tang and his field commanders resorted to a highly irregular and likely illegal practice to exact crop contributions from the people in Henan. They issued paper slips known as *dai gou mai* (literally, wheat purchase coupons) requiring the people to supply the troops with wheat; these coupons were supposed to be redeemed after the end of the Chinese-Japanese war. The coupons, issued in regular intervals and exacting heavy wheat contributions, were never redeemed; they caused widespread resentment. This author was a direct witness to this practice as his family, native of Henan, regularly received the coupons.

[15]He Chengxun, Superintendent of Department of Military Justice from 1942 to 1945, recorded in his diaries numerous corruption cases. Whenever a case was brought to his attention, Chiang almost invariably ordered execution, even for minor offenses. Yet many cases were not reported to him, and many known culprits escaped punishment. See He Chengxun, *He Chengxun Jiang Jun Zhan Shi Ri Ji* [*General He Chengxun's Wartime Diaries*], Taipei: Zhuanji Wenxue Chu Ban She, [1986].

[16]*The New York Times*, December 28, 2009.

[17]The Communists have recently recognized that the Nationalist army bore the brunt of the war against Japan. Yet they still claim that they led the Chinese to victory in the war while the Nationalist army was more focused on fighting them than the Japanese. Ironically, two publications from mainland China seem to refute this claim. One of these, published by the People's Liberation Army Press, listed more than one hundred Nationalist generals as having died in the battles with Japan. See Dang Dexian and Yang Yuwen, *Kang Ri Zhan Zheng Guo Min Dang Zhen Wang Jiang Ling Lu* [*Record on Nationalist Generals Having Died in the Anti-Japanese War*], Beijing: Jie Fang Jun Chu Ban She, 1987. In contrast, only one Communist general was killed in the war; he was Zuo Quan, Deputy Chief of Staff of the Eighth Route Army, in a battle in Shanxi in 1942. The other publication revealed that the Nationalist army suffered more than 3.2 million casualties (death and wounded) during the war, whereas the comparable figure for the Communist army was more than 580,000—a 85 to 15 ratio. Guo Rugui and Huang Yuzhang, *Zhongguo Kang Ri Zhan Zheng Zheng Mian Zhan Chang Zuo Zhan Ji* [*Record of the Frontline Battles of the Chinese-Japanese War*] (Nanjing: Jiangsu Ren Min Chu Ban She, 2001), Vol. 1, p. 45. Relying on several accounts of war casualties—primarily Zhou Enlai's report to Stalin during the war—Jay Taylor estimated the ratio at 90 to 10. Taylor, *The Generalissimo*, pp. 169-70, 297-98; notes No.123 and No. 124 on p. 629.

[18]*The New York Times*, October 7, 2010, p. A1.

[19] Adopted by the Sixth Plenary Session of the 11th Central Committee of the Communist Party of China on June 27, 1981.

[20] Robert E. Bedeski, "China's Wartime State," in Hsiung and Levine, *China's Bitter Victory*, p. 48.

[21] James C. Hsiung, "The War and After: World Politics in Historical Context," in ibid., pp.295-96.

[22] Garver, "China's Wartime Diplomacy," p. 28.

[23] William C. Kirby, "The Chinese Party-State under Dictatorship and Democracy on the Mainland and Taiwan," in William C. Kirby, ed., *Realms of Freedom in Modern China* (Stanford: Stanford University Press, 2004), p. 113. Yu-Shan Wu has made a similar point. In a theoretical exposition on the various models of political and economic development that China has adopted since the Republican Revolution of 1911, he points out the model adopted by the government on the Chinese mainland today quite resembles that of the Nationalist regime under Chiang. Wu makes then an astute observation: "The mainland [today] has moved into Taiwan's institutional past." Yu-Shan Wu, "Sun Yat-sen Thought, Centennial of the ROC, and Development Models in Taiwan and Mainland China: A Macro Analytical Framework" (A paper presented at the 53rd Annual Conference of the American Association for Chinese Studies, University of Pennsylvania, Philadelphia, October 15, 2011), pp. 1 and 25.

[24] Li Baoming, *Liang An Jing Ji Guan Xi 20 Nian: Tu Po yu Fa Zhan Li Cheng de Shi Zheng Fen Xi* [*Twenty Years' Cross-Strait Economic Relations: An Empirical Analysis of Their Breakthrough and Development*] (Beijing: Ren Min Chu Ban She, 2007), p. 72; and Zhu Zhengming and Sun Mingde, eds., *Zhong Guo Jing Ji Kai Shi Ju, Liang An Guan Xi Chuang Xin Ji* [*New Opportunities for the World and Taiwan Rising from Chinese Economic Development*] (Taipei: Taiwan Jing Ji Yan Jiu Yuan, [2005]), pp., 407, 410.

[25] Li, *Twenty Years' Cross-Strait Economic Relations*, pp. 58-59; and Peter Drysdale and Xinpeng Xu, "Taiwan's Role in the Economic Architecture of East Asia and the Pacific" in Julian Chang and Steven M. Goldstein, eds., *Economic Reform and Cross-Strait Relations: Taiwan and China in the WTO* (Hackensack, NJ: World Scientific, 2007), p. 153.

[26] See David Barboza, "China Overtakes Japan to Become No. 2 Global Economic Power," *The New York Times,* August 16, 2010, Section B, pp. 1, 3.

[27] See International Institute for Strategic Studies, *The Military Balance 2007*, pp. 332-33, 346-50; Richard D. Fisher Jr., *China's Military Modernization: Building for Regional and Global Reach,*

Westport, Conn.: Praeger Security International, 2008; You Ji, *The Armed Forces of China,* London: I. B. Tauris, 1999. For details on Chinese nuclear weapon inventory as of 2008, see "Nuclear Force Guide," Http://www.fas.org/ nuke/guide/summary.htm.

[28] Since the 1911 Revolution that created the Chinese Republic, all the government leaders prior to Chiang and Mao had a short tenure of service and exercised authority in only part of China. These included Sun Yat-sen, who served as Provisional President of the Republic for three months; Yuan Shikai, head of the northern government; and several warlords taking turns to control the regime in Beijing.

[29] Of course, mainland China and Taiwan have been ruled by two separate governments since1949. But the fact that Taiwan is part of China has been recognized by Chiang and Mao and by the international community. Even the independence-minded Democratic Progressive Party in Taiwan has repeatedly affirmed that the Republic of China governs the island.

APPENDIX

CHIANG KAI-SHEK'S CONFESSION AND REDEMPTION

Character Flaws

Early in his adult life, Chiang Kai-shek was often troubled by his character flaws, which he once, in a confession mood, wrote down as "being cunning, greedy, and lustful" (CKSD, 1/8/18). Subsequently, he identified many additional ones, including "hot temper," "arrogance," "hypocrisy," and "vanity" and pounded himself mercilessly for what went wrong with his behavior.

Two of these flaws that troubled him the most were his insatiable sexual desire and fiery temperament. He warned himself, "Lust is a great evil; it must be stopped" (CKSD, 8/17/18). And he went on with an exposition of his love life: "In the past, I found that love came with the sight of a beauty, but beauty could also appear because of love. So, whenever I saw a beauty, I fell in love. Yet love breeds desire, desire leads to misconduct, and misconduct results in hatred....In the last seventeen or eighteen years, I could not count with the fingers of my hand the sins I had committed. I cannot wash myself clean with all the water of the East Sea" (CKSD, 10/5/19)! In his diary entries from 1919 to 1921, he jot down at least fifty-three times about his problematic sexual behavior.[1]

Similarly, Chiang was perturbed by his inability to moderate his impetuous and impulsive temper. He warned himself sternly, "With my hot temper not under control, it has become the root cause of my troubles" (CKSD, 7/27/20). Yet, "with repeated effort, I just could not control it" (CKSD, 12/27/20). In numerous of his diary entries, he recorded instances in which how his irascibility caused quarrels with others, including his closest colleagues, and even resulted in fracas with such persons as rickshaw pullers and hotel and bathhouse attendants (CKSD, 6/12/18; 12/19/18; 7/10/19; 10/1/19; 3/3/20; 3/12/20; 9/3/20; 10/10/20; 12/27/20; 12/31/20; and 4/18/21).

Of particular concern to him was that Sun Yat-sen, whose leadership position in the Nationalist Party he eagerly sought to succeed, recognized this problem of his. In a letter to Chiang dated October 29, 1920, Sun warned, "You have a fiery temper....Thus you often have difficulties with others, not easy to get along with them. Yet in order to shoulder the heavy responsibilities of our party, you must not insist on holding fast your opinions but have to make compromise with others."[2]

For his troubled behavior pattern and for his drifting military career in the late 1910s and early 1920s, Chiang at times felt despondent. He regarded his future as hopeless (CKSD, 10/22/19); he considered "my mind is like dead ashes, without one trace of life in it" (CKSD, 10/24/19); he lamented, "My appearance has turned old; my spirit has faded away; my courage has vanished!...I seem to have lost myself, without a sense of self-control. What a terrible pity" (CKSD, 6/21/20)!

Regimen for Self-Improvement

Around the mid1920s Chiang began to devise a regimen for self-improvement in order to correct his flaws. It was not an integrated program but one consisting of four specific actions that he implemented with extraordinary tenacity from then until his old age.

His first action was to *rise early*, which he regarded as essential to a disciplined life and efficiency at work. He was normally out of bed at 4:30 to 6:00 in the morning. Excepting when he was sick or when he was in honeymoon, he would not tolerate any late rise. "Getting up at 8 O'clock," he warned, "is a sure way to becoming a useless person" (CKSD, 12/16/26). He once wrote down a statement of censure on himself for a delayed rise (CKSD, 12/24/26). He remained an early riser till his last years in Taiwan.

A second action Chiang took with equal regularity was *meditation*. He generally meditated for an hour once a day but on occasions twice or even three times. He meditated anywhere, at his residence or during travel. He also did it in the battlefield. During his service with the Chen Jiongming army, he recorded in his diary entry one day, "Up for mediation at four, for 25 minutes; arrived at the artillery field at five; started bombardment at 6:30" (CKSD, 10/3/18). He practiced it with religious devotion and consistency. As he noted in 1938, "I have practiced meditation for 20 years, in the morning and evening without fail" (CKSD, 12/31/38, Yearend Review). He used meditation to assay his character flaws, to calm down his spirit, and to purify his mind.

A third action he took for self-improvement was to devise and observe many Neo-Confucianism-inspired *mottos* as guidance to his conduct. He wrote down the mottos nearly everyday in the header of his diaries. Two mottos appearing more frequently were: *"Jing Jing Dan Yi"* and *"Li Zhi Shuai Qi."* The former meant: reverence, tranquility, asceticism, and single-mindedness. The latter can be translated as, "Let aspiration command spirit." Other mottos appearing in his diaries included *"Jin Yan Shen Xing" "Cheng Fen Zhi Yu," "Wu Shi Qiu Zhen," "Ren Ru Fu Zhong,"* and *"Ju Shen Zhi Pu,"* which meant, respectively, "be careful with words and deeds," "restrain anger, curtail desire," "emphasize fact, seek truth," "tolerate insult, bear burden," and "live simply and frugally." These mottos were intended to free his mind from improper thoughts and to curtail tendencies of wrongdoing. In his diaries—and sometimes, in his other writings—he reviewed and commented on his behavior by reference to the mottos.

Finally, he immersed himself in *reading*—a subject that has been extensively treated in Chapter Two. What may be recited here are his motivations for learning: "I'm ashamed I was not well educated. I can never spare enough time for reading" (CKSD, 3/13/28). He also shared a belief in the ancient Greek adage that "knowledge is virtue," as he instructed himself, "Pursuing studies without letup will improve my moral character. If I want to be a man of strength and integrity, I must obtain learning from studies" (CKSD, 12/20/30).

Transformation of Character

How effective were Chiang's strivings for self-improvement? He appeared to have redeemed himself by the late 1920s and the early 30s by a transformation of his character. He followed a sort of code of daily conduct: rising and turning in early, eating sparingly, abstaining from alcohol, drinking nothing but boiled water, and refraining from smoke. He never again indulged in the excesses of "feasting, drinking, gambling, and womanizing." He scrupulously maintained an appropriate appearance: wearing attires clean and neatly pressed, standing and sitting straight, with his chest sticking out, his eyes focused, with an intense gaze. In a way, one can conjure up an image of him as a pagoda—balanced, immutable, and centered round an axis running from the top to the bottom. People having chance of observing him closely, such as his secretaries, bodyguards, and physicians, can all testify to his changed lifestyle.

With respect to his sexual life in particular, he put an end to his licentious activities when he married his third wife Ch'en Chieh-ju in 1921. And after marrying his fourth wife Soong May-ling in 1927, he was as faithful to her as she was devoted to him in their 48-year-long marriage, the recurrent rumors to the contrary notwithstanding.[3]

In politics and in military affairs, he had learned the necessity for restraining his temper in order to accommodate with others. At various times, he appointed many of his erstwhile adversaries—including Feng Yuxiang, Yan Xishan, Zhang Xueliang, Wang Jingwei, and Sun Fo, among others—as well as many of these people's subordinates to high administrative and military positions. Still, he was given to occasional emotional outbursts against persons flouting his will.

Chiang did not appear to have rid of another flaw of his, "cunningness." After becoming the national leader in 1928, he continued to scheme and manipulate against his adversaries and even his colleagues to gain an upper hand. He considered it prudent to offer these individuals "high ranks" and "substantial enumeration" to insure their allegiance (CKSD, 9/14/36). He played the divide-and-rule game with consummate skills. And in his diplomatic engagements, he endeavored to exploit foreign powers' desires, fears, and vulnerabilities to his advantage.

NOTES

[1] Yang, *Secret Archive on Chiang*, pp. 43-48.

[2] Text of Sun's letter is quoted in Mao, *Chiang Kai-shek prior to 1926*, p. 97.

[3] In 1944, Chiang was so incensed by the rumors about his extramarital affairs that he took an unusual step to clear his name. He hosted a tea party for the heads of the five branches of the government, cabinet ministers, and American and British guests (totaling some 60 people), at which he resolutely refuted the innuendos and rumors about his married life. At his side, Soong May-ling also spoke, vouching for her husband's faithfulness (CKSD,7/4/44;7/6/44).

INDEX

571 Project, 190, 191
Acheson, Dean, 226, 257, 258; delimiting American defense perimeter in Asia, 226
Ames, Robert T., 48, 60, 122
Anti-A B Corps campaign, 177
Anti-Comintern Pact, 212
Art of the possible: as supplementary instruments of governance, x, 100-202
Barnett, A. Doak, 306, 317
Barrel of the gun: as symbol of primary instrument of governance, x, 41-63
Barrel of the pen: as symbol of primary instrument of governance, x, inspiring trust, 64-99; establishing orthodoxy and guidance, 79-99
Bo Yibo, 303, 316
Bolshevik Revolution, 16, 23, 24, 35, 94, 173
Borodin, Mikhail, 17
Boxer Rebellion, 2, 204, 244
Brezhnev, Leonid, 269, 274
Britain: abolition of unequal treaties in China, 216; British-Chinese negotiations in wartime, 214-216; recognition of the People's Republic of China, 226; support of China's war objectives, 215-216
Central Investigation and Statistical Bureau of the Nationalist Party (Zhong Tong), 126, 127, 128, 129, 130, 143, 151, 165
Central Military Investigation and Statistical Bureau (Jun Tong), 126, 127, 128, 129, 130, 143, 165, 168
Chang, Jung, and Jon Halliday, 11, 12, 169, 182, 193, 198, 202, 278, 319, 332
Chen Boda, 65, 190
Chen Bulei, 64, 120, 149, 168
Chen Cheng, 120, 141, 144, 297, 298, 299
Ch'en Chieh-ju, 6, 31, 37, 123, 139, 162, 359
Chen Duxiu, 16, 18, 28, 31, 183
Chen Jian, 243, 260, 284, 286

Chen Jiongming, 14, 24, 42, 43, 117, 332, 358
Chen Lifu, 128, 131
Chen, Nai-ruenn, xii, 198, 317, 318
Chen Yun, 302, 304, 310, 319
Ch'i, Hsi-sheng, xii, 245
Chiang Ching-kuo, 7, 9, 12, 44, 127, 133, 145, 149, 236, 252
Chiang, Elizabeth, xiv, 7
Chiang Kai-shek and economic development: approach to policymaking, 293-300; concept of growth, 290-292; differences from Mao's experience, 308-311; export process zones, 299, 312; industrialization programs in Taiwan, 299-300; land reform programs in Taiwan, 299-300; path to prosperity, 311-312; political craftsmanship in economic achievements, 336; record of performance (Nanjing period and Taiwan Miracle), 304-306, 317
Chiang Kai-shek and Mao Zedong: as comrades in early political life, 18; as co-rulers of China, ix, xiv, 39, 40; as first generation national rulers of Repulican China, ix, building up China as a big power, 280-282; common goals, 345-347; comrades for an emerging superpower, ix, 345-350; from enemies to comrades, x, xii, 322-356; handling diplomacy, 204-289; path to prosperity, 311-312; perceiving China as an organic entity, 18; prosperous and strong China as long-term goals, ix, x, 2, 18, 203; removing warlordism and imperialism as short-term goals, 23, 281; same path to power, 13-47; seeking national wealth, 290-321; shared traits in diplomacy, 205-207; uncanny similarities, viii, 1-37
Chiang Kai-shek as ruler: achievements, 332-336; failures, 338-341; leadership characteristics, 322-324;

362

Index 363

leadership style, 327-330; overall assessment, 343-345
Chiang Kai-shek diaries, xi, xiv, xvi, 68-70, 236
Chiang Kai-shek's appeal to emotions: xii, 101-116; celebrating the living, 113-114; honoring the dead, 108-113; pseudo-family relations, 107-108; sworn brotherhood, 101-107
Chiang Kai-shek's barrel of the gun: 42-46; bravery, 24, 43-44; encirclement campaigns, 26, 31, 42, 43, 51, 53, 56, 61; losing wars to Mao, 56-58; strategic talents, 24, 44-45, 333-334
Chiang Kai-shek's barrel of the pen: 41-63, citizens' code of conduct, 82, 98; ideology, 80-83; moralizing political leadership, 65-70; sloganeering, 87-91
Chiang Kai-shek's belief in Christianity, 68-70
Chiang Kai-shek's causes for losing China to the Communists, 56-58, 339-341
Chiang Kai-shek's concept of rulership, 67
Chiang Kai-shek's confession and redemption: 67, 357-361; character flaws, 357-358; regimen for improvement, 358-359; transformation of character, 359-360
Chiang Kai-shek's cunning practices: 117-146, action of removal (assassination), 122-127; art of withdrawal, 135-141; dictatorship in the guise of democracy, 131-135; divide and rule, 127-131; purchasing loyalty, 117-122; secret shipment of gold to Taiwan, 140-141
Chiang Kai-shek's ideology. *See* Chiang Kai-shek's barrel of the pen
Chiang Kai-shek's life: as naughty kid and studious adult, 4-5; as southerner, 3-4; birth and death, 2-3; political posterity, 7-8; loyal wives, 6-7

Chiang Kai-shek's multi-power diplomacy, 1931-1945: xii, 207-225, achievements, 222-225; bargaining wih Britain, 214-216; bargaining with United States, 216-220; dispute with Stilwell, 218-219, 246-248; domestic dividends, 220-222; multi-nationalizing conflict with Japan, 209-212; policy guideline, 207-208; seizing Soviet fear of two-front wars, 212-214
Chiang Kai-shek's path to power: 13-37; history-mandated goals, 18-23; reading books, 27-30; resorting to arms, 23-27; rising above others, 31-32; Soviet factor, 16-18; starting point, 13-15
Chiang Kai-shek's purge of the Chinese Communists, 25, 35, 105
Chiang Kai-shek's single-power (United States)-dependency diplomacy, 1945-1975: 225-242; attempts to recover the mainland, 232-233; declining diplomatic efficacy, 240-242; from euphoria to despondency, 225-227; handling Quemoy crises, 227-237, 262-267; Taiwan in international community, 233-236; U. S.-Nationalist China security treaty, 228-229; unexercised Soviet option, 236-240
Chiang Kai-shek's strategic talents, 44-45, 333-334
Chiang Kai-shek's wills, 43, 44, 66
Chiang Wei-kuo, 6, 7, 44, 103, 107, 149, 162, 353
China: accounting for a quarter of world's population, xiv; hitsorical growth, 19-23; historical union-disunion cycle, 22-23
China's Destiny, 5, 80, 81, 313
Chinese Academy of Social Sciences in Beijing, x, xii, xiii, 36, 352
Chinese Communist Party, 15, 16, 17, 28, 31, 33, 34, 40, 41, 47, 53, 65, 82, 85, 94, 98, 99, 124, 151, 155, 160, 164, 166, 167, 168, 169, 177, 191, 193, 196, 199, 200, 225, 255, 269, 293, 302, 344, 348; fourth generation leadership, 312, 320

Chinese Communist Party-Chinese Nationalist Party alliance, 18
Chinese Expeditionary Army to Burma, 215, 221, 224
Chinese-Japanese war, 1937-1945, 45, 46, 48, 50, 54, 58, 70, 77, 80, 88, 102, 104, 109, 110, 112, 120, 121, 125, 129, 133, 157, 207, 208, 210, 211, 212, 213, 214, 220, 221, 244, 248, 280, 295, 304, 305, 323, 326, 332, 334, 335, 336, 342, 344, 346, 347, 351, 354
Chinese National Resources Commission, 294-295, 314
Chinese Nationalist Party, xvi, 7, 13, 14, 16, 17, 18, 25, 31, 33, 34, 35, 82, 87, 91, 98, 103, 104, 105, 107, 122, 123, 126, 128, 131, 132, 134, 135, 137, 138, 144, 151, 167, 173, 292, 300, 335, 344, 345, 352, 357; *see also* Kuomintang
Chinese population accounted for quarter of mankind, xiv
Chinese Republican Revolution, 1, 2, 5, 13, 15, 17, 23, 24, 42, 80, 101, 102, 103, 125, 126, 355
Chongqing peace talks, 39, 225
Churchill, Winston, viii, 214, 216, 217, 222
CMRC, xi, xvi, 11, 33, 36, 60, 144
Cold War, 82, 94, 227, 232, 243, 247, 248, 249, 251, 252, 254, 256, 283, 284, 285, 286, 289, 341, 347
Comintern, 16, 17, 31, 34, 212
Communist China, 230, 231, 232, 233, 234, 235, 236, 237, 239, 251, 252, 281, 283, 287, 288, 306, 317
Confucianism, 4, 5, 6, 20, 27, 38, 67, 68, 69, 77, 79, 80, 81, 112, 179, 184, 194, 314, 317, 328, 358, 329
Confucianism and Economic Development, 317
Cultural Revolution, 1, 4, 7, 38, 95, 148, 172, 178, 186, 188, 189, 191, 192, 193, 194, 195, 197, 201, 270, 301, 303, 307, 318, 330, 343, 344
Dai Jitao, 103, 107, 149
Dai Li, 126, 128, 143
Dalai Lama, 13th, 111
Dalai Lama, 14th, 104

Deutsch, Karl W., 331, 352
Dorn, Frank, 123-124,
Dulles, John Foster, 228, 229, 230, 231, 249, 250, 251, 267
Dikötter, Frank ,175, 198
Eastern Expedition, 24, 31, 43, 44, 103, 108
Eastman, Lloyd E., 305, 317, 331
Eckstein, Alexander, 306, 315
Eifler, Carl F. , 123, 143
Eisenhower, Dwight, 112, 228, 229, 230, 231, 250, 266, 267, 285, 286, 333
Encirclement campaigns, 26, 31, 42, 43, 51, 53, 56, 61
Feng Yuxiang, 14, 43, 44, 45, 46, 87, 104, 105, 107, 114, 117, 118, 119, 121, 124, 125, 137, 159, 160, 323, 328, 346, 360
First National Congress of the Chinese Nationalist Party, 16, 18
Foreign powers' privileges and aggression in China, 20
Formosa Resolution, 229, 231, 232, 342
Four Little Dragons, 306, 308, 311, 317
Four Old Marshals' Report, 273-274
Fudan University, x, xiii, 352
Fu Zuoyi, 111, 158-159
Gandhi, Mahatma, 112, 215, 352
Gang of Four, 7, 192
General Line of Socialist Reconstruction, 301, 302, 318
Germany: anti-Comintern Pact, 212; assistance to China 314, providing advisers to China, 244, 337
Gorbachev, Mikhail, 279
Great Leap Forward, 86, 87, 95, 96, 172, 174, 175, 176, 184, 185, 186, 187, 194, 198, 201, 268, 301, 302, 304, 307, 310, 316, 318, 342-343, 344
Great Wall, 19, 60, 71, 293
Guerrilla war, 26, 32, 46-50, 47, 48, 49, 50, 55, 56, 57, 58, 83, 85, 152, 168, 184, 185, 310, 326, 330, 335, 336, 341
He Yingqin, 128, 136, 139, 141
He Zizhen, 6, 7, 8, 148
Hoover Institution (of Stanford University), x, xi, xii, xiii, 36, 76, 236, 246, 248, 352

Index 365

Hu Hanmin, 31, 131, 132, 137, 138, 139, 328
Hu Jintao, 312, 320
Hu Shih, 89, 111, 114, 224
Hu Zongnan, 53, 54, 62, 128, 140, 147, 150, 163, 164, 221, 251, 326
Hua Guofeng, 178
Huntington, Samuel P., 56, 144
Huo Qubing, 19, 332
Jiang Jieshi, xv, 11, 12, 33, 36, 59, 61, 76, 98, 142, 144, 145, 166, 244, 245, 283, 313, 352, 353; *see* also Chiang Kai-shek
Jiang Qing, 6, 7, 8, 147, 148, 191, 192, 261, 284
Jinggang Mountain, 26, 46, 47, 148
Joint Commission on Rural Reconstruction, 297, 299, 315
Jun Tong, 126, 127, 128, 129, 130, 143, 165, 168
Khrushchev, Nikita, 185, 186, 188, 264, 265, 266, 267, 268, 269, 285, 286, 330
Kim, Il-sung, 257, 258, 259, 262, 267, 341
Kirby, William C., 204, 244, 288, 348, 355
Korean War, 7, 50, 51, 60, 94, 148, 184, 185, 227, 228, 232, 233, 257, 260, 261, 262, 263, 274, 281, 283, 284, 326, 330, 342, 347
Kosygin, Alexei, 239, 271
Kung, H. H., 121, 128, 129, 130, 293, 309, 339
Kuo Tai-chun, xii, 351
Kuomintang, viii, xvi, 13, 144, 196, 217, 250, 317; *see* also Chinese Nationalist Party
Lasswell, Harold D., 38
League of Nations, 208, 294
Lee Teng-hui, 297
Legislative Yuan, 7, 104, 128, 132
Li Dazhao, 16, 18, 31
Li Kwoh-ting, 295, 296, 298, 300, 309, 311, 315, 319
Li Lishan, 26, 27, 31
Li Min, 8, 9, 12, 166
Li Na, 8, 147
Li Xiannian, 201, 303, 307, 310, 319

Li Zhisui, author of *The Private Life of Chairman Mao*, x, xi, 10, 12, 36, 166, 285, 332
Li Zongren, 14, 56, 104, 107, 119, 131, 136, 137, 138, 139, 141, 143, 323, 328, 346
Liang Shuming, 179, 194, 199
Lin Biao, 51, 55, 65, 149, 178, 183, 185, 186, 188, 190, 191, 194, 195, 198, 200-201, 260
Lin Hsiao-ting, xii, 142, 248
Little Red Book, 178, 189
Liu Ding, 156-157, 164, 168
Liu Fei, 152-153, 164
Liu Shaoqi, 96, 174, 175, 176, 183, 184, 185, 186, 188, 189, 192, 195, 283, 307
Long March, 7, 27, 29, 31, 53, 59, 61, 71, 74, 75, 92, 148, 156, 183, 184, 201, 302, 303, 330
Louis, Victor, 236, 237, 238, 239
Ma Yinchu, 180, 199, 300
MacFarquhar, Roderick, xiii, 193, 197, 201, 287
Madison, James, 170, 196
Manchu Dynasty, xvi, 11, 13, 43; *see* also Qing Dynasty
Manchuria, xv, 20, 21, 34, 43, 44, 45, 55, 58, 66, 88, 93, 94, 105, 106, 110, 119, 124, 137, 139, 148, 153, 156, 158, 161, 183, 193, 202, 205, 207, 208, 209, 210, 212, 213, 214, 215, 218, 222, 223, 225, 244, 255, 256, 259, 260, 262, 270, 302, 305, 335, 339
Manchurian Incident, 43, 207, 218, 219
Manzhouguo, 124, 210
Mao Anqing, 8, 9, 148, 168
Mao Anying, 7, 9, 148, 166, 168, 261, 262, 284, 326
Mao Zedong: a man devoid of emotions, 147-150; a powerful communicator, 96-97, achievements, 336-338; failures, 341-343; Report of an Investigation into the Peasant Movement in Hunan," 25, 41, 99; setting quota of counter-revolutionaries to be killed, 173; overall assessment, 343-345

Mao Zedong and economic development: approach to policymaking, 300-304, 315, 316; concept of growth, 292-293; differences from Chiang's experiences, 308-311; path to prosperity, 311-312; record of performance, 306-307

Mao Zedong as ruler: achievements, 336-338; failures, 341-343; leadership characteristics, 324-327; leadership style, 330-331; overall assessment, 343-345

Mao Zedong's barrel of the gun: 46-51; guerrilla war, 32, 46-50; how he won wars against Chiang, 51-58; the people's war, 54, 58, 59, 69

Mao Zedong's barrel of the pen: concept of contradictions, 40, 83, 196, 197, 201; empowering poems, 70-75; ideology (thought of Mao Zedong), 83-87; more powerful communicator than Chiang, 96-97; New Democracy, 40, 86, 99, 292, 301, 336; One Hundred Flowers movement, 94, 181, 195, 32; paper tiger, 92-96, 267; sloganeering, 91-96; "Snow" (poem), 71-72

Mao Zedong's campaigns of struggle: x, 170-202; cultural revolution, 191-193; disciplining intellectuals, 178-183; forging submissive cadres, 176-178; list of campaigns, 172; methods of conflict resolution, 170-172; reaching limit of the art of the possible, 194-195; removing the most powerfuls (Lin Biao, 188-191, 200-201; Liu Shaoqi, 186-188; Peng Dehuai, 184-186); taming the masses, 172-176

Mao Zedong's diplomacy: 253-289, battling mind with Nixon, 274-278; dealing with Third World, 271-273; development of nuclear weapons, 267-268; grand strategy, 253-273; handling Korean War, 257-262; handling Quemoy crises, 262-267; handling Vietnam War, 272, 275-278; negotiations for a Sino-Soviet security in Moscow, 254-257;

Shanghai Communiqué, 277-280, 289, 327; Sino-American détente and strategic triangle, 273-280; Sino-Soviet split, 264, 268-271

Mao Zedonng's ideology. *See* Mao Zedonng's barrel of the pen

Mao Zedong's life: as naughty kid and studious adult, 4-5; as southerner, 3-4; birth and death, 2-3; political posterity, 7-8; loyal wives, 6-7

Mao Zedong's path to power: 13-37; history-mandated goals, 18-23; reading books, 27-30; resorting to arms, 23-27; rising above others, 31-32; Soviet factor, 16-18; starting point, 13-15

Mao Zedong's spy warfare: xii, 147-169; dagger in the heart, 164-165; infiltration of the Nationalist Central command, 152-155; massive underground network, 150-164; penetration of the Nationalist field commands, 156-164

Marshall, George, 153, 225-226, 333

Maring, H., 16

Marxism and Leninism, 16, 54, 83, 183, 292

May Fourth Movement, 16, 80, 81

Mu Bei, 198

Nathan, Andrew J., xi, 60

National Revolutionary Army, 24, 25, 43, 44, 59, 104, 118, 119, 136, 139, 141, 154, 332

Nationalist China, 36, 142, 206, 228, 232, 234, 235, 236, 237, 238, 240, 245, 247, 248, 251, 252, 263, 266, 279, 280, 281, 331, 342, 351

Neo-Confucianism, 68-69

New Democracy, 40, 86, 99, 292, 301, 336

New Life Movement, 5, 82, 88

Nixon, Richard M., 8, 11, 90, 151, 233, 235, 236, 241, 251, 271, 274, 275, 276, 277, 278, 279, 280, 289, 327, 330, 331, 347; battling mind with Mao, 274-278; normalization of relations with People's Republic of China, 235-236; Shanghai Communiqué, 277-280, 289; Sino-

American détente and strategic triangle, 273-280, 289
Northern Expedition, 23, 24, 25, 28, 35, 43, 44, 45, 57, 59, 82, 87, 104, 117, 118, 119, 120, 121, 124, 125, 135, 136, 139, 142, 244, 293, 303, 323, 332, 334, 336, 344, 346
One-Hundred-Day Reform, 80
One Hundred Flowers Movement, 94, 181, 195, 326
Open Door policy, 204
Opium War, 20, 80, 223
Outer Mongolia, 34, 190, 213, 223, 234, 235, 240, 241, 244, 249, 256, 333
Paper tiger, 92, 96
Peaceful Coexistence, 263, 269
Peng Dehuai, 147, 175, 183, 184, 185, 186, 187, 188, 189, 192, 194, 198, 199, 261, 262, 266, 316, 326
People's Republic of China. See Communist China
People's war, 46, 50, 51, 60
Positional warfare, 42, 43, 45, 50, 56, 335, 341
Qin Shihuang, 79, 343, 345
Qing Dynasty, xvi, 20, 21, 22, 79, 94, 222, 337; *see* also Manchu Dynasty
Rectification Campaign in Yan'an, 177
Red Guards, 96, 186, 188, 189, 193, 194, 336
Report of an Investigation into the Peasant Movement in Hunan, 25, 41, 99
Republic of China. *See* Nationalist China
Revisionism/Revisionist, 96, 176, 182, 186, 188, 269, 274
Roosevelt, Franklin D., v, viii,112, 123, 214, 216, 217, 218, 219, 222, 223, 224, 231, 246, 247, 324
Rule by gun. *See* Chiang's barrel of the gun and Mao's barrel of the gun,
Rule by pen. *See* Chiang's barrel of the pen and Mao's barrel of the pen,
Rule by appealing to emotions. *See* Chiang Kai-shek's appeal to emotions
Rule by cunning practices. *See* Chiang Kai-shek's cunning practices
Rule by campaigns of struggle. *See* Mao Zedong's campaigns of struggle

Rule by espionage. *See* Mao Zedong's spywarfare
Rural communism, 3, 26, 27, 42, 46, 58, 84, 85, 336
Schoenhals, Michael,193, 197
Second Historical Archives of China, Nanjing, x, xiii, 59, 77, 243
Second World War, xii, 9, 126, 164, 183, 184, 222, 223, 231, 241, 248, 256, 270, 294
Self-Strengthening Movement, 80, 81, 204, 290
Sheng Shicai, 120, 221, 346
Sino-Soviet split, 264, 268-271
Smedley, Agnes, 59, 157
Snow, Edgar, 9, 15, 47, 61, 84, 168, 331
Soong May-ling, xv, 6, 7, 44, 65, 136, 149, 339, 359, 361
Soong, T. V., 65, 66, 76, 119, 120, 121, 128, 129, 130, 140, 217, 222, 223, 246, 248, 293, 309
Soviet assistance to the Chinese Nationalist Party, 17
Soviet impact on the formation of Chinese Communist Party, 17
Soviet military assistance to China, 1937-1941, 213
Soviet renunciation of privileges in China, 16, 17, 33
Soviet Russia in China, 82, 98
Soviet Union, xii, 6, 9, 10, 12, 14, 16, 17, 34, 37, 73, 76, 82, 87, 94, 104, 126, 136, 149, 185, 186, 190, 205, 209, 210, 211, 212, 213, 214, 217, 219, 220, 221, 223, 224, 228, 232, 234, 236, 238, 239, 240, 241, 251, 252, 253, 254, 255, 256, 257, 258, 262, 263, 264, 265, 266, 268, 269, 270, 271, 273, 274, 275, 277, 278, 279, 280, 281, 286, 287, 289, 327, 338, 339, 347
Stalin, Joseph, 85, 94, 149, 205, 223, 224, 245, 254, 255, 256, 257, 258, 259, 262, 264, 267, 268, 283, 284, 327, 330, 331, 341, 354
Statitistics on population: the world and China, xiv
Stilwell, Joseph, 112, 123, 143, 218, 219, 224, 227, 246, 247, 324, 337, 351; uncarried out assassination

368   Index

plans against Chiang Kai-shek, 123-124
Sun Chuanfang, 14, 44, 45, 136, 346
Sun Yat-sen, xv, 1, 10, 11, 13, 14, 17, 23, 24, 29, 30, 31, 34, 41, 43, 44, 59, 67, 72, 81, 82, 102, 103, 105, 107, 113, 127, 131, 159, 169, 247, 291, 300, 301, 333, 345, 355, 356, 357
Tai Hung-chao, xi, 35, 252, 315, 317; see also Paul H. Tai
Tai Minchuan, 110
Tai, Paul H., i, 246, 247, 252, 289, 351; see also Hung-chao Tai
Taiwan, 228 Incident, 133-134; Democratic Progressive Party (DPP), 335, 356; economic miracle, 305-306, 317; electoral process, 132, 335-336; export process zones, 299, 312; industrialization programs, 299-300; land reform programs, 299; Reign of White Terror, 133-134; self-rule of local government, 335-336
Taiwan Relations Act, 280
Tang Enbo, 140, 161-162, 340
Taylor, Jay, xiii, 143, 145, 214, 331, 354
The Federalist, 170, 196
The International Development of China, 291
Three Kingdoms, 2, 11, 152, 165
Three Principles of the People, 81, 105, 291, 295, 313
Tibet, 20, 21, 104, 111, 173, 193, 20, 206, 216, 220, 221, 222, 243, 244, 246, 248, 346
Tito, Josef, 256, 264, 265
Tong Men Hui, 14
Trade Space for Time, 45, 89, 334
Truman, Harry, 225, 226, 227; order of neutralization of Taiwan Strait, 225
Unequal treaties, 16, 20, 216, 217, 222, 244, 346
Unit 8341, 188, 194, 200, 201
United Nations: admission of Outer Mongolia, 234-235; replacing Republic of China's delegation with People's Republic of China's, 234-235, 347

United States: dispatching George Marshall mission to China, 225-226; Formosa Resolution, 229, 231, 232, 342; normalization of relations with People's Republic of China, 235-236; order of neutralization of the Taiwan Strait, 1950, 225; possible use of nuclear weapons in the Taiwan Strait area, 229, 231, 250, 251; security treaty with Nationalist China, 228-229; uncarried out assassination plans against Chiang Kai-shek, 123-124; *White Paper* on China of 1949, 226
Univeristy of California, San Diego, Library system, xiii
Van de Ven, Hans, xiii, 139, 146, 244, 245, 247, 351
Vietnam War, 59, 252, 293, 296, 300, 303, 372
Wang Dongxing, 188, 200
Wang Hongwen, 192
Wang Jingwei, 31, 37, 91, 120, 125, 127, 135, 136, 137, 138, 139, 141, 328, 360
Wang Ming, 26, 27, 31, 53, 183
Wedemeyer, Albert, 219, 337
Wei Lihuang, 157-158, 159, 168
Wen Jiabao, 312, 320
Weng Wenhao, 128, 129, 294, 309
Whampoa Military Academy, 6, 13, 18, 23, 24, 34, 43, 82, 103, 107, 108, 117, 125, 128, 153, 163, 337
Wu Guozheng, 128, 129, 144
Wu Han, 59, 191, 192
Wu Peifu, 14, 44, 45, 346
Wu Shi, 154, 155, 164, 167, 359
Wu Sing-Yung, xiii, 140, 146
Wuchang Uprising, 13, 15
Xi'an Incident, 43, 65-67, 76, 88, 104, 106, 110, 157, 168, 322, 323, 324, 329
Xinjiang, 19, 20, 120, 173, 193, 205, 214, 220, 221, 238, 244, 256, 268, 270, 281, 335, 346
Xiong Xianghui, 150-151, 153, 164, 167
Yalta Agreement, 213, 214, 234, 239, 255, 256
Yan Jiagan, 144, 295, 298, 309, 311

Yan Xishan, 14, 43, 44, 45, 46, 87, 104, 105, 111, 117, 118, 119, 121, 125, 137, 207, 323, 328, 346, 360
Yang Hucheng, 65, 106, 156, 168
Yang Jisheng, 198
Yang Kaihui, 6, 73, 148, 166
Yang mu (open conspiracy), 182-183, 195, 201, 326
Yao Wenyuan, 191, 192
Yin Zhongrong, 295, 298, 300, 309, 311
Yoffe, Adolf, 17
Yongfeng Warship Incident, 43
Young, Arthur N., 305, 314, 317, 337
Yuan Shikai, 1, 13, 23, 24, 101, 102, 103, 104, 356
Yudin, Pavel, 264-265
Zhang Chunqiao, 192
Zhang Guotao, 31, 183
Zhang Jingjiang, 102, 107, 136, 294
Zhang Qun, 102, 103, 107, 128, 141, 149, 163
Zhang Xueliang, 65, 105, 107, 110, 117, 119, 121, 125, 156, 157, 168, 323, 329, 346, 360
Zhang Zuolin, 14, 31, 44, 105, 110, 166, 352, 354
Zhenbao (Damansky) Island, 237, 270, 273, 287
Zhenwu Military Academy, 4, 42, 102
Zhong Tong, 126, 127, 128, 129, 130, 143, 151, 165
Zhongshan Warship Incident, 31, 37
Zhou Enlai, 31, 83, 85, 98, 143, 148, 151, 156, 157, 159, 184, 185, 239, 253, 256, 259, 260, 271, 275, 307, 328, 354
Zhu De, 26, 31, 184, 185, 261
Zhuanji Wenxue, (*Biographical Literature*, in Taipei, Taiwan) xv, 115, 116, 143, 166, 352, 354
Zunyi Conference, 27, 83, 177

www.ingramcontent.com/pod-product-compliance
Lightning Source LLC
Chambersburg PA
CBHW062122280526
45788CB00001B/19